France under Fire

"We request an immediate favor of you, to build a shelter for us women and small children, because we have absolutely no place to take refuge and we are terrified!" This French mother's petition sent to her mayor on the eve of Germany's 1940 invasion of France reveals civilians' security concerns unleashed by the Blitzkrieg fighting tactics of World War II. Unprepared for air warfare's assault on civilian psyches, French planners were among the first in history to respond to civilian security challenges posed by aerial bombardment. *France under Fire* offers a social, political, and military examination of the origins of the French refugee crisis of 1940, a mass displacement of 8 million civilians fleeing German combatants. Scattered throughout a divided France, refugees turned to German Occupation officials and Vichy administrators for relief and repatriation. Their solutions raised questions about occupying powers' obligations to civilians and elicited new definitions of refugees' rights.

NICOLE DOMBROWSKI RISSER is Associate Professor of History at Towson University in Maryland. She is editor of *Women and War in the Twentieth Century: Enlisted With or Without Consent* (1998).

Studies in the Social and Cultural History of Modern Warfare

General Editor
Jay Winter, *Yale University*

Advisory Editors
Omer Bartov, *Brown University*
Carol Gluck, *Columbia University*
David M. Kennedy, *Stanford University*
Paul Kennedy, *Yale University*
Antoine Prost, *Université de Paris-Sorbonne*
Emmanuel Sivan, *Hebrew University of Jerusalem*
Robert Wohl, *University of California, Los Angeles*

In recent years the field of modern history has been enriched by the exploration of two parallel histories. These are the social and cultural history of armed conflict, and the impact of military events on social and cultural history.

Studies in the Social and Cultural History of Modern Warfare presents the fruits of this growing area of research, reflecting both the colonization of military history by cultural historians and the reciprocal interest of military historians in social and cultural history, to the benefit of both. The series offers the latest scholarship in European and non-European events from the 1850s to the present day.

A full list of titles in the series can be found at: www.cambridge.org/modernwarfare

France under Fire

*German Invasion, Civilian Flight, and
Family Survival during World War II*

Nicole Dombrowski Risser

CAMBRIDGE
UNIVERSITY PRESS

CAMBRIDGE
UNIVERSITY PRESS

University Printing House, Cambridge CB2 8BS, United Kingdom

Cambridge University Press is part of the University of Cambridge.

It furthers the University's mission by disseminating knowledge in the pursuit of education, learning and research at the highest international levels of excellence.

www.cambridge.org
Information on this title: www.cambridge.org/9781107521254

© Nicole Dombrowski Risser 2012

This publication is in copyright. Subject to statutory exception and to the provisions of relevant collective licensing agreements, no reproduction of any part may take place without the written permission of Cambridge University Press.

First published 2012
First paperback edition 2015

A catalogue record for this publication is available from the British Library

Library of Congress Cataloguing in Publication data
Risser, Nicole Dombrowski, author.
    France under fire : German invasion, civilian flight and
    family survival during World War II / Nicole Dombrowski Risser.
        pages   cm. – (Studies in the social and cultural history
        of modern warfare)
    Includes bibliographical references and index.
    ISBN 978-1-107-02532-5 (hardback)
    1. France – History – German occupation, 1940–1945.   2. War –
    Protection of civilians – France.   3. World War, 1939–1945 – Civilian
    relief – France.   4. World War, 1939–1945 – Refugees.   5. World War,
    1939–1945 – France.   I. Title.
    D802.F8R564 2012
    940.53´44–dc23
    2012016904

ISBN 978-1-107-02532-5 Hardback
ISBN 978-1-107-52125-4 Paperback

Cambridge University Press has no responsibility for the persistence or accuracy of URLs for external or third-party internet websites referred to in this publication, and does not guarantee that any content on such websites is, or will remain, accurate or appropriate.

For Jim

Contents

Illustrations

Maps

Tables

Acknowledgments

Many institutions and individuals have made the research and writing of this book possible.

First, I warmly thank Lewis Bateman and, especially, Michael Watson at Cambridge University Press. I would also like to thank the anonymous readers for their valuable suggestions on the manuscript and supporting the book's publication.

Two years of research in Paris, Corrèze, and the Marne were funded by a Chateaubriand administered French Government Research grant and the Franco-American Bicentennial Fellowship. An Andrew W. Mellon Junior Faculty Research Award allowed me to return to France for a summer to complete the final dissertation research. The Prize Teaching Fellowship at New York University (NYU) funded me through two years of writing. Supplemental research was funded by Princeton University's Committee for Research in the Humanities and a Princeton Faculty Summer Research Award. A Towson University Faculty Development Research Award funded a semester of sabbatical in Paris, allowing me to complete the book's final research.

I wish to acknowledge Patricia M. E. Lorcin and Daniel Brewer for permission to reprint, as part of Chapter 8, my contribution, "In Search of Civilian Safe Spaces: Re-evacuation of Nord and Pas-de-Calais in Response to British Bombing, September 1940–March 1941," to their edited volume, *France and Its Spaces of War: Experience, Memory, Image* (2009: 59–72). Martin S. Alexander generously shared his current research, "The Republic at War: The French Army and the Fight for France, 1939–1940."

In Paris at the Archives nationales, Chantal Bonnazi helped me identify key collections. Thanks to the generosity of Pierre Petitmengin, I enjoyed two years of access to the library at the École normale supérieure, rue d'Ulm. Jean-Pierre Azéma and Michel Winock welcomed me into their seminar on wartime France at the Institut d'études politiques de Paris, and offered advice on research and secondary sources. Michelle Perrot allowed me to attend her seminar on Women in Modern France at Université de Paris Diderot (VII). In Reims, I received valuable aid from Jean-Pierre Husson, affiliated with the Université de Reims. In Corrèze, Guy Quincy at the Archives départementales familiarized me with local archival collections and offered me daily rides up the little mountain to the archives.

A number of French families in Reims hosted me for several months and placed me in contact with participants of the exodus. I especially thank Maurice and Marie-Pascale Cérisola and their children, Thomas, Adeline, Timothy, and Charlotte. The Cérisola's were supreme hosts and connected me to many individuals in Reims. Pierre Husson and Christelle Pierre introduced me to veterans of the exodus and helped me locate sources at the Bibliothèque Carnegie de Reims. Thierry and France Gosset connected me to Renaud Poirer and other individuals in the champagne world. The family of Anne D'Argent kindly hosted me.

In Corrèze, Louis Dalm introduced me to families who had hosted refugees. Régine and Alain Kaneko welcomed me in Nyons and introduced me to many participants in the war, especially René Brès who shared his stories of resistance and inspired my initial interest in wartime France.

In Paris I also enjoyed a supportive community of young American scholars. I thank Clare Crowston, Cynthia Cupples, Lisa DiCaprio, Jennifer Hecht, Hilary Jewett, Cheryl A. Koos, Janine Lanza, Mindy Roseman, John Savage, Lynn Sharp, and Victoria Thompson. Parisian friends and colleagues guided me through the cultural divides that often confront Americans in Paris. Laure Léveillé, Jack and Marie-Jo Léveillé, Frédéric Attal, Thomas Hafen, Carolle von Ins, Cécilia Bouzard, Olivier De Col, and their families made sure that I enjoyed the best of French life and cuisine. I can never thank them enough for entering into our Franco-American friendship.

In New York a vibrant group of friends and colleagues discussed history and politics and helped with revisions. I thank Aline Baehler, Caitlin Barbakoff, Valentjn Bivank, Deborah Brody, Anne-Sophie Cerisola, G. Daniel Cohen, Mark Giaimo, Savario Giovacchini, Carolyn Helmke, Matthew Hockenos, Wendy Holliday, Jennifer Homans, Steve Hubbell, Sarah Judson, Edward Kastenmeier, Dan Katz, Peter Lang, Nancy Mykoff, Timothy Pytell, Marybeth Shaw, Amy Sittler, Tracy Tullis, and especially Iris Derbsch.

At NYU, I enjoyed the privilege of excellent faculty readers. Herrick Chapman commented on the last draft of my dissertation. Susan Ware helped me think more critically about women's history questions. Jerrold Seigel pushed me to re-conceptualize key interpretive ideas.

Marilyn Young allowed me to hold a conference on women and war, which helped me contextualize French civilians' experience in a more global framework.

At Princeton University I met Arno Mayer, who not only deepened my love of European history, but as a survivor of the exodus from Luxembourg, shared his memories with me. Arno read through my entire manuscript and saved me from several errors. Most importantly, he reminded me that as a historian, "chronology was my friend." Robert Darnton shared with me stories about his mother's career as a young female journalist in Paris and inspired me to read American journalistic accounts of the war. I deepened my understanding of the Third Republic precepting in Philip Nord's course on Modern France. Stephen Kotkin insisted I think more politically about historical structures in a comparative framework. William Chester Jordan invited me to present a chapter to the Princeton faculty. I received helpful feedback from a number of colleagues, especially David Allyn, Ben Alpers, Hilary Bernstein, Peter Lake, and Suzanne Marchand.

At Towson University and in the greater Baltimore–Washington DC area, I have enjoyed invaluable collegial support. Cindy Gissendanner and Mark Whitman supported two separate semesters of maternity leave. Former deans, Dan Jones and Beverly Leetch approved both leaves. I received generous support for graduate research assistance from the Towson University College of Liberal Arts. Dorian Cole, Lisa Hammond, Peter Krause, and Hugh Weigel helped with research. Christine Adams, Linda Bishai, Rita Costa-Gomes, Julie Fette, William Friend, Marion Hughes, Joshua Humphries, Michael Korzi, Paul Miller, Tracy Miller, Katharine Norris, and Ronn Pineo have read and commented on various chapters or offered support. Professor Emeritus Karl Larew provided a stream of invaluable wartime novels and memoirs. Benjamin Zajicek has been a great sounding board at the end of this process. Emily Daugherty, our secretary, has provided unmatched administrative assistance.

A trio of incredible women has inspired me intellectually and professionally. Sally Charnow, Jair Kessler, and Molly Nolan have guided me along at different stages of this work. Sally and Molly have read significant portions of versions of this manuscript and made critically important comments. Without Jair Kessler none of the research, travel, or career advancement would have been possible. Jair has not only guided the Institute of French Studies at NYU and helped manage the Remarque Institute as its administrative director, but she has facilitated the encounter and advancement of a generation of graduate students and scholars. Three invitations to Remarque Institute seminars in

Vienna (1995), New York (1996), and Kandersteg (2011) introduced me to a group of international scholars whose work has especially pushed me to understand French history in the larger European framework. I wish to especially thank Katherine E. Fleming for organizing the 2011 Kandersteg seminar honoring Tony Judt, which brought together many of his students and colleagues, inspiring me through the final revisions of this book.

Two scholars have had the greatest impact on my life and work, but are certainly not responsible for any of this work's failings, which are solely my own. Jack Fruchtman, Jr. has mentored me since I became an assistant professor at Towson University. Jack has been instrumental in helping me see this book through to publication. I thank him for his inspiration and guidance.

I had the greatest fortune to study at NYU under Tony Judt. Tony helped me conceptualize this project from its beginnings. He insisted that I travel to local archives, read local histories, and meet with exodus veterans. He also ensured the financial support necessary for such travel. Throughout the long revision process Tony read and re-read many versions and offered criticism and valuable comments. He was always generous with his advice, time, and friendship. My debt and thanks to Tony is immeasurable, as is the amount I miss him.

My family has lived with this project for many years, patiently accompanying me on trips to France, allowing me time to cloister myself to "write." I thank my parents, Jerome and Sue Ellen Dombrowski for their unwavering support. My children, Olivia and Michael, have forced me to strive for a balanced and joyous lifestyle. However, in writing this book, I have been reminded daily that, with the exception of Olivia's first year, our nation has been at war throughout my children's young lives. As a mother, I have appreciated being able to raise them in a relatively safe environment despite 9/11 and its consequences. I cannot help but recognize how many families elsewhere in our world live in war-torn societies, motivating me to complete this book, if for no other reason than to honor the sacrifices of the millions of families who struggled to survive the twentieth century's brutal wars.

The completion of this work would not have been possible without my husband, Jim Risser's steady encouragement. He has read and commented on the entire manuscript many times, sustaining me through the years of research and revision. His patience and love for our family allowed me to finish this work. I thank him and lovingly dedicate this book to him.

Abbreviations

AN	Archives nationales de la France
ADC	Archives départementales de la Corrèze
ADM	Archives départementales de la Marne
AMBG	Archives municipales de Brive-la-Gaillarde
AMVR	Archives municipales de la ville de Reims
BDIC	Bibliothèque Documentaire Information Contemporaine
DGGFTO	Délégation générale du Gouvernement français pour les territoires occupés
IDP	internally displaced person
MBF	Militärbefehlshaber in Frankreich
MBH	German Military Administration in Belgium
PCF	Parti communiste français
PSF	Parti socialiste français
PoW	prisoner of war
PTT	Poste télégraphe et téléphone
RAF	Royal Air Force
SHAT	Service historique de l'armée de la terre
SFIO	Section française de l'internationale d'ouvrière
SNCF	Société Nationale des Chemins de fer français (French National Railway)
UN	United Nations
UNHCR	United Nations High Commissioner for Refugees

Introduction: no more "behind the lines"

Total War, Endangered Civilians, and the French Exodus of 1940

For a thousand years man has been taught that women and children are to be shielded from war. War is a matter for men only. The village mayors are full of this law of society; their clerks know it; the school teachers know it. Assume that suddenly they receive orders to stop the evacuations, which is to say, force women and children to remain in the zone of bombardment. It will take them a month to adjust their conscience to this sign of a new age.

Antoine de Saint-Exupéry, *Flight to Arras*, 1942[1]

The deliberate attack and maiming of unarmed civilians is terrorism pure and simple, whatever the cause.

Kofi Annan, United Nations Secretary General, July 13, 2006[2]

On May 10, 1940, flying at a low altitude and shadowing an impressive constellation of ground forces, German Heinkel and Dornier bombers ripped through northern European skies. In seven key attacks, the Luftwaffe unleashed its hailstorm of bombs. From Delfzijl and Rotterdam in the Netherlands, to Brussels and Antwerp in Belgium, to Luxembourg, the attacks shattered the deceptive tranquility that cloaked France and the Benelux countries. Along the River Moselle, the French returned "a hurricane of defensive fire from small arms and anti-aircraft guns."[3] British pilots joined the fight over Belgium, skipping over a "swarm of refugees who preceded the German line" and loosing "small bombs and sprays of machine gun bullets" onto the German divisions. Reaching Paris on May 11, German bombers

---

[1] Antoine de Saint-Exupéry, *Flight to Arras*, trans. Lewis Galantière, illustrated by Bernard Lamotte (New York: Reynal & Hitchcock, 1942), 129. The author thanks Karl Larew, Professor Emeritus of Towson University, for Saint-Exupéry's memoir.

[2] Kofi Annan, Secretary-General's press encounter following working luncheon with Italian Prime Minister, Romano Prodi, Rome, Italy, July 12, 2006, see http://www.un.org/sg/offthecuff/?nid=903.

[3] "British Airmen Hit Nazi Columns; Raid is Reported at Essen in Ruhr: The Mark of the Bomber Left on Paris and Nancy by Raiding Reich Warplanes," *New York Times*, May 12, 1940, 1.

1

hit French airfields and rail stations, as well as crushing civilian residences in Méry-sur-Oise on the outskirts of the capital. In one night, 148 French civilians died.[4]

The ensuing six weeks brought murderous fighting deep within French borders. On the ground, gritty combat consumed troops in the Ardennes forest, at the Moselle, the Meuse, and the Somme, places that still bore the scars from the ravages of World War I. The British Expeditionary Force was evacuated from Dunkerque on May 28, leaving French troops to fight on alone. By June 22, the German Wehrmacht had captured nearly two million French soldiers and killed an estimated 100,000.[5] The "swarm" of refugees that first amassed in the Benelux countries marched along with the German troops into France. Terrified, residents of France's north-eastern departments joined their ranks. By the time the "exodus" of refugees cleared Paris on June 14, their numbers had swollen to between 8 and 11 million.[6] During the rout, the Germans captured the husbands of 790,000 French women, leaving them as the sole providers for their families.[7] Millions of refugee women retreated with children, grandparents, and the few household possessions they managed to hastily pack. German bombers and fighter planes trailed the mass of humanity and retreating French troops, who co-mingled with civilians on the way to Orléans, Tours, Rennes, and Bordeaux. Unwilling, or unable, to distinguish combatant from non-combatant, German pilots fired upon the civilian innocents, claiming another 100,000 victims before the battle's end. British expatriate, W. Fortune, living in France wondered, "Had any army up to that date suffered so many casualties in so short a time?"[8]

The government collapsed as quickly as the military front. On June 16, the Cabinet of Ministers voted fourteen to six against Prime Minister Paul Reynaud and for inquiring about German terms of an armistice. Reynaud chose to resign rather than end the fight, but he recommended to President Albert Lebrun that he name Marshal

---

[4] "British Airmen Hit Nazi Columns," *New York Times*, May 12, 1940, 1.

[5] G. and W. Fortune, *Hitler Divided Europe: A Factual Account of Conditions in Occupied France from the Armistice of June 1940 up to the Total Occupation in November 1942* (London: Macmillan, 1943), 16–17. Fishman reports that the Red Cross estimated 1,605,000, while the Germans claimed 1,929,000 captive soldiers. Sarah Fishman, *We Will Wait: Wives of French Prisoners of War, 1940–1945* (New Haven, CT: Yale University Press, 1991), xv.

[6] Fortune, *Hitler Divided Europe*, 1. The larger number was reported at the time. The accepted number is the lower.

[7] Fishman, *We Will Wait*, xv.   [8] Fortune, *Hitler Divided France*, 16.

Philippe Pétain, hero of the battle of Verdun, as his successor. Pétain favored an armistice. On June 17, Pétain declared via radio: "Stop the fighting." Historians have amply documented these events. The armistice that took effect on June 25 dealt France its most stinging blow since Waterloo. It stipulated that the country would be governed by a German Military Administration in the "Occupied Zone," and by a French state in a "Free Zone." The agreement made no mention of a formal partition of the nation by a "Line of Demarcation."[9] But within the week, the German Army began laying barbed wire and establishing checkpoints: France would be divided.

The defeat produced several immediate crises. Militarily, much of the French Army had been captured and soldiers, detached from their units, had deserted. Politically, the government had collapsed and was moving from German-occupied Bordeaux, to a spa town in the "Free Zone," Vichy, where Pétain would win the case for assuming full governing powers on July 10. The greater crisis unfolded on the roads and in towns along the Atlantic coast, and in the Massif Central and southwestern departments of France. The millions of residents who had fled the invading German forces, now found themselves homeless, without food, transportation, or news of lost family members. Universally called "refugees," these populations created an unprecedented humanitarian crisis spanning both administrative zones.

The principal problem challenging the new government at Vichy was to "repatriate" French, Benelux, German, and Jewish refugees to their homes.[10] The task of repatriation was immediately complicated by the German sealing of the Line of Demarcation and by the destruction to rails and roadways. Communication between the two zones was prohibited. Refugees crowded into town halls, schools, churches, train stations, and barns for shelter. Food shortages arose as municipalities tried to feed the surplus populations. The inadequacy of sanitary facilities threatened public health. In their desperate attempt to escape German bombing and contact with enemy combatants, civilian refugees found themselves engaged in a struggle for survival.

How had France come to this point in her history, where her population stood scattered across the country intermingled with her broken army? How would a newly formed government, heir to a partitioned,

---

[9] Eric Alary, *La ligne de démarcation: 1940–1944* (Paris: Perrin, 2003), 33.
[10] The original argument regarding repatriation and the core of the research in this volume are drawn from the author's dissertation, Nicole Ann Dombrowski, "Beyond the Battlefield: The French Civilian Exodus of May–June 1940," Ph.D. dissertation, New York University, 1995.

defeated nation, address the needs of millions of internally displaced civilians and foreign refugees? What challenges did women in particular face as displaced heads of households, forced to provide for children whose fathers were captured or wandering about somewhere in northern France?

Several postwar studies have investigated the causes of France's defeat in 1940.[11] We know much about the weaknesses of interwar military planning and production.[12] Philippe Burrin and Robert Paxton helped to forge a body of scholarship that details forms of political, economic, and cultural collaboration between the Vichy regime and the Germans.[13] This broad spectrum has defined activities that ranged from the ideological embrace of German fascism and criminal enforcement of its politically repressive and racist policies, through daily accommodation with the military administration, to active armed resistance anchored in anti-fascist and communist ideals. The historiography of Gaullist resistance and liberation remains the standard lens to view and commemorate the war's end.[14] Within the last two decades, historians have mined the rich terrain of daily life under the Occupation, casting light

---

[11] See Jean-Pierre Azéma, *1940 l'anné terrible* (Paris: Seuil, 1990); Martin Alexander, "The Fall of France, 1940," in Gordon Martel (ed.), *The World War II Reader* (New York: Routledge, 2004), 7–40; Marc Bloch, *The Strange Defeat: A Statement of Evidence Written in 1940* (New York: Norton, [1948] 1968); Julian Jackson, *The Fall of France: The Nazi Invasion of 1940* (Oxford University Press, 2003); Jean-Baptiste Duroselle, *L'Abîme 1939–1945* (Paris: Imprimerie nationale, 1982); Henry Dutailly, *Les Problèmes de l'armée de terre française (1935–1939)* (Paris: Imprime nationale, 1980); André Geraud, *The Gravediggers of France: Gamelin, Daladier, Reynaud, Petain, and Laval* (Garden City, NY: Doubleday, Doran, 1944); Erich von Manstein, *Lost Victories: The War Memoirs of Hitler's Most Brilliant General*, ed. Martin Blumenson (Munich: Bernard & Graefe Verlag, [1955] 1982).

[12] Herrick Chapman, *State Capitalism and Working-Class Radicalism in the French Aircraft Industry* (Berkeley, CA: University of California Press, 1991); Talbot Imlay, *Facing the Second World War: Strategy, Politics and Economics in Britain and France 1938–1940* (Oxford University Press, 2003); Roxanne Panchasi, *Future Tense: The Culture of Anticipation in France between the Wars* (Ithaca, NY: Cornell University Press, 2009).

[13] Philippe Burrin, *France under the Germans: Collaboration and Compromise*, trans. Janet Lloyd (New York: The New Press, 1993); Robert O. Paxton, *Vichy France: Old Guard and New Order, 1940–1944* (New York: Columbia University Press, 1982); Julian Jackson, *France, The Dark Years, 1940–44* (Oxford University Press, 2002); Robert Gildea, *Marianne in Chains: Daily Life in the Heart of France during the German Occupation* (New York: Metropolitan Books, 2002); Bertram M. Gordon, *Collaborationism in France during the Second World War* (Ithaca, NY: Cornell University Press, 1980); John Sweets, *Choices in Vichy France* (New York: Oxford University Press, 1986); Richard Vinen, *The Unfree French: Life under the Occupation* (London: Penguin/Allen Lane, 2005). Robert Zaretsky, *Nîmes at War: Religion, Politics and Public Opinion in the Gard, 1938–1944* (University Park, PN: Pennsylvania State University Press, 1995).

[14] For a synopsis of Gaullist scholarship, see Fondation nationale des sciences politiques et la Fondation Charles de Gaulle, *Le rétablissement de la légalité républicaine (1944)* (Bruxelles: Éditions Complexe, 1996).

on women's experiences.[15] The research that weaves France's wartime history most directly into the broader European experience of German Occupation is the shameful treatment of European Jews through policies of discrimination, round-up, detention, deportation, forced labor, and extermination. In this field, Holocaust history in France has intersected with the study of postwar memory of the Occupation.[16]

Imbedded within these subdivisions of France's wartime history is the topic of civilian survival during and in the aftermath of combat exposure. This subject falls in line with new approaches linking civilian and military experience under total war.[17] Specifically, civilian evacuations and the problems associated with mass flight and internal displacement of domestic and foreign refugees offers historians a vast panorama for exploring the relationship between state military planning, civilian

[15] Clare Gorrara (ed.), *Modern and Contemporary France*, Special Issue, "Gendering the Occupation," February 1997; Sarah Fishman, *The Battle for Children: World War II, Youth Crime, and Juvenile Justice in Twentieth Century France* (Cambridge, MA: Harvard University Press, 2002); Hannah Diamond, *Women and the Second World War in France, 1938–1948: Choices and Constraints* (London: Longman, 1999); Margaret Collins Weitz, *Sisters in the Resistance: How Women Fought to Free France, 1940–1945* (New York: John Wiley, 1995); Nicole Chatel, *Des femmes dans la résistance* (Paris: Juilliard, 1972); Ania Francis, *Il était des femmes dans la résistance* (Paris: Stock, 1978); Miranda Pollard, *Reign of Virtue: Mobilizing Gender in Vichy France* (University of Chicago Press, 1998); Fabrice Virgili, *Shorn Women: Gender and Punishment in Liberation France*, trans. John Flower (Oxford: Berg, 2002); Dominique Veillon, *La mode sous l'Occupation* (Paris: Payot, 1990); Paula Schwartz, "*Partisanes* and Gender Politics in Vichy France," in Gordon Martel (ed.), *The World War II Reader* (New York: Routledge, 2004), 296–316.

[16] Denis Peschanski, *La France des camps: l'internement, 1938–1946* (Paris: Gaillmard, 2002) and *Vichy 1940–44: contrôle et exclusion* (Bruxelles: Éditions Complexe, 1997); Renée Poznanski, *Jews in France during World War II*, trans. Nathan Bracher (Hanover, NH: University Press of New England, 2001); Adam Rayski, *Le choix des juifs sous Vichy entre soumission et résistance* (Paris: la Découverte, 1992); Rita Thalmann, *La mise au pas. Idéologie et stratégie sécuritaire dans la France occupée* (Paris: Fayard, 1991); Annette Wieviorka, *Déportation et génocide: Entre la mémoire et l'oublie* (Paris: Plon, 1992); Susan Zuccotti, *The Holocaust, The French, and The Jews* (New York: Basic Books, 1993); Paul Webster, *Pétain's Crime: The Full Story of French Collaboration in the Holocaust* (London: Macmillan, 1990); Yves Soulignac, *Les camps d'internement en Limousin, 1939–1945* (Saint-Paul: Soulignac, 1995); Dan Michman, *Belgium and the Holocaust: Jews, Belgians, Germans* (Jerusalem: Yad Vashem, 1998); Serge Klarsfeld, *Vichy–Auschwitz. Le rôle de Vichy dans la solution finale de la question juive en France, 1942* (Paris: Fayard, 1983); Claude Singer, *Vichy, l'université et les juifs. Les silences et la mémoire* (Paris: Les Belles Lettres, 1992); Bernard Delaunay, *Mémorial de la Résistance et de la déportation en Corrèze 1940–1945* (Édité par le Comité de la Corrèze de l'Association nationale des anciens combattants de la Résistance et ses amis. Brive: ANACR, 1995).

[17] Tammy M. Proctor, *Civilians in a World at War, 1914–1918* (New York University Press, 2010); Nicholas Atkin (ed.), *Daily Lives of Civilians in Wartime Twentieth-Century Europe*, "Daily Life through History" Series (Westport, CN: Greenwood Press, 2008); John N. Horne and Alain Kramer, *German Atrocities, 1914: A History of Denial* (New Haven, CT: Yale University Press, 2001).

security provisioning, and humanitarian crisis management. These areas of modern state activity have received much attention from government planners, scholars of international law, and human rights activists, but have only recently attracted attention from historians.[18]

The origins of France's refugee crisis stem from French interwar approaches to national defense and civilian security, which national officials developed in response to the breakdown of the international order crafted at Versailles. Until May 1940, planning streamed from the national to the local level, but civilians lived the consequences of the successes and failures of national programs in their towns and villages. The French Ministry of Interior and National Defense crafted interwar civilian protection strategies: bomb shelters, evacuation plans, relocation schemes, population transfers, and civil defense. Most civilians learned about the state's security plans as well as the war's progress in their local newspapers. The Bureau of Civil Defense (Défense passive), attached to National Defense and the Ministry of the Interior, imagined zones of civilian vulnerability and attempted to generate sets of uniform policies; however, implementation of policies differed from one region to another. While Paris concentrated its greatest efforts on the border departments within Alsace and Lorraine, it prepared other north-eastern departments for secondary evacuations. By 1936, the Défense passive had planned for the transfer of large populations to interior departments in the Massif Central and south-western regions, whose prefects planned for the reception of potentially large evacuee populations.

Selecting the department of the Marne for close examination of the erosion of civilian confidence and a site of mass departures, and Corrèze as a host department designated to receive evacuees; this study highlights the interaction between threatened civilians and their local government officials. The Marne sits just outside Alsace and Lorraine and was designated in 1936 to host future Alsatian and Lorrainer evacuees. However, the Marne also developed a plan to evacuate its own residents in the case of deeper German military encroachment. The Marne was thus more similar to the vast majority of northern French departments, also designated to host potential evacuees, but aware of their own population's eventual vulnerability. During World War I, the

---

[18] Eric Alary, *L'exode: Un drame oublié* (Paris: Perrin, 2010); Hanna Diamond, *Fleeing Hitler* (Oxford University Press, 2007); Julia S. Torrie, *"For Their Own Good": Civilian Evacuations in Germany and France, 1939–1945* (New York: Berghahn Books, 2010); Laura Lee Downs, "'A Very British Revolution'? L'évacuation des enfants citadins vers les campagnes anglaises 1939–1945," *Vingtième Siècle. Revue d'Histoire*, 89, January–March 2006, 47–60.

Marne witnessed some of the heaviest fighting, and its civilian population carried the memory of the devastation caused by German land invasion and aerial bombardment; a memory which played a role in civilians' decisions to flee.[19]

Corrèze forms the south-eastern tip of the Limousin region, located in France's Massif Central. A gateway to France's south-western departments and Spain, isolated, rural, and lightly populated, Corrèze was chosen by civil defense planners as an ideal retreat for northern evacuees. Already in 1936, Corrèze and the surrounding departments of the Limousin and Aquitaine received directives to prepare evacuee reception centers. Corrèze, with a major train hub at Brive-la-Gaillarde, thus emerged as a final destination for evacuees, and a major transfer point for evacuees traveling further south. Corrèze also emerged as a magnet for refugee relocation after repatriation, due in part to a political heritage which favored communalism, shared public responsibility, and a predisposition against right-wing politics.[20]

The earliest questions posed by French historians about the exodus, written in the immediate aftermath of the war, focused on the impact that the dispersal of civilians had upon French military maneuvers.[21] Jean Vidalenc's classic study, *L'exode de mai–juin 1940* (1957), asked whether the exodus evolved as a deliberate plot of German agents implanted within France to stir up public anxiety and trigger a mass civilian flight that would encumber French troops.[22] Vidalenc provisionally concluded that: "It is still not possible to confirm whether the initial exodus ... was the work of local enemy agents (sleepers) already in place, ready to act without direct orders from superiors."[23] The sleeper thesis received widespread support in popular fiction written during and after the German Occupation. Lion Feuchtwanger's 1944 resistance novel, *Simone*, first distilled the sleeper thesis as a collaborator named Prosper opined that: "the alleged French official orders to evacuate additional territory really came from the Boches [Germans]

---

[19] Jean-Pierre Husson, *La Marne et les Marnais à l'epreuve de la Seconde Guerre mondiale*, vols. 1 and 2 (Reims: Presses universitaires de Reims, 1995), 87.

[20] Laird Boswell, *Rural Communism in France 1920–1939* (Ithaca, NY: Cornell University Press, 1998), 221. Boswell states that Communists controlled thirty-three rural villages in Corrèze by the mid-1930s.

[21] Jean-Louis Crémieux-Birlhac, *Les français de l'an 40: ouvriers et soldats*, vol. 1 (Paris: Gallimard, 1990); Pierre Miquel, *L'exode de 10 mai–20 juin 1940* (Paris: Plon, 2002); Paul-André Lesort, *Quelques jours de mai–juin 40: Mémoire, témoignage, histoire* (Paris: Seuil, 1992).

[22] Jean Vidalenc, *L'exode de mai–juin 1940* (Paris: Presses universitaires de France, 1957), 67–8.

[23] Vidalenc, *L'exode de mai–juin 1940*. Translated from the French by the author.

for the purpose of increasing the confusion. At any rate, the panic was contagious, half of France was now in flight, all roads were jammed, preventing military movements."[24]

Vidalenc and the historian Jean-Louis Crémieux-Brilhac took as a starting point the description of civilians' new reality as military targets. But Vidalenc puzzled that, "One is at a loss to explain certain bombings and machine guns 'randomly fired' far from any military target ... Such a tactic sought to create panic on back roads and alleyways, which cannot be explained except by an orientation toward a psychological form of war."[25] Many scholars in the 1950s had trouble integrating civilians' experiences into the traditional historical paradigms of military and political history. Still, Vidalenc's work presented one of the first attempts at a social and cultural history of France's defeat. Historian Marc Bloch, who did not survive the war, identified bombing of civilians as an end in and of itself. Bloch outwitted the Gestapo long enough to pen these conclusions: "the fact is that this dropping of bombs from the sky has a unique power of spreading terror. They are dropped from a great height, and seem, though quite erroneously, to be falling straight on top of one's head."[26] Accepting the spreading of terror as one of the intentions of bombing, and examining its other consequences – civilian death, social demoralization, mass displacement, economic paralysis, humanitarian crisis, political and social destabilization, infrastructure collapse – deepens our understanding of what "total war" means for the destruction of civilian life. American historian John Dower was among the first to reconfigure the historian's approach to the civilian experience of bombing. Histories of Hiroshima and Nagasaki, Dower writes, "leave out the fate of nuclear victims."[27] Dower insists that the paucity of information about the effects of atomic bombing resulted from an intentional suppression of eye-witness accounts and a reluctance to make documentation of civilian experience available to the public in the aftermath of the war. Retrieving, comparing, and legitimizing eye-witness accounts of embattled civilians, must, as Dower argues, serve as the keystone for historical analysis of civilian experience of World War II and of modern warfare in general. Within this revised approach to the history of bombing, *France under Fire* seeks to offer a more detailed account of the daily impact of bombing's violence

[24] Lion Feuchtwanger, *Simone*, trans. G. A. Hermann (New York: Viking Press, 1944), 36.
[25] Feuchtwanger, *Simone*, 68.
[26] Bloch, *The Strange Defeat*, 57.
[27] John Dower, "The Bombed," in Michael J. Hogan (ed.), *Hiroshima in History and Memory* (Cambridge University Press, 1996), 124.

upon women and children and refugees most frequently discursively gendered as female. Such an approach may help contemporary readers to appreciate what Tony Judt has described as: "the trauma that lay behind the images of desolation and hopelessness that caught the attention of observers in 1945," helping to launch postwar reforms to the laws of war and human rights.[28]

To understand non-combatants' wartime experience, historians must excavate the sources of fear and realize that civilians caught up in combat lack the training of soldiers prepared to encounter military violence. Civilian fears grew in the context of growing frustration with French government civil defense planning, poor military communication, misleading journalism, and unexpected aerial attack. Focusing on the sources of fear contributes to the revision of earlier accusations that refugees were traitors, cowards, or victims of foreign agents, and allows us to pinpoint many of the structural sources of civilian flight.

Recent studies have acknowledged the consequences of civilian fear and allowed for a larger role of the civilian upheaval in France's defeat. Julian Jackson's *The Fall of France*, Robert Gildea's *Marianne in Chains*, and Richard Vinen's *The Unfree French* discuss the refugee crisis as an episode in France's defeat and connect it to French support of the armistice. Yet the deep impact on family survival and relief institutions begs further exploration. Hanna Diamond's *Fleeing Hitler*, has recently tapped oral histories and literary women's recollections to paint a picture of refugees' fear, and also gives women's voices a more prominent role in narrating the exodus. Anchored in archival research, *France under Fire* mines ordinary women's letters, written during the crisis to all levels of French officials, in attempts to explain the sources of their fear and to influence policy to improve their security. By examining women's experience through their letters and postwar testimonies, we see that mass flight was both an expression of fear and frustration with women's failed efforts to lobby local officials and national civil defense planners during France's march toward war. Throughout the crisis we find women appropriating the political language of social entitlements and collective rights that was used by pronatalists to win family allowances as a universal benefit during the Popular Front era (1936–1938).[29] The model of state subsidies paid to families helped French women to imagine structures that would limit war's devastating impact upon families.

---

[28] Tony Judt, *Postwar: A History of Europe since 1945* (New York: Penguin, 2005), 16.
[29] Susan Pedersen, *Family, Dependence, and the Origins of the Welfare State, Britain and France, 1914–1945* (Cambridge University Press, 1993), 358, 387, 410.

Since civilian women engaged the state during all three phases of the displacement crisis – the Phoney War's period of selective evacuations, the moment of invasion and exodus, and the period of repatriation and resettlement – we find them active as citizens, motivated as war's victims, struggling as refugees, and advocating for access to social, economic, and human rights guarantees. As such, the exodus and its aftermath represent a notable episode not only in France's history, but in the history of French women's emergence into modern citizens.

Swept up into the war, civilian women were "called to action" in the arenas within French society where they had participated since 1914. As emerging citizens, they lobbied local and national politicians, circulated petitions, volunteered for relief services, supported national defense when given the opportunity, and tried to preserve the rights they had gained in the interwar period.[30] Miranda Pollard has shown how Vichy capitalized on the defeat to enact a systematic reversal of women's interwar political and economic achievements. Pollard shows that some women resisted and rejected policies that limited their gains in the face of authoritarianism and occupation. This study complements Pollard's work, identifying how Vichy's policies extended to the refugee population, and shows that civilian refugees engaged the state throughout the dictatorship, actively defying the narrowing scope for female participation in public life.

As shapers and beneficiaries of the interwar welfare state, civilian women pressed for the enhancement and extension of entitlements under the new conditions of war. Capitalizing upon their status as war workers, many civilian women tried to relocate to industries operating out of harm's way and find jobs that would contribute to national defense. Contiguous with interwar efforts to establish economic independence, female civilian workers attempted to use their employment status to improve their wartime physical security.[31] As heads of families, French women mobilized in the context of economic collapse for the basics: food, clothing and shelter, as well as the return of their captive husbands.[32] The refugee crisis forced women to engage with the state for subsistence needs prior to the full imposition of the Occupation.

---

[30] Pollard, *Reign of Virtue*; Rita Thalmann (ed.), *Femmes et fascisme* (Paris: Éditions Tierce, 1986).

[31] For women's interwar workplace activity see Laura Lee Downs, *Manufacturing Inequality: Gender Division in the French and British Metal-working Industries, 1914–1939* (Ithaca, NY: Cornell University Press, 1995).

[32] Lynne Taylor, *Between Resistance and Collaboration: Popular Protest in Northern France, 1940–1944* (Basingstoke: Macmillan, 1999).

Under the Occupation, historians have found that women engaged in a spectrum of activity ranging from collaboration to resistance.

Civilian refugees were the first to challenge the enforcement of French territorial partitioning and the exclusionary policies of German border patrols. The refugee crisis and partition also escalated the dangers confronting French and foreign Jewish civilians. The Line of Demarcation allowed the Germans to introduce policies of ethnic and racial cleansing, discrimination, and exclusion. Families in host communities engaged in some of the first acts of resistance, sheltering excluded refugees or ignoring the regime's insistence on enforcing racial policies.[33]

As victims of war, French women, and sometimes male household heads, expressed anger over the encroachment of war into the home front, fleeing aerial bombing, suffering hunger, dehydration, and rape, but demanding as citizens' and as displaced refugees their rights to compensation for their wartime suffering.[34] The French civilian population experienced the deprivation of their human rights and responded by demanding protection from war and access to domestic and international relief. French civilians articulated their security concerns within a historically emerging framework, herein labeled "the politics of civilian protection," which gave rise to a civilian-centered concept of "national security."[35]

Part II of this book explores the management of the refugee crisis amid competing German and French interests at the onset of occupation and reconstruction. In the context of state partition, military occupation, and the establishment of an authoritarian French state, civilian refugees organized in the south in an attempt to influence policies impacting their long-term displacement and repatriation. Two important French studies by Eric Alary and Philippe Souleau weigh the benefits and liabilities of national partition on French economic recovery.[36] Both works corroborate Robert Paxton's earlier thesis that

---

[33] Dominique Veillon, *La Collaboration. Textes et débats* (Paris: Hachette, 1984); Weitz, *Sisters in the Resistance*; Schwartz, "*Partisanes* and Gender Politics in Vichy France," 296–316; Diamond, *Women and the Second World War*; Shannon L. Fogg, *The Politics of Everyday Life in Vichy France* (Cambridge University Press, 2009).

[34] Downs, "A Very British Revolution?"; Fishman, *We Will Wait*.

[35] Susan Grayzel, *Women's Identities at War: Gender, Motherhood, and Politics in Britain and France During the First World War* (Chapel Hill, NC: University of North Carolina Press, 1999); Annette Becker, *War and Faith: The Religious Imagination in France, 1914–1930*, trans. Helen McPhail (New York: Berg, 1998); Helen McPhail, *The Long Silence: Civilian Life under the German Occupation of Northern France, 1914–1918* (London: I. B. Tauris, 1999).

[36] Alary, *La ligne de démarcation: 1940–1944*; Alary, *L'exode un drame oublié*; Philippe Souleau, *La ligne de démarcation en Gironde: Occupation, Résistance et société 1940–1944* (Périgueux: Fanlac, 1998).

partition allowed prefects a greater degree of freedom in managing local crises.[37] This study uses local and national archival sources to examine Vichy negotiations with the Germans to allow fluid passage between the two zones and how national objectives quickly narrowed the ability of Free Zone prefects to craft independent policies toward refugees. Department archives also reveal the role refugees played in trying to influence crisis management.

Examining refugee relief in Corèzze offers several advantages. Prefects and mayors in Corrèze structured refugee relief, administered government relocation subsidies, and launched refugee employment programs as stipulated in national directives. However, they also developed unique applications from some surrounding departments, which is reflected in interdepartmental correspondence and sheds light on the growing imprint of Vichy ideology on refugee relief and repatriation policy. This slightly comparative approach throws into relief Vichy's recovery objectives for the Occupied Zone, which hinged upon a quick and thorough refugee repatriation program. The exploration of the conditions of return reveal the linkages between repatriation policy and the early implementation of the policies of civilian categorization that resulted in political, racial, and national exclusion, and ultimately prepared local mechanisms for the round-up, arrest, and deportation of political "undesirables" and Jewish refugees. Hence, this work contributes to the research on exclusion notably advanced by Denis Peschanski and Shannon L. Fogg.[38] Fogg's *The Politics of Everyday Life* has explored how Limousin officials coped with the long-term refugee presence, in part by enforcing policies of exclusion of Jews and Gypsies.[39] *France under Fire* reinforces Fogg's work on material shortages and political propaganda, but further explores the role played by Vichy's economic and political ambitions for the Occupied Zone in shaping the "insider" and "outsider" refugee dynamic.

Finally, by following refugees through the repatriation process from Corrèze to the Occupied Zone, we can learn how refugee women experienced the return to bombed-out, hostile territory. Repatriated refugees continued to engage the state, demanding assistance for reintegration

---

[37] Paxton, *Vichy France*. In Alary in *L'exode* dedicates two chapters to the return policy.
[38] Peschanski, *Vichy 1940–44*.
[39] Shannon L. Fogg, "Refugees and Indifference: The Effects of Shortages on Attitudes towards Jews in France's Limousin Region during World War II," *Holocaust and Genocide Studies* 21(1), Spring 2007, 31–54; Fogg, "'They are Undesirables': Local and National Responses to Gypsies during World War II," *French Historical Studies* 31(2), Spring 2008, 327–351; Robert Zaretsky, *Nîmes at War*; Sweets, *Choices in Vichy*.

and reconstruction costs. Following returnees to the Marne, as well as Pas-de-Calais and Nord, we find refugee returnees reassuming the role of endangered non-combatants, disappointed about continued British bombing and demanding with new clarity that German occupying authorities abide by the requirements of the laws of war to ensure their security.

Reintegration offers a lens to view how returnee refugees, and women especially, had learned to articulate their demands with a more pointed reference to the emerging language of human rights and the rights of the displaced. We can ask to what degree did French civilians, like their counterparts across the globe, succeed in creating a consciousness among national and world leaders of the necessity to revise the laws of war, and codify their suffering as "crimes against humanity"? Or did French civilians' wartime suffering go unregistered or misunderstood by the postwar authors of international law? *France under Fire* joins the efforts of historian G. Daniel Cohen in linking World War II's displaced civilians' wartime petitions, struggles, and demands to the inauguration of postwar international refugee rights' claims.[40] But it also identifies a link to postwar nation-states' and international institutions' emerging obligations to provide civil defense and social welfare guarantees to civilians displaced by war.

The book is organized chronologically. However, particular themes have emerged that are linked to the chronological phases of the crisis. In some cases, it is necessary to jump chronologically to explore a theme fully. Part I of the book treats the issues surrounding the build-up to war and the unleashing of the refugee crisis. Part II treats the topic of administering refugee relief and the policy of repatriation. Chapter 1 traces French state planning for home-front defense in the interwar years, which focused on Alsace and Lorraine. Civilians' and local officials' response to invasion in the Marne forms the subject of Chapter 2. Chapter 3 follows the exodus to Paris and analyzes the French government's decision to leave the capital. The emptying of Paris shocked the world and prompted spectators to wonder if European civilization sat on the precipice of a tragic end. Eric Sevareid at the Columbia Broadcasting desk in Paris delivered France's eulogy to an American audience: "By noon, dark smoke obscured the sun and crept in streamers along the Champs Élysées … it hung like a giant

---

[40] Gerard Daniel Cohen, *In War's Wake: Europe's Displaced Persons in the Postwar Order* (New York: Oxford University Press, 2011). For a chronology of women refugees' claims to international protection see Heaven Crawley, *Refugees and Gender: Law and Process* (Bristol: Jordan Publishing, 2001).

shroud over the dying city."[41] Chapter 4 describes refugees' survival on the roads of France, co-mingled with a rapidly demobilizing French Army. The chapter also documents how gender influenced experiences for male and female refugees on the road, examining cases of feared and reported sexual violation.

The chapters in Part II examine how partitioning, combined with refugee repatriation, exposed displaced civilians to the potential abrogation of their economic and political rights; and subjected targeted communities to ethnic and political cleansing. It shows that in the aftermath of partition, refugees followed different paths: returning to the destruction in the Occupied Zone, remaining permanently displaced, or fleeing into exile. Chapter 5 focuses on refugee relief in Corrèze, where the arrival of 200,000 to 250,000 refugees doubled the population during the summer of 1940.[42] Chapter 6 recounts the story of the negotiations between the representatives of the newly installed Vichy government and the German Armistice Commission over the repatriation of approximately 7 million refugees from the Free Zone to the Occupied Zone. Chapter 7 examines more deeply the impact of ethnic cleansing measures on "undesirable" refugees who were refused the right of return. Chapter 8 examines how the subdivision of the Occupied Zone into smaller "Restricted Zones" created refugee crises within the northern departments too, frequently reproducing the same dynamics of refugee competition that had existed in communes and villages in the south, and robbing returnees of their desire to find an end to war's disruption.

A final note on language: French officials used the term "evacuee" prior to May 10, 1940 to designate individuals who had official authorization to relocate from their home department. In host communities, individuals and state officials referred to "evacuees" as refugees or evacuees. After the exodus, previously relocated individuals as well as the recently displaced civilians were nearly universally referred to as "refugees." However, policy makers soon tried to distinguish between evacuees, who they considered to be Alsatian and Lorrainers, and refugees, who were targeted for repatriation. This book generally follows the contemporary usage, but adopts the terms used in policy reports cited from either period.

---

[41] Eric Sevareid, *Not So Wild A Dream* (New York: Atheneum, [1946] 1976), 145.
[42] AN F/1a/3660, Service of Refugees, Report, June 1940. The highest concentration of permanent refugees in Corrèze on a single report is 120,000. However, with transfers through the department, the total number of refugees hosted as permanent or short term ranged between 200,000 and 250,000.

Part I

Civilians in the line of fire

1   Securing the homeland

Managing civilian vulnerability

Marthe Vluggens might never have appeared in the historical record of the twentieth century. She held no political office, claimed no great fortune, and could not even vote. Little about her life in Colombes, a town north of Paris, would have attracted historical attention. Then, on September 1, 1939, Germany invaded Poland. On September 2, the French Army drafted her husband, and the next day France declared war on Germany. During three months of the Phoney War – a deceptive title given to the period of quiet conflict prior to the Blitzkrieg – air raids, the loss of her husband's income, and a broadening combat zone transformed Vluggens' sense of personal security. Hence, she took a financial risk and sent her daughter to a boarding school in Brive-la-Gaillarde, a city situated in Corrèze, deep within France's interior.

By December 1939, the war's toll and her dwindling finances led Vluggens to put pen to paper to register a complaint, and hence place herself and her family's experience in the annals of twentieth-century history.[1] She wrote to the mayor of Brive, explaining that since her husband had been drafted, she alone worked to finance their household. Her salary could not cover her rent, transportation to work, clothes for herself and her child, and care packages for her husband. Moreover, employment rendered her ineligible for the military benefit paid to most soldiers' wives. Her letter made an urgent request to receive the "evacuee allocation" paid by the government to Alsatians and Lorrainers relocating to France's interior, which she hoped to use to pay her child's room and board.

"Why," simply because she had taken the initiative to move her own daughter out of harm's way, "should [she] not also receive public

[1] AMBG H/IV, Mme Marthe Vluggens to mayor of Brive-la-Gaillarde, December 12, 1939. Colombes (Seine).

assistance from the government to help cover the cost of essentially maintaining two households?", she argued. "I too must eat!"[2]

Madame Vluggens received a form letter from the mayor. He regretted that national policy tied his hands, and explained that only residents of Alsace and Lorraine and military designated urban centers were eligible for government assistance for evacuation and relocation expenses. Living outside these "official evacuation zones" (Map 1), Vluggens and her child did not qualify for assistance. The correspondence ended there. No record of Madame Vluggens' daughter remains in the municipal archives of Brive-la-Gaillarde. We do not know whether she passed the rest of the war under the shelter of Brive or returned to the more vulnerable Parisian suburbs, only to retreat again once Germany invaded in May 1940.

Marthe Vluggens' family arrangement resembled situations experienced by millions of other civilians who endured the population upheavals common to France and Europe in the first half of the twentieth century.[3] Once caught in the mix of boundary reconfigurations, territorial acquisitions and resettlements, or simple unorganized flight, Europeans struggled to maintain control of individual and family destinies, sometimes by appealing to government or private organizations for assistance, or sometimes by eschewing them. Hundreds of mothers, grandparents, and even some fathers, residing in northern France, authored letters revealing mounting public anxiety. Despite the relative tranquility along French borders during the Phoney War, which lasted from September 3, 1939 to May 10, 1940, population relocation produced a state of perpetual agitation behind the lines. During this period, thousands of French civilians traveled back and forth between homes in eastern border regions and designated safe havens in France's interior. Compared with the massive population upheaval of France and Benelux countries in the spring of 1940, these earlier relocations unfolded, on the surface, in a calm and planned manner. Yet civilian migrations during the Phoney War evidenced the growing restlessness and discontent with government civilian security programs.

Vluggens, and thousands of other French civilians, recorded a spiraling historic phenomenon. They registered their consciousness of their vulnerability and demanded improved civilian protection

---

[2] AMBG H/IV, Mme Marthe Vluggens to mayor of Brive-la-Gaillarde.
[3] These forced refugee migrations must be situated within the larger phenomenon of voluntary and forced migrations in Europe during the period from 1900 to 1953.

Map 1. Map of divided France

programs. The government bureau, Défense passive, processed hundreds of civilian complaints during the Phoney War.[4] The Défense passive struggled to respond to the exigencies of department prefects and city mayors stretched beyond their experience and resources in

---

[4] In 1931 the Ministry of the Interior established the Commission supérieur de la défense passive to plan for eventual civilian evacuations. See Torrie, *"For Their Own Good"*, 25.

confronting the escalating crisis. By writing her letter and moving her daughter, Vluggens, along with other women during World War II, began to reconfigure the perception of the state's responsibility to protect civilians from harm in times of war. The actions of civilians contributed to defining and pioneering what contemporary international law refers to as the "politics of protection."[5] From the interwar period, throughout the period of invasion, partition, and occupation, the "politics of protection" emerged in conjunction with French prewar and wartime national security policies and transformations in warfare. Women of all backgrounds engaged the state to try to gain improved access to civil defense, linking protection to perceived economic or social rights. Women, overwhelmingly more than men, wrote letters as household heads – perhaps because women had received more elementary education, or because wives tended the domestic sphere. In the context of long-term conflict and displacement, family heads came to judge various forms of state wartime assistance as their "due." Assistance included: building air-raid shelters; relocating populations; subsidizing children's boarding-school fees; distributing gas masks; furnishing stipends to equip kitchens; subsidizing utility bills; and paying for gasoline.

Throughout the war, "protection" encompassed a wide variety of state programs linked to shelter, evacuation, forced displacement, flight, and repatriation. The successes and failures of wartime civil defense planning factored into the speed and scope of the collapse of the French home front. Historians of wartime home fronts, such as Julie S. Torrie, are developing a consensus that links "civilians' reactions to evacuation ... to the degree of popular consent for the domestic and foreign policies of the government."[6] Throughout the war in France, civilian contentment with civil defense planning influenced the population's response to German and Allied military attacks and conditioned their survival strategies under national partition and foreign occupation.

---

[5] Most scholarly research on refugee women and civilian evacuees is found in the field of international law. Much of this focuses on the internationally displaced and ignores internally displaced people. Heaven Crawley argues for focus on refugee women because, "the experiences of women differ significantly from men because women's political protest, activism and resistance may manifest itself in different ways": Crawley, *Refugees and Gender, Law and Process*, 2–3. See J. Greatbach, "The Gender Difference: Feminist Critiques of Refugee Discourse," *International Journal of Refugee Law* 3(3), 1989, 585–605, quoted in Crawley, 5.

[6] Torrie, "*For Their Own Good*," 7. For the German experience Torrie references Marlis Steinert, *Hitler's War and the Germans: Public Mood and Attitude during the Second World War*, trans. Thomas E. J. de Witt (Athens, OH: Ohio University Press, 1977).

Interwar civil defense planning

In spring 1936, the Germans raised the stakes for French civil defense planners and northern French civilians when they launched their remilitarization of the Rhineland. Occupation reawakened civilian security concerns and reopened sensitivities about national loyalty in the border regions of Alsace and Lorraine.[7] Many inhabitants of the former German Imperial territories had taken comfort from the Treaty of Versailles, which prohibited Germany from quartering troops, or building fortifications along the left bank of the River Rhine, or within 50 km of the right bank.[8] The signing of the Treaty of Locarno in 1925 demonstrated France's commitment to preventing German remilitarization and reannexation of the Rhineland, a protective buffer between Alsace and Lorraine and its former German master (see Map 2). Hitler denounced the Treaty of Locarno, and when France moved toward ratifying a defense pact with the Soviet Union in May 1935, Germany cried encirclement, mobilized troops along the Rhine and voided the treaty.[9] News of the Reichwehr's reoccupation of the Rhineland and rumors that residents of the region had eagerly greeted German troops stunned French political and military authorities. On March 8, 1936 France moved 50,000 troops toward the Rhineland frontier to back up the 100,000 troops already stationed in border forts.[10] At the same time, the French Foreign Minister Pierre-Étienne Flandin, registered France's disapproval of Germany's treaty violation with the Secretary General of the League of Nations Council.[11] In a speech to the French people,

[7] Laird Boswell, "From Liberation to Purge Trials in the 'Mythic Provinces': Recasting French Identities in Alsace and Lorraine, 1918–1920," *French Historical Studies*, 23(1), Winter 2000, 152, 161–162. Boswell describes how France aggressively attempted to cleanse the German past from Alsace and Lorraine "to allow underlying French national sentiment ... to resurface."

[8] Treaty of Versailles, 1919 (Arts. 42 and 43). Article 44 stipulated: "In case Germany violates in any manner whatever the provisions of Articles 42 and 43 (regarding the demilitarization of the Rhineland), she shall be regarded as committing a hostile act against the Powers signatory of the present Treaty and as calculated to disturb the peace of the world," see www.firstworldwar.com/source/versailles.htm.

[9] Jean-Baptiste Duroselle, *Politique étrangère de la France: La décadence 1932–1939* (Paris: Imprimerie nationale, 1979), 157–161. In fact, the Franco-Soviet Pact of May 1935 lacked any force. Poland's refusal of Soviet troops to defend against the Germans slowed interwar progress toward a military agreement between Britain, France and the USSR. See Paul Reynaud, *In the Thick of the Fight 1930–1945*, trans. James D. Lambert (New York: Simon & Schuster, 1955), 211–233.

[10] "50,000 Men March in Alsace-Lorraine: French Troops Pour From Metz and Other Garrisons on Trek to Rhine Frontier," *New York Times*, March 9, 1936, 3.

[11] P. J. Phillip, "Paris Bars Berlin Offers: Refuses Parleys 'Under Menace' of Troops in Rhineland," *New York Times*, March 9, 1936, 1.

Prime Minister Albert Sarraut articulated French resolve to ensure the region's security: "I declare in the name of the French Government that we intend to see maintained the essential guarantee of French and Belgian security, constituted by Locarno ... We are not disposed to allow Strasbourg to be under the fire of German cannon."[12]

Behind the scenes preparations to secure civilians in Alsace and Lorraine intensified after the remilitarization of the Rhineland. "Protection" soon embraced a policy that was broader than mere military fortification.[13] French politicians insisted that military leaders should adopt a plan for preserving civilian safety and maintaining the allegiance of the vulnerable constituency. In response, the army drew up detailed evacuation plans for the departments stranded east of France's Maginot fortification, a perimeter barrier designed to delay a future German invasion and afford French troops time to mobilize. Once construction began in 1930, the government expanded the Défense passive to address the wide range of potential dangers to the civilian population in the event of war. It oversaw everything from bomb shelter construction and policing of the blackout regulations, to the sock knitting campaigns for soldiers. From its inception, the Défense passive focused on the departments located near the Maginot Line, including the five departments bordering Germany, Meurthe-et-Moselle, Meuse, Moselle, Bas-Rhin, and Haut-Rhin, that hosted the barrier.[14]

Over the summer of 1936, the Défense passive began updating older plans and scripting new schemes for moving eastern residents to safe spaces away from the border. By fall, the military authorities had finalized evacuation plans for the eastern population which threatened to encumber military operations in the event of a new war. The population envisioned for relocation totaled approximately 500,000.[15] The scope of the proposed transfer represented one of the most ambitious

[12] Phillip, "Paris Bars Berlin Offers," *New York Times*, March 9, 1936, 2.
[13] For interwar planning see Panchasi, *Future Tense*.
[14] See J. Hughes, *To the Maginot Line: The Politics of French Military Preparedness in the 1920s* (Cambridge, MA: Harvard University Press, 1970), quoted by R. F. Crane, "Maginot Line," in Bertram M. Gordon (ed.), *Historical Dictionary of World War II France: The Occupation, Vichy and the Resistance, 1938–1946* (Westport, CT: Greenwood Press, 1998), 230.
[15] Paul Vaucher, "Evacuation in France," in Richard Padley and Margaret Cole (eds.), *Evacuation Survey: A Report to the Fabian Society* (London: Routledge, 1940), 289. The population of Strasbourg is reported as 181,000 and the department of the Moselle is estimated at 306,000. Bas-Rhin transferred 76,000 to Dordogne.

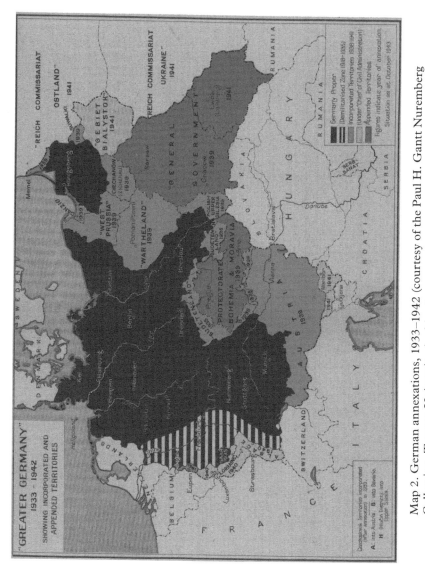

Map 2. German annexations, 1933–1942 (courtesy of the Paul H. Gantt Nuremberg Collection, Towson University Archives)

planned European evacuations of the twentieth century, comparable to the World War II resettlements realized in the Soviet Union.[16]

The legislative elections of May 1936 also impacted national and civilian security programs as voters elected a new government in the context of the spread of fascism. The Popular Front government developed a loosely united coalition of anti-fascists, including socialists led by Léon Blum, Radical-Socialists led by Édouard Daladier, and French communists (Parti communiste français, PCF) led by Maurice Thorez. For one critical year from June 1936 to June 1937, the Popular Front attempted to lessen the growing tensions that jeopardized French security on both her eastern and south-western boarders. Within one month of coming to power, the Popular Front confronted a deepening international crisis when civil war erupted in Spain. Spain's nationalist and fascist, military opposition attacked the Second Spanish Republic, shattering any illusion that France or the League of Nations could preserve peace in Europe. The war in Spain presented Blum's government with a series of intractable problems. Spanish Republican refugees began crossing into France along the Pyrénées creating overcrowding in south-western towns and heightening awareness of civilian vulnerabilities. Blum backed his party's sentiment of "arms for Spain," but as Tony Judt has observed, "he was truly constrained; not only at home, where Conservatives and Radicals alike counseled caution, but abroad, where the Conservative government of Britain, France's only strong ally in a hostile continent, urged him not to 'intervene'."[17] Unable to lend a strong hand abroad, Blum's government sharpened its focus on securing the home front.

The Défense passive's population relocation model certainly had holes, but was nonetheless progressive for the time. Problematically, a loosely centralized chain of command formed whereby the army, Défense passive, and later the Service of Refugees drafted policies in Paris and relied upon departmental and municipal leaders to define operational details. Early evacuation plans designated travel timetables, allocated trains to departments, estimated evacuee food requirements, and identified lodging and travel costs. The 1936 plans attempted to respect the good will and material sacrifices required of host communities. Preservation of community cohesiveness guided

---

[16] In 1941, the Soviets transferred 1,500 enterprises to the east. Nearly 10 million Soviets were transferred east of the Volga, effectively relocating the manufacture of the Soviet steel industry. See Geoffrey Hosking, *The First Socialist Society: A History of the Soviet Union from Within* (Cambridge, MA: Harvard, 1985), 283.

[17] Tony Judt, *The Burden of Responsibility: Blum, Camus, Aron and the French Twentieth Century* (University of Chicago Press, 1998), 47.

relocation schemes in the hope of maintaining order, ensuring continuity of experience, and protecting individuals or small evacuation groups from exploitation.[18] Thus, the plans paired each town within the five designated evacuation departments to towns in France's interior. In addition, these plans identified graduated "retreat points" for "first wave" and "second wave" evacuations. These retreat points fell within departments scattered between the "Red Zone," and the final receiving centers located in the south-west. These prewar placements of intermediary retreat points revealed how French military defense thinking remained fixed on the World War I idea of fighting a slow-moving war of entrenchment.[19]

The events in Spain in the spring of 1937 should have compelled French military and Défense passive planners to reconsider the premise that combat could be geographically limited and spatially contained. On April 26, 1937, German planes bombed the civilian population of Guernica, Spain. The Spanish fascists defended the bombing as an attack on a munitions plant. On May 1, *Ce Soir*, the Parisian daily, published photographs of civilian casualties from Guernica estimated at between 200 and 1,654 victims of a population of 5,600.[20] Hoping to generate worldwide condemnation of the fascist rebels, the struggling Spanish Republican government commissioned Pablo Picasso to commemorate the suffering of the Basque country victims. The Paris International Exposition opened on May 25, 1937, and Picasso delivered *Guernica* to the Spanish Exposition Hall in June. The mural-size painting captured aerial warfare's destruction of civilian sanctuaries, depicting the horror of bombing. At Guernica, the Germans served notice of their technological capability and tactical plans to bomb civilian populations; forever shattering the obsolete idea of spatial distinction between combat zone and home front that had barely lingered beyond World War I. Historian Tammy Proctor convincingly argues that World War I's mobilization of civilians into wartime production, combat support, mental and physical rehabilitation of soldiers had already destroyed any distinctions between home front and combat zone. The two became

---

[18] AN F/23/223, prefect of the Marne to the Minister of the Interior and the Director General of National Security and the Police, December 12, 1936.

[19] Torrie concludes that, "In the prewar period, discussion about protecting civilians had been dominated by fears of the 'airborne menace,' rather than land invasion," Torrie, *"For Their Own Good,"* 32. Military correspondence with the Défense passive (AN F/23/223) suggests the opposite: from 1936 to 1938 French military operations focused on land invasion and tailored evacuations to that scenario.

[20] Historians debate the number of casualties. For widely accepted figures see: www.rfi.fr/actufr/articles/088/article_51333.asp.

interdependent from that time.[21] In France, government officials and military leaders absorbed partial lessons from Guernica's experience.

Almost a year later, on March 13, 1938, international events further troubled French security concerns. Prefects in the northern departments of retreat re-evaluated their security in response to Germany's march into Austria and declaration of an Anschluss, or "peaceful union." In the Marne, Île-de-France, Aisne, and Oise, departments designated to host the "first wave" of Alsatian and Lorrainer evacuees, prefects worried that their own populations risked aerial bombardment. They considered that their residents might require relocation to the interior. The prefect of the Marne, André Jozon, rushed a letter to the Minister of National Defense and War in Paris, copying the headquarters of the army's 4th Bureau, 1 Section A charged with the Marne's protection. Jozon challenged the practicality of relocating Alsatians and Lorrainers in a staging center recently built in the Marne.[22] He pointed out the logistics: the Marne was located directly on the western border of the department of the Meuse, one of the five departments targeted for total evacuation. The Marne, he reminded the army, had witnessed two of the most deadly battles of World War I. The first, in September 1914, claimed civilian lives as well as the lives of 250,000 French soldiers.[23] Then on July 15, 1918 the Germans again invaded the Marne, attacking Reims directly. The Marnais defended their territory; forcing the Germans to a final retreat on August 3, 1918.[24]

Given her history, why was the Marne not included in the "Red Zone"? Prefect Jozon had only arrived in the Marne in 1938 and had not participated in drafting the 1936 plans; but he understood the heavy toll that the destruction of World War I had taken upon the Marne and its population. Jozon noted that the Marne's economy had only recently showed signs of recovery from its dramatic World War I losses. The census of 1921 recorded a loss of 69,500 inhabitants, dropping the population to 366,700, the same level it had been in 1840.[25] The disproportionate death of young men during World War I widowed mothers and left single women without husbands, unable to reproduce an

---

[21] Proctor, *Civilians in a World at War 1914–1918*, 13–39.

[22] AN F/23/223, prefect of the Marne to the Minister of the Interior and the Director General of National Security and the Police, December 12, 1936.

[23] See Michael Duffy, "First Battle of the Marne," the Germans did not report casualties. The British reported 12,733, see www.WorldWarI.com.

[24] Duffy, "Second Battle of the Marne," military casualties: France, 95,000; Britain, 13,000; United States, 12,000. Germany sacrificed 168,000 soldiers trying to divert French troops from Flanders, see www.WorldWarI.com.

[25] The wars of 1870–71 and 1914–18 hastened the Marne's demographic decline. See Husson, *La Marne et les Marnais*, 26–27.

entire generation. Destruction to the land further forced many farmers to seek employment in other sectors of the economy, leading many to migrate to Paris.[26] Only in 1936 did the department's census finally show a population rebound that brought the total number of inhabitants to 410,238.[27]

With the Marne's record of German invasion, Jozon sidestepped interdepartmental correspondence, sending his objections directly to the office of the Minister of the Interior. He demanded that the minister amend the 1936 plan, which failed to secure residents of the Marne or evacuees from Alsace and Lorraine. Instead, the French High Command responded to Germany's occupation of Austria by ordering an immediate evacuation of 22,000 residents from the communes of Stenay and Montmedy located near Verdun (Meuse) to refugee facilities outside the perimeter of Reims, the commercial capital of the Marne and the greater champagne region. Jozon protested vigorously.[28] A frank correspondence transpired between the Minister of War, the army commander of the four bureaux, and Jozon.[29] Jozon insisted, "It is absolutely impossible for me to shelter these populations [Alsace and Lorraine] in the countryside surrounding the city of Reims (Marne). In reality, I must reserve the entire area outside the city of Reims for the relocation of residents of the city of Reims itself."[30] He requested, as did other prefects, the direct transfer of Alsatians and Lorrainers to the less populated south-western departments of Dordogne, Lot, and Gironde, which were considered more suited than the densely populated northern departments to absorb masses of evacuees whose stay might extend indefinitely.[31]

Jozon's objection to the placement of refugees in the Marne did not reflect a visionary understanding of the reach of aerial bombing and the need for long-distance evacuations. Instead, he, too, expected a land invasion and planned for internal department displacements. He estimated that 113,017 residents of the city of Reims would have to be

---

[26] Husson, *La Marne et les Marnais*, 26–27.

[27] Husson, *La Marne et les Marnais*, 26–27. The 11.8 percent increase was twice the national average.

[28] AN F/23/223, prefect of the Marne to Minister of National Defense and the War (Army Chief of Staff, 4th Bureau, 1 Section A), Châlons, March 29, 1938.

[29] Husson, *La Marne et les Marnais*, 63–64, 101.

[30] AN F/23/223, prefect of the Marne to the Minister of National Defense, March 29, 1938.

[31] By April 1940, when Alsatians and Lorrainers were resettled in the south-west, citizens of Vienne made mocking reference to the refugees celebrating Hitler's birthday. See Boswell, "Franco-Alsatian Conflict and the Crisis of National Sentiment during the Phoney War," 552.

evacuated to the nearby countryside. His studies predicted that the area surrounding Reims could absorb 41,535 evacuees, leaving him with another 60,000 to transport elsewhere.[32] Small villages on the outskirts of Reims, such as Ville d'Ay, would become overpopulated without even including evacuees from eastern departments, he argued. Jozon thus refused to accept evacuees from departments further east. In April 1938, Jozon's analysis won the day, and national civil defense planners agreed to relocate Alsatian and Lorrainer evacuees elsewhere.

In July 1938, the French National Assembly passed the War Powers Act. The law formalized war preparations, but further increased tensions between mayors and prefects in the east and their colleagues in the interior, as the latter became truly fearful of a deluge of evacuees. East of the River Meuse, military authorities also reassessed the potential duration of evacuations. Prefects of designated host departments within France's interior voiced concerns about long-term evacuee displacement, fearing a severe drain on the financial resources of host communities. The revised assessments of evacuees exceeding 500,000, relocated for stays lasting beyond one year, spurred debate and negotiation among host department officials, who increasingly called upon national planners to referee interdepartmental negotiations and establish national standards for burden-sharing. By the winter of 1938, authorities at every level were engaged in attempts to amend the 1936 plans. Gradually as war approached, civilian and military planners began to abandon the idea of intermediary evacuations and agreed to shift all long-term evacuee reception centers to France's south-west. Unfortunately, this change came at the same time that south-western departments were accommodating increasing numbers of Spanish exiles whose population had reached approximately 400,000.[33]

The reduction in the number of intermediary resettlement centers reduced the time that prefects of south-western departments and center regions had to prepare to receive "officially approved" evacuees. For most northerners, the region's history and culture were more unfamiliar than that of Germany. The Massif Central sits at the northernmost tip of France's south-west, bordering the Dordogne. For many mid-century Frenchmen, this swath of worn mountain tops remained a haven of peasant traditions and wilderness.[34] Alsatians and Lorrainers

---

[32] Boswell, "Franco-Alsatian Conflict and the Crisis of National Sentiment during the Phoney War," 552.

[33] On Spanish refugee camps in France see Peschanski, *La France des camps*.

[34] In 1938 the departments comprising this region included Corrèze, Dordogne, Cantal, Lot, Aveyron, Creuse and Haute-Vienne. South-west France includes the departments of Gironde, Landes, Lot-et-Garonne, Tarn-et-Garonne, Haute-Garonne, Tarn, Gers, Charente, and Charente-Maritime.

recognized Bordeaux wine and might recently have learned of the Revolution's upheavals in the Gironde, but strained relations between host communities and refugees emerged immediately as shortages fostered competition between regional natives and evacuees, who Shannon Fogg describes as being viewed as "outsiders."[35]

Population shuffles were not reserved for France in 1938. In September, Édouard Daladier, France's new premier met in Munich with Britain's Prime Minister, Neville Chamberlain, and Adolph Hitler to encourage the Germans to respect the peace and borders of Europe. The "Munich Accords" went into effect at midnight on October 1, 1938. They permitted Germany to enter into the Czechoslovakian border territory called the Krumau Zone, which before 1919 had formed part of Upper Austria. Hitler argued that the Czech territory "completed" the Austrian annexation. Capitalizing on the Czech state's fragility, Poland then demanded from the Czechs the disputed area of Teschen. Referencing shared ethnic and historical ties, Poland claimed the population of the Czechlands "beyond Olza," and Germany claimed her right to Sudetenland. Thousands of inhabitants resisting these historic ties fled to Prague to escape Hitler and the Poles.[36]

Annexation of Austria and her former borderlands advanced Hitler's goal of German ethnic unification. The Third Reich rejected Otto von Bismarck's nineteenth-century compromise for unifying Germany under the "small" Germany model, which relinquished Austria. Alsace and Lorraine, however, had been a basic component of *both* models and were unlikely to be left out of Hitler's ethnic unification scheme. The German claims to "historic Germanic territories" further alarmed residents of Alsace and Lorraine, who read the writing on the wall and stepped up demands to be evacuated to safe and historically non-disputed French territory.[37] Returning from Munich, Daladier was met by cheering crowds; most likely not Alsatians or Lorrainers. They applauded the preservation of the peace. Privately he called appeasement supporters, "blind fools," and admitted, "This is only a respite, and if we don't make use of it, we will all be shot."[38]

For French civil defense planners the Sudeten crisis complicated civilian evacuation planning. Guernica offered a lesson about German

---

[35] Fogg, *The Politics of Everyday Life in Vichy France*, 58.

[36] Wireless, "Czechs are Bitter over Poles' Stand; Political Circles say Munich Agreement on General Peace Already has been Broken; Evacuation Underway," *New York Times*, October 2, 1938, 29.

[37] Otto von Bismarck claimed Alsace and Lorraine as part of the First German Empire after France's defeat in the Franco-Prussian War (1870–71).

[38] Thomas R. Christofferson, with Michael S. Christofferson, *France during World War II: from Defeat to Liberation* (New York: Fordham University Press, 2006), 17.

air power: urban centers that hosted munitions manufacturing facilities could become targets of strategic bombing. The annexation of Austria and the Sudetenlands presented a different lesson: German territorial and ethnic unification offered the greatest threat to French civilians living in the historically swapped border regions. Where should French civilian security planners focus their resources? Confronted with the prospect of evacuating the entire northern territory of France, planners considered limiting civilian evacuations. A dominant school of thought contended that civilians living in large urban manufacturing centers outside the Red Zone might not be as *endangered* by the threat of bombs as Alsatians and Lorrainers were threatened by German territorial reabsorption. Which danger would the government prioritize in structuring civilian evacuations?

In Paris civil defense privileged the threat to Alsatians and Lorrainers. However, they also responded to the protestations of such prefects as André Jozon. In the fall of 1938, the Paris bureau issued maps to mayors in Alsace and Lorraine designating rail departure routes to southwestern relocation centers, thus superficially dispensing with the idea of intermediary resettlement. Within these officially defined routes, the towns of Poitier in Vienne and Brive-la-Gaillarde in Corrèze emerged as two of the most important transfer stations linking passengers from the north to routes continuing to the south. By December, refugees began transferring trains in Corrèze, or settling there temporarily while waiting for trains. An informal system of evacuee resettlement took root in rail hub departments for which the department prefects had not planned. Evacuees' improvised resettlement placed unexpected pressures on the Limousin and Massif Central regions.

Meeting in Corrèze to craft a coherent policy for accommodating the mass infusion of evacuees, host community leaders identified problems in short-term relocation plans: would the national government, the department of evacuee origin, the host department, or the host municipality absorb relocation costs? How would evacuees be politically represented? Who would employ them? For national planners, the logistical questions had mattered more than philosophical human rights issues, as would occur throughout the displacement crisis. Host community authorities wrongly assumed that the Défense passive would finance evacuee services, and sketched relief paradigms based on expectations of evacuees' remaining for only thirty days to six months.

The six-month period between the Sudeten crisis in October 1938 and Germany's full-blown invasion of Czechoslovakia on March 15, 1939, witnessed an explosion of population movement in France and Europe. The *New York Times* correspondent, P. J. Philip, reported from

Paris that: "There is no public alarm here over the situation, which is regarded as entirely different from that of last September, when France was engaged to undertake to help the Czecho-Slovak Republic if attacked."[39] Perhaps the French foreign office muted its comment about the fate of the young Czech nation, but on the ground, civilians expressed their discontent with their feet. On March 15, the International Bureau for the Right of Asylum issued an appeal to the democratic governments of Europe and the Americas. The Bureau petitioned these nations to open their consular buildings in Prague to asylum-seeking refugees. The organization also called upon France and Britain to establish a neutral zone in Poland where the refugees could seek diplomatic protection.[40] In New York, the chairman of the spontaneously formed New York United Jewish Appeal for Refugees and Overseas Needs, Henry Ittleson, estimated that 250,000 Jewish refugees were involved in the Czech crisis and another 14,000 remained displaced from the Sudeten affair.[41]

In France's eastern border departments and in Paris waves of Jewish and non-Jewish refugees arrived from Germany, Austria, Sudetenland, Poland, and the former Czecho-Slovak Republic. By the end of 1938 the French had naturalized 48,630 foreign applications for citizenship and would handle 58,100 more in 1939, primarily from German refugees.[42] This influx of foreign refugees augmented the French population demanding aid and relocation in the capital. Their presence produced a desire and need among civil defense planners and host prefects to distinguish between French evacuees and foreign refugees.

Throughout the winter of 1938–1939, increased international and domestic dangers forced military and civilian planners to expand the scope of evacuations and begin the allocation of services and benefits to evacuees, including foreign refugees. The military expanded the number of eastern departments whose residents qualified as "official evacuees" beyond the initial five. The first expansion included the departments of Haute-Alpes, Doubs, Jura, and Ain. Civilian unrest throughout the north contributed to the changing scope of national evacuation plans. Residents in northern urban centers, like Martha Vluggens, who did not qualify as "official evacuees" but felt threatened,

[39] P. J. Philip, "France Watching Poland's Reaction," *New York Times*, March 14, 1939, 16.
[40] "A Nation Disappears," *New York Times*, March 15, 1939, 1.
[41] "Ittleson to Head Refugees' Appeal; New Crisis Abroad to Spur Three Agencies' Efforts to Meet Emergency," *New York Times*, March 16, 1939, 22.
[42] See Anne Grynberg, *Les camps de honte: les internés juifs des camps Français (1939–1944)* (Paris: Éditions La Découverte, 1991).

began to relocate themselves or family members to the interior *without* government approval. These "unofficial" or "voluntary" evacuees did not qualify for state-paid relocation funds. The mixing of planned and improvised evacuations muddied well-intentioned protection theories grounded in republican ideals of the state's responsibility to offer equal protection to all members of one national community. Operational realities and international crises tested the abilities of host prefects and mayors to guarantee "voluntary evacuees" relief benefits as rights due to French citizens. Foreign asylees entered into competition for assistance with "official" Alsatian and Lorrainer evacuees.

First-generation rural migrants figured prominently among "voluntary" evacuees as they sought to exercise a "right of return" to their familial homes in the interior. This return amounted to a slow reverse migration beginning in 1938 and expanding throughout 1939 and 1940. Because prefects could not officially count them, few hard numbers exist for these voluntary returnees, but we do know that their presence was sufficient for host departments to turn away large numbers of military-approved evacuees. Unlike evacuees from the east, who relocated in large communities and resorted to previous forms of community representation, returning relatives acted as individuals, employing familial connections to advance their desires to relocate and tap into evacuee privileges. Because "voluntary evacuees" did not technically qualify to receive evacuee benefits, they could not access cash subsidies and special housing considerations. However, voluntary evacuees played their local connections. Relatives lobbied mayors and prefects to issue benefits to "native sons" before accommodating "foreigners" from Alsace and Lorraine. Far from Paris, mayors and prefects in the south-west acted with a wide margin of personal discretion, and had few incentives to accommodate strange evacuees from border departments. They preferred to extend assistance to the returning kin of their departments' residents. Thus, voluntary "returnee" evacuees formed one of the first groups of "unofficial" evacuees to compete with Alsatians and Lorrainers for receipt of state-funded relocation monies and refugee benefits.

A 1938 episode in Cantal typified the general problem created by voluntary evacuees. A week prior to Christmas, the prefect of the Cantal wrote to his counterpart in Ain on the Swiss border. He informed the prefect of Ain that due to the "flood" of Cantalese-born "voluntary evacuees" returning to their native region, he would have to limit the number of officially authorized evacuees admitted to Cantal relocation centers from Ain. The Cantal, in his mind, could not accept any refugees exceeding the number of residents who had been called up to military service, a total of 50,000.[43] Furthermore, the prefect of the Haute-Alpes had already requested Cantal to accept 114,000 refugees. The prefect concluded that Cantal could no longer accept any evacuees from Ain.[44]

As the evacuation grew more complex, host department prefects also stumbled over military representatives charged with overseeing evacuee transportation. Corrèze's prefect, Alfred Papinot, identified a set of enduring operational and jurisdictional concerns in a letter sent to the commander of the 13th Region of the army overseeing Corrèze. He accused the military of intruding into civilian affairs and advanced a principle of the primacy of civilian oversight regarding evacuee resettlement operations. He objected to the French Army sending personnel to administer evacuation facilities and direct management of refugee populations. Papinot emphasized that Corrèze had established a department commission to protect the rights of evacuees, and to ensure respect for their "human dignity." The mayor of Brive-la-Gaillarde headed the commission, which included one member of the municipal council of the evacuated community, one member of the municipal council of the host community, the commissioner of police, the director of the office of public health, and the director of charity. The commission had responsibility for the establishment of housing, health care, food distribution, and employment.[45] Papinot stressed the importance of including representatives of the evacuee communities in the resettlement process; however, as indicated by the composition of the commission, the balance of representation tilted toward the host community. Ensuring fair representation of the refugee community seemed important, but was secondary to Papinot's chief objective of maintaining civilian control over a local jurisdiction.

In Corrèze the relocation process, as throughout the south-west area, began with Alsatians and Lorrainers. Each step of the relocation and resettlement involved coordination between national, regional, departmental, and municipal administrations. To accommodate evacuees experiencing lengthy delays, train hub towns dispatched evacuees into department communes where they camped in schools, residents' homes, hospitals, hotels, or community centers. At receiving stations, local relief workers and railway employees grouped evacuees according to their host commune destinations. Host department prefects

[43] AN F/23/222, Cantal prefect to Ain prefect, December 17, 1938.
[44] AN F/23/222, Cantal prefect to Ain prefect, December 17, 1938.
[45] AN F/23/222, Corrèze prefect to Commander of the 13th Region of the Army, September 27, 1938.

coordinated with regional military commanders to arrange transportation from stations. Women volunteers served cold dinners to evacuees while they waited. Authorities in Corrèze grappled constantly with the difficulties of synchronizing train connections, and as a consequence established several temporary welcome centers spread throughout the department to ensure availability of sanitation services and refreshments for evacuees awaiting transfers to final destinations.[46]

Despite state involvement, socioeconomic realities conditioned all the experiences of evacuees. Wealthy Alsatians and Lorrainers stayed in hotels and ate at restaurants; but not all evacuees enjoyed such financial means. Papinot wrote to the Défense passive to indicate that in Corrèze the department would happily provide lodging to temporary evacuees whose resources could not afford them the luxury of a hotel room. However, the prefect also saw opportunity in evacuees' hard circumstances. Papinot informed national authorities that evacuees receiving local subsidies were expected to volunteer for local work projects. The exchange of refugee labor for sanctuary introduced the concept of evacuee "responsibilities" accompanying the language of evacuee "rights." Host residents also bore responsibilities: on July 5, 1938, at a staging center in the north, the prefect of the Eure-et-Loire reminded his population that any bother that might result from the arrival of evacuees "must be borne like a duty imposed upon them not unlike a requisition."[47] Attempting to console critics, he noted that any evacuees passing through the Eure-et-Loire would likely be en route to destinations in the south, and that these refugees "constituted a reservoir of manual labor which no one should hesitate to employ, particularly in departments suffering from labor shortages."[48] Local politicians understood the need to assuage the fears of their residents who anticipated the arrival of hardships, competition, and even illness, with the influx of outsiders.[49]

Prior to and during the Phoney War, evacuees who encountered derision from locals, and took unwanted or unpleasant local jobs suffered little more than insult. However, when the war exploded in September 1939, and new refugees entered into these southern communities, more rigid hierarchies of inclusion and exclusion emerged that jeopardized host community tolerance of evacuees, exacerbated the

[46] AN F/23/222, Corrèze prefect to Commander of the 13th Region of the Army, September 27, 1938.
[47] AN F/23/222, Eure-et-Loire prefect to department mayors, July 5, 1938.
[48] AN F/23/222, Eure-et-Loire prefect to department mayors, July 5, 1938.
[49] Corrèze's health authorities mandated vaccinations for all arriving refugees.

divide between voluntary and official evacuees, and eroded residents' openness to foreign refugees.

Following the Czech crisis of 1939, the military expanded the number of eastern departments whose residents qualified for evacuation, bringing the total evacuation to approximately 800,000 evacuees to be absorbed into rural, south-western communities.[50] When the military added the departments of Doubs, which bordered Switzerland, and the Hautes-Alpes on the Italian border, local authorities began circumventing the Défense passive, entering into direct negotiations with neighboring departments to arrange evacuee swaps and burden-sharing.

By August 24, 1939, one week before France formally declared war, centralization of the evacuation effort was crumbling. The prefect of Tarn-et-Garonne, Louis Boucoiran, circumvented the office of the Minister of the Interior to plead with the prefect of Lot to assist in accommodating some of 304,000 evacuees from Doubs. Referencing plans from 1936 that designated the Lot as primarily responsible for sheltering evacuees from Doubs, Boucoiran declared that he could not possibly absorb this number of evacuees.[51] The prefect of Lot retorted that, in June, he had indicated to the Minister of the Interior his intention to limit Lot to 80,000 evacuees from Doubs. He did accept 1,000 hospitalized refugees who could not find sufficient bed space in Tarn-et-Garonne.[52] The Minister of the Interior finally settled the dispute between Lot and Tarn-et-Garonne. Lot would accept 80,000 refugees from Doubs, including the 1,000 hospitalized evacuees from Tarn-et-Garonne. In return, the Minister of the Interior relieved Lot of responsibility for accommodating an unspecified number of hospitalized evacuees from Paris. The correspondence left unsettled the fate of 223,000 Doubs evacuees.

The clash of interests between the prefects of Lot and Tarn-et-Garonne seriously delayed the transfer of Doubs' population. On September 12, 1939, Lot's prefect reported that not a single refugee from Doubs had arrived. Thinking it a shame to leave prepared facilities empty, he reported to the Minister of the Interior's office that he had allowed recent evacuees from the Paris region to occupy the facilities set aside for Doubs evacuees.[53]

---

[50] Défense passive estimated 500,000 Alsatian and Lorrainer evacuees and considered transferring 300,000 from Doubs.

[51] AN F/23/226, Prefect Boucoiran of Tarn-et-Garonne to Lot prefect, August 24, 1939.

[52] AN F/23/226, Lot prefect to Tarn-et-Garonne prefect, August 26, 1939.

[53] AN F/23/226, Lot prefect to Minister of the Interior, Director General of National Security and the Police, September 12, 1939.

The plight of Madame Zenot, a voluntary evacuee from Reims (Marne), illustrates the difficulties evacuees encountered when prefects enforced relief distribution guidelines. On September 2, 1939, the army mobilized Zenot's husband. Pregnant with her second child and a thirteen-year-old daughter in her care, Madame Zenot moved in with her mother-in-law who lived in Bougneau (Charante-Inférieure). The prefect of Charante-Inférieure refused to add Zenot to the evacuee relief rolls because she came from the Marne, which was not located in the Red Zone. On September 7, per instructions from the prefect of Charante-Inférieure, Madame Zenot wrote to the prefect of the Marne, André Jozon, to request that he send her an evacuee allocation since she had not received her husband's military allocation, and could not work because she was pregnant. Jozon denied her request, explaining that she did not qualify for evacuee assistance because the military did not consider the Marne "necessary to evacuate."[54]

Evacuation of war industry workers

The lead up to war also pressured the industrial sector. In 1938, French rearmament moved into high gear. Former senator, Guy la Chambre, assumed direction of the Air Ministry, launching an aggressive production schedule after March 15, 1938. La Chambre pressed the aircraft industry to increase production drastically in order to build 2,617 frontline aircraft and 2,122 reserve planes.[55] Keeping wartime production safe and on schedule meant evacuating labor and equipment. French aviation plants were primarily located in the south-west, but other ancillary industry required relocation. Industrial relocation first targeted the iron and steel industries of Alsace and Lorraine, but quickly spread to Paris-based munitions plants. Beginning in 1938, the military controlled plans for moving important industries to the interior. The headquarters of the army's 6th Region issued orders governing the relocation of heavy industry from Alsace and Lorraine, but Albert Sarraut at the Ministry of the Interior also assumed a lead role in shaping worker evacuations. Following discussions with the Ministry, army leaders issued precise orders to industrial leaders to ensure that families of relocated workers remained together. In January 1939, the 6th Army issued a directive stressing the importance of grouping workers

---

[54] ADM, Reims depot, Nos. 411–420, Refugee letters, 1939–1940. Mme Zenot to the prefect of Charante-Inférieure, forwarded to prefect of the Marne, September 7, 1939.
[55] Chapman, *State Capitalism and Working-Class Radicalism in the French Aircraft Industry*, 156.

and their families in the same communes: "To separate workers from their families at this moment would be purely illusory and generate unrest."[56] This injunction resulted from complaints by workers whose families had been prohibited from joining them. By February 1940, word of worker dissatisfaction had reached the highest levels of government, resulting in one deputy from Alsace and Lorraine writing to the French prime minister to remind him that workers served the nation in as important a capacity as soldiers. If wives and children could not join relocated workers, "whose labor is the ransom for their liberty," he wrote, then, at the very least, the government should grant workers vacation time and finance visits to their families.[57]

Actually, the government bore less responsibility for the relocation of war industry workers than it did for evacuation of civilian residents. Private industry shared the financial burden, with many enterprises building or paying for housing for relocated workers. Also, war industry workers did not initially qualify for relief allocations because they earned salaries. However, hosting war industry workers taxed community resources in other ways. Their children enrolled in public schools, placing pressure on space and teachers. Extended family networks frayed, as relocation schemes excluded grandparents who had provided care for small children. Despite the provision of housing, workers' quarters frequently lacked basic amenities. Typical refugee relocation centers consisted of cinder block or wooden barracks with tin roofs. Many lacked heating and indoor plumbing. Fortunate evacuees purchased propane burners for cooking and heating. Few facilities provided private family suites with men and women often sleeping and dressing in the same room.

The prefect of the Eure and future resistance martyr, Jean Moulin, challenged the logic of factory relocation. In a March 1940 correspondence with Albert Sarraut's office, Moulin stated his case against war industry relocation.[58] Already, thirty-one industries had moved to the Eure, nineteen of which contributed directly to national defense. When family members were included, the total "foreign population," as host residents called war workers, approached 40,000, doubling the population of some smaller communities like Varron and Beaumont-le-Roger.

---

[56] AN F/23/223, "Procès Verbal de la réunion ayant eu lieu à l'état-major de la 6éme région," November 8, 1938. Circulated to Alsace and Lorraine prefects, January 9, 1939.

[57] AN F/23/230, Chamber of Deputies, Commission of Alsace and Lorraine to the President of the Council, February 28, 1940.

[58] Albert Sarraut served twenty-six times as a minister under the Third Republic including six terms as Minister of the Interior. Husson, *La Marne et les Marnais*, 111.

Moulin worried that continued relocation of defense industry workers to the Eure marked his department as a target for German bombardment.[59]

Sarraut's plans rested on relatively progressive ideas about family unity and community relocation. Despite Moulin's complaint that evacuating workers' families along with workers increased the drain on local resources, Sarraut insisted on preserving less fiscally tangible values like family unity. He ordered that Moulin and others keep families together at all costs, and lobbied prefects to place refugee families in local residents' homes. When such arrangements proved impossible, he suggested that small groupings of refugees worked best. Sarraut warned that large assemblies of refugees in public buildings risked exposing children to epidemics.[60] He instructed prefects to make as many improvements in living conditions as possible, ordering: "Above all, I insist that you make the question of heating your first priority, an obvious necessity at the beginning of a winter season."[61]

Declaration of war brings Robert Schuman to lead the Service of Refugees

The combustible diplomatic atmosphere that spurred industrial production prior to September 1939 heightened domestic security concerns, intensifying pressures on an already fragile and fragmented civilian security system. The August signing of the non-aggression pact between Germany and the Soviet Union, and Germany's declared designs on Polish territory drew Prime Minister Édouard Daladier's attention away from civil defense. Soon after meeting with military and diplomatic advisors, and President Albert Lebrun and the Cabinet council, Daladier issued a statement committing France to declare war against Germany in the event of an invasion of Poland. Peace rested in German hands as far as Daladier was concerned. In contrast, Hitler placed the burden of the peace on Poland, vowing to invade if Poland did not peacefully yield Danzig and German-populated Pomerania. Threatened German military action and promised French reprisals

---

[59] AN F/23/227, Minister of the Interior, Inspector General of Administrative Services to the Secretary of State and the Vice President of the Council mentioning the prefect of the Eure's complaints, March 1, 1940.

[60] ADM R/2749, Paris, Circular from Minister of Education and Public Health, Minister of the Interior, Albert Sarraut, Minister of National Education, Yvéon Delbos, Minister of Public Health, Marc Rucart to all prefects, September 25, 1939.

[61] ADM R/2749, Paris, Circular from Minister of Education and Public Health.

shifted policymakers' focus away from civilian security and toward the issue of Polish sovereignty.

Realizing the need for focused leadership to clarify and centralize civilian evacuation policy, Daladier named the stalwart deputy from the Moselle, Robert Schuman, to a cabinet post as Under Secretary of the Service of Refugees. Before the outbreak of war, cabinets of the Third Republic had treated civilian relocation as a chore for department and municipal leaders, without strong coordination or assistance from national-level agencies. The Minister of the Interior and the Minister of War set national policy guidelines, but allowed individual prefects to tailor evacuation schemes for their department. Daladier counted upon Schuman to command civilian security administration with the same purpose he expected from his military generals.

The appointment of the Catholic Lorrainer, a defender of the regional interests of Alsace and Lorraine, indicated that the government still considered evacuations an issue primarily concerning the formerly German populations of eastern France. National politicians and Défense passive planners increasingly adopted an approach that virtually designated Alsatians and Lorrainers as an "ethnic minority." Interwar policies, which resulted in issuing identity cards to Alsatians and Lorrainers, indicated, as Boswell argues, "that in the eyes of the state, Frenchness in the border provinces was determined by blood, and they intimated that the attribution of citizenship [to Alsatians and Lorrainers] would not follow the same rules as in the rest of the nation."[62] However, compared with treatment of minorities elsewhere in Europe in 1939, Alsatians and Lorrainers formed a privileged and protected minority. Within the realm of evolving civilian protection policies, their "threatened status" helped advance civilian protection schemes during a new phase of modern warfare. Meanwhile, "regular French" civilians living in urban centers still did not appear to national government leaders as a group at high risk of exposure to enemy fire. Schuman, perhaps because of his origins, would broaden civil defense plans to include the urban populations of other departments.

Schuman's biography shaped the policies he pursued and, hence, French and European history.[63] The statesman issued from the cross-cultural union of Jean-Pierre Schuman, a veteran of the Franco-Prussian

[62] Boswell, "From Liberation to Purge Trials in the 'Mythic Provinces,'" 160.

[63] My approach draws from Martin Brozat's work, *The Hitler State*, which marries structuralist perspectives with the enduring, sometimes troubling, power of individual will. See Martin Brozat, *The Hitler State: The Foundation and Development of the Internal Structure of the Third Reich*, trans. John W. Hilden (New York: Longman, 1981).

war who emigrated to Luxembourg after the German Empire annexed Alsace and Lorraine, and the Luxembourgess, Eugenie Duren. Raised initially in Luxembourg, then in the German Empire after a family move, Schuman inhabited a bilingual world located at the intersection of two enemy empires. During World War I, Schuman served as an auxiliary soldier in the German Army, repeatedly writing to his friends and family that he desired the victory of good over evil, rather than Germany over France.[64] This seeming neutrality earned Schuman the respect of Mosellian elders, and in 1919, the new French citizens of Moselle elected him to France's National Assembly. During his Third Republic career, which lasted until July 1940, Schuman crafted a unique pro-republican form of politics that remained firmly rooted in matters concerning Lorraine. In 1939, after having advocated accommodation with Germany since 1935, Schuman accepted Daladier's invitation to lead the government initiative to evacuate Alsace and Lorraine, and ensure the loyalty and security of this region. In a letter written a few months after his appointment, Schuman defined his understanding of his mission. He urged that: "this bloodied soil which has borne such damage, must be materially protected against even worse damage, because it would be gravely serious if certain propaganda could make use of the awful argument that: 'Hitler caused less damage to our region than the evacuation and its consequences.'"[65]

Thus, at the outset of Schuman's tenure as Under Secretary of Refugee Relief, national policy continued its focus on evacuating Alsace and Lorraine. Schuman's top priority rested in rapidly and efficiently finalizing the safe passage and successful absorption of Alsatians and Lorrainers into host communities. To this end, he established offices at the departure end in Metz (Moselle) and at the receiving end in Poitier in the department of Vienne where he hoped to resettle 300,000 Mosellians.[66] Shortly after Schuman assumed office, the mounting challenges to the narrowly focused, regionally based evacuation scheme escalated. After September 3, civilians in cities like Paris, Lille, Amiens, and Reims began to demand that protections be extended to the entire northern population. In response, Daladier encouraged Schuman to prepare a full-scale evacuation of children from the Paris region by the end of September, dramatically expanding Schuman's constituency and task.

---

[64] Raymond Poidevin, *Robert Schuman, homme d'État, 1886–1963* (Paris: Imprimerie nationale, 1985), 35.
[65] AN F/23/230, Robert Schuman to prefect of the Dordogne, February 28, 1940.
[66] Poidevin, *Robert Schuman*, 132–135.

The mid-September announcement of plans for partial evacuations of Paris and urban centers located outside the "Red Zone" marked a reversal by Daladier, who had maintained that the war could be contained within the border regions of eastern France. Schuman faced the undesirable task of informing the population of plans to evacuate children from Paris and northern urban centers. His public announcement invoked the powers of the military to order an evacuation. Schuman explained how evacuations differed from a "retreat," a measure adopted only under threat of invasion and issued by order of the Minister of the Interior. A "retreat" was further distinguished from the current "temporary relocation." Any evacuation order for the general population, Schuman warned, must follow an approved plan, drawn up during peacetime by military authorities, in conjunction with prefects and representatives of the national railway.[67] In short, Schuman's communiqué declared that no one was allowed to move anywhere unless expressly ordered to do so by the proper authorities. French military authorities continued to emphasize the difference between "evacuation" and "retreat" until a week prior to full capitulation in the hopes that they could prevent an unauthorized mass civilian exodus.

In reality, many Frenchmen, and more so women, ignored the government's commands to remain stationary. By November 1939, conservative estimates suggest that over 500,000 French civilians lived in relocation centers. Estimates of schoolchildren's departures range from 88,000 to 93,000 for Paris alone.[68] Reports submitted to the Prefect of Paris in March 1940 estimated that 271,966 persons left Paris in September 1939 – including many unauthorized adults. School-age children represented 34 percent of that number, bringing mass disruption to the commencement of the school year.[69] Mothers received train tickets to transport school-age children to holiday camps. Not everyone made use of the government-subsidized train tickets offered to young children to move them out of danger. A survey of the 12th arrondissement, a working-class neighborhood, reported that only 4,000 children had claimed rail passes in a school district comprising 44,000. Yet only 1,000 students remained in class. At least two explanations seem plausible: the 39,000 missing students thought that the evacuation meant that the education authorities had closed Parisian schools; or, parents,

---

[67] AN F/23/229, Memo, September 1939.
[68] AN F/23/229, "Un rapport suisse sur la défense passive de Paris et le problème de l'évacuation," prepared for the prefect of Paris, March 12, 1940. Paul Vaucher's estimate was 88,000, slightly smaller than 93,000.
[69] AN F/23/229, "Un rapport suisse sur la défense passive de Paris et le problème de l'évacuation."

unwilling or unable to send their children to evacuation centers, kept their children at home for fear that authorities would send their children away if they attended school.[70] The evacuation of Parisian children presented a host of problems and multiple contradictions. One reporter observed that Parisians displayed "a certain opposition," to the orders because no real danger of war seemed to exist.[71] Yet segments of the population had previously expressed outrage at the priority placed upon the evacuation of Alsace, Lorraine, and other Red Zone departments. Regardless of the policy pursued by the government, critics emerged among all constituencies except for the children, most of whom experienced evacuations as an extension of the summer holiday.

Despite the massive efforts, government authorities received low marks for managing the "exodus of children." Laura Lee Downs describes one socialist, Henri Sellier, as having, "fulminated against the bureaucratic stupidity with which the entire operation unfolded."[72] Sellier believed in small-scale placements that matched children with rural families. Parents also levied a multitude of complaints: education authorities should not have overseen the evacuation; there was insufficient planning for placing children in local families or summer camps; no warning was given to pack winter clothes; there was no medical assistance available to children; no blankets; no heaters. However, parents' greatest complaints concerned the length of their children's absence. Government authorities promised that evacuations would last no longer than a few weeks, but some separations dragged on into the winter of 1939. Many parents eventually disobeyed government orders and traveled substantial distances to reclaim their children. Upon arrival at refugee centers near Orléans, parents expressed exasperation upon finding boys and girls learning to make pillows and mattresses from straw rather than memorizing their multiplication tables.[73] Fear and frustration combined to force authorities and parents alike to rethink the wisdom of mass evacuations. After the September exercise, the first truly centralized attempt to evacuate Paris, Schuman scaled back future plans to relocate urban residents.

---

[70] Richard Padley and Margaret Cole (eds.), *Evacuation Survey: A Report to the Fabian Society* (London: Routledge, 1940), 289.

[71] AN F/23/229, "Un rapport suisse sur la défense passive de Paris et le problème de l'évacuation."

[72] Laura Lee Downs, *Childhood in the Promised Land: Working-Class Movements and the Colonies de Vacances in France, 1880–1960* (Durham, NC: Duke University Press, 2002), 190.

[73] AN F/23/229, "Un rapport suisse sur la défense passive de Paris et le problème de l'évacuation."

Still, by late September Schuman's administration had transferred over 374,000 Alsatians to destinations in the south-west.[74] In Poitiers (Vienne), where Schuman opened a Refugee Service office, the prefect, Henri Moulongue, alerted the local population to the arrival of eastern refugees. Moulongue encouraged his constituents to extend a "fraternal" welcome to the displaced, urging townspeople to "respect the mother tongue of these Lorrainers ... who have remained profoundly attached to France during the German occupation [1871–1918], and whose hearts have always beat in unison with our own."[75]

Volunteers stayed behind in Alsace and Lorraine to manage the problems arising in the "ghost towns" of the border. One Strasbourg report suggested that the population had "lost its head" upon departure. Residents left without closing windows and shutters. Potted flowers stood unattended on windowsills. Outhouses emitted a stench that suggested a potential health threat. A Swiss observer noted that, "some women even left their laundry drying on the wash line."[76]

Strasbourg policemen and firemen worked to prevent the collapse of infrastructure, visiting each house to extinguish central heating and empty trash, and installing pumps to keep pipes from freezing and bursting in winter. Preventing theft became a primary responsibility of municipal police and the military. Lingering residents carried identity passes and obeyed a curfew and were forbidden from burning oil or lamps after dusk.[77] Signs of the massive disruption to the economy, homes, and even to animal life suggested the end to a once vibrant civilization. Cats scampered from trash can to trash can, competing for remains; yet despite the cats, the rat population multiplied unchecked. The large plaza at the city hall resembled a giant Parisian flea market where furniture and household objects of evacuated families sat like refugees themselves waiting for the next train out of town. Municipal officials worked daily to fetch household items, drive them to the train station, and send them on their way to distant owners in the interior. By spring 1940, the military authorities were voicing concern about using rail resources for such trivial purposes; but Schuman insisted that refugees should endure no greater hardships than any other French citizen. This initiative stopped once the invasion began, but in 1941, the Service of Refugees launched an elaborate program of Alsatian and Lorrainer property reunion in cooperation with the German

[74] Poidevin, *Robert Schuman*, 132.
[75] AN F/23/230, Poitiers poster, prefect of Vienne, Henri Moulongue, September 6, 1939.
[76] AN F/23/230, Poitiers poster, prefect of Vienne, Henri Moulongue.
[77] AN F/23/230, Poitiers poster, prefect of Vienne, Henri Moulongue.

occupying authorities.[78] As we will see, property relocation and restitution remained a constant demand of *all* displaced French civilians
throughout the war and in the aftermath of Liberation.

Policy and attitude adjustments follow a failed dress rehearsal

During his first two months leading the Service of Refugees, Schuman
accomplished a significant transfer of Parisian children; a substantial
achievement in ensuring civilian protection even by today's standards.
The tone of complaints revealed, among other problems, the gender and
class biases embedded in assistance policies. While the state financed
transportation costs and housing expenses, working-class families
could ill afford the additional supplies required for a relocated child.
Military mobilization of fathers forced working-class mothers to find
employment, but then required many to choose between keeping a job
and releasing their child to the state, or giving up work to accompany
their child.

Schuman realized the need to address existing and emerging inequal-
ities in evacuee assistance programs. From October 1939 to May 1940,
he worked to improve delivery of government services, protect the rights
of evacuees, and resolve animosities between department prefects. His
most daunting problem rested in determining eligibility for refugee
relief, the cornerstone of successful long-term relocation.[79] Explicit
national guidelines existed for determining who qualified for assistance, but prefects altered policy to suit local particulars. The uneven
application of national guidelines fueled debate and policy adjustments.
Evacuees demanded clarification of policies in several areas:

- Who could legitimately evacuate and who was eligible for assistance?
- Were benefits the same for all refugees regardless of wealth or income?
- Were evacuated women with conscripted husbands eligible for a refu-
gee stipend in addition to a military spouse's stipend?

[78] AN F/23/230, Poitiers poster, prefect of Vienne, Henri Moulongue.
[79] In 1951 the United Nations Convention Relating to the Status of Refugees outlined postwar principles for determining eligibility for political asylum and international refugee aid. The Convention emphasized a definition of refugee predicated
upon the crossing of international borders. On December 18, 1961 the UN created
UNHCR's good offices to recognize "prima facie refugees," as a category of displaced person. Often "prima facie refugees" did not cross borders and were entitled
to material assistance in the case of displacement, but not necessarily to legal protection. See Jennifer Hyndman, *Managing Displacement: Refugees and the Politics of
Humanitarianism* (Minneapolis, MN: University of Minnesota Press, 2000), 8–12.

- Could children from outside designated evacuation areas, whose parents sent them to live with relatives, receive state assistance for schooling, room and board?
- Could servants of foreign nationality accompanying refugees receive stipends?
- Could people without an official military evacuation order receive assistance?

Schuman's office worked up to the moment of defeat on June 18, 1940 to resolve these questions.

Together with Albert Sarraut from the Ministry of the Interior, Schuman revised and clarified refugee relief policy. The Service of Refugees issued a universal scale for cash payments. Still, vast differences emerged between guidelines drafted in Paris and actual applications in locations as far away as Dordogne. Schuman instructed departments to establish local planning committees to oversee evacuee services distribution. The committees' work included ensuring equitable distribution of aid, avoiding the outbreak of epidemics, identifying employment opportunities, placing evacuee students in schools, and minimizing disruption to local communities.

As national policy established guideposts for assisting evacuees, host community administrators enforced revised policies. By January 1940, host department prefects began limiting cash aid dispersals, in some cases withdrawing assistance from "voluntary evacuees." Authorities applied rationalized scales of entitlement, disqualifying "double-dippers" – mainly wives of soldiers who drew both military and refugee benefits. Military wives' refugee allocations were halved, but children of soldiers continued to receive full payment from both allocations.[80]

Watchdog organizations appeared advocating on behalf of evacuees. One evacuee newsletter, *Le Lorrain*, placed pressure on host community authorities to respect the rights of the displaced. An article, "Visits with Evacuees," reported that a citizens' group, Social Services of Lorraine, had visited eighty-seven towns in departments of relocation and interviewed 280 families. The reporter claimed that the newspaper's presence increased the success rate in obtaining improvements in lodging, particularly for large families.[81]

Refugees constantly submitted complaints to mayors about the amount of cash aid, the quality of housing, assistance in paying energy bills, and access to medical benefits. In January 1940, Madame Simone,

[80] AN F/23/230, Notice, prefect of Dordogne and the Service of Evacuees of Bas-Rhin, Périgueux, January 4, 1940.
[81] AN F/23/230, *Le Lorrain*, February 9, 1940.

an "official evacuee" from Metz, wrote to Prefect Jozon of the Marne. She began, "I demand my right to a refugee allocation that the prefect has denied to me since my arrival in Châlons-sur-Marne."[82] She explained that the military had relocated her, her husband, and two children from Metz to Châlons-sur-Marne. The army had discharged her husband, declaring him unfit for service. Thus, he drew no military pension. Monsieur Simon found a job in Châlons that paid 1,200 francs per month. In Châlons, Madame Simon paid 350 francs per month for the family's two-room apartment, while the Syndicate of Landlords of Metz required her to continue to pay her full 200 francs per month rent in Metz. Her estimated 100 francs per month utility costs left her approximately 550 francs per month for living expenses. "Do you think," she asked, "that what remains is enough for four people to live on? How would you like me to buy milk and shoes for my children?"[83]

In fact, 1,300 francs per month became the maximum monthly payment allotted to a family of four, according to a scale developed in the Dordogne and adopted by Schuman's Refugee Service.[84] Madame Simon rightly demanded her additional 100 francs. Employing a language of rights to request her due, Madame Simon's letter underscores the degree to which expectations for displacement compensation had become common among Alsatian and Lorrainer refugees. Evacuee allocations surpassed the concept of ordinary entitlements; they had become compensatory rights owed to evacuees.

Soldiers' wives invoked patriotism in battles to retain the full payment of both refugee and military benefits. Madame Mallet of Channy wrote a fierce letter to the President of the Commission of Appeals at the Office of Refugee Assistance in Tulle (Corrèze): she explained that she was an evacuee from the Paris region and mother of a large family.[85] Still, the authorities refused her request for an evacuee allocation because her husband served as an army officer. Mallet disagreed with national officials who judged that officers' wives received a military benefit sufficient to meet family needs: "Children are considered the future of this country. It is inadmissible that anyone would refuse me assistance at this moment simply because the father of three

---

[82] ADM, Reims depot, Nos. 411–420, Refugee letters, 1939–1940. Mme Simon to the prefect of the Marne, Châlons-sur-Marne, January 22, 1940.
[83] ADM, Reims depot, Mme Simon to the prefect of the Marne.
[84] AN F/23/230, Notice, prefect of Dordogne and the Service of Evacuees of Bas-Rhin.
[85] Mallet used the term, "famille nombreuse," which signified an officially recognized category of family entitled to many state benefits. See Françoise Théabaud, *Quand nos grandes mères donnait la vie: La maternité en France dans l'entre-deux-guerre* (Lyon: Presses universitaires de Lyon, 1986).

Table 1. *"Minimum for family existence"*

Number in family	Francs per month
1	800
2	900
3	1,000
4	1,300
5	1,600
6	1,900
7	2,200
8	2,500
9	2,800
10	3,100

children ... is himself sacrificing his life for this country!"[86] Clearly Mallet felt that, having left her home and her husband, she deserved double compensation.

Schuman worked with host department prefects to address evacuee complaints of unfair policies and to ensure equitable distribution of cash assistance to qualifying refugees. His office circulated a standardized allocation table with a scale that allotted 10 francs per day to adults over age twelve and 7 francs per day to children below age thirteen. In sum, the government agreed to pay each adult 300 francs per month and each child 210 francs per month. But because authorities feared that refugees would grow dependent upon allocations, they adopted payment caps in order to encourage pursuit of employment. Refugees who worked still qualified for a refugee allocation equal to the difference between their salary and the allotted maximum allocation per family (Table 1).[87]

Problems immediately arose due to the misleading title, "Minimum for family existence." Evacuees concluded that the numbers indicated the minimum the state would pay to each family. However, refugees needed to read the fine print. The notes accompanying the table instructed department officials to terminate state aid to families when private sources of income equaled or exceeded the prescribed ceilings (*not* minimums). An example accompanied the table. The allocation

---

[86] AMBG H/IV, Mme Mallet de Channy to the President of the Commission of Appeals, Office of Refugee Assistance in Tulle (Corrèze), December 9, 1939.

[87] AN F/23/230, Notice, prefect of Dordogne and the Service of Evacuees of Bas-Rhin.

for a family of four including two children over age twelve would be 1,200 francs per month (four adult family members at 10 francs per day times 30 days). Per the plan, this family could earn up to 1,300 francs per month and still collect government assistance. In the example, the family earned 1,100 francs per month, so the family could receive a refugee benefit of 200 francs per month or, for 30 days per month, 7 francs per day (6.6 francs per day rounded up).[88] In this manner, the state made a contribution to the family and, it hoped, inspired evacuees to seek employment. Many refugees experienced these guidelines as an infringement on their perceived rights to allocations. The system engendered confusion, dispute, and undoubtedly a bit of abuse.

The payment policies outlined other contingencies. Displaced government employees such as railway, postal, and electric company workers, along with government pensioners could, in addition to their refugee allocation, collect 10 percent of their government salary or stipend provided the additional funds did not result in a larger total monthly income than fully employed government workers living in the host region.[89] This 10 percent policy drew complaints from relocated state workers who wanted to draw a full refugee benefit.

Despite Schuman's adoption of the refugee allocation table, distribution of refugee allocations never achieved the desired uniformity or equality. In mid-March 1940, the mayor of a small hamlet near Strasbourg, evacuated with his constituents to Vienne, wrote to Schuman's office demanding more uniformity in the refugee allocation process, "to help avoid the deplorable situation among the evacuated populations."[90] Finally, on April 16, Schuman issued revised guidelines for relief distribution. Refugees working in the local economy could now collect 25 percent of their allocation regardless of their family's total income. All pensioners and recipients of social security, due to previously defined dependencies, now qualified for hardship subsidies. However, the government would no longer provide money to those refugees for the previously covered costs of electricity, housing, gas, and clothing. In this regard, Schuman exerted fiscal discipline, urging private agencies to fill the gap. "If situations of particular difficulty should appear," Schuman warned, "they [refugees] should from this time forward turn to charitable organizations of either the refugee or

---

[88] AN F/23/230, Notice, prefect of Dordogne and the Service of Evacuees of Bas-Rhin.
[89] AN F/23/230, Notice, prefect of Dordogne and the Service of Evacuees of Bas-Rhin.
[90] AN F/23/226, Mayor of Freyming (Moselle) to Robert Schuman, Moselle deputy, March 18, 1940.

the host community."[91] Certainly non-government organizations did exist. The Red Cross, Secours National (National Assistance), and regionally based mutual aid societies tried to assist evacuees; but no relief organization could cover the electrical bills of hundreds of thousands of refugees. Perhaps because the cold winter months had passed, Schuman allowed that refugees who paid for their lodging and heating could submit requests for reimbursements for up to 2 francs per day to help meet their energy costs.[92]

The details of these distribution schemes may seem nettlesome, but the fair distribution of refugee relief represented one of the most important government policies crafted during this period. A large percentage of the French population based their strategies for wartime survival on receipt of refugee relief. A family's ability to pay for food, shelter, and energy determined how long it could stay healthy, maintain a safe distance from the war, and, in the end, stay alive. The refugee allocation system represented the cornerstone of an internally generated politics of humanitarian aid.

Women challenge relief limitations

In spring 1940, Schuman adopted new limitations for relief eligibility, supporting the government's desire to discourage further unauthorized civilian departures from Paris and other urban centers. The Service of Refugees specified that only three categories of individuals from Paris and Lyon would be eligible for refugee assistance: children aged 14 and under; mothers or guardians of young children; and pregnant women.[93] Also, persons aged over 70 could continue to receive refugee allocations only if they had been registered on the allocation rolls prior to April 10, 1940. Schuman specified that by May 1, 1940, "You [prefects] must refuse assistance to all persons not belonging to the above categories."[94]

As the principal beneficiaries of state aid and the guardians of children's benefits, women engaged every level of government in attempts to influence evacuation plans, expand eligibility for relief, and gain assistance in relocating their children or family. In an interesting way, the distribution of refugee relief opened a door for women to interact with the government. They entered that door not only with an open

---

[91] AN F/23/226, Robert Schuman to all prefects, April 16, 1940.
[92] AN F/23/226, Robert Schuman to all prefects, April 16, 1940.
[93] ADC 528/W/3, Robert Schuman to all prefects, Paris, April 10, 1940.
[94] ADC 528/W/3, Robert Schuman to all prefects, Paris, April 10, 1940.

hand, but also with a charged mind, filled with observations and comments about the economic and political events of the day. For example, Madame Broch, the widow of a World War I veteran and mother of three, found herself alone in Paris in the spring of 1940, faced with managing the fate of her family. In a letter to the mayor of Brive-la-Gaillarde (Corrèze), Broch explained that her children could no longer bear the terror of nightly air raids. She desired to relocate her family to Brive where she hoped to escape danger. Without a hint of shame, she requested that the mayor provide free lodging and food to assist her family's transition. She also inquired whether her granddaughter, currently enrolled in a middle school certificate program could enroll in a similar program in Brive so as not to "interrupt her studies."[95] Another woman from Bagnolet (Seine), aged 28 and the mother of a small child, wrote to the mayor of Brive in February 1940, seeking assistance with finding employment in Brive. Her reason for relocating stemmed from her husband's fear. "We need to find shelter," she insisted, "to calm the morale of my husband who is tormented by fear for the safety of his wife and small child."[96]

Parisian wives and mothers expressed strong opposition to the government's policy of reserving evacuation assistance for "official evacuees" of Alsace and Lorraine. Madame Gabrielle Thorne of Paris explained that since September 1939, her daughter, accompanied by grandparents, had taken refuge in Brive. While the grandparents came from an designated evacuation region; her child, a resident of Paris, did not qualify for state aid. In order to keep her job, Thorne had remained in Paris, but faced the hardship of paying to shelter her child on top of financing her own household. "It is impossible for me to take care of myself and support my child," she lamented. "Could you find some way to assist me?" ended her vague, but desperate request.[97]

Prolonged separation of parents from children increased financial hardships, adding fiscal concerns to fears for the well-being of their children. Madame Lucie Pouyard of Comté Vannes (Seine) expressed her worry in a letter written on April 26, 1940. Entreating the mayor of Brive to extend refugee benefits to her son, she painted a picture of a mental and material struggle. Madame Pouyard supplemented her monthly military benefit by earning 120 francs doing cleaning and odd jobs, but sent 15 francs per day to her son and also sent money to her

---

[95] AMBG H/IV, Mme Vve. Broch to mayor of Brive, Paris, Tuesday April 9, 1940.
[96] AMBG H/IV, to mayor of Brive from resident in Bagnolet (Seine), February 1, 1940 (sender's name illegible).
[97] AMBG H/IV, Mme Gabrielle Thorné to mayor of Brive, Paris, March 26, 1940.

husband. "I am alone," began her letter. "I have a right to a refugee allocation. It's the law," she declared. Her letter evidenced other pains. She had not seen her son since November 1939 because she could not afford the train fare to Brive. In an effort to claim her perceived legal right she boldly transferred authority to Madame Guillaume (apparently her son's guardian) to collect her son's refugee allocation on her behalf.[98]

The burden of making ends meet and fulfilling the parental role to protect pushed many women to challenge hierarchies of authority or to transgress boundaries of class and region. Working-class women wrote letters despite their poor grammar and young mothers traveled to remote parts of the country in efforts to improve their children's chance of surviving the war. Because policies regarding evacuees seemed to be generated at both the national and local levels, evacuees learned to navigate the zones where competing authorities converged. If a mother did not like the response she received from a municipal official, she addressed her concerns to higher-ups. Madame Buge, for example, attempted to circumvent the authority of the mayor of Brive by addressing her complaint to the Minister of Agriculture in Paris. It is not clear why she thought this branch of the government might be helpful, but from her perspective a national ministry surely had greater authority than a small-town mayor. In September, Buge's husband had been mobilized as a defense industry worker and she and her son had moved from Alfortville to Corrèze, her husband's native department. During this period she continued to collect a military benefit, but paid 15 percent in taxes, covered her husband's rent and laundry costs, and paid for lodging in Brive. Having found themselves in "thin circumstances" even before the war, Buge's budget met further challenges due to her son's liver and intestinal illness. Having met with a negative response to her request for a refugee allocation from the mayor of Brive, she entreated the Minister of Agriculture to come to her aid. "Other people in my same condition receive an allocation," she added in her defense.[99] In this case, the office of the Minister of Agriculture simply forwarded Buge's letter back to the mayor of Brive.

Less frequently, but no less emphatically, men pleaded their families' cases. Jean Louis Lachand, veteran of World War I, invoked his service to France in an attempt to secure passage for his wife and grandchildren. "Our family includes a grandfather, a mother, five children and

[98] AMBG H/IV, Mme Pouyarde, Louis née Léger Lucie to mayor of Brive, Comte Vannes (Seine), April 26, 1940.
[99] AMBG H/IV, Mme Buge to the Minister of Agriculture, Brive, November 22, 1939, forwarded to mayor of Brive, November 24, 1939, from Minister of Agriculture.

two grandchildren whose father is in the army," began Lachand's letter to the mayor of Paris. Lachand's family had lived in Saint-Ouen, a suburb of Paris, until September 1939 when the army ordered their evacuation to a small village about 15 km away. Lachand explained his family's difficulties, including that they could not find wood to warm themselves nor a doctor to care for one of the granddaughters who suffered from paralysis; and his grown children could not find work. Lachand hoped that the mayor would facilitate the family's relocation to Corrèze. "Being natives of Corrèze, we would like to return to our country," pleaded Lachand. "I personally am a wounded veteran sergeant of the 326th Army division from Brive,"[100] Lachand concluded, clearly hoping that his past sacrifices might gain special consideration. The mayor of Paris forwarded the letter to the mayor of Brive.

When urban northerners did succeed in relocating to the interior as "official" evacuees, they confronted new problems. Finding work proved more of a challenge than government policies recognized. Madame Gagneki, who had resided in Brive since the beginning of the war, wrote to the mayor on several occasions in an attempt to find supplemental work. The mayor's office notified her in February 1940 of jobs advertised at the La Marque munitions factory. Unfortunately, La Marque's manufacturing headquarters were in Tulle, located about 15 minutes from Brive by train. Gagneki replied to the mayor that, "to my great regret, it is impossible for me to go all the way to Tulle to work since I have a newborn baby in my care." "I'm not refusing to work," she insisted, "I just prefer to work in Brive."[101] The mayor kindly responded that he would ask La Marque if they might place her in their plant in Brive.

Conclusion

Robert Schuman's appointment to head the Service of Refugees in August 1939 brought the political weight needed to resolve the disputes and disparities arising from an evacuation policy that had been cobbled together between 1936 and 1939. His effectiveness in finalizing the evacuation of his native region, Alsace and Lorraine, exceeded that which he demonstrated in attempting to extend the protections offered by evacuations to a larger segment of the population, particularly residents of industrialized urban centers. He fell short of his main goal: to achieve a uniform application of refugee relief. Schuman tempered

---

[100] AMBG H/IV, M. Jean Louis Lachand to mayor of Paris, February 28, 1940.
[101] AMBG H/IV, Mme Gagneki to mayor of Brive, February 26, 1940.

disputes between prefects of interior, host departments and those from the eastern regions. He began to halt the self-initiated voluntary evacuations from Paris and other urban centers. He addressed, but did not resolve, the competition for access to refugee relief between "official evacuees," and "voluntary evacuees." The distinction between the two groups of French civilians seeking protection from war remained a source of tension across the interior, pitting Frenchmen against Frenchmen in a battle for scarce resources.

To address this increased pressure on the resources of the Service of Refugees, Schuman began in April 1940 to narrow the eligibility criteria for refugee assistance. This tack generated more confrontation, particularly from mothers attempting to make ends meet and protect their children from exposure to war. By May 1940, the expanding awareness of a program that sponsored civilian evacuations energized a broad spectrum of civilians interested in relocating their families from potentially dangerous urban centers. The evacuation programs competed with military orders to civilians to stay put and ready themselves to confront the enemy.

Inadequate as Schuman's evacuation program may have been, it did lay the fundamental structure for accommodating masses of displaced civilians. On May 10, 1940, the German Wehrmacht invaded Belgium, Luxembourg, the Netherlands, and French airspace. Fear of the invasion spread rapidly through the northern departments of Ardennes, Marne, Pas-de-Calais, Aisne, Nord, Somme, Oise, Val-d'Oise, Seine-Saint-Dénis, Seine-et-Marne, Hauts-de-Seine, and Île-de-France – all located outside the evacuated Red Zone. As we have seen, the government offered limited assistance to residents in these departments and forbade civilians from participating in the "official evacuation." Within a week of the German attack, a deluge of Belgian refugees entered France, carrying personal belongings and the most reliable reports of German movements. As bombs fell on urban centers, an exodus from northern France amassed millions of civilian refugees. Like the French State, the organized evacuation structure that Schuman had thoughtfully rebuilt, collapsed.

2   Mothers move against military and bureaucratic entrenchment

Germany's "method of modern super-Blitzkrieg," reported George Axelsson of the *New York Times*, "caused 'lasting damage'" to French airfields at Metz, Saint-Omer and Vitry-le-François.[1] According to French and British estimates, the Germans flew 1,000 planes into battle on May 10 and lost 200 as bombing campaigns spread to Reims, Épernay, and Châlons-sur-Marne, towns located in the Marne.[2] Local newspapers in the Marne did not report attack details to the same degree, but French civilians became conscious of their position within the Luftwaffe's firing range. The day's official reports put the number of civilian wounded from air raids at 337.[3] Understandably civilians feared for their lives, but French military and Défense passive authorities broadcast orders for civilians to remain calm and in place. One very concerned woman, Madame Maria Parmentier of Reims, resided in a working-class neighborhood less than half a mile from the railroad station. At the close of World War I, German pilots bombed Reims' train station and 80 percent of the city. The cathedral of Notre Dame, a holy site for the crowning of French kings, reigned tall about a mile from her house. Demolished in World War I, the cathedral's restoration had only been completed in 1937. Now, twenty-one years later, Reims faced renewed air assault. Based upon history and contemporary events, Parmentier logically concluded that she lived in a war zone. Military authorities disagreed.

Determined to rattle local leaders, Parmentier began to knock on the doors of her neighbors, inviting them to sign a petition. We can imagine her conversation with fellow Rémois: "Had they heard the air-raid sirens last night?" "What did they plan to do if the Germans

---

[1] George Axelsson, "Border Resistance Broken, Nazis Say, 'Furious Attacks' Reported with Fliers over a Broad Front," *New York Times*, May 10, 1940, 1.
[2] Felix Belair, Jr., "America Angered Says Roosevelt," *New York Times*, May 10, 1940, 34 and Associated Press, "The Mark of Bomber Left on Paris and Nancy by Raiding Reich Warplanes," *New York Times*, May 12, 1940, 32.
[3] Associated Press, "The Mark of Bomber Left on Paris," 32.

reached Reims?" "Where would they go to find shelter with their children?" "Were they aware that no bomb shelter had been built for their block?" We know that she successfully stirred enough concern among her neighbors to persuade them to sign her petition, which she delivered to Deputy Mayor Paul Marchandeau, so titled because he had also been elected to the National Assembly's Chamber of Deputies. Parmentier's petition bluntly stated its concern: "We request an immediate favor of you, to build a shelter for us women and small children, because we have absolutely no place to take refuge and we are terrified!"[4]

The petition included the following signatures of residents of Parmentier's neighborhood:

Mme Maria Parmentier
Mme André Brodeir, one granddaughter, aged 4
Mme Joseph Helein, two children
Mme Gastin Memessen, three children
Mme C. Norart, one child
Mme Marcel Wargnier, two children
Mme Louis Pacot, one child
Mme N. Duforer, two granddaughters, aged 2 and 6
Mme Lemaoine, two children
M. and Mme Lavillonnière
M. Dandolf
Mme Hermenter
Mme Boulle, two children, aged 6 and 15
Mme Michandon
M. Domart
M. and Mme Rousiot
M. and Mme Calmenes
M. and Mme Haurenter
Mme Emil Wylocke, two children
M. and Mme Pourchten
M. and Mme Potin
M. and Mme Grégoire and Mme Guillaume
Mme Bonnet
M. Follmer, four children
Docteur Person
Mme Framer
Mme Saussette

[4] AMVR, Series Secrétariat Général, No. 3214, Mme Parmentier to Mayor Marchandeau, May 12, 1940.

Mme Masson
Mme Baudelet
Mme Melchior

The names on Parmentier's petition not only recorded the identity of the women and the few men living in thirty households on Parmentier's street, rue de Pévy, but also showed something of the demographic profile of Reims at the outbreak of war. Of the twenty-five adult women petitioners, ten headed households with children; eight lived alone without children; another seven women lived with their husbands; and one, Madame Guillaume, lived with a married couple, perhaps her parents, Monsieur and Madame Grégoire. Eleven men and twenty-three children also lived on the block. Of the seven married couples residing on the street where a man remained, none claimed any children, suggesting possibly that they were older. Only four children lived with a single man, all under the roof of Monsieur Follmer, presumably the children's widowed father. In short, if rue de Pévy shared demographics with the rest of the town, women and the elderly composed the majority of the population of war-threatened Reims.

In France, the "petition" has long been a cherished tool of intellectuals and the people for registering their voice with government representatives perceived to have failed the people's interests.[5] At the very moment that France's government sat on the precipice of collapse, disenfranchised women attempted to engage government representatives and urge responsiveness from France's ailing institutions. Unlike Marthe Vluggens of Paris, Parmentier and her neighbors did not initially demand the "right" to evacuate; rather they demanded a way to safely remain in Reims, in a bomb shelter.

The actions of Parmentier and Vluggens share a commonality: their interventions are responses to the intensified experience of air war, or "modern super-Blitzkrieg." While the women of France's various communities shared no evident political, social, or economic commonality, they formed part of an emerging contingent community: militarily threatened civilians. Fear of exposure to military invasion, aerial bombardment, and even displacement created common concerns and anxieties, which generated a new set of demands upon the state to ensure civilian protection. Political scientist Michael Shapiro describes how new experiences generate new shared languages that gain political currency: "Innovative political action ... consists in linguistic action, in

---

[5] See Jean-François Sirinelli, *Intellectuels et passions françaises: Manifestes et pétitions au XXe siècle* (Paris: Fayard, 1990). Sirinelli focuses on intellectual appeals, but discusses the impact of petitions.

changing the rules that link what we say to our experience ... Politics and language are intimately commingled ... one must analyze language as a domain of political relations."[6] Indeed, the predicament of multi-faceted military invasion propelled civilians to formulate a language of complaint and entitlement to advance claims upon the state for wartime protection. This language of protection began acquiring sufficient force to mint a newly formulated "right": a civilian security right.[7]

Marchandeau responded to the petitioners the following day. He informed Parmentier that the nearest shelter sat at the intersection of Boulevard Albert 1er and rue Léonard de Vinci, two blocks west and one block north of rue de Pévy. He also noted that the city of Reims had requested funding from the office of the Défense passive to construct an additional shelter located about a block closer than the current shelter. The city had not yet received authorization from the Défense passive to build the shelter. Marchandeau promised to authorize construction to begin despite national officials' failure to act.[8] Three days into the German invasion, such news could hardly have reassured Maria Parmentier.

In the 1950s, French politicians and historians, attempting to make sense of France's defeat, debated whether the German military consciously sought to foment civilian panic and flight in order to interfere with French military operations. Historian Jean Vidalenc concluded that existing evidence was insufficient to determine whether enemy agents organized the initial stages of the exodus. A strong possibility existed, he argued, that once the exodus began, enemy agents in north-eastern towns capitalized on the civilian departures to encumber French military operations.[9] The martyred French historian, Marc Bloch, writing while in captivity in his Gestapo prison cell in 1940, believed it did not matter whether the Germans targeted civilians or not.[10] The mere

---

[6] Michael Shapiro, *Language and Political Understanding: the Politics of Discursive Practices* (New Haven, CT: Yale University Press, 1981), 23, quoted in Hilary Footitt, *Women, Europe and the New Languages of Politics* (London: Continuum, 2002), 11.

[7] Civilian "rights" to security have evolved in relation to international human rights and international law, gaining force initially with the 1897 Hague Accords and in the 1920 Geneva conventions. Only recently have historians begun to link the histories of civilian security rights and human rights. See Helen Kinsella, "The Image before the Weapon: A Genealogy of the 'Civilian' in International Law and Politics," Ph.D. dissertation, University of Minnesota, July 2004; Samuel Moyn, *The Last Utopia: Human Rights in History* (Cambridge, MA: Belknap Press, 2010).

[8] AMVR, Series Secrétariat Général, No. 3214, Marchandeau to Mme Parmentier, May 13, 1940.

[9] Vidalenc, *L'exode de mai–juin 1940*, 67–69.

[10] For recent studies on the trauma of bombing, see Sven Lindqvist, *A History of Bombing* (New York: The New Press, 2003); Ben Shephard, *A War of Nerves: Soldiers and Psychiatrists in the Twentieth Century* (Cambridge, MA: Harvard University Press, 2002).

sound of enemy planes unnerved civilians as well as soldiers. Bloch's own words best evoke this terror:

No, the fact is that this dropping of bombs from the sky has a unique power of spreading terror ... The combination of weight and altitude gives them an appearance of almost visible violence which no shelter, however thick, seems capable of resisting.[11]

Bloch concluded that the best-trained soldier feels "utterly defense-less."[12] Thus, we can easily understand the validity in civilians' sense of vulnerability in the face of this new brand of psychological air warfare.

Providing adequate security, such as bomb shelters, offered a way to assuage civilian fears. Whether bomb shelters actually provided the required protection from falling bombs seemed less important than the mere existence of shelters within reasonable proximity to threatened neighborhoods. Civilians and government officials expressed aware-ness of the role shelters should play in the defense of the home front. In an interview with famous journalist and novelist, Blaise Cendrars, and published in *Paris-Soir*, a female munitions plant worker testified to civilian concerns: "I work in a gunpowder plant 40 metres beneath the earth. You think it is reasonable do you?," asked the woman. "I work in a government job. Every morning I go to work in a fortified château ... and each night I return to my home in Paris. What a funny war it is! One is protected in a shelter to work, but not at home."[13]

Until May 16, Rémois civilians read about aerial bombardment in Marchandeau's own newspaper, *L'Éclaireur de l'Est*. Newspapers not only tracked the progress of air and land battles, but provided read-ers with the language to describe war's new technologies. On May 11, *L'Éclaireur de l'Est* reported on the bombing of Nancy, located an hour east of Reims. One story described how German planes had bombed civilian homes and a school.[14] Thirteen civilians died and thirty were wounded. Yet another report detailed the bombing of Lyon, where a German bomb had fallen on the home of Virgile Dubois. His wife and eight-month-old child, Marcel Janin Dubois and little Virgile Dubois, died in the attack.[15] Paul Reynaud, called by President Albert Lebrun to serve as prime minister on March 21, 1940 issued a solemn note of sympathy to the French people.[16] He recognized that, "serious concerns

---

[11] Bloch, *Strange Defeat*, 57.   [12] Bloch, *Strange Defeat*, 57.
[13] Blaise Cendrars, "Je travaille dans une poudrerie à quarante mètres sous terre," *Paris Soir*, September 21, 1939.
[14] *L'Éclaireur de l'Est*, May 11, 1940.
[15] *L'Éclaireur de l'Est*, May 11, 1940.
[16] Reynaud led a small, moderate group in the Chamber of Deputies called the Centre Républicain. He had been a member of the Alliance Démocratique, a group of parties

occupy each home, each village and every unit of the army."[17] Reynaud asked that the French turn to "moral fortitude" to help see them through the dangerous turn of events.

While the prime minister urged calm, Reims police posted warnings alerting civilians to the existence of unexploded bombs. In the event of the discovery of an unexploded bomb near an apartment complex or building, police instructed residents to "evacuate the premises immediately and notify the police."[18] Throughout the week, tensions within Reims mounted. Again on May 15, L'Éclaireur de l'Est published a reminder that: "City Hall is under constant inquiry as to whether the city of Reims has been ordered to evacuate," admitted the announcement, but continued, "Only the military authority has the power to order an evacuation ... There exists absolutely no reason to order the evacuation of Reims."[19]

Monsieur P. Devin wrote to the mayor "in the name of the valiant mothers that I witness during air raid alerts, who act calmly and dignified with their children." He urged the mayor to recognize the legitimacy of civilians' fears and realize that local officials' actions actually aggravated civilian unrest. Devin observed that it was, "necessary and humane," to warn the population of the need to evacuate Reims. Furthermore, he requested that military leaders intensify air defense around Reims. Repeated air alerts took their toll he said: "workshops interrupt work, stores close, and traffic draws to a halt during the air alerts." The perpetual disruption to daily life harmed the economy and wore on civilians' nerves. Ordering an evacuation, Devin believed, would allow Rémois to focus on "participating in the defense of our city."[20]

Streams of civilian letters pressed the mayor to petition the military to alter their strategy for safeguarding Reims. Otherwise, residents argued, the mayor should break with military orders and satisfy civilian concerns. A sample of approximately three dozen letters mailed between May 10 and May 15 shows that two groups felt a strong need to express their feelings: mothers and business owners.

representing the moderate Right and the Center. He resigned from the Alliance in September 1938, in part because Flandin, the president of the Alliance Démocratique, had supported the publication in La Liberté of a pacifist editorial. Reynaud, Thick of the Fight, 194.

[17] L'Éclaireur de l'Est, May 11, 1940.
[18] AMVR, Series Secrétariat Général, No. 3214.
[19] L'Éclaireur de l'Est, May 15, 1940.
[20] AMVR, Series Secrétariat Général, No. 3602, M. P. Devin to Reims mayor, May 15, 1940.

Police reports confirmed Devin's claims of increased anxiety. On May 14, police searched rue Trudaine and found a metal fountain pen engraved with the word, "Germania." They submitted the pen to the Pyrotechnic Service of Reims. Alarmed by the "device," agents at police headquarters sounded the air raid sirens. Monsieur Abel Kuhn, an employee of the railroad, and an evacuee from Charleville (Ardennes), reacted to the alarm system by running through rue Diderot crying, "Gas attack!"[21] Kuhn, who had donned a helmet and a gas mask, ran through public walkways and into courtyards, terrifying women and children. Police arrested Kuhn for uttering "alarmist and demoralizing slogans."[22]

Less hysterical circumstances prompted city officials to intensify efforts to segregate refugees arriving from departments north and east of the Marne and, by week's end, from Belgium, Holland and Luxembourg. Monsieur Houdin, assistant to Marchandeau and a member of the city council, coordinated efforts with Captain Chabaudet of the police department to send trucks to pick up "road refugees" and transport them to the train station, so as to limit their contact with residents. Assistant Mayor Houdin and Captain Chabaudet also ordered police to question refugees about movements of the French and German armies, because official channels of communication were failing to keep municipal authorities apace of military events.[23] In fact, few national officials understood precisely how the war at the front – an ever changing geographical designation – proceeded.

The military situation surrounding the Marne

Military histories of the battle of France abound, debating the role of tactics, personality, and technical application of military machinery in Germany's victory. For an understanding of how military events conditioned civilian flight, it serves to recall how the battle encroached beyond the "combat zone." Ultimately "news" of the advance of the Wehrmacht, as much as the German Army's actual proximity, fueled civilian flight, forcing the French military and civilian command to reconsider the delay of issuing evacuation orders.

German General Erich von Manstein's memoir provides the perspective of one of the Wehrmacht's chief architects of the Ardennes

---

[21] AMVR, Series Secrétariat Général, No. 3184, Reims Municipal Police Report, May 14, 1940.
[22] AMVR, Series Secrétariat Général, No. 3184, Reims Municipal Police Report.
[23] AMVR, Series Secrétariat Général, No. 3161, Captain Chabaudet at the station of Reims to the mayor and M. Hodin, May 14, 1940.

invasion.[24] The Ardennes forest is located approximately 60 miles north of Reims, and many German strategists thought it impenetrable. The traditional plan, not dissimilar from Schlieffen's World War I plan, would have had the Germans invade with a frontal assault in Belgium with the limited goal of securing the Channel coast. However, the blueprint for the Germans, championed by Colonel-General Gerd von Rundstedt and von Manstein, envisioned a coordinated attack on Belgium and northern France. Their plan exceeded more modest plans for achieving partial victory in the west, setting the final goal as the complete capitulation of continental allied forces.

Germany's military intentions mattered in terms of the allied military and civilian response they provoked; but they also mattered in terms of how the allies judged them after defeat. On October 6, 1945, at the International Military Tribunal in Nuremberg, the allies held court, charging Nazi Party leaders and Wehrmacht officers with four counts of war crimes. The invasion of the Low Countries figured in Count One: The Common Plan or Conspiracy, which specified in Part IV, Section F, No. 5, "Expansion of the war into a general war of aggression: planning and execution of attacks on Denmark, Norway, Belgium, the Netherlands, Luxembourg, Yugoslavia, and Greece."[25] For American chief prosecutor, Robert H. Jackson, the charge of conspiracy to wage aggressive war by invading foreign countries constituted "the crime which comprehends all lesser crimes in the crime of making unjustifiable war."[26] France, having declared war on Germany after the Wehrmacht violated Belgian neutrality was referred to, but not principally named in the aggressive war clause.

In 1949, a British Military Tribunal found von Manstein guilty of nine counts of war crimes. One included: "Deliberately and recklessly disregarded his duty as a military commander by failing to insure respect for human life, as a result of which Jews and others were exterminated."[27] Von Manstein's ambitious entry through the Ardennes surprised contemporary observers, but his 1955 memoirs revealed that much like Hermann Goering, he never accepted the criminality

[24] Von Manstein, *Lost Victories*.
[25] "Indictment," International Military Tribunal (IMT), *Trial of the Major War Criminals before the International Military Tribunal, Nuremberg, 14 November 1945–1 October 1946*. 42 vols. (Nuremberg: International Military Tribunal, 1947), extracted in Michael R. Marrus (ed.), *The Nuremberg War Crimes Trial 1945–46: A Documentary History* (Boston, MA: Bedford/St Martin's Press, 1997), 62.
[26] Telford Taylor, *The Anatomy of the Nuremberg Trials* (Boston, MA: Little, Brown, 1992), 54.
[27] United Press, "Manstein Guilty of Crimes, Gets 18 Years' Imprisonment," *New York Times*, December 19, 1949, 1, 19.

of waging aggressive or total war. At his trial, Goering rejected the authority of the 1906 and 1907 Hague Conventions governing modern warfare arguing that: "the regulations on land warfare of the Hague Convention are in my opinion not an instrument which can be used as a basis for a modern war, because they do not take into consideration the essential principles of this war; the war in the air, the economic war, and the war of propaganda."[28]

The principal attack through the Ardennes necessarily imperiled civilian lives and Goering included civilian dispersal as an aspect of the new definition of warfare. He justified it in a comparison with World War I: "A war at that time [of the Hague conventions 1906–1907] between one army and another, in which the population was more or less not involved, cannot be compared with today's total war, in which everyone, even the child, is drawn into the experience of war through the introduction of air warfare."[29]

While von Manstein's plan focused on ground operations, its success depended upon air support. His two-pronged plan had Army Group B marching through northern Belgium for the expected frontal assault on French and British troops, while Army Group A would form a strong southern attack on France. With forty infantry divisions, Group A would penetrate the Ardennes forest, cross the River Meuse at Sedan and Charleville, circle north to the Channel and trap the retreating allied troops. Part of Group A would then proceed east to Abbeville on the Somme estuary, encircling the French and British northern wings in the maneuver that forced the evacuation of allied troops from Dunkerque on May 27, 1940. Other Group A divisions would split off in the direction of Paris and Reims, while the 16th Army, also part of Group A, would march through Luxembourg to meet French forces concentrated between the end of the Maginot fortification and Sedan.

On May 27, von Manstein entered France to secure the lower Somme. Despite the "brave" fighting at the Somme, von Manstein later noted: "One thing that struck us was the relative inactivity of the enemy artillery, which was quite out of proportion to the number of batteries we had identified."[30] He attributed French passivity to the fact that, "French gunners were still far too, 'Maginot-minded.'"[31] French general Maxime Weygand, had declared that France's fate rested on the outcome of

[28] Hermann Goering, "Testimony on the Applicability of the Hague Convention of 1907," IMT, *Trial of Major War Criminals*, vol. 9, 362–364, in Marrus, *The Nuremberg War Crimes Trials*, 180.
[29] Marrus, *The Nuremberg War Crimes Trials*, 181.
[30] Von Manstein, *Lost Victories*, 106.
[31] Von Manstein, *Lost Victories*, 106.

the battle of the Somme. Reynaud had once tried to replace General Maurice Gamelin with Weygand on May 9 after Gamelin refused to lend support to Norway.[32] However, the Secretary of War refused to decommission the honorable veteran. The following day, Gamelin declared, "Germany has engaged us in a struggle to the death."[33] But on June 5, after nearly a month of dwindling French success, Reynaud appointed Weygand, hoping for a miracle on the Somme.

Weygand planned intensified fighting in north-eastern France. He envisioned the entrapment of the Germans at the Somme, drawing upon Pétain's plan. In 1934, the National Assembly had questioned then Secretary of War, Marshal Pétain, about the possibility of a German advance through the Ardennes. Pétain had replied, "Nothing to fear. If the German army passes that way, we'll trap them coming out."[34] Indeed, in the first week of June, the mass of German troops lay between Paris and the Channel, sandwiched between Allied troops to the north and south. Weygand envisioned the northern and southern divisions of the Allied armies coming together at the Somme like a "locking jaw." Unfortunately, the general lacked the requisite manpower. The Wehrmacht outnumbered the Allies three to one.

Already on May 29, Weygand had issued a not inaccurate memorandum suggesting that the army would likely crumble if the battle of Somme went against them. "The British government should be warned," he wrote, "to prepare for the consequences of defeat."[35] Some postwar critics argue that such expressions of defeatism before a decisive battle warranted Weygand's immediate removal. However, since so many in the French military agreed with the general's assessment, Reynaud would have needed to exercise significant imagination to find Weygand's replacement. The talented, but unproven young strategist, Charles De Gaulle, had received a recent promotion, but no one considered him experienced enough to command all of France's forces. William C. Bullitt, US Ambassador to France, wrote favorably to President Roosevelt after his first meeting with De Gaulle complementing: "Two weeks ago this General was a Colonel in the tank corps. He showed great initiative and courage in stemming the German

---

[32] Reynaud explained his choice of Weygand to the Commission Charged to Investigate the Events Which Happened in France from 1933 to 1945, established by the National Assembly and convened June 11, 1947. See *Rapport de la Commission Chargée d'Enquêter sur les événements survenues en France de 1933 1945*, vol. 6, No. 2344, 114.

[33] G. H. Archambault, "This is France's Battle," *New York Times*, May 11, 1940, 1.

[34] Pétain quoted by Paul Reynaud, *Rapport de la Commission Chargée*, 114.

[35] Pertinax, *The Gravediggers of France*, 221.

advance on Paris ... He is a young man who appears to be vigorous and intelligent."[36]

The British meanwhile attempted to defer France's defeat. At a meeting of the War Cabinet in Paris, attended by Reynaud, Weygand, Darlan, Churchill, and Clement Attlee, they petitioned Bullitt to press President Roosevelt for aid. The evacuation of British and French troops across the Channel had damaged or sunk several allied destroyers. At Churchill's request Bullitt pressed Roosevelt, "to turn over 24 old destroyers immediately to the French Navy."[37] Such assistance could not arrive in time to save France.

One of the most important facts for French civilians about the military details of the first two weeks of the battle of France rested in the simple reality that they did not know of them! The censor forbade accurate, detailed, or "defeatist" reporting of military maneuvers. Although censorship was a standard practice among the western democracies during wartime, French papers withheld details that, if released, could have better prepared the population for the German advance. The French government allowed newspapers to describe the methods and horrors of the new German warfare, but forbade papers to present battle logistics or pessimistic accounts of the moving front. Hence, knowledge of the worsening position of the allied forces could not guide local civilian planners in making decisions about evacuations. By choosing to allow only small morsels of information to leak to the press, government information officers permitted civilians and their overseers to draw their own conclusions from eyewitness accounts, which differed dramatically from "approved" reports. Had Défense passive planners aggressively pressured the military to permit a public discussion of the deteriorating state of the battle, civilians might have resisted the impulse to flee. Government candor and suggestions as to how civilians might actively, rather than passively, endure or resist the invasion, might have mobilized civilians to hold their ground. Balancing the interests of national security intelligence against the obligation to inform a potentially threatened citizenry of impending disaster presents an enduring dilemma for modern governments. In 1940, withholding information to "protect" national security ultimately weakened home front stability.[38]

---

[36] William C. Bullitt, "Telegram to Franklin D. Roosevelt," June 6, 1940, 6 pm, in *For the President: Personal and Secret Correspondence between Franklin D. Roosevelt and William C. Bullitt*, ed. Orville H. Bullitt (Boston, MA: Houghton Mifflin, 1972), 452.

[37] Bullitt, "Telegram," May 31, 1940, 6 pm, *For the President*, 444.

[38] See Eric V. Larson and Bogdan Savych, *Misfortunes of War: Press and Public Reactions to Civilian Deaths in Wartime* (Santa Monica, CA: RAND Corporation, Project Air Force, 2007).

The rush of refugees and the fly of rumors

On May 12, while Gamelin still held his command, a Portuguese citizen and evacuee from Neufchateau, Antonio Moraes, reported to the Marne police that the Germans had broken through the French line. Moraes fled Neufchateau of his own initiative after he had learned that the burgermeister had escaped to France. Moraes' deposition registered a cheering and triumphant testimony of the valor of French troops trying to push back the German advance on Arlon. Many Belgian refugees celebrated the courage of the French troops, especially the 5th Regiment of the Motorized Dragoon Division which Moraes witnessed at battle.[39] The Rémois police lacked the communications to verify Moraes' and other refugee reports. Yet the police cited Moraes' optimistic observations of French valor when justifying postponement of the evacuation of Reims.

With the battle concentrating to the north and east of Reims, larger populations from both directions flowed into Reims. Their accents and ancestry often fueled local suspicions. The peculiar rituals of Charles Walter, a refugee of Mulhouse, drew police interest. Born as a German in Strasbourg in 1887, and married to Suzanne (née Becker) from Pleuheim, Germany, Walter lived at the factory of Longuaux, working as ground security. Despite several rebukes by local police, Walter placed a light in his window each night. After refusing to extinguish his night light, which police said could act as a reference point for enemy aircraft, police seized the couple's passports and arrested the Walters under suspicion of espionage. The couple were then turned over to the head of the 2nd Army office of the 6th Region in Châlons.[40] Local tensions were running high.

Police files from May 1940 confirm that many Rémois already felt under siege well before the Germans arrived. Refugees from other departments, along with foreigners, stirred their suspicion. On May 13, police papered the town with instructions urging civilians to keep their eyes and ears open for potential traitors. The poster warned that enemies practicing "shady and criminal dealings," certainly existed. Any time a local resident noticed an unfamiliar person who might seem to be stirring up panic or asking specific and suspicious questions, the resident should "discreetly" point that person out to the police. Conversely, the poster's final warning contradicted its initial message: "Don't see a spy everywhere and in everything."[41] But on the

---

[39] AMVR, Secrétariat Général, No. 3184, Police report to the mayor, May 12, 1940.
[40] AMVR, Secrétariat Général, No. 3184, Police report, May 25, 1940.
[41] AMVR, Secrétariat Général, No. 3214, Municipal poster, May 13, 1940.

panic front, Marchandeau's team, like the French Army, engaged in a losing battle.

On May 15, *L'Éclaireur de l'Est* announced that German troops were moving toward Reims. In an air attack the preceding night, German bombers had pummeled the Ardennes, wounding 240 civilians and soldiers; the largest attack reported in the local paper to date. The number must have shocked readers. Now the censors made little effort to disguise the rapaciousness of the German tactics. The newspaper editors, however, balanced the dismal news with a prominently positioned story noting French and British successes. In Sedan, British aircraft and French troops fought bravely; the paper celebrated. The RAF retaliated, destroying two bridges and levying heavy losses upon enemy personnel.[42]

Newspaper reports in the United States differed from the French in the amount of detail released. The *New York Times* minced few words in describing German violence against fleeing refugees. One witness said that fleeing peasants "had been machine-gunned mercilessly."[43] Soon afterward, the planes returned to gun down horses and cattle. Refugees stopped at the Belgian border had become standing targets.

"The Germans send over reconnaissance planes which, detecting where cars were parked, would immediately disappear," testified an observer. Shortly after, "bombers appeared to drop their load on the parked cars."[44] One unidentified survivor testified: "We dived into ditches, where we remained some time, waiting for them to return. They did. This time seemingly they saw us, though we dressed for the occasion in dark clothes."[45] The planes flew over four times, "machine-gunning each time until French chasers appeared."[46]

Mayor Marchandeau detailed the escalating Ardennes crisis in a memo to Marne prefect, André Jozon. Approximately 100,000 refugees from Belgium and the Ardennes, including some army deserters, clogged the streets around Reims. Refugee relief stations, intended to protect the inhabitants of Reims, were saturated, and few, if any, Rémois occupied them. "Under no condition can they [Belgians and Ardennais] be sheltered here," Marchandeau emphasized.[47] Marchandeau contemptuously

---

[42] "L'activité des bombardiers de la Royal Air Force dans la région de Sedan," *L'Éclaireur de l'Est*, May 15, 1940, 2.

[43] "Refugee Attacks: Laid to Germans: Planes Machine Gun Autos Far North of Paris," *New York Times*, May 16, 1940, 1.

[44] "Refugee Attacks," *New York Times*, May 16, 1940, 1.

[45] "Refugee Attacks," *New York Times*, May 16, 1940, 1.

[46] "Refugee Attacks," *New York Times*, May 16, 1940, 1.

[47] ADM, Reims Annex, Series 6W/R2747, deputy prefect of Reims to the Marne prefect, Conversation summary with the mayor of Reims, May 19, 1940.

described deserters, "whose accounts seed panic and stir up the desire within the city to evacuate." He complained that "foreign elements" benefited from the abandoned homes. "Increasingly they infiltrate the city of Reims itself." He concluded with a warning, "Combined, they constitute a very real danger!"[48]

Marchandeau's focus on the "foreign" refugee threat to civilian order referenced his interwar politics.[49] As Minister of Justice under Daladier in 1939, he had attached his name to legislation called the Marchandeau Law. This emergency measure forbade attacks in the press of a racial or religious nature. The law was a tool to fight growing anti-Semitism, supposed to be linked to the influx of Jewish refugees from Germany. Many German interwar refugees attempted to raise awareness in France of the menace posed by fascism and Hitler. But French anti-war activists and non-interventionists resented German Jews encouraging France to adopt a confrontational foreign policy toward the Nazi regime.[50] Historian Vicki Caron argues that, despite the fact that Marchandeau's name designated a law of tolerance for foreign Jews, he actually displayed a consistent pattern of anti-Semitism and xenophobia. Marchandeau believed that strict distinctions should be applied to differentiate "desirable" from "non-desirable" refugees. His position would have restricted the number of asylum-seekers eligible for residence in France in 1939. Now, faced with an influx of foreign refugees into the Marne, Marchandeau curiously labeled the foreign refugees agents of defeatism and instigators of exodus. One might expect that Marchandeau would have welcomed the refugees' pessimistic tales, since their accounts reinforced his inclination to order the evacuation of Reims. However, like many French politicians whose ideas stretched across the entire political spectrum, Marchandeau continued to search for ways to balance past optimism with the new gloomy reality.

By May 16, eight months after the French declaration of war against Germany, Rémois civilians had fled. A few Rémois and Marnais voluntary evacuees had trickled out of the area immediately upon learning of the German advance on Belgium. These were mainly people of wealth, with summer homes, cars, and finances that supported an

---

[48] ADM, Reims Annex, Series 6W/R2747, Conversation summary with the mayor of Reims, May 19, 1940.

[49] In 1934 as Minister of the Interior, Marchandeau sought to censor political agitation by foreigners. See Mary Dewhurst Lewis, *The Boundaries of the Republic: Migrant Rights and the Limits of Universalism in France, 1918–1940* (Stanford University Press, 2007), 141.

[50] Vicki Caron, *Uneasy Asylum: France and the Jewish Refugee Crisis, 1933–1942* (Stanford University Press, 1999), fnn. 201, 238. Cited in Secretary General of the Confédération des Syndicats Médicaux Français, speech of February 15, 1939.

early retreat to west coast destinations. At the opposite end of the economic spectrum, as discussed in Chapter 1, day laborers from industrial towns such as Lille, Amiens, and Paris retreated to family villages
in the countryside. Between the two groups of urbanites with links to
provincial retreats, the mass of refugees simply poured out onto the
national highways leading toward Paris and beyond.

Resilient class structures in a crumbling society: the bourgeoisie depart first

Madame Thienot of Reims belonged to the privileged bourgeoisie. The
daughter of a fabric manufacturer, and married to a well-placed manager in the champagne industry, Madame Thienot benefited from the
security available to a bourgeois woman. Her husband owned a town-
house in Reims, a car, and a family summer home in Brittany. The
Thienots departed from Reims immediately after they received word of
the German invasion of Belgium. Leaving a few days before the mass
departure, and several days prior to Marchandeau's legal evacuation
order, the Thienots avoided crowded roads on the way to the Brittany
coast. Despite Madame Thienot's socioeconomic advantages, she faced
a serious health concern: she was pregnant and legitimately worried
that the vibrations from a car ride might precipitate a second miscar-
riage. To reduce this risk, she rested horizontally in the back seat of the
car while her husband drove. Needing to stop frequently to rest, the
Thienots soon exhausted their food supply and resolve. Unable to find
a restaurant or hotel, they found themselves dependent upon peasant
hospitality.

In the aftermath of the exodus, urban refugees offered differing
commentary on their interaction with rural peasants. The Thienots'
first experience engraved a favorable memory: "We stopped in an area
completely deserted. There was only a little farm, no hotel, nothing,"
Madame Thienot recalled. The couple approached a farmhouse. "They
welcomed us in a most kind manner. The family sat gathered around
the hearth. They were actually cooking in the hearth, in a pot above the
fire," she marveled. "They gave us a bedroom, very comfortable, with a
large duvet, very thick. We were just fine," she reassured herself.[51] After
a restful night, the Thienots arrived at the family home in Châtillion
the next day. Their escape from Reims had transpired smoothly without any consequences for Madame Thienot's pregnancy. Having driven

---

[51] Mme Thienot, interview with author, Reims, 1993.

his wife to safety, Monsieur Thienot departed the following day for England via Spain, later joining up with de Gaulle's group in London.

Similar testimonies corroborate the initial comfort enjoyed by bourgeois women who embarked on the exodus in comfortable cars. The richly detailed personal memoir of René Carré provides a fuller perspective on the advantages of affluence. In 1940, Carré was the Director of Pommery Champagne, then owned by the flamboyant aristocrat, the marquis de Polignac. As recorded in his journal, the exodus from Reims struck Carré as a tragedy of historic proportions.[52] Carré's journal documented the swift unraveling of a local economy once the evacuation reached full throttle. Told from the perspective of a father of a large family – Carré had seven children, three of whom were in the French military – the memoir documented the entanglement of family, economic, and national destinies. On May 16, the Pommery, Carré, and Poirier families met to determine their departure route. Hoping to conserve cars so as to assist in the rescue of the champagne stocks, the families pooled together in a luxury sedan and a black pick-up truck donated to the cause by Madame la marquise de Polignac. In Carré's words, "Thanks to Madame la Marquise, my wife and daughter, in the care of my son, Jack, were evacuated."[53] Carré bid farewell to his family and friends, who included Marius Poirier, then chief chemist of Pommery and Poirier's wife and son, Renaud. After exchanging good-bye kisses, the families departed for their summer homes in Biarritz (Pyrénées-Atlantiques), the popular Rémois coastal retreat. Having safely evacuated his family, Carré could now lead the remaining men in protecting Pommery's valuable champagne stock.[54]

Marchandeau finally issues evacuation order

The less fortunate of Reims, like Maria Parmentier, held their ground until the situation seemed doomed. On May 16, the mayor publicly recognized the dire situation, but withheld a fully articulated order for evacuation. Marchandeau admitted, via his own newspaper, that a dispersal of a large majority of the population of Reims seemed necessary. Since many bourgeois families had already departed, the message primarily reached the remaining working-class and peasant families.

---

[52] I am indebted to Renaud Poirier of Reims for permission to quote from René Carré's journal manuscript written in 1940.

[53] Rene Carré, unpublished journal, 6.

[54] For a popular account of France's wine industry under German Occupation, see Donald Kladstrup and Petie Kladstrup, *Wine and War: The French, the Nazis, and the Battle for France's Greatest Treasure* (New York: Broadway, 2002).

Families wishing to send their children to protected areas of the interior received instructions to go to school. Mothers wishing to accompany their children to refugee centers were told to make a formal request. Grandparents residing with a child received instructions to accompany the child to school, where they would receive their train's departure time and destination. Mothers of children not yet of school age, elderly people without grandchildren, young people living alone, and parents of invalids were instructed to report to City Hall. The latter population would all be driven to their destinations or to train stations. However, due to the reduced fleet of vehicles available for civilian transport, all other categories of civilians were ordered to walk to their evacuation destination. The mayor encouraged the population to keep baggage to a minimum and pack one-and-a-half day's supply of food for each person.[55] Marchandeau qualified the exercise as a "partial" evacuation.

Authorities expected all able-bodied men to remain in Reims to oversee operations of the city and to continue providing services. In fact, only on Saturday, May 18, two days after Marchandeau allowed for partial evacuation of women, children, and the elderly, did Albert Sarraut, Minister of Education, close all French public schools.[56] Sarraut charged teachers and clergy to convert schools and rectories into refugee welcome centers.

The *L'Éclaireur de l'Est* continued publication for several more days. The headline of May 17 quoted General Gamelin: "Conquer or Die! We Must Conquer!" Meanwhile in Paris, undisclosed to the public, Prime Minister Reynaud weighed Gamelin's future. In what observers have recorded as a "calm voice," Gamelin had informed Reynaud the previous morning that the Germans might reach Paris by nightfall; such was the commander-in-chief's own pessimism.[57] Reynaud ordered the seat of government moved to Tours and the burning of the archives of the Ministry of Foreign Affairs. Later in the day, however, battle news improved and Reynaud canceled the orders.

Reims' local newspaper remained operating long enough to document the civilian retreat. The feature article of the single-sheet paper informed any remaining readers of Marchandeau's evacuation order. Civilians left by any means available. As in Strasbourg, homes and businesses sat empty, prompting the newspaper to remind readers that pillage, theft, or redistribution of property was subject to capital punishment. Yet the

---

[55] *L'Éclaireur de l'Est*, May 16, 1940, 2.
[56] ADM, Reims Annex, Series R/2686, A. Sarraut, Minister of National Education to departmental prefects, rectories and school superintendents, Paris, May 18, 1940.
[57] Pertinax, *Gravediggers of France*, 76.

reporter urged readers to "avoid listening to depressing rumors" and opined, "We are a long way from singing victory hymns, but also from dark pessimism."[58] The editorial writer instructed: "Reims knows what it means to be at war. Certainly the scope of battle, the bitterness of the fighting is such that emotions are profoundly stirred. But nothing explains why the cold-blooded calm of the population of Reims that has served us since the beginning of the war, should suddenly cease to fortify our morale."[59] The conclusion to the day's opinion rested its case for civilian restraint: "As President Herriot said in the Chamber yesterday, France remains proud of herself. Her army does its job. Have confidence in the army and remain level-headed."[60] Herriot's comment may have marked the first expression of an evolving political formula: departure = treason.

In Paris, refugees from the north who had departed without an official evacuation order flooded the capital. Paris still held on to the faint hope that the French military could defeat the Germans at the Somme, and the shortage of space in *L'Éclaireur* left no room to report on the refugee situation. However, censored reports seeped into the foreign press.[61] Their stories captured the chaotic nature of the situation and emphasized the lack of coordination of information and services at all levels. International relief organizers tried to harvest the sympathy of foreign observers. From Paris, Winthrop Aldrich, chairman of the French and British Relief Funds, issued a plea to the American people: "I am appealing for a particular and vital need, that of the American Hospital in Paris," he beseeched. "The facilities are being taxed to the utmost by the wounded soldiers and thousands of refugees – French, Belgian and Dutch – who are pouring into the city."[62] Invoking a tradition of Franco-American fraternity, Aldrich insisted: "This hospital, founded by Americans and supported by Americans, is in immediate and desperate need of funds to help care for these refugees and for the wounded."[63] Similarly, Norman H. Davis of the American Red Cross announced that his organization would immediately establish headquarters in Paris to address the growing crisis.

---

[58] *L'Éclaireur de l'Est*, Friday, May 17, 1940, 1.

[59] *L'Éclaireur de l'Est*, Friday, May 17, 1940, 2.

[60] *L'Éclaireur de l'Est*, Friday, May 17, 1940, 2.

[61] "For Paris Red Cross Unit: American Division Moves to Help Belgian, French Refugees," *New York Times*, May 19, 1940, 1.

[62] "American Hospital in Paris Needs Aid: Appeal Issued Here for Funds for Overburdened Center," *New York Times*, May 19, 1940, 1.

[63] "American Hospital in Paris Needs Aid," *New York Times*, May 19, 1940, 1.

Relocation of Rémois municipal offices

The "partial evacuation" of Reims simply provided an official stamp of approval for a policy being dictated to municipal officials by disaffected citizens. With mayoral approval for the partial evacuation, Rémois civilians were now eligible, as "official evacuees," to collect refugee relief. The admission that the danger had become sufficient to order partial evacuations prompted discussion between local and military authorities about ordering a full-scale evacuation. A complete evacuation order would authorize the departure of infrastructure maintenance and emergency personnel such as electric and sewage workers, firefighters, and policemen, as well as elected officials. On May 19, Marchandeau increased pressure upon Prefect Jozon to persuade military commanders to order a full-scale evacuation of Reims so that these groups might join their departing families. Marchandeau's correspondence and published circulars attest to his growing impatience with the military command.

Monsieur Philip, deputy prefect (sous-préfet) of Reims, the department's second-in-command, reported to Jozon that Marchandeau had embarked on "an independent mission" to obtain a military order to evacuate all of Reims. According to Philip, Marchandeau sent several telegrams to the Minister of the Interior in an attempt to gain access to the military leaders responsible for the Marne. After much difficulty, the General Secretary of the Marne, appointed by the Minister of the Interior to act as go-between for Marchandeau to the High Command, reported that, "the military authority has categorically refused to consider ordering any (full-scale) evacuation of Reims."[64] The obstinate reply of the military fell on the heels of six days of intensive battle. The Germans had nearly crushed the 9th Army and repelled the 2nd Army, leaving the 6th Army the job of blocking the road to Paris. That task became easier when the Germans changed direction and moved toward the Channel. This northward shift in the enemy's advance may, in part, account for the military's stubborn belief that Reims was not in danger.[65]

However, only 100 km north of Reims at Cambrai, the international wire reported heavy bombing of civilian concentrations. P. J. Philip, special reporter to the *New York Times*, filed his eye-witness testimony:

[64] ADM, Reims Annex, Series 6W/R2747, deputy prefect of Reims to the prefect of the Marne, Reims, May 19, 1940.
[65] Pertinax, *Gravediggers of France*, 77.

Cambrai [two words censored] was ferociously bombed twice just after 9 o'clock yesterday morning. It was full of refugees, and when I left the town two hours later by bicycle, because no other means of transportation was available, heavy smoke clouds rose from [four words censored] buildings, and a few miles away, Douai, Arras, and Peronne presented the same spectacle.[66]

Marchandeau may or may not have had full knowledge of the hostilities transpiring to his immediate north, but unlike his departmental and military superiors, he had finally accepted the nature of the conflict. Pre-empting Jozon, he issued a statement via the *L'Éclaireur de l'Est* notifying remaining Rémois that the city government would transfer operations and services to Nevers (Nièvre), its designated point of retreat. Relocated municipal officials would assist refugees in obtaining permanent shelter and finding lost family members and friends. The announcement testified to the problems already being reported to the mayor's office. Transportation disruptions, inadequate lodging, and bombings forced families to split up. Calls to the mayor's office already registered complaints and inquiries about how to go about finding lost children, wives, and grandparents.

Relocation of the municipal operations of Reims did not result from any well-conceived interwar plan – these had designated Reims as a refugee *reception* center, *not* a department to be evacuated. Marchandeau himself severely criticized bureaucrats charged with drawing up evacuation plans in his testimony before members of the city council of Reims, reconvened in Nevers. Since October 1939, Marchandeau had submitted repeated requests to the Minister of the Interior to designate a department of retreat for Reims, as had been assigned to Charleville (Ardennes) located 50 miles north of Reims. Marchandeau's requests met sustained rejections. Finally, in March 1940, the Ministry of the Interior agreed to establish a "partnership" between the departments of the Marne and Nièvre, assigning Nevers as the sister city to Reims.[67] The time between March and May had not allowed officials to prepare a detailed evacuation scheme. Improvising, municipal authorities in Reims packed crates and people onto trucks and shipped them off to Nevers, hoping they would arrive safely.

While preparing the unauthorized departure of Rémois municipal operations, Marchandeau continued corresponding with Jozon. Jozon finally telegraphed a report of living conditions in Reims to General

[66] P. J. Philip, "Nazi Dive Bombers Terrify Refugees: Witness Describes Confusion as Planes Spread Death Among French Civilians," *New York Times*, May 19, 1940, 1.
[67] AMVR, "Procès-verbaux du Conseil Municipal de Reims, Séance du mecredi," *Bulletin Municipal*, June 12, 1940.

Touchon, whose 6th Army had not experienced the heavy casualties that the Germans had levied upon the 9th Army fighting to the north. Jozon described how daily bombardments had spurred citizens to flee Reims, leaving abandoned bakeries, butcheries, and general stores. Civilians who remained under order of service – firemen, police officers, postal workers, and other government employees – found it impossible to feed themselves. Hence, Jozon requested that Touchon send supplies to help sustain the remaining population.[68] In fact, Marchandeau had ordered a locksmith to break into abandoned stores so that officials might confiscate any remaining food.

Finally, on May 19, Touchon agreed to honor Marchandeau's request. In a letter addressed personally to the mayor, Touchon said that, given the situation, he agreed that it was "wise" to order the complete evacuation of Reims. However, he asked that Marchandeau leave the necessary personnel to ensure the operation of telephone and telegraph services.[69] He also assured Marchandeau that he would assign an infantry battalion to keep watch over the city. Since reports of pillaging had increased, Touchon specifically reminded Marchandeau to repeat that theft or pillaging were subject to capital punishment. On the evening of May 19, Jozon signed the evacuation notice for Reims. Marchandeau did not wait for daybreak. Firemen, municipal employees, and police officers plastered posters throughout the city. The evacuation siren sounded. More than two centuries of city archives and official records sat already packed and loaded into a truck. Before dawn, records of births, deaths, marriages, property rights, and divorces – all the instruments that provided the legal architecture for the civil life of Reims – departed for Nevers.

Marchandeau's staff, on the other hand, had not received authorization to leave the department of the Marne. Absurdly, the evacuation notice signed by Jozon ordered municipal employees of Reims, particularly water, electricity, fire, and police service employees, moved to the seat of the prefecture, Châlons-sur-Marne, located about twenty minutes to the south by train. Touchon had agreed only to the evacuation of Reims, not the entire department of the Marne.[70] On May 20, Jozon ordered a reminder posted to alert other residents of the Marne that military orders required they remain in the department. According to

[68] ADM, Reims Annex, Series R/2747, Prefect Jozon to General Touchon, Châlons-sur-Marne, May 18, 1940.
[69] ADM, Reims Annex, Series R/2747, General Touchon, 6th Army, 3rd Bureau, Staff Officer, No. 87/3 to Paul Marchandeau, mayor of Reims, May 19, 1940.
[70] ADM, Reims Annex, Series 6W/R2747, Deputy prefect of Reims to the prefect of the Marne, Reims, May 19, 1940.

Jozon's notice, if it became necessary to notify the population to move to a more secure place, "the responsible authorities and me would not leave it to the care of any other person to speak to you with frankness and clearness about the truth of the situation."[71] He concluded with the enjoinder that: "No military pressure places the territory of our department in danger."[72] Technically, Jozon's statement was correct. Completing their push through the Ardennes, the Germans intended to secure the area surrounding Reims, but move toward their final objective – encirclement of French troops near the Somme–Oise–Aisne waterway. Even if Jozon had known that Reims and the Marne were not German military targets, the region's military commanders should have understood the panic that word of the Wehrmacht's advance continued to unleash.

The first direct attack on Reims hit near the railroad station on Sunday, May 19. The Germans might not send tanks immediately, but bombs could be easily unloaded without the presence of ground troops. Working to relocate the reserve stock of Pommery champagne to a secure location, Carré recorded the apocalyptic scene. Around 10 o'clock in the morning, two near-by towns, St. Léonard and Brimont, triggered their sirens. A formidable shaking could be felt. "It was as if the entire neighborhood had just exploded," recorded Carré.[73] Suddenly Carré and his colleague Mousty witnessed smoke billowing up from the bridge of Laon. A few minutes later, the windows in the Pommery offices began quaking. Camille Corpart, Carré, and Mousty ran to the office of the marquis de Polingac and watched from his window as a large building in the Sarlino district bellowed a black, dense smoke.[74] One can only hope that the families of rue de Pévy, situated near the station, had already left their homes.

Despite official rejoinders demanding that civil servants report to work, the lieutenant prefect of Reims, Monsieur Philip, reported that many of his employees failed to return to their jobs. Growing rates of absenteeism provoked a letter to Jozon requesting the authority to levy stiff penalties against government employees who "cowardly abandoned their post." "In my opinion," wrote Philip, "such actions should be met with strict sanctions going as far as dismissal."[75] The irony of Philip's

[71] ADM, Reims Annex, Series R/2747, Poster, signed A. Jozon, prefect of the Marne, May 20, 1940.
[72] ADM, Reims Annex, Series R/2747, Poster, signed A. Jozon.
[73] Carré, unpublished journal, 74.
[74] Carré, unpublished journal, 74.
[75] ADM, Reims Annex, Series 6W/R/2747, Deputy Prefect M. Philip to Prefect M. Jozon, Reims, May 22, 1940.

threat to dismiss state employees who had left their posts before ordered to do so was twofold. First, the employees calculated that without their lives, jobs would be meaningless. Second, beginning on June 4, 1940, a fiscal crisis forced Jozon to "let go" most prefectoral employees who had stayed to fulfill their duty.[76]

Among the civil servants who failed to report to work, Philip named four of the five judges of Reims and the concierge of the Palais du Justice, who departed with the only set of keys to the building. The "cowardly," in Philip's words, even included a World War I veteran, the assistant controller of the PTT. Of the forty-eight employees listed as absent, thirty-one were men, fourteen were married women, and three were single women. The large percentage of men, suggests that government services employed a larger number of men than women, a situation that was not at all exceptional in 1940. Among the women, more married women than single women "abandoned" their post, most likely as a response to the needs of their families. From this small sample, we may suppose that maintaining family unity played a critical role in constructing civilian escape strategies. Unlike the bourgeois stakeholders, male civil servants had decided to leave Reims with their families intact.[77]

In the large picture, absenteeism or "abandonment" remained relatively low, according to the homage made to public workers by Marchandeau in Nevers on June 12. Marchandeau applauded public employees, saying, "We have had the comfort of noting, since circumstances began to take on a grave character, the excellent resilience of a personnel who, in the realm of 98% if not more, have remained at their post despite the exodus of the population and the repeated bombing raids."[78] Lauding their courage, he assured the audience that each employee would be nominated for official recognition honoring his or her service to the city of Reims and to France.

While the military had finally ordered the evacuation of Reims, a few Rémois found themselves unable or unwilling to comply with the order. Of the 120,000 residents of Reims, an estimated 5,000 to 6,000 remained as of May 20. The case of the widow Camille Juillemin illustrates the predicament faced by civilians who did not join the mass exodus. On June 6 she wrote to Marchandeau in Nevers, explaining her

[76] AMVR, *Bulletin Municipal*, 238.

[77] ADM, Reims Annex, Series 6W/R.2747, Deputy Prefect M. Philip to Prefect M. Jozon, Reims, May 22, 1940.

[78] AMVR, "Procès-verbaux du Conseil Municipal," *Bulletin Municipal*, June 12, 1940, held at Nevers, 237–238.

situation. Upon issue of the order to evacuate Reims, authorities moved Juillemin and her eighty-two-year-old mother to the nearby hamlet of Rilly-la-Montagne. The couple could travel no further. Juillemin's mother, having been paralyzed and bedridden for over four years, could not move. In fact, rescue aids had carried the mother to Rilly on a stretcher. Now the mayor of Rilly, Monsieur Hoche, ordered the complete evacuation of Rilly. "It is absolutely impossible to transport my mother any further," insisted Juillemin. "She is not moveable. I beg of you, Monsieur Mayor, to please intervene on my behalf with Mayor Hoche, so that we may stay."[79] We do not know Juillemin's fate.

Police reports recorded many similar refusals to honor the evacuation order. A gendarme discovered a note with the body of an unnamed elderly man who chose to commit suicide rather than flee. The man's note explained that he had not fled the German invasion of World War I and concluded, "My dog and I are too old. I take my life so that the Germans may not take it from me."[80] The man used a gas stove to end his life. His dog rested beside him in death.

The civilian exodus caught both the military and the national government by surprise. Without much coordination, a patchwork of policies and attempts at rescue emerged from the various ministries in Paris. On May 18, Camille Chautemps, Vice President of the Cabinet of Ministers, telephoned Henri Queuille, Senator of Corrèze and Minister of Supply. He requested that Queuille send provisions to the hungry refugees in the region of Compiègne and the Oise.[81] The Ministry of Supply was unprepared for the refugee crisis in part because Queuille had opposed efforts to establish a policy of food requisitioning and a rationing system during the Phoney War. Now the Minister of Supply could not meet the demands of a burgeoning refugee and humanitarian crisis. Queuille thus began to incorporate the provisioning of refugees into his already failing efforts to supply the army and sedentary civilian population. Within a week, his ministry organized the delivery of flour and sugar to areas in need. With the assistance of the farmers and citizens of Rouen, Queuille located and transported 2 million hard-boiled eggs from Rouen to positions on the roads leading to Vernon and other southern passageways.[82] Over the

---

[79] AMVR, No. 3161, Vve. Camille Juillemin to the mayor of Reims, Rilly-la-Montagne, June 4, 1940.

[80] AMVR, No. 3161, Police report to the mayor's office, June 6, 1940.

[81] Francis de Tarr, *Henri Queuille en son temps 1884–1970* (Paris: La Table Ronde, 1995), 280.

[82] De Tarr, *Henri Queuille en son temps*, 280.

next several weeks, Queuille spearheaded efforts to ensure the delivery of food from England. By May 29, stocks had dwindled, but Queuille's communications with the United States suggested that foreign aid would be forthcoming.[83]

At about this stage in the exodus, Ambassador Bullitt, still at the US Embassy in Paris, placed another urgent call to the White House, requesting that President Roosevelt dispatch immediate aid to France via the Red Cross. Roosevelt pledged, according to Bullitt, that he would request that Congress immediately dispatch US$20,000,000 to France to help support Belgian and French refugees.[84] While the aid did not arrive in time, awareness of the dire situation in northern France began to spread beyond the boundaries of the embattled nation.

Efforts to mitigate economic disaster

While a core of mostly male civilians like Carré had remained behind in Reims for several days to transfer stock to safe houses, retreating business owners attempted to maintain communication with municipal officials in the hope of mitigating economic losses from afar. Unlike Térmand Duenardl, the Director of Victor Clicquot, who wrote to Marchandeau on May 16 to inform him that upon his departure, 1,200,000 francs worth of Clicquot champagne stock would remain vulnerable. "I hope it will suit the appointed authorities to take every available measure to protect our stocks of wine in our cellars," urged Duenardl.[85]

Similarly, on May 21, Madame Sadot, the manager of the Boulangerie Petizon in Reims wrote from Roanne (Loire). Having read in the Paris daily, *Paris-Soir*, that Marchandeau remained in Reims, Sadot requested that he send his staff to her shop to requisition fifty-two sacks of flour. She recommended using the flour to feed French troops.[86] Amazingly, the letter reached Reims, but only after the mayor had departed and France had fallen.

The case of Monsieur Viennet, Director of the Charcuteries de Champagne meat processing plant, highlights the difficulties faced by agro-businessmen. "I have remained in Reims to make sure that the refrigeration at the plant continues to work and that the perishable stock of meat is conserved," Viennet explained, justifying his refusal to honor the evacuation order. Viennet claimed that he had repeatedly

[83] De Tarr, *Henri Queuille en son temps*, 281.
[84] Bullitt, "Telegram," June 11, 1940, 3 pm, *For the President*, 462.
[85] AMVR, No. 3165, Térmand Duenardl to Paul Marchandeau, May 16, 1940.
[86] AMVR, No. 3165, Mme Sadot to Paul Marchandeau, May 21, 1940.

asked for assistance to move the factory's machinery as well as its stock, but had received insufficient help. He estimated that the value of his meat products stood at approximately 100,000 francs.[87]

Such economic casualties generated criticisms of the evacuation order and of Marchandeau himself. The police commissioner of Sézanne sent a telegraph to inform Jozon of criticisms against the evacuation and Marchandeau's administration. Apparently, Rémois residents from all social and economic levels reported to his office the day after the evacuation order. "However wrong or right they may be," wrote the commissioner, "they say that Monsieur Marchandeau only issued the evacuation order so that he himself might depart."[88]

The organization of the evacuation evidenced a myriad of problems attributable to several causes: the Minister of the Interior's initial refusal to establish a department of retreat for the Marne; the tardiness of Touchon's evacuation order; and the inability of municipal and departmental administrators to anticipate the complexity of the evacuation. Lesser mistakes further aggravated an already dire situation. For example, on May 19, Marchandeau notified citizens of Reims that municipal offices would be relocated to Nevers. On May 20, however, in an open letter to those who remained in Reims, he warned that, while his office had moved to Nevers, other Rémois should not regroup there unless ordered to do so. "Nièvre cannot receive any new refugees," the poster informed readers. "Instead everyone should abide by the evacuation order specifically issued to their group and report to their assigned retreat points, not to Nièvre."[89] The warning came too late as many Rémois had followed their mayor, only to be turned away upon their arrival by that department's administration. As a consequence of the overpopulation of Nièvre and the acceleration of the German advance, Marchandeau scouted a more distant retreat point for Rémois refugees. He tapped his native roots in southwestern France, enlisting help from the towns of Albi and his native Gaillac (Tarn).

Meanwhile, on May 21, General Germain, interim commander of the 23rd Army Corps, sent orders to Lieutenant Prefect Philip to evacuate the civilian population in the communities north of Reims. Jozon, who later expressed anger that Germain had not contacted him

[87] AMVR, Secrétariat Général, No. 172, M. Viennet to Mayor Marchandeau, Reims, May 21, 1940.

[88] ADM, Reims Annex, Series R/2747, official telegram, Police Commissioner of Sézanne to Prefect Jozon, May 23, 1940.

[89] AMVR, Secrétariat Général, No. 3161, Circular, Paul Marchandeau.

personally with the order, could obtain no information about where residents had been sent. The evacuation of the northern Marne, coupled with sustained bombing in Reims, meant that the population had fled without Jozon being able to assign guards to protect property. Unverifiable reports of destruction and pillaging trickled into his office. Jozon expressed his distress to the Minister of the Interior, particularly because Germain's order had resulted in a renewed attempt by farmers in the southern Marne to join the exodus.[90]

French morale suffered another blow when King Leopold of Belgium capitulated on May 27, ordering Belgian military forces to cease resistance. The news refreshed the flight of refugees out of Belgium. In an attempt to manage the escalating evacuation and maintain order within his department, Jozon posted a circular: "I demand instantly that the population of Châlons remains at home."[91] The poster warned that any Marnais evacuating the department without an official order would become ineligible to receive refugee allocations. Few constituents remained behind to read Jozon's notice.

Eventually, Jozon succeeded in communicating with Général Charles-Léon Huntzinger, France's youngest general and leader of the 2nd Army which had fought unsuccessfully at the defense of Sedan. On June 2, looking beyond the seemingly inevitable collapse of his military, Huntzinger ordered Jozon to prepare for a full-scale evacuation of the Marne. "The recent circumstances force me to envision a new evacuation measure," he wrote. Huntzinger cautioned Jozon that the evacuation of the Marne would have to proceed more smoothly than the evacuation of Reims; noting that it was, "absolutely necessary: (a) to maintain a representative in place as long as possible; (b) to group and cage all livestock in order to transport them safely to the interior, including equestrian livestock."[92] Huntzinger's plan called for the total evacuation of Châlons-sur-Marne and its surrounding cantons at 7 pm on June 13.[93]

On June 12, the German 19th Panzers Corps broke through the front in Champagne, out-pacing fleeing civilians as tanks rolled through Châlons-sur-Marne, then Troyès and past Nevers, actually trapping

---

[90] ADM, Reims Annex, Series 6W/R/2747, Prefect Jozon, Châlons-sur-Marne, May 29, 1940.

[91] ADM, Reims Annex, Series 6W/R/2474, Prefect Jozon to Marne mayors, Châlons-sur-Marne, June 2, 1940.

[92] ADM, Reims Annex, General Huntzinger, Commander of the 2nd Army, 4th Bureau to Prefect Jozon, June 2, 1940.

[93] ADM, Reims Annex, General Huntzinger to Prefect Jozon, June 2, 1940.

the few Marnais and other refugees attempting to escape to the south.[94] The orderly evacuation that Huntzinger had envisioned fell to pieces. In many cases, Germans and civilians marched together toward Paris and then south to the Loire. So swiftly had the Germans descended upon Châlons-sur-Marne that notable residents such as the Abbé Gillet and Monsieur Heller, inspector of the local academy, were unable to escape before the Germans arrived. Châlons' municipal services, however, had already marked their retreat for Corrèze.

French women and families vote with their feet; result: "no confidence!"

In a historical eruption of popular disapproval ("voting with their feet," to employ Eric Hobsbawm's description of Europeans' collective expression during the Velvet Revolution of 1989) the disempowered and, in many cases, politically disenfranchised civilians of north-eastern France packed their bags and resoundingly rejected a fate of quiet submission to invasion. The flight from the Marne and the surrounding departments eventually engulfed the majority of France's population living north of the Loire, whisking them into a current of human motion whose force and momentum no government or army could control.

The examination of the Marne offers some complex, but compelling answers to how and why this exodus unfolded as it did. French Défense passive planning failed for a number of reasons. Obviously, military defense strategy influenced plans to ensure civilian security. The belief that the Germans would enter near the Maginot Line and move rapidly to re-take Alsace and Lorraine, permeated home front security preparations. Hence, the Service of Refugees executed, prior to May 1940, a rather elaborate evacuation of Alsace and Lorraine. To be sure, Alsatian and Lorrainer evacuees complained; but in hindsight, they clearly had less about which to complain than civilians who lived in the departments of the Ardennes and Aisne where the Germans actually attacked. Understandably, national authorities resisted pressure from prefects and mayors in the north-east to expand evacuation schemes. The logistics of whole-scale population removal and relocation seem unmanageable and unaffordable. Perhaps most importantly, German airpower moved so swiftly through French airspace, that planes began unleashing bombs on urban centers across the north within a few short hours of the start of the invasion. Even von Manstein expressed surprise

---

[94] Husson, *La Marne et les Marnais*, 89.

at the weakness of French anti-aircraft defenses, which failed to intercept bombers before they reached heavily populated urban centers.

Not all civilians initially embraced evacuations as an ideal security model. While a majority of letters written to mayors and prefects from September 1939 to May 1940 requested permission to move to the interior, a significant number of residents expressed the desire for improved security at home. Municipal and departmental officials distributed occasional brochures about the location of bomb shelters and procedures for dimming lights at night, but these instructions appeared to many residents as small bandages over a growing wound. Urban dwellers wondered why the government, both at the local and national level, did not do more to protect them. The passive nature of the Défense passive caused the government to forgo the opportunity to harness the support of the populations who were willing to defend France. The uncoordinated use of the fire and police services of Reims offers just one stunning example of how civilian resources were squandered.

Civilians clamored for protection at home and, more remarkably, expressed a right to it. Women, whose education often stopped at sixth grade, were emboldened to write to officials to demand the right to security for themselves and their families. The evidence strongly suggests that an echo of the social rights movements of the mid-1930s reverberated during the Phoney War, expanding the arena for the application of the language of entitlements and human rights in order to advance civilian protection in wartime. Thus, the eve of the exodus is not only an important moment in France's wartime history, but is also a major milestone in the evolution of the demand for universal human rights during wartime. Unfortunately, the inability of the state to ensure and deliver such universal protections to its citizens resulted in their mass flight.

Conclusion

The spontaneous flight of French civilians from the Marne unraveled in chaos for three main reasons. The first factor was that civilians and local officials lacked accurate information regarding the military campaign. This problem resulted from government efforts to challenge defeatism and boost home front morale by censoring accounts about German advances and the state of the French Army's resistance. Many journalists and editors contributed to this effort by withholding editorial comments and refusing to disclose facts about the ferocity of the German assault and the weakness of the French military position. By failing to accurately, and honestly, report the rapid advance of German troops, the government and journalists reduced the amount of time civilians had to mentally and physically prepare for invasion. These actions of the government and media were a *de facto* abdication of their responsibility to fuel open debate and act as stewards in the flow of information in a democracy – albeit a democracy at war. This abdication opened the door to the ascendancy of a culture of rumors. Rumors, however, often provided more accurate accounts of the German advance as retreating Belgian, Dutch, and Luxembourgeois refugees delivered eye-witness accounts of destructive German bombings unleashed on their homes and on fleeing refugees.[95]

A second factor in the collapse of the home front arose from poor planning and coordination of civilian security on the part of the military, national ministries, and local governments. The failure of military authorities to heed the requests of municipal officials to plan for civilian evacuations in regions outside Alsace and Lorraine undermined the ability of local authorities to maintain the confidence and respect of northern residents. The army rationalized that broadening evacuation schemes would spread defeatism among the civilian population and interfere with military maneuvers. In the end, the failure to prepare civilians for defeat and confrontation with the enemy contributed to mass flight, which, in some cases, impeded military mobility.

Civilian politicization during the Phoney War provided the third factor that contributed to the collapse of France's home front. Maria Parmentier's experience, like millions of other women in northern France and the Benelux countries, demonstrated the growing resolve of women to take action to protect their families from war's violence. Despite their marginalization from official French decision-making institutions, French women articulated their understanding of the transformations in modern warfare and Germany's willingness to wage aggressive war. Northern women wrote letters to their hometown mayors, to mayors in the south, and to officials of the Défense passive in

---

[95] Might we argue that the freedom to flee is a mark of civilian freedom in the West? Karma Nabulsi argues that for nineteenth-century France, "Civilians under occupation were confronted with a loss of freedom, autonomy, and national sovereignty, and forced to accept foreign rule." Acceptance of foreign rule has been contingent upon the cessation of hostilities. European states, Nabulsi points out, have had difficulty defining exactly when fighting ends and occupation begins, thus requiring civilians to cease resistance. As a result of nineteenth-century foreign occupation in France, civilian resistance became galvanized by republican principles of democracy, thus weaving resistance into what she considers to be the "customs of war," that continued into the twentieth century. The problem with this particular "custom of war" is that participation in resistance by others erodes the sanctity of civilian space. See Karma Nabulsi, *Traditions of War: Occupation, Resistance and the Law* (Oxford University Press, 1999), 65.

Paris, demanding improvements in civilian security programs. They embraced the hallmarks of active citizenship to challenge the policies of government passivity, objecting to being forgotten in the formulation of national security planning, and insisting upon the state's responsibility to deliver them from war's violence.

In a broader sense, French women helped pave the way for international recognition of the need to expand human rights protections and civilian protection in the postwar period. Their concerns preceded postwar changes to international law, later codified in the Geneva Conventions' prohibition of waging war against civilian non-combatants. In the short term, French women's activities to ensure their families' security by challenging military policy prohibiting mass evacuations resulted in a change in local French officials' views of the importance of evacuations. In the long term, French women laid the groundwork for a larger global acceptance of redefining civilian refugees' rights to asylum. Indeed, in a loose application of the concept, French civilians' requests for relocation embodied a form of application for internal asylum motivated by the belief that they stood in harm's way. In this regard, they acted within the parameters of international legal norms of their day. J. C. Hathaway clarifies that: "it was generally assumed that a person compelled to flight should make reasonable efforts to seek protection within a safe part of her own country (if one exists) before looking for refuge abroad."[96]

As we will see in later chapters, the exodus cycle of retreat-return-retreat evidenced populist 1940's expressions of a poorly articulated, but deeply felt desire for asylum from combat and the threat of German occupation.[97] Unfortunately, the flight and the tragedy of many refugees who encountered violence on the road meant that women's pre-invasion wisdom was not fully recognized until after the martyrdom of refugees arose from the roadside ditches where many continued to perish as a consequence of Germany and Italy's campaign of "aggressive war." Historical recognition of their collective complaint against air

---

[96] J. C. Hathaway, *The Law of Refugee Status* (Toronto: Butterworths, 1991), 18–19 quoted in Hyndman, *Managing Displacement*, 13.

[97] The difficulty in international law in the postwar era has come from an inability to adopt universally accepted criteria defining "persecution" that would admit civilians to the protections afforded by asylum. To complicate matters women have had a particularly difficult time applying for asylum because, much like the women of 1940 France, postwar female asylum applicants frequently come from countries where they lack political rights. See Crawley, *Refugees and Gender, Law and Process*, 9. In addition, Jennifer Hyndman has shown that internally displaced persons have traditionally, even in the postwar period, had narrow access to claims for protection or asylum.

warfare emerged mutedly at the Nuremberg War Crimes Trials in 1945, where Allies trying German leaders sought to avoid invoking their own air strikes against the Axis powers.[98] Having opted for flight, without much forethought as to destination or long-term survival, civilians soon learned that under the new conditions of total war, security would be hard to find.

[98] Marrus emphasizes that the Tribunal prohibited any mention of unlawful Allied air bombardment of Germany. Marrus, *Nuremberg War Crimes Trials*, 183.

3   Pulling the plug on the city of lights

By June 10, Reims and surrounding areas of northern France lay barren. The daily rituals of private life and the machinery of commerce ceased. The nomadic wanderings of civilians, soldiers, and animals along the roads and railways of north-eastern France created a human tragedy paralleling the military and political drama. Recalling the view from his reconnaissance plane, Antoine de Saint-Exupéry wrote, "Somewhere in the north of France a boot had scattered an ant-hill, and the ants were on the march. Laboriously. Without panic. Without hope. Without despair. On the march as if in duty bound."[1] During early June, the forces of war destroyed the resolve of Parisians and laid a shroud of darkness over Europe's city of lights. The southward rush of refugees and military personnel presented a worsening refugee crisis; this, at the very moment when the nation's infrastructure and military teetered toward collapse.

The first instance of siren alerts in Paris sounded at 4.55 pm on May 10. For three hours, the sirens warned Parisians of German air assaults. Suburban residents reported hearing cannon fire and the explosion of bombs.[2] At 7.30 pm Oscar Frossard, the Minister of Information, addressed Parisians via radio and announced that, "the real war had begun."[3] On Sunday, May 13, sirens blared again. Parisians, enjoying a weekend promenade, ran to the tunnels of the Metro for cover. About 100,000 Parisians waited out the alert below the city's emptied streets. Historian, Jean-Louis Crémieux-Brilhac reports estimates of 6,000 people in the Metro tunnels at Republic and Pigalle, 6,500 at Madeline, Sèvres-Babylone, and Place-des-Fêtes and 5,000 on the line between Havre-Caumartin and l'Hôtel de Ville. However, by 5 pm cafés had reopened; romantic couples waltzed under the evening sky at Moulin de la

[1] Saint-Exupéry, *Flight to Arras*, 118.
[2] Police and Défense passive reports cited by Jean-Louis Crémieux-Brilhac, *Les Français de l'an 40, vol. II: La guerre oui ou non?* (Paris: Gallimard, 1990), 541.
[3] Crémieux-Brilhac, *Les Français de l'an 40*, 541.

Galette; and the controversial politician from the Marne, Marcel Déat, reportedly enjoyed tea at the intellectual watering hole, Deux-Magots.[4] Indeed, accounts from early May suggest that Parisians, despite being annoyed by daily siren alerts, could not be bothered to stop their daily rituals to accommodate a war that they most assuredly did not want.

Parisians managed their nerves for over a month, but their determination to stubbornly remain in their capital gradually eroded. Why? Refugees passed through in increasing numbers, first via the Parisian suburbs, then over the city's railways. Initially, observers discounted the mass upheaval as a uniquely Belgian tragedy. However, news of the expanding crisis reached Paris with the evacuation of Dunkerque, which drew international media attention. Overseas' dailies began running stories about US or British civilians trapped inside France, suffering alongside the French civilian population. One American expatriate, Lloyd Stark, reported from Malo-les-Bains, a resort town near Dunkerque, how he had survived a German air attack that destroyed his home. Stark, was seriously wounded, recovering in a near-by hospital, when he wired the American Embassy in Paris to request, "full publicity and aid to homeless and desolate here as result of German savagery."[5]

By June, rumor of the German advance stirred Parisian fears. Witnessing the capital's emergence from denial to consciousness of the grave situation, Eric Sevareid recorded:

Paris knew now. Paris knew what the northern cities knew: how it is to sit in the corridor of the dank cellar holding tight to the children who cry with fright at the look in their parents' eyes while droning like that of a million bees fills the sky; how it is to feel the old house quiver, to see the plaster peel itself from the wall ... to have the acrid smell of cordite in the nostrils, to see an old woman on her hands and knees at the doorstep, mopping up the blood of her husband with the parlor curtain.[6]

Sixteen-year-old Jackie Golter and her family knew that fear. They gathered with neighbors for the last time in their apartment building to discuss the previously unthinkable, leaving Paris. Fifty years after the event, Golter vividly remembered the urban backdrop of, "a very black fog" engulfing an apocalyptic sky. Only later, she learned that the "fog" was smoke emanating from bombings. The adolescent memory still

---

[4] Crémieux-Brilhac, *Les Français de l'an 40*, 542.
[5] "Nazi Bombs Wound American in France: Lloyd R. Stark of Mystic, Conn., Loses Home Near Dunkerque," *New York Times*, June 2, 1940.
[6] Sevareid, *Not So Wild a Dream*, 145.

haunted the adult: "At this moment, maybe because of the fog, I knew that we had to leave this hell. Everyone knew that the Germans were fearsome." In the comfort of her living room, half a century removed from the war, Golter vividly remembered the beginning of a conflict that eventually consumed the lives of several family members.[7]

Most eye-witness accounts confirm the horrifying impression made by the plumes of black smoke. One report surmised German responsibility, "He [the enemy] is also now using smoke-screens on a large scale, and Parisians had evidence of this during the last few days; a thick pall drifting, sinister and silent, over the city has made the use of torches necessary in the late afternoon."[8] Another hypothesized more positively that Allied bombing had been so detrimental to German forces that the enemy employed smoke screens to obscure the few bridges remaining intact. British pilots flying over Paris concluded that the haze must be artificially generated, "It is not the usual sort of smoke barrage but a kind of mist attained by some chemical means ... One can hardly see across the Place de la Concorde, and the Eiffel Tower is invisible except for brief seconds when the breeze whirls away the smoke."[9]

More than the smoke, the stubborn refusal of the government to communicate with civilians and a complete invisibility of action by the Défense passive, spurred Parisians to join the mass of refugees now retreating toward the River Loire. One neighbor in Golter's apartment building encouraged everyone to leave warning, "I don't want my daughter to serve as a welcome mat for the Germans."[10] With the growing consensus about civilian endangerment, Golter's family agreed that her mother and her sixty-eight-year-old grandmother would leave on foot immediately in the direction of Chartres, the cathedral town near the River Loire.

For men and women alike, bombs and smoke caused worry, but fears of rape drew upon deeply imbedded memories of World War I. Survivors of German occupation of north-eastern France during World War I, passed down stories to their grandchildren about the barbaric behavior of the German boches (cows). One horror recounted to French youth of the 1930s, described how German soldiers had cut off the hands of little French children.[11] Such tales find their place among European

---

[7] Jackie Golter, interviewed by author at Franconville, June 23, 1992.
[8] "Struggle for Rheims: Heavy Enemy Losses," *The Times*, June 13, 1940, 6.
[9] "The Threat to Paris: Defence from the Air: Smoke and An Exodus," *The Times*, June 14, 1940, 7.
[10] Golter interview.
[11] Ruth Harris, "The Child of the Barbarian," *Past and Present* 141, October 1993, 170–206.

folk tales; but in the context of the expanding violence of the war, such stories served as prudent reminders of potentially dangerous encounters. Grandmothers and civilian veterans of World War I carried with them memories about the commission of atrocities against their generation the war. Staying the ground in 1915–1916 had resulted in costly encounters with "German barbarians."[12] Much interwar ink recorded the real and recreated experiences of German-impregnated French girls forced to choose between having an illegal abortion or giving birth to a Germanic child. Such stories certainly motivated French women to avoid a re-encounter with the German conqueror.[13]

As in the Marne, administrative disorganization prevented engagement of brave civilians in a coordinated defense of Paris. Golter's uncle and father had resolved to enlist in the army to help defend Paris after sending their wives, children, and mothers ahead while they remained behind to combat the Germans. In the 1930s, both Golter's parents and grandparents emigrated from Odessa following the Bolshevik Revolution in Russia. The decision to leave their adopted city weighed heavily upon their sense of national loyalty. Like the Carrés and Poiriers of Reims, Golter's father and uncle promised to rejoin their families at a later date. Once the women had departed, the men reported to the local recruitment station, only to find it had already closed. After several failed attempts to enlist in the army or some type of civil defense activity, the men joined the departing masses.

Other examples of independently initiated evacuations abound, sparked in large measure by the failure of government direction. Parisian school officials reactivated the dormant plan to evacuate children, beginning an evacuation of children via rail and bus on June 6.[14] However, unlike the Paris evacuation of September 1939, parents now insisted that they accompany their children.[15] Despite these activities the Parisian dailies remained virtually silent on the issue of evacuation.

---

[12] Grayzel, *Women's Identities at War*, 66–83.

[13] Grayzel, *Women's Identities at War*, 66–83. Stéphane Audoin-Rouzeau and Annette Becker in their study of the Great War, *14–18: Retrouver la guerre, Bibliothèque des Histoires* (Paris: Gallimard, 2000) argue that the memory of atrocities of World War I did not survive in interwar memory. Instead atrocities became what they call "mythicized," to such an extent that the real horror went uncommemorated. Grayzel's work suggests that, at least in fiction, this was not the case. For a review of discussions of women civilians' experience of World War I, see Belinda Davis, "Review Article: Experience, Identity, and Memory: The Legacy of World War I," *The Journal of Modern History* 75 March 2003, 111–131.

[14] Chief of Service of the 5th Section of the SNCF for the south-east regional division, "Report" quoted in Vidalenc, *L'exode de mai–juin 1940*, 252.

[15] Jean Poyet, "Exode d'enfants," unpublished manuscript cited in Vidalenc, *L'exode de mai–juin 1940*, 252.

On June 6, *Le Figaro* granted just 1 inch of front-page column space to: "Evacuation of small Parisians." The article offered no evacuation information, but reported that many children remained in the capital. The writer evidenced some dissatisfaction with the authorities in one possibly critical sentence: "Until now, those in high places have contented themselves to act through persuasion in inviting families to evacuate their small children."[16] One previous notice about evacuations had appeared on May 24, when *La Victoire* published government warnings to state workers not to leave the city. No articles reported on parliamentary debates about the merits or liabilities of a civilian evacuation.

Le Figaro did report on the refugee crisis, but as if it was happening to other countries. Reporters emphasized the large populations of Belgian, Dutch, and Luxembourgeois refugees. When reporting on the plight of French refugees, the June 4 edition focused on farmers from the northeast. The story made the tragedy seem like a uniquely rural phenomenon. Readers did learn about the agricultural crisis in the north as farmers abandoned all cultivation, leaving crops, livestock, tools and, of course, their property. Rural families harnessed their horses to carts in attempts to save some property and refugees walked 35–40 km a day. By June 4, many had traveled 600–700 km before passing through Paris, and faced as many as twenty-five more days on the road before they might reach safety.[17] And yet, the same edition of *Le Figaro* buried a report on the previous night's bombings of the Paris suburbs at the bottom of page 2. Warning sirens had sounded throughout the day, starting at 1.10 pm, yet most of the population had remained calm. Small signs of panic shadowed optimistic reporting. Some Parisians ran through the streets. Others forgot to extinguish all their lights. Curious observers looked for bombers from their windows. Other than admonishing citizens who did not obey air raid orders to stay in their homes and away from windows, neither the newspaper nor the government offered any advice to a tense population.

At Matignon, Prime Minister Reynaud's cabinet publicly stood determined to defend Paris. Behind closed doors, however, it considered an evacuation of France's capital. The ambivalence of the government about issuing an evacuation order ultimately unleashed the chaotic flight of Parisian civilians. Military leaders first introduced the question of evacuating Paris on June 7. In a secret memo, General Joseph Vuillemin informed General Weygand that all his information indicated that the Germans would bomb Paris with the "utmost

---

[16] "L'évacuation des petits Parisiens," *Le Figaro*, June 6, 1940, 1.
[17] "Nos paysans chassés de leur terre," *Le Figaro*, June 4, 1940, 1.

severity."[18] Hence, Vuillemin concluded that two actions must follow: Paris should be evacuated and fighter aircraft would have to be withdrawn from the battle to conserve them for the defense of Paris. Other ministers worked behind the scenes to prepare for the impending retreat, but internal divisions slowed plans. Under Secretary of State for Refugees Schuman pressured Minister of Supply Queuille to begin the evacuation of all livestock from the Paris region so as to be able to feed the growing multitude of refugees and keep the herds from falling into the hands of the Germans. Queuille fiercely opposed Schuman's plan for two reasons. First, only the army had the capacity to move such a massive and dispersed load, and the army, noted Queuille sarcastically, "had another job at the moment."[19] Second, Queuille argued that one could not just move livestock without moving the farm, reasoning, "a farm is more than a cow."[20] Queuille's unwillingness to plan for evacuation of cattle meant that, once the government did order the evacuation, it was too late to move the region's livestock.

Two days later, on June 9, Weygand discussed the problem of evacuating Paris with Reynaud, saying, "I cannot for myself advise any other step than a withdrawal from Paris of children under sixteen years."[21] Actually, the evacuation of Parisian children had started three days earlier. The debate in the highest circles of government subordinated a discussion of civilian evacuation, prioritizing debates about policies to evacuate government officials and offices. Weygand believed that top government officials should stay in Paris and allow themselves to be taken prisoner. His June 9 memo stressed, "the Commander-in-Chief must point out to him [the President of the Council] that, in view of the military situation, he considers it wise to carry out this evacuation without including the ministers whose presence the President of the Council thinks necessary in the capital up to the last moment."[22] That evening the Council of Ministers met on the issue of evacuation. In Reynaud's brief words, "I decided to leave the capital."[23]

Minister of the Interior, Georges Mandel, argued strongly for a government retreat to Touraine. Mandel waged a behind-the-scenes crusade to evacuate the entire political body to remote areas outside the enemy's grasp. On June 10, Mandel addressed the municipal representatives of

[18] Reynaud, *In the Thick of the Fight 1930–1945*, 479.
[19] De Tarr, *Henri Queuille en son temps*, 283.
[20] De Tarr, *Henri Queuille en son temps*, 283.
[21] De Tarr, *Henri Queuille en son temps*, 480.
[22] Reynaud, *In the Thick of the Fight*, 480.
[23] Reynaud, *In the Thick of the Fight*, 480.

Paris and asked them to follow the example of the Council of Ministers and issue an evacuation order. The President of the Representatives of Paris, Louis Peuch, led a motion echoing Mandel's wish, but moved to insert a contingency. In order to preserve order, Peuch suggested the formation of a permanent commission to stay in Paris and represent the people in "whatever be the circumstances."[24] Peuch appointed the men who would essentially serve as Paris' first ambassadors to the Third Reich: Jean Chiappe, Georges Contenot, René Fiquet, Maurice de Fontenay, Marcel Héraud, Noël Pinelli, and André le Troquer.[25]

Ironically, Mandel objected to plans to evacuate Paris' civilian population. Reynaud's postwar testimony reported that Mandel, "ordered the civilian authorities to oppose such a movement, and in any case not to take part in it."[26] Mandel actually took actions to punish prefects, mayors, and police commissioners who ordered evacuations or assisted fleeing civilians. On May 21, Mandel dismissed the lieutenant prefect of Mondidier (Nord) for lending assistance to departing civilians. On May 26, he fired eight police commissioners in the Nord for similar infractions.[27]

As the government formalized its departure plans, the military began to alter its plan for Paris. Reynaud's recollections admit to his indecision about evacuating the capital. From a strategic perspective, he wanted the military to defend the city and fight the Germans to the end. Emotionally, he wanted to spare Paris and her citizens needless destruction and bloodshed. His memoirs bitterly record the belief that Weygand and Pétain had never intended to mount a military defense of Paris. On June 10, *fait accompli*, Reynaud received news from Weygand that Paris had been declared, "an open city." Weygand's memo stressed that Paris would fall within a defense zone whose front lay 30 km from the city, and explained that no "defensive organization" would be mounted around the city's old fortifications to ensure that the Germans believed that the city was left "open."[28] Reynaud's memoir suggests that Weygand acted independently in declaring Paris an "open city"; but also testifies that he, as the head of government, was unwilling to mobilize the city's citizens to defend Paris. Despite the change in military strategy, newspapers continued to report that the government would defend Paris to the end.

---

[24] Reynaud, *In the Thick of the Fight*, 481.
[25] Reynaud, *In the Thick of the Fight*, 481.
[26] Reynaud, *In the Thick of the Fight*, 483.
[27] Reynaud, *In the Thick of the Fight*, 483.
[28] Reynaud, *In the Thick of the Fight*, 481.

Weygand's reorganization plan created "The Army of Paris," with General Héring in command, but this was a meaningless gesture, since he had decided to allow the German Army free passage. More reflective of his intention to initiate transition of Paris from French to German control was his naming of General Dentz, commander of the army of the Paris region, as governor of Paris. On June 12, Weygand telephoned Dentz informing him: "Paris is declared an open city, and every measure has been taken to ensure, in all circumstances the safety and provisioning of the city."[29] Weygand left the task to Héring, prior to leading his army on a retreat to the Loire, to paste notices throughout Paris alerting the population: "Paris is declared an open city."[30]

Reynaud later defended his position claiming: "I knew the people of Paris too well to feel the slightest doubt that they would not be ready to sacrifice everything for the welfare of their country. But what right had we to ask it of them when Weygand assured me that such an act of abnegation and heroism was useless?"[31] Contemporary memoirs testify to the unwillingness of the French authorities to harness civilians to resist the Germans. Radio correspondent, Eric Sevareid, recalled the missed opportunity the day Mussolini declared war: "They [Parisians] waited for words that would give them strength and courage and defiance, and they heard only the funereal voice of Premier Reynaud, sealing their doom, informing them that Mussolini had broken his pledges and had that day declared war upon France."[32] After the war, while testifying at the trial of Pétain, Weygand assumed responsibility: "I [Weygand] myself, therefore, assumed the responsibility for declaring Paris an open town, I took the initiative in this, and I claim full responsibility. I told Monsieur Paul Reynaud what I had done."[33] In the context of disagreement between government officials about what to do with Paris, Parisian families like the Golters took their fate into their own hands. They left Paris behind.

Hopes fade as eyes turn across the Atlantic

While Parisian civilians were giving up the fight, Reynaud prepared for continued resistance, pressing the United States for intervention. In his last act before leaving Paris on June 10, the prime minister wrote a letter to President Roosevelt, pleading with him to take France's case

---

[29] Reynaud, *In the Thick of the Fight*, 482.
[30] Reynaud, *In the Thick of the Fight*, 482.
[31] Reynaud, *In the Thick of the Fight*, 483.
[32] Sevareid, *Not So Wild a Dream*, 146.   [33] Sevareid, *Not So Wild a Dream*, 146.

to the people of America. Reynaud clarified why the French government had chosen to leave the capital: "I am making ready to leave for the front. That will be to intensify the struggle with all the forces which we still have and not to abandon the struggle."[34] At that moment, the "front" was now the French Army's newly designated last line of resistance, the River Loire. Implicating not only France's future, but that of all free peoples, Reynaud sought to stir Roosevelt to action: "May I ask you, Mr. President, to explain all this yourself ... to all the citizens of the United States saying to them that we are determined to sacrifice ourselves in the struggle that we are carrying on for all free men."[35]

Meanwhile, at the American Embassy, Ambassador William Bullitt, who had taken up his post in Paris in September 1936, refused to retreat. Bullitt stayed on to advocate on behalf of Reynaud, transmitting to Roosevelt the details of the ever-growing exodus and the tiring military resistance. Bullitt had already narrowly escaped death during the invasion. On June 4, while holding a cocktail glass at a luncheon at the French Ministry of Air "One bomb came through the roof, pierced each successive floor, and rolled at their [Bullitt's group] feet."[36] Roosevelt received a barrage of telegrams from Bullitt that bluntly spelled out the situation in France and urged US assistance. Bullitt showed a keen understanding of the civilian and military disaster gripping France and Europe, but, unfortunately, he had few supporters in the US Congress or State Department. On June 11, he re-issued a plea to the President for assistance, demanding that Roosevelt place "personal and political" reservations aside and seek immediate relief for the French population. "The evacuation of Paris has added a million to the number of men, women, and children who are moving into southwestern France whose lives can be saved only by American aid," he warned.[37]

Bullitt reminded Roosevelt that exactly a week earlier, he had requested via telephone that Roosevelt petition Congress for US$20,000,000 in refugee relief to help "keep them alive."[38] Contrary to the agreement to send the aid, Bullitt learned that Roosevelt had deferred making the request to Congress until the Red Cross had completed a fundraising drive. Norman H. Davis, Red Cross Chairman, reported on June 2 that the charity had only raised US$5,410,983 toward the needed US$20,000,000.[39] Since refugee numbers were already nearly

[34] Paul Reynaud to President Roosevelt, June 10, 1940. Telegram forwarded by William Bullitt, reprinted in Orville H. Bullitt, *For the President*, 460–461.
[35] Bullitt, *For the President*, 460–461.   [36] Sevareid, *Not So Wild a Dream*, 145.
[37] Bullitt, Telegram No. 1149, dated June 11, 3 pm, Bullitt, *For the President*, 462.
[38] Bullitt, *For the President*, 462.
[39] "Red Cross to Buy Some Surplus Food," *New York Times*, June 2, 1940, 1.

6 million and would reach 8 million, donations amounted to less than US$1.00 per refugee. Private and corporate contributions testified to American generosity, but fell short of the needed amount. In one day the US national chapter of the Red Cross received gifts amounting to US$665,640. Bernard M. Baruch and Chrysler Corporation each donated US$25,000; New York Life Insurance Company collected US$3,872.70 in home-office employee contributions; Mrs. George Vettlesen of Manhattan pledged US$5,000. Other corporate donations included US$16,000 from the Firestone, Goodrich, Goodyear, and General Tire companies; US$750 from Brooklyn Union Gas; and US$500 each from the South Brooklyn Savings Bank and the South Brooklyn Ladies' Benevolent Society. A more modest contribution of US$1.00 came from a New York City apartment dweller, writing: "The rent is unpaid here, but thank God I am at least safe from bombs and horror and send this as an expression of this thankfulness."[40]

American giving was not entirely self-sacrificing, however. Davis had brokered a deal with the US Department of Agriculture whereby the Red Cross would purchase US surplus farm products at a favorable price. The first Red Cross "mercy ship" would carry 5,881,000 lbs of wheat flour, 1,250,000 lbs of corn meal, 750,000 lbs of lard, and 800,000 lbs each of prunes and raisins.[41] The Secretary of Agriculture commented on the mutually beneficial nature of the exchange: "we can assist United States producers through the increased distribution ... at the same time that we are making it possible for the Red Cross to accomplish greater humanitarian ends with its available funds."[42] Indeed, General George C. Marshall would build upon the same aid formula for postwar reconstruction.

American women of society mobilized swiftly in a genuine display of compassion and solidarity with French refugees. Mrs. Erstein, Mrs. L. Alchevsky, and Mrs. S. E. Fitzgibbon of New York City staffed war relief centers established by the American–French War Relief, Inc., organizing debutantes and any willing volunteers to collect donations of clothing, blankets, food, medical supplies, or cash. Mrs. Frederick Ecker, president of the organization, assisted Mrs. Alchevsky in directing a workroom where New York women came to knit, sew, and make

---

[40] "Red Cross to Buy Some Surplus Food," *New York Times*, June 2, 1940, 1. On July 13, 2002 I attended a ceremony hosted by the Sapeurs et Pompiers during Paris' Bastille Day celebration that honored the courage of NYFD fire fighters who contributed relief to the 9/11 disaster. Paris city officials invoked the historic friendship between New York and Paris, citing as examples the Statue of Liberty and the support of New Yorkers and Americans for France and Paris during World War II.
[41] "Red Cross," *New York Times*, 1.   [42] "Red Cross," *New York Times*, 1.

surgical dressings. For those women who wished to volunteer, but could not spend time in the workroom, Fitzgibbon had set up a purchasing department where women could purchase wool, flannel, and material to take home to sew finished articles to return to the center for shipment to France.[43] In Britain, similar efforts raised the London relief agency's totals to £1,553,000. US Ambassador to Britain Joseph P. Kennedy and his wife contributed £1,000 toward the purchase of ambulances for France.[44] Unfortunately, without well-established international systems to transfer refugee relief, the efforts of American women achieved local glory but few concrete overseas' results. Despite all the charitable activity, as of June 11, neither a Red Cross shipment nor any other US funds had arrived in Bordeaux, the designated receiving port for US aid.[45] To add to this problem, British Red Cross relief workers in northern France had to abandon £40,000 worth of supplies and medical equipment due to German advances upon their stations.[46]

Throughout the day of June 11, Bullitt fired off a series of telegrams urging Roosevelt to remove responsibility from the Red Cross for assisting in the exodus: "I am now convinced that the officials of the Red Cross are incompetent to organize relief on the scale demanded." Despite an occasional flare of exaggeration, Bullitt fully tried to convey the magnitude of the disaster, writing: "The problem is as great as the problem of feeding and supplying the entire French Army."[47] Later that day, Roosevelt called upon the US Congress to appropriate the needed monies to the Red Cross, writing in his request: "I feel the Congress would receive nation-wide support, if it were to add an appropriation to the relief bill in the sum of at least $50,000,000 as a token of our deep-seated desire to help not only Americans but people who are destitute in other lands."[48]

Responding to Roosevelt's initiative, Count Bertrand Clauzel, Vice-President of the French Red Cross, hailed and thanked Americans saying: "The American generosity, which touches us deeply, is really equal to the tragic circumstances through which we are passing."[49] Directors of relief agencies spoke in defense of Roosevelt's proposal. Clarence

---

[43] "Relief Center to Aid Refugees Will Open," *New York Times*, June 2, 1940, 1.
[44] "Red Cross A Heavy Loser: Abandons Stores in Retreat," *New York Times*, June 2, 1940, 1.
[45] Bullitt, Telegram No. 1149, dated June 11, 3 pm, Bullitt, *For the President*, 462.
[46] "Red Cross A Heavy Loser," *New York Times*, 1.
[47] Bullitt, *For the President*, 463.
[48] "Franklin D. Roosevelt asks $50,000,000 to Aid Refugees," *New York Times*, June 12, 1940, 1.
[49] "Asks $50,000,000 to Aid Refugees," *New York Times*, 1.

Pickett, Secretary of the American Friends Service Committee, announced at the meeting of the board of directors of the American Committee for Christian Refugees that: "The thing has come so fast, voluntary organizations are no match for the problem ... America can meet its responsibility only by Congressional appropriations."[50]

In an effort to conceive of a workable plan for delivering the necessary aid, the Ambassador proposed that Roosevelt dispatch two ships per week to Bordeaux as part of a regular delivery schedule to bring US$1,000,000 per shipment. (Bullitt's aid calculation for the entire year of 1940 had increased to US$100,000,000.) Bullitt realized that even if Congress agreed to the aid request that very same day, supplies would not reach France until the end of June. The only shipments from the United States that actually arrived in Bordeaux during the June crisis carried twelve Thompson submachine guns ordered by Bullitt who incorrectly feared a communist insurrection. "There is every reason to expect that if the French Government should be forced to leave Paris, its place would be taken by a communist mob," opined the Ambassador.[51] Even as the Nazis prepared to conquer France, senior US diplomats, as well as some French leaders, clung to the belief that communism represented a greater evil than fascism.

Roosevelt and Bullitt's final exchanges before the collapse of France remind the reader of just how politically unprepared was the United States in 1940 to deliver France from her fate. In a reply telegram marked "rush" sent from Washington at 10 pm, Roosevelt assured Bullitt, "We are doing everything possible in regard to your dispatches about Red Cross arrangements."[52] Roosevelt's concerns actually focused on maintaining contact with the French government currently preparing to leave Paris; but Bullitt threatened to defy Roosevelt's orders to leave Paris. In a characteristically thespian declaration, Bullitt defended his desire to stay in Paris: "since the age of four I have never run away from anything however painful or dangerous when I thought it was my duty to take a stand."[53] He secured the transfer of diplomatic powers to Tony Biddle, a career foreign service officer, who followed Reynaud's government to Tours.

[50] "Refugee Aid Held Duty of Congress: Secretary of American Friends Group Calls Problem Too Big for Relief Agencies," *New York Times*, June 11, 1940, 1.
[51] Bullitt to the Secretary of State (Cordell Hull), Telegram No. 1098, June 8, 9 pm, Bullitt, *For the President*, 455.
[52] Roosevelt to Bullitt, Telegram dated June 11, 10 pm, Bullitt, *For the President*, 465.
[53] Bullitt to Roosevelt, Telegram No. 1157, June 12, 11 am, Bullitt, *For the President*, 466.

On June 12, Bullitt informed Roosevelt that Héring was prepared to issue an order of retreat, an order that did not include a mandated departure of civilians. As envisioned by Weygand, only Dentz would remain, accompanied by the gendarmerie to protect against fires or mobs. Despite persistent hopes to the contrary, the inevitability of defeat could not be deferred much longer.

All systems fail: communication and leadership look beyond the civilian crisis

Serious shortcomings in communication influenced the trajectory of France's defeat. Military commanders, elected government representatives, appointed government administrators, editors, and reporters faced difficult judgments regarding the release of sensitive information. Distilling information to produce the appropriate mix of maintaining military secrecy and creating a public awareness of wartime dangers without stirring public panic demanded delicate decisions. Civilians received information about the military campaign, government policies, and international events from the radio, newspapers, and government decrees posted in public squares. Because newspapers remained a key source of public information, their stories chronicled the war's events, marked its geographic location, and ultimately provided the language by which readers discussed the war. Both newspapers and government announcements prescribed guidelines and behavior for civilians. Civilians not only applied that information and instruction to their own choices, but also to what they thought about the war and its prosecution.

A central feature of the World War II experience on the European continent was the absence of an uncensored press. The fact that all warring nations practiced censorship does not diminish the impact that the filtering of security facts had on shaping local and national experience. The growing consciousness among the population about the gaps between their daily experience of the war and the information they received from government and media outlets may have played a pivotal role in shaping events, especially in May to June 1940. Indeed, by 1943 some critics charged that the press' complicity in sanitizing the methods and results of waging war actually contributed to the escalation of violence. Writing in England in 1943, Vera Brittain castigated government censorship and media complicity around bombing arguing: "The propagandist Press descriptions of this bombing and its results skillfully conceal their real meaning ... by such carefully chosen phrases as 'softening-up' an area, 'neutralizing the target', 'area bombing', 'saturating the defences' and 'blanketing an industrial district."[54] Brittain argued that the euphemisms used in the press to describe the horror of bombing prevented readers from understanding the human consequences of modern military strategy. She advanced that throughout history, "wrongs have been committed, or evils gone too long unremedied, simply because we did not perceive the real meaning of the suffering which we had caused or failed to mitigate."[55] Brittain concludes that only a fully-informed citizenry can change government policy.

In the Marne, the failure of newspapers to accurately report and question the government's program of civil defense, contributed to the collapse of the provincial home front. This phenomenon reproduced itself in Paris. It is difficult to assess the failure of French and international news reporting to inform civilians of the destructive power and rapid advance of German troops. Historians can and should ask a few obvious questions. First, would accurate reporting have better prepared civilians to confront invasion and occupation? Second, if officials and civilians had confronted the invasion soberly, could some civilians have been more responsibly and safely moved to designated shelters?

American journalist, Eric Sevareid, recognized the dilemma facing French war reporters. Sevareid and his French and English-speaking colleagues worked creatively from the outbreak of war to evade the heavy hand of the French censor, but Sevareid himself acknowledged a serious ethical problem. After the evacuation of Dunkerque, obtaining accurate and verifiable information from the front became nearly impossible. French newspapers, and British ones too, inflated Allied successes, quoting French military officials who mentioned "terrible German losses."[56] Sevareid and his colleagues knew that such positive reports masked observable reality, but they could not seem to confirm the opposite. He also confessed that: "We were all victims of 'wishful thinking', true, but of something else too; the effects of our professional compulsions."[57] To report the news accurately fed into German propaganda: "The French stood defeated, but should the paper report so?"[58]

On the eve of June 10, rumors of government evacuation plans began to circulate through Paris. *New York Times* correspondent P. J. Philip broke the story in the international press and commented on the macabre feeling that cloaked Paris on the eve of the government's

---

[54] Vera Brittain, "Seed of Chaos: What Mass Bombing Really Means" (1943) in Shirley Williams (ed.), *One Voice: Pacifist Writings from the Second World War* (London: Continuum, 2005), 95.
[55] Brittain, "Seed of Chaos," 95.   [56] Sevareid, *Not So Wild a Dream*, 142.
[57] Sevareid, *Not So Wild a Dream*, 143.
[58] Sevareid, *Not So Wild a Dream*, 143.

departure: "The night was made mysterious and somewhat sinister by the movements in the dark of persons carrying cases and boxes of all kinds out of offices and loading them onto army or private trucks."[59] In the morning, the government refused to issue an official evacuation order, but strongly advised parents to take their children to the outskirts of the city immediately since, "there are too many tender faces exposed to massacre by the Nazi assassins."[60] A few banks reportedly stayed open to curb mass panic, but also to accommodate residents' attempts to clean out their bank accounts before vacating the city. Guaranty Trust Company, Morgans, and most notably the Bank of France remained open throughout the night and into the following day. Authorities debated whether to relocate the Paris stock exchange to a different city, while embassy agents, legations, and ministries – Europe's diplomatic core – all evacuated the majority of their personnel.

Despite civilian departures and French military leaders' claims to the contrary, the French daily, *Matin*, insisted that the city would be defended. Miscommunication, bordering on disinformation, between the government, the newspapers, and the population remained a staple of Parisian life to the bitter end. Newspapers erroneously informed civilians that: "All roads leading into the city were barricaded and preparations were made to defend the capital street by street and block by block in its first direct siege since 1870."[61] Official discourse could not stand more opposed to daily life. The presence of heavy smoke and noise from unceasing artillery fire testified to the fierce battle being waged on the outskirts of the city. Parisian suburbs endured heavy bombing throughout the night of June 10. In the Seine valley, German bombers destroyed two towns leaving few survivors. "Scarcely a single house in them has escaped. The streets are piled high with stones and bricks and no one is left alive in these pleasant riverside villas," lamented one of the last American reports from Paris.[62]

Local eye-witness accounts confirmed civilian anxiety: "Whether this [residential bombings] will happen to Paris last is still uncertain," questioned a late breaking report.[63] Most civilians were not eager to wait and find out what the Germans had in mind. Word that tanks approached the city propelled civilians into the streets. The June 10

[59] P. J. Philip, "Packing Made Sinister," *New York Times*, June 11, 1940, 3.
[60] "Barricades Put Up in Streets of Paris: Army Prepares to Defend City to the Last –Great Exodus From Capital Continues," *New York Times*, June 12, 1940, 6.
[61] "Barricades Put Up in Streets of Paris," *New York Times*, 6.
[62] Philip, "Packing Made Sinister," *New York Times*, 3.
[63] Philip, "Packing Made Sinister," *New York Times*, 3.

bombings seemed intended to offer French officials a preview of the destiny awaiting Paris if the government backed up its rhetoric to resist the assault and defend the capital. Trying to muster public morale, a morning editorial vowed: "In the worst of storms, Paris was not subdued. Paris will never bow."[64] German spokesmen also entered the war of words, warning the French: "If Paris were defended, it would be bombed and shelled without mercy."[65]

The flight of the press signaled the crumbling of the institutions and foundations of the Third Republic. Weighing the decision to leave, one American reporter explained: "The choice is a difficult one – to stay here and be bombed would not matter if one could get news, but it is certain that there will be no news available except of these bombings."[66] The *New York Times* closed its Paris offices on June 11, and moved to a location where news could be supplied and communication with the United States could be assured.[67] A single reporter, Lansing Warren, remained behind to communicate news of the "last newspaper to be printed in Paris." Warren's censored article, identified as originating from "Somewhere in France," sounded the final bell, reporting: "The last newspaper to appear was, either symbolically or ironically, Gustave Hervé's *La Victoire*."[68]

As institutions folded, Parisian train stations experienced a forceful rush. On June 11, rail stations with lines serving France's southern regions sealed the doors between the station ticketing galleries and the tracks for fear that a mad push to board departing trains would result in the unstoppable crush of refugees. Montparnasse, gateway to the west coast, closed all its exterior doors; Gare de Lyon, with trains running southbound to Marseilles, and Gare d'Austerlitz, with lines extending toward Switzerland, closed temporarily on June 12 in an effort to disperse pushing crowds.[69] Limiting access to ticketing counters aggravated civilian anxiety. The "special correspondent" from *The Times* witnessed:

Now and again I would come across a solitary little bunch of refugees making their way across the city from the Gare Saint-Lazaire or the Gare du Nord, some of them white-haired women pushing children and their scanty

---

[64] "Barricades Put Up in Streets of Paris," *New York Times*, 6.

[65] "Swastika in Paris," *New York Times*, June 16, 1940, section 4, 1.

[66] Philip, "Packing Made Sinister," *New York Times*, 3.

[67] Philip, "Packing Made Sinister," *New York Times*, 3.

[68] "Tours is Jammed; Refugees Pitiful: Substitute French Capital Is Scene of Confusion," *New York Times*, June 14, 1940, 4.

[69] Testimonies cited from P. Fontiane, *Last to Leave Paris*, 41 and J. de la Hire's, *La crime des évacuations*, 27 in Vidalenc, *L'exode de mai–juin 1940*, 257.

belongings in perambulators or wheel-barrows, or a great lorry would lurch through piled high with refugees and their belongings.[70]

Some refugees camped on sidewalks, surrounded by mounds of luggage and children. Like their rural counterparts, urban refugees attempted to save animal life too, as one British reporter described: "Some had even brought their canaries and their goldfish."[71]

Crowds and confusion inevitably spawned individual tragedies. Parisian newspapers documented the hazards faced by children embroiled in the exodus. *Le Journal* printed a dialogue overheard between two women at the Paris train station, Gare de l'Est: "Excuse me madame," interrupted the desperate mother. "You wouldn't have happened to see a little girl? Five years old? Blond. She would have been alone," explained the mother. "Her name is Mariette. She's mine. I've lost her." The reporter described the mother as a strong, large woman with a forceful stature who stood curled over from carrying an enormous bundle described as, "so big that it seemed impossible that the back of a woman alone could bear such an unbelievable load."[72] The papers emphasized civilians' grief, but did they also contribute to it? By privileging stories of loss and displacement rather than investigating government activities to mount a civil defense or to provide for refugees suggests French papers' complicity with government failure to publicize disaster relief measures. Newspapers hawked stories about the civilian defeat; they were forbidden to report on the military defeat. Newspapers "sold" tragedy not information until the war forced editors of the Parisian dailies to stop the presses.

Perhaps in keeping with Mandel's orders, police and civil defense agencies provided little assistance to Parisian refugees planning their departures. Small isolated efforts suggest that some police and city employees worked to offer improvised assistance to departing cohorts. British reports describe the limited successes to feed refugees congregated around train stations: "Buffets were besieged by thousands who could have had little hope of getting food or drink for the journey."[73] As the Wehrmacht advanced, however, German agents working for the National Society for the People's Welfare (NSV) trailed, serving cold and hot meals to displaced refugees. Julia Torrie found that: "NSV assistance was supposed to encourage French and Belgian civilians to

[70] "The Flight from the Capital: Three Days' Flow of Refugees," *The Times*, June 14, 1940, 6.
[71] "Threat to Paris: Defence from the Air: An Emptying City," *The Times*, June 14, 1940, 7.
[72] *Le Journal*, May 14, 1940, 1.   [73] "Threat to Paris," *The Times*, June 14, 1940, 7.

think of the Germans as generous friends, not enemies, and to smooth the road for occupation."[74] The NSV claimed to German newspaper reporters to have served, "27 million portions of cold food, 15 million hot meals, 8.5 million servings of milk for children and mothers, and 3 million loaves of bread," figures Torrie suggests were exaggerated.[75]

Congestion around train stations grew as buses and taxis, requisitioned as they had been in World War I, deposited women and children rescued from the war zone. The frantic movement of vehicles throughout the city created gridlock, and in some cases interfered with rescue efforts. Descriptions conveyed the sense of circus: "Mingling with the taxis were cars and lorries, even horse-drawn vehicles, in which whole families and their pets had packed themselves for the journey to a new home."[76] The variety of vehicles was stunning, "a steady stream of every conceivable kind of vehicle, from farm carts to the most expensive make of cars, is pouring southward from Paris."[77] In these circumstances, however, fortunes reversed. Of the owners of horse-drawn carts, a commentator noted their advantage: "they are lucky, since they [the horses] do not need petrol."[78] Owners of cars soon ran out of gasoline and found roadside pumps had also run dry.[79]

Slow processionals, symbolically evocative of funeral marches, jammed Parisian roads, as well as the arteries surrounding the city. "Land operations have been further hampered and confused by the headlong rush from Paris which has blocked the roads to the south for many miles, holding up ammunition convoys from the factories and reinforcements for the troops for days," one reporter charged. Indeed, military authorities and historians would debate for a decade whether the exodus impeded the French from mounting a successful defense of the River Loire.[80] Clearly, congestion not only threatened military operations, but stymied rescue efforts as well. *The Times* noted that: "supply lorries are experiencing the greatest difficulty in reaching the most overcrowded areas," thus jeopardizing the delivery of Red Cross and other institutionally funded relief aid.[81]

Inside train stations, populations competed for access to departing cars, "As one train pulled out hundreds of people were left to catch the

---

[74] Torrie, *"For Their Own Good,"* 43.
[75] Torrie, *"For Their Own Good,"* 42.
[76] Torrie, *"For Their Own Good,"* 42.
[77] "Germans in Paris," *The Times*, June 15, 1940, 6.
[78] "Germans in Paris," *The Times*, June 15, 1940, 6.
[79] "The Flight From the Capital," *The Times*, June 14, 1940, 6.
[80] "Germans in Paris," *The Times*, June 15, 1940, 6.
[81] "Germans in Paris," *The Times*, June 15, 1940, 6.

next."[82] Buses evacuated persons easily grouped together from major institutions such as prisons, hospitals, and homes for the elderly. One Parisian bus transported half a dozen nurses and twenty to thirty tiny children. "It seemed probable that they had been carried straight from a maternity hospital," concluded the observer.[83]

Boarding a bus or a train did not ensure passenger safety. Miss Berth, of Nancy, explained how she passed through a countryside riddled by violence before reaching her destination of Avignon (Vaucluse). Her train departed on June 15. It stopped every quarter of an hour, rolling occasionally at a snail's pace. After a morning of stop-and-go passage, the train pulled into Epinal. From Epinal to Dijon the train moved at express speed, but at 5 pm on the outskirts of Bains-les-Bains, planes bombed the tracks. Passengers disembarked from the train, scattering throughout the forest until the attacks ceased. Soldiers and railroad personnel worked together to repair the badly damaged tracks, and passengers re-boarded the train. After a jerky start, the train regained locomotion, moving swiftly away from Aillevillers (Haute-Saône). Beyond her window Berth could see the town burning, but took reassurance in her train's continued flight beyond the scene of destruction.[84]

Madeline Gohier departed with her family from Franconville, but separated from them in Paris. She planned to join up with them in Tanné (Nièvres). Madeline's remembrances, recorded in 1992, hit upon a frequent survivor theme of, "having caught the 'last train' to leave Paris." She arrived at the Gare de Lyons on June 6, intent on catching a train to Nièvres. Suddenly the air sirens blared. The loudspeaker announced the cancellation of all departures. "I was so distraught that I didn't want to believe it … I ran all the same to my train's departure platform," she excitedly recalled.[85] Luckily Madeline's train was still at the platform. She hurried into one of the cars and the train soon departed: "I don't know but I think it was the last train to leave that day."[86] Like Berth, Madeline witnessed a panorama of destruction from her cautiously moving train. Passing under cover of night through the countryside, her train ran through a station engulfed in flames. "We couldn't tell if the building was on fire or if it was just some straw because it was nighttime, but it was a spectacular sight," she ruefully testified.[87] The next morning Madeline regrouped with her family at Tanné.

---

[82] "Threat to Paris," *The Times*, June 14, 1940, 7.
[83] "Threat to Paris," *The Times*, June 14, 1940, 7.
[84] AN Papers, Jean Vidalenc, Mlle Barth, "Nancy à Avignon: Exode du 14–19 juin."
[85] Madeline Gohier, interview at Franconville, June 1992.
[86] Gohier, interview.   [87] Gohier, interview.

Accounts describing Paris emphasized a certain tranquility: "Many persons have already left the city, but those still here went about their business as usual. There was not the remotest suggestion of panic. People sat on café terraces, chatting and sipping their drinks," according to one observer.[88] But by June 13, a remorseful stillness cloaked the Parisian boulevards. The now sparse population began, "settling down to await events with calm in spite of its anxiety."[89] Prefect of Police, Roger Langeron, ordered all bakeries, food shops, and pharmacies to remain open. As had been the case in Reims, few merchants remained to obey the directive. A British journalist, reporting from Tours and counting himself among the last to leave, commented on Paris' final day of liberty: "I had felt the sinister silences of Strasbourg and Rheims [sic], but this was a nightmare by comparison. Could this really be Paris? There were no newspapers, except one composite sheet, and only guarded announcements on the wireless, to dispel the fear that the city might already be encircled."[90]

Government relocation

The government's retreat continued in stages, temporarily re-settling at Tours and later moving on to Bordeaux. The General Headquarters had long ago moved from Château Vincennes near Paris, to the Varangeau Estate around Briare. Thinking the quarters too small, Weygand transferred his staff to Château du Muguet, located 10 km east of Briare. News reports could not confirm Tours as the government's new seat; however, refugees spoke of it knowingly. Reports hinted to civilian readers that the President of the Republic, Albert Lebrun, and Prime Minister Reynaud had retreated further south. Despite the absence of the top leaders, Tours remained a center of information for the international press and refugees. Communications remained open due to the foresight of the editors of the Parisian dailies and the operators of the Press Wireless, which provided the only information to US newspapers. One report drew a vivid parallel suggesting, "Tours as a substitute for Paris is as if the population of New York had suddenly been added to that of Washington and cramped in the latter city."[91]

On June 16, the wireless services reported that the French Council of Ministers, meeting in Bordeaux, had voted to surrender. Prime

---

[88] Philip, "Packing Made Sinister," 3.
[89] "Struggle for Rheims," *The Times*, June 13, 1940, 6.
[90] "The Flight From the Capital," *The Times*, June 14, 1940, 6.
[91] "Tours is Jammed," *New York Times*, 4.

Minister Reynaud resigned as a consequence of the decision. At the postwar investigations into the causes of France's defeat, Lebrun asked Reynaud why he had resigned. Reynaud responded: "How could I have pursued this policy, I who had concluded the agreement forbidding any separate armistice?" Lebrun, as if not quite understanding the value of honor, blandly replied, "That is true."[92]

Despite the cessation of hostilities, the refugee crisis expanded as the population accelerated its push in a south-westerly direction. Panicked refugees now fled toward the port city of Bordeaux in pursuit of the new government. "Ladies bent on saving themselves and their lapdogs, refugees of all kinds, rich and poor, French and foreigners, civilians and military, turn in a ceaseless maelstrom of cars ranging through Bordeaux," described a British report.[93] On June 19, Minister for Refugees Schuman also resurfaced in Pau (Pyrénées-Atlantiques). He temporarily assumed his post under a new government and under increasingly desperate conditions. By now the Service of Refugees could do little to provide national assistance in the crisis. Instead, Schuman attempted to assess the magnitude of the disaster. He reported that the estimated number of refugees in France had increased to 6 million. These numbers continued to swell as news of the collapse spread and people who had previously sheltered refugees now fled to save their own lives.[94]

When German troops marched down the Champs Elyseé on June 14, they entered an eerily vacant city. Berlin reported that the swastika flag, planted on the Arc de Triomphe on the first day of the Occupation, had already been removed. German occupying troops showed tolerance for Parisian displays of the tricolor. By June 19, shops in Montmartre and the district between Boulevard des Italiens and the Panthéon had reopened. Even the Galleries Lafayettes, the grand department store preferred by the Parisian bourgeoisie, had reopened its doors. No French cabinet official remained to meet the German commander, General von Studnitz; but, as a disapproving British report noted, US Ambassador Bullitt, "is apparently subject to no restraint, for he has twice called on Lieutenant General Bogislav von Studnitz."[95] *The Times* published accounts of French prisoners of war being paraded through Paris and crying out upon viewing the American flag outside the US embassy: "Why in hell didn't you help us out?"[96] Bullitt's efforts and

---

[92] Reynaud, *Thick of the Fight*, 554.
[93] "Refugees Crowding into Bordeaux," *The Times*, June 20, 1940, 6.
[94] "6,000,000 Refugees Adrift in France," *The Times*, June 19, 1940, 4.
[95] "Semblance of Life," *The Times*, June 19, 1940, 4.
[96] "Semblance of Life," *The Times*, June 19, 1940, 4.

the Allied landing in Normandy to launch the liberation of France and Europe four years later would never entirely erase the memory and feeling of abandonment felt by French troops at their moment of bitter defeat in June 1940.

Conclusion

Parisians, like the Rémois of the Marne, faced the invasion of their city without much guidance or support from municipal or national authorities. Reynaud's postwar testimony reveals that, as the Germans descended upon Paris, his focus was military resistance, not civilian retreat. However, Reynaud also wished to spare Paris a bloody fight, a goal seemingly at odds with his desire for resistance. The decision to declare Paris "open," an act Reynaud attributed to Weygand, weakened the argument for ordering a civilian evacuation. Undoubtedly, Reynaud followed the advice of Minister of the Interior Mandel, who had lobbied hard to evacuate the government. Mandel instructed elected municipal representatives to join the national government in retreat, recommending that the City Council leave behind a few representatives to negotiate with the Germans. He also stressed that the civilian population of Paris should stay in place. By the time the evacuation was ordered on June 13, Parisians had already fled.

Had military and cabinet ministers taken civilian evacuations more seriously, the government might also have mitigated the dangers that civilians encountered on the open roads. The government certainly could have taken better control of road and rail congestion had it actively organized civilians to leave Paris at the outbreak of the attack in May. In the end, the lack of preparation proved detrimental to all civilians. The failure to adequately prepare for invasion lay in part with the government, in part with the military, but also importantly with the press. Without information, and in the absence of debate, civilians made decisions in the dark. By failing to report on the French government's poor emergency management performance, the press played a significant role in the collapse of home front security.

What feasible alternative policies might the French have pursued to avoid a mass exodus from Paris? One alternative would have been to arm the Parisian populace. The lack of preparation for a civilian assisted defense of Paris suggests that Parisians would not have seen the same success as the residents of Leningrad, Stalingrad, and London in resisting the German advance. Would the eruption of street by street combat in Paris have produced anything short of a massacre in 1940? The loss of civilian life in both Soviet cities forces historians to reconsider definitions of "success." While approximately 200,000 French men and women perished during the battle of France and in the exodus, resistance in the Soviet Union caused hundreds of thousands of civilian casualties. If saving lives defines "success," then perhaps flight was the best option. However, the answer is complicated. If Parisians had stayed in Paris and surrendered, it is possible that fewer civilians would have lost their lives under the heavy fire from German and Italian planes that rained down mercilessly upon the fleeing masses.

Rather than conclude that Mandel, Reynaud, and Weygand shared a callous disregard for civilian security, one might adopt a more historically contextualized interpretation. French officials simply did not anticipate the impact that changes in warfare would have upon the civilian population. Memoirs and testimonies of French leaders such as Reynaud, Weygand, Queuille, and Mandel reveal that they did not share a common understanding about the magnitude of the unfolding humanitarian crisis. In contrast, US Ambassador Bullitt, in early May, interpreted the exodus as a harbinger of worse events to come and as a tragedy in its own right. He spent all his political capital with Roosevelt in a desperate effort to push the United States to widen its commitment to send France humanitarian aid. Unfortunately, Weygand and Reynaud did not see as sharply as did Bullitt the centrality of the civilian security component in the invasion crisis. Weygand arrived very late at a decision to evacuate Parisian schoolchildren under the age of sixteen. Not until June 9, two days after Parisian school officials initiated their own plans to evacuate schoolchildren, did Weygand approach Reynaud about making the order "official." Why did Weygand wait a week after German bombers had entered Parisian airspace to approve the evacuation of schoolchildren? He did not plan to defend Paris, but still believed that the Germans would bomb the city "mercilessly," despite the fact that the Germans had dropped propaganda leaflets from planes stating that if France surrendered, the Germans would discontinue hostilities. Weygand's intelligence officers must have considered the Germans insincere in their pledge; French civilians did too.

As the next chapter recounts, one of the few national leaders who did acknowledge the centrality of the exodus within the larger events of defeat was Marshal Philippe Pétain. Admittedly, he did so to advance his desire to sign the Armistice and end hostilities with Germany.

4   Civilian survival on the open road

German exile writer and exodus refugee, Lion Feuchtwanger, opened his 1944 novel, *Simone* with a chapter titled "The Refugees." Written in California, after Feuchtwanger's escape from France's Free Zone in the autumn of 1940, *Simone* presented international readers with one of the first wartime literary interpretations of the exodus. Describing the arrival of the French refugees in her hometown of Saint-Martin in Bourgogne, the novel's heroine, Simone Planchard, a fifteen-year-old French girl, comprehends her country's defeat as she observes the flow of refugees: "Resigned, in awkward discomfort, they [the refugees] all squatted in the sultry heat where they had stopped, old and young, men and women, soldiers and civilians, wounded and whole, in sweating, hopeless stupor."[1] Feuchtwanger's description of the road refugees, painted by his fictional heroine, Simone, memorialized the destitution that the invasion had wrought on France's civilian population, enshrining for the postwar era, the image of the refugee among the war's most vulnerable victims. Indeed, refugees of all classes and regional backgrounds met and became lost in a random reconfiguration of family and nation. In the context of this disorder, refugees desired family reunification most, and soon demanded it as their right. The language of a politics of civilian protection, which at the outset of hostilities had articulated the "right" to evacuation and access to bomb shelters, now broadened to include the demand for family reunification.[2] As refugees confronted the growing realization that flight exposed them to new dangers, they engaged in acts of self-representation, resignation, compassion, and camaraderie, as well as selfishness in order to meet the challenges of survival.

Eye-witness accounts, wartime and postwar novels, and letters written to officials capture the dynamics of survival on the road during

---

[1] Feuchtwanger, *Simone*, 5.
[2] Torrie suggests that France and Germany considered evacuations a "privilege not a right." Torrie, *"For Their Own Good,"* 2. I believe the French saw evacuations as a last resort, to be planned for, but avoided wherever possible.

the weeks before refugees settled in host communities. The sources compiled here present common themes generated by mass displacement expressed at the time of the crisis and in the postwar period. Individual testimonials and memoirs evidence an evolving collective conscious-ness about the exodus, contrasted occasionally by singularities of expe-rience and isolated counter-currents to dominant collective memory. While no unified and seamless narrative of the exodus can capture the experience of millions of homeless refugees, the identification of domi-nant and alternative exodus story lines helps us to distinguish better how class, gender, and race did differentiate refugee survival strate-gies. The flight narratives of the Parisian teenager, Jackie Golter, and the Rémois businessman, René Carré, continue to help establish two detailed accounts of key phases of the displacement crisis. They provide two exodus accounts against which to compare a variety of recorded refugee experiences.

The recollections of Golter and Carré illustrate the ways civilians transitioned from the threatened space of home to the unanticipated dangers of the road. Their narratives sketch out a range of civilian anxi-eties about physical harm, slippage from civilization into a world of brutality, and elusive security. Carré's memoir is distinguished from Golter's by time and position. Writing in 1940, immediately following the defeat, Carré's motivation in recording his experiences was to cast blame for the exodus. A prominent Catholic and businessman, who managed a large staff and advised the owner of Pommery champagne house, Carré resented orders to leave Reims, but encouraged his family to comply. His typewritten, unpublished memoir blasted the French authorities and fleeing refugees, implicating both in France's fall. Carré records a story of French ineptitude, contrasted against German capability, a dominant thesis in refugee narratives. His memoir is fur-ther distinguishable from Golter's in that Carré's chronicles the war's destruction of private property.

Golter's narrative, in contrast, recounts the tale of the destruction of a Parisian Jewish family and the pleasures of an adolescent's daily rou-tines. Golter was a young girl studying for her high school Baccalaureate in 1940, with hopes of becoming a teacher. Her family, Russian Jewish immigrants who had fled to France in the 1920s, had mostly assimilated into French secular society. Golter told her story in 1992, a retired, divorced, middle-school teacher, who shared her archived experiences of World War II including her rationing cards and identification papers. Her memory of the exodus remained strong and well documented, in part owing to her love of France and history, but also as a consequence of her family's particular experience of racial persecution. Under the

Occupation, the Gestapo arrested Golter's father, later deporting him to Auschwitz where he died. For Golter, the exodus marked the end of life in one kind of asylum-offering France and the beginning of life in a partitioned, racially segregated country that forced her and her family members to reconsider their own individual and collective identities.[3]

Golter's story differs from Carré's in another significant way: Golter offers the perspective of refugee women. She articulates themes that include women's particular fears, challenges, and anxieties over their sexual vulnerability on the road. Much of contemporary knowledge about France under the German Occupation comes from works written during the period of "great obsession," as Henri Rousso has identified the postwar years of 1975–1994.[4] During these years, the writing of French history and fiction attempted to "re-create the 'truth' of the past."[5] Historians, novelists, and filmmakers excavated documents, recorded eye-witness accounts, and published previously suppressed information to draw a clearer picture of who was responsible for France's military defeat, for Franco-German collaboration, and the internment and deportation of European Jews. Postwar fiction and history attempted to "reconstruct an absence," according to William VanderWolk.[6] Golter's account enters into this work of reconstructed absent narratives, which not only shed light on the Occupation, but allow us to create a link between the effects of the displacement crisis and the emergence of policies that eroded French national solidarity and facilitated the geographic and political fragmentation of the nation.

Golter and Carré's narratives emphasize the vast differences in the "truth" about the French defeat and yet share important similarities, which help to identify points of commonality of a shared national past. Both narrators assume a wide distance between themselves as agents of history, and the mass of refugees whom both describe as victims of history. Both Golter and Carré claim higher reasoning skills as the factor that distinguished them from the "hysterical" crowd. Carré defines

[3] Selections of Jackie Golter's testimony first appeared in Nicole Ann Dombrowski, "Surviving the German Invasion of France: Women's Stories of the Exodus of 1940," in Nicole Ann Dombrowski (ed.), *Women and War in the Twentieth Century: Enlisted with or without Consent* (New York: Garland Publishing, 1999 (Routledge, 2004)), 116–135.

[4] Henri Rousso, *Le syndrome de Vichy: 1944–198...* (Paris: Seuil, 1987) in William VanderWolk, "Whose Memory is This?: Patrick Modiano's Historical Method," in Martine Guyot-Bender and William VanderWolk (eds.), *Paradigms of Memory: The Occupation and Other Hi/stories in the Novels of Patrick Modiano* (New York: Peter Lang, 1998), 60.

[5] VanderWolk, "Whose Memory is This?," 61.

[6] VanderWolk, "Whose Memory is This?," 60.

rationality as the determination to remain level-headed and committed to routine in the face of wartime chaos. Golter views her rationality as having forced her to accept the invasion as dangerous and threatening. Although she and her family joined the exodus, Golter carefully indicated how she and her mother made important, life-saving choices to depart from the masses. Because Golter retold her tale nearly fifty years after her experience, her narrative reconstructs the experiences of a teenager. She juxtaposes memories of tragedy and remembered fear, such as the application of mustard to her body to discourage potential rapists, against lush descriptions of pleasurable moments of reverie, as when during heavy air bombardment she lay in a ditch eating strawberries. As a teenager during the exodus, its origins strike Golter as less interesting than its consequences. For Golter and her family, the war's chief tragedy was not the exodus, but the Occupation.

For Carré, the exodus was the original sin, the precursor to the Occupation. He assigns responsibility for the disaster; but in doing so, removes responsibility from himself. He identifies his "heroic actions," as "rational" acts of resistance to *French* incompetence. Carré's critique echoes the criticisms of many wartime writers. When Lion Feuchtwanger sat in an internment camp in Les Milles (Var) on the eve of the exodus, he encountered the "devil in France." This devil was responsible for the internment of well-credentialed, anti-fascist refugees. This devil hastened France's defeat. As Feuchtwanger explained in his 1940 escape narrative, *The Devil in France*:

I do not think that the Devil with whom we had to deal in France of 1940 was a particularly truculent devil who enjoyed practical jokes of a sadistic nature. I am inclined to think that he was the Devil of Untidiness, of Unthoughtfulness, of Sloth in good-will, of Convention, of Routine, the very Devil to whom the French have given the motto, "je m'en fous" – "I don't give a damn.[7]

For the average French refugee families, the worst "devil" was the involuntary separations that occurred in the chaos and terror of flight. Nearly every exodus narrative recorded at the time or in the postwar era mentions how family separations eroded the nation's resolve to continue the fight. Voluntary separations, by contrast, occurred in two controlled phases. First, women, children, and the elderly separated from fathers and husbands. Under the strain of the journey, many elderly people chose to end their evacuation, hoping to reunite with their families at some unknown place and time. Involuntary separations, usually

---

[7] Lion Feuchtwanger, *The Devil in France: My Encounter with Him in the Summer of 1940* (New York: Viking Press, 1941), 40.

of children from mothers or guardians, occurred when aircraft fired on refugees, forcing them to scatter into shelter and roadside ditches.

Lesser separations occurred even prior to departure. Choices involving selecting which items to carry on the road or to leave behind generated anxieties as departing civilians chose between survival necessities and cherished mementoes. Surveying her trove of possessions, Golter labored with her emotions to prepare her departure. "How does one determine what is the most precious possession in life?" she pondered retrospectively. Golter chose a book, *La Joie des Moeurs*, and, wisely, a new pair of boots. Preoccupied by more practical concerns, her mother packed a suitcase with kitchen utensils. The Golter men and women promised to reunite in the cathedral city of Chartres, made emotional declarations of love and bid each other farewell. Three generations of women then began the 80-km hike to Chartres. Beyond the "gates of Paris," they took notice of earlier refugees' abandoned possessions and came upon a wheelbarrow: "We picked it up and pushed the thing."[8] Happy to have found some assistance in carrying their supplies, the women pressed forward.

Farm families defined "valuables" differently than urban families and often had the capacity to move more cargo. Owning large wagons, they often attempted to save everything, including livestock. Refugees from rural France arrived on the outskirts of Paris accompanied by goats, cattle, and ewes. One family, featured in a photo printed in *France Magazine*'s issue of May 28, 1940, transported a large uncovered wagon, trailed by a child's chariot, a cow, and a goat shepherded by seven children. In the wagon, the family had packed a dresser, two louvered doors, a hen cage, a four-poster bed frame, a rack of clothes with winter coats, and framed pictures, all topped with hay. In the children's chariot the family had rolled up a mattress, packed several pillows, and stashed more canvas bags and clothes.[9] Unsightly in urban eyes, rural family possessions could ease the burdens of displacement. Initially, Parisians viewed refugees' plight with a kind of distant empathy, but by June the pillars of their own civilized, protected existence crumbled. The exodus turned rapidly from an image of pioneers breaking frontier ground, to a parade of urban sophisticates struggling to trade in their high fashion for more durable hiking apparel.

---

[8] Golter interview.

[9] Gerard Giuliano, Jacques Lambert, and Valerie Rostowsky, *Les Ardennais dans la Tourmente: De la mobilisation à l'évacuation* (Charleville-Mezieres: Editions Terres Ardennaises, 1990), 308. *Les Ardennais* assembles an excellent collection of personal testimonials, newspaper clippings, family photos, and government documents.

Prioritizing valuables entered into the process of recognizing the reality of social breakdown and the disintegration of "private life."[10] Nine-year-old Janine Flanet lived with her sister and parents in an apartment building in Paris. She confessed that her memories of her family's departure held no ominous forebodings of doom. Rather, fifty years later, Flanet still delighted in the memory of an adventure. "My mother packed everything in the kitchen," remembered Janine.[11] "We couldn't pack another thing into the car, I experienced all that as though we were going on a grand camping trip, really" (Figure 1).[12] Despite leaving with a car, the vehicle did not long remain useful. Once the car ran out of gas a few kilometers outside Paris, the family continued their journey on foot, but only after pushing the car for several kilometers. Flanet witnessed others' discarded possessions and experienced losses of her own. Her most vivid and sad memory pertained to an abandoned puppy: "We saw the puppy sitting among a pile of abandoned objects ... We carried it along to the next village (Eva Maron), but then, when we put it down, the puppy ran away all alone in the direction from which we had come."[13] Another item Flanet lamented losing was her beloved gas mask. As a schoolgirl, Flanet had carried the gas mask to and from school daily. Her mother frequently reminded her daughters: "Don't forget your gasmasks."[14] Flanet remembered experiencing the loss with as great a sense of regret as if it were a favored toy. Perhaps unconsciously the mask had also come to represent a reliable protection to a child bewildered by the uncertainty of war.

Children's sense of adventure and lack of understanding of war's consequences could be used to adults' advantage. Madame Thienot, who had escaped from Reims, recalled how her father rescued the family fortune from German capture by capitalizing on his nephew's sense of play. An aged man, Thienot's father brought his entire fortune in cash and various objects with him. Having reached his first destination, an aunt's home on the Atlantic coast, the old gentleman dug a hole in the garden. Placing the money and other treasures inside, he covered the hole and returned to the house. According to Thienot, the

---

[10] Michelle Perrot (ed.), *A History of Private Life: From the Fires of Revolution to the Great War*, trans. Arthur Goldhammer (Cambridge, MA: Belknap Press, 1990), 671. Perrot argues that, "the declaration of war in 1914 abruptly reminded everyone of the primacy of the public and the limits of private life"; but alludes to the opportunities created by World War I for new interwar re-entrenchment into the private sphere.

[11] Janine (née Flanet) De Col, interviewed by the author in Paris, June 1992.

[12] Janine (née Flanet) De Col, interview.

[13] Janine (née Flanet) De Col, interview.

[14] Janine (née Flanet) De Col, interview.

Figure 1. Janine Flanet, Paris 1942 (reproduced with the permission of Olivier De Col).

Germans arrived within hours and occupied the grounds. Unwilling to completely disturb the family, the soldiers set up camp in the backyard. Watching anxiously from his window, the father noticed a German soldier begin to dig a small hole around the tree for his personal relief. Thienot described the hysterical state of her father who insisted that the family continue their flight, after first rescuing the treasure. His solution pivoted on the help of his small nephew, whom he instructed to take a pail and shovel and play about in the yard. The boy's uncle told him that, while the soldiers looked elsewhere, he should dig up the treasure near the tree and bring it immediately to the house. Excited by the mission, the young boy set off to play. He successfully exhumed the fortune, returning it to the anxious old man.[15]

On the surface, Thienot's story is an amusing tale of the adventures of an old man and a young boy. However, children's heroism became a dominant theme in refugee narratives and postwar French fiction. In the popular 1950's children's book, *Jerry dans l'ombre*, a boy, Tom, and three other children are separated from their mother who becomes ill during the exodus. Tom must learn to drive the car.[16] The story emphasizes the children's resourcefulness and the adventure that characterized their struggle to feed themselves, reunite with their mother, and escape death or capture. For a period devoid of adult heroes, French children became the only eligible heroes of the recent French past and the near future.

Interviewed in her Manhattan apartment in 1994, Madame Fanny Racine, also a child of Russian Jewish immigrants, described how she, her mother, and her sister smuggled family heirlooms out of Paris and eventually under the noses of French border guards in Marseilles. A family shaped by the upheavals of twentieth-century Europe, the Racines had honed their escape strategies: "The girls removed each stone from our family jewels and wrapped them in individual ribbons. We then sewed the ribbons on to our garments as buttons." In this way the family managed to salvage part of their wealth and eventually finance the purchase of ocean liner tickets to the United States.[17] Like the Thienots and Carrès, the Racines enjoyed a higher economic status than the families of Golter and Flanet. Bourgeois families relied upon their wealth to create a wider range of survival and escape options. However, prewar economic advantages diminished as the conflict endured, especially when, as for the Racines, Golters, and Flanets, Jewish identity entered into the survival equation.

Madeline Gohier, like Jackie Golter, shared her memories of the exodus at the women's shared Franconville home in 1992. Madeline had just started student-teaching in 1940 in the Parisian suburbs. Daily, her family witnessed processions of refugees marching on the national

15 Interview with Mme Thienot.
16 Madeline H. Giraud, *Jerry dans l'ombre* (Paris: La Bibliothèque Suzette, 1954).
17 Fannie Racine and Nadine Gill, interviewed by author, New York, April 1994.

highway that passed through Franconville. Madeline grew accustomed to seeing, "lots of automobiles pass by, many wrapped with mattresses roped to the roofs to shield against machine gun bullets."[18] But in June, Madeline's family employed the same method of protection for their car, joining the eclectic parade of mattresses. The family departed to a summer home in Tanné, while Madeline took temporary refuge in Paris until she passed her Baccalaureate.

Golter, in contrast, remained with part of her family throughout June 1940. However, after only a day on foot and still far from Chartres, Golter's grandmother decided she could walk no further. She ended her flight from Bolsheviks and fascists, taking a seat along the road and watching the exodus. Unwilling to completely abandon the grandmother to circumstances, Golter and her mother petitioned fellow refugees traveling in cars. After many rejections, the family found a willing driver. The women helped the grandmother into the car and planned a rendezvous for dusk at a hotel near the Chartres train station. Reflecting upon their naive optimism, Golter concluded, "We had no sense of reality."[19] The family, who were among the more fortunate, would not reunite until after the signing of the Armistice.

Similarly, Janine and Hélène Flanet recalled their family's reluctance to abandon a car that had run out of gas, but "had everything packed into it, including Grandma."[20] The sisters laughed from a distance of time and place. However, this family, too, eventually separated from their grandmother. Often grandparents pre-empted fate. Madeline Gohier's grandparents remained behind in Tanné arguing that, "the elderly risked less than the youth."[21]

Not all elderly people *chose* to stay behind. Renaud Poirier, son of the chief chemist of Pommery, told a story that reveals a different method of setting priorities.[22] Arriving halfway between Reims and his destination, Biarritz, where he would join his family and the marquis de Polignac, Poirier, telephoned the marquis. The marquis instructed Poirier to return to Reims to retrieve a forgotten ivory cigarette case from Japanese Emperor Hirohito. Following orders, Poirier turned back, meeting the advancing German troops on the way. The Germans could not be bothered to stop him. Upon his return to deserted Reims, Poirier retrieved the irreplaceable trinket. He also took the opportunity to salvage some other possessions and rescue the family's elderly

---

[18] Madeline Gohier, interviewed by author, Franconville, June 23, 1992.
[19] Gohier interview.
[20] Janine (née Flanet) De Col and Hélène Flanet interview.
[21] Gohier quoting her grandmother.
[22] Renaud Poirier entrusted the author with René Carré's journal.

schoolmistress, who had mistakenly been left behind. After wedging everything, including Chinese porcelain, into the car, Poirier judged that only enough space remained for either the family dog or the school-mistress. He remembered, without much regret, that he chose to take the dog and leave the spinster behind once again.[23]

"Voluntary separations" had a veneer of cool-headedness, but surely created stress and anxiety. "Involuntary" or "accidental" separations, usually involving loss of a child, shattered families, and intensified the sense of collective tragedy weighing heavily upon the hearts of fellow travelers. The entanglement of children in the chaos and violence of war became enshrined in national memory, symbolized by the experi-ence of women hopelessly searching for lost children or trying to find shelter for their families.

In his personal memoir, Jean Gaultier, a French soldier who observed civilian disintegration on the road, remembered a distraught grand-mother who had lost her daughter and grandchild: "Have you seen a woman with a baby walk by this way" the grandmother asked Gaultier. He observed, "We had seen so many that it had become impossible for us to distinguish one unfortunate woman with a baby bottle in her hand from another."[24]

In a compelling, fictionalized memoir published in 1943, Anne Jacques rued, "Oh how I witnessed the loss of children!"[25] Jacques encountered one mother who desperately attempted to return home, because, dur-ing a bombing attack that destroyed all the houses on the street, she had managed to save five of her six children, but had forgotten her baby sleeping in its cradle. "She could not stop from declaring her guilt," wrote Jacques. Haunted by the maddening image of a baby left alone to die, the mother could not muster the mental strength to continue the exodus with her five surviving children.[26] The fiction did not exaggerate the lived tragedies. Rather, wartime authors attempted to commemor-ate, offer sympathy, and record for posterity the crimes suffered by the French people. The nation's loss found its most riveting symbol in the image of a home collapsed atop the cradle of an abandoned newborn baby. Not surprisingly, as Miranda Pollard's work has shown, the soon-to-be authoritarian regime appropriated the displacement of French families to reorganize enthusiasm for French natalist-familialism under

---

[23] Renaud Poirier, interviewed by author in Reims, February 1992.
[24] AN 72/AJ/623, Papers of Jean Vidalenc: Jean Gaultier, "Souvenirs personnels sur mai–juin 1940: Extraits de mon journal de route." 126th RI, unpublished manuscript.
[25] Anne Jacques, *Pitié pour les hommes* (Paris: Éditions Seuil, 1943), 44–45.
[26] Jacques, *Pitié pour les hommes*, 44–45.

the Vichy regime.[27] In marshaling the German assault on French civilians to bolster the cause of anti-feminist conceptions of family and tradition, Vichy missed an opportunity to apply the emerging language and laws of human rights and war crimes to describe and decry Germany's violation of the Geneva Conventions.

For many refugees, departing from the dead proved as emotionally challenging as separating from the living. Scouts sent out by A. Pioger, a regimental commander in Picardé, brought him a person they believed to be an enemy parachutist disguised as a woman. In fact, the person was a woman, dressed in men's clogs. She seemed to them deranged, repeating, "I must find my daughter! She must attend the burial of her father!"[28] Pioger could never decide whether the woman's husband had indeed just died, or if the trauma of the evacuation had reawakened previously experienced horrors. When the soldiers attempted to board the woman onto a truck of elderly refugees, she escaped into the forest. Such images and memories of destroyed families traumatized many French civilians and served to ready them not only for military capitulation, but for deployment of traditionalist paradigms for family reconstruction.[29]

Food and shelter: low in supply, high in price

Competition for food and water coincided with struggles to secure shelter, find gasoline, and replace lost or stolen supplies such as blankets, cooking utensils, and clothing. Hunger began to set in early in the upheaval. Food rationing had been relatively stringent since early spring with newspapers publishing weekly dietary restrictions. For example, for the week of March 12, 1940 eliminations included:

Tuesday – no meat, no alcohol including an aperitif, no pastry, no chocolate, no candies, no cookies; Wednesday – no pastries, no chocolate, no candies, no cookies; Friday – no meat, no lunch meat or sausages, no tripe, no pastries, no chocolate, no candies, no cookies; Saturday – no alcohol, no aperitif; Sunday – no restrictions.[30]

In the south, mayors and prefects began to supply refugees' basic needs. However, government directives to evacuees had not anticipated

---

[27] Miranda Pollard, *Reign of Virtue*, 40.
[28] AN 72/AJ/623, papers of Jean Vidalenc, Picardé file, A. Pioger, Director of Supplementary Supplies, Le Mans, ex-commandant of 361ème area, essential supplies: RG 161.
[29] Pollard, *Reign of Virtue*, 31.
[30] "Calendrier des restrictions," *La Victoire*, March 12, 1940, 2.

the duration of the crisis, leaving refugees undersupplied with regard to food. In May, Marchandeau had ordered Rémois to pack food for a day and a half, but as the exodus endured, provisions carried from home shrank. Profiteering proliferated. Reynaud issued orders to merchants to avoid price inflation, but not everyone complied. Peasants felt squeezed by the arrival of urbanites who, in many cases, demanded handouts or attempted to trade in what peasants deemed worthless: currency. Refugees created a black market among themselves, especially in fuel and water. Organizations such as the Red Cross and the Nationalsozialistische Volkswohlfahrt (NSV), trailed invading German troops establishing soup kitchens along the route. In mid-June, the NSV claimed to have 283 volunteers servicing the exodus.[31] Flanet remembered how efficiently the Germans responded to the crisis: "The Germans made soup for all the people on the road who didn't have anything. You had all these people on the road to Orléans, at the relief center, which was a gymnasium near the market of Orléans. They [the Germans] seemed full of good intentions."[32] Flanet also indicated that after feeding the refugees, the Germans encouraged people to return to their homes.

Refugees' memories fixed upon eating or finding food as scarcity spread. In 1991, Claudine Breton, daughter of a Parisian interior designer, explained how she and her parents managed to feed their family on their flight from Paris. After several days on the road the family had exhausted their provisions. Tired and hungry, they searched for shelter in order to sleep and avoid thinking about hunger. Unable to locate any hotel vacancies or empty barns, the family settled in a field with other refugees. Miraculously, in the small area the family had selected to make camp, Breton discovered an immense, abandoned pot of honey and a few crusts of bread. "It served as our food for the next two days," she fondly recalled.[33] Similarly, one of Golter's extraordinary memories involved ripe strawberries. On the way to Chartres, she and her mother survived an aerial bombing of civilians: "There were no military personnel among us, absolutely nothing threatening, but they [the Germans] didn't risk anything, massacring these people on the road ... for me that experience ... typified the 'unreality' of the period."[34] Golter jumped into a roadside ditch to secure protection, and despite, or because, of the horrors and violence surrounding her, she

[31] Torrie, *"For Their Own Good,"* 41.
[32] Janine (née Flanet) De Col interview.
[33] Claudine Breton, interview with author, Barbenteune, December, 1991.
[34] Golter interview.

began consuming a basket of strawberries she had been rationing out to herself. She remembered, "I just ate the strawberries," one after the other she motioned successively with her hands, "while the planes fired. I ate strawberries ... you see how extraordinary it was!"[35]

Fantastic memories of finding food come from witnesses who were still children or teenagers. Adults, by contrast, experienced the challenge of feeding their families with great anxiety. Their memories of exodus deprivations fold into remembering the shortages and rationing that persisted throughout the Occupation and beyond. Mothers especially suffered, offering food first to children. The Flanet women recalled their mother's dramatic weight loss as a check to their happier memories of exodus adventure: "Mama, who was a strong, large woman when we left weighed about 80 kilos. She lost about 30 kilos during the exodus ... boy she was skinny."[36] Madame Thienot recalled that her first child, born shortly after her exodus from Reims, weighed less than all her subsequent children. She linked weight loss to the disappearance of entire categories of food from the national diet. Her family, for example, did not see or eat an orange again until after 1944. Occupation literature lionized the altruistic refugee mother. In *Pity for Humanity*, Anne Jacques described refugee mothers: "Famished, they watch their children eat without taking even a crumb. Thirsty, they sipped from the glass where only a drop remained – everything was for their children."[37]

By contrast, refugees of some financial means could still buy meals in restaurants throughout much of the crisis. Léon Werth, celebrated friend of Saint-Exupéry, noted the price paid for such disappearing luxuries. Werth recalled: "already we began feeling the price of respite, of refuge, of hospitality. These people were no mercy givers, no inn keepers ... out of decency they *only* made us pay double the normal price of a regular meal."[38]

Disputes proliferated about the relationship between price gouging and anti-patriotic politics. One fictionalized memoir, authored by Madame Tellier, placed food at the center of a debate about patriotic commerce. Tellier owned a small fruit and vegetable store. She debates with herself and her neighbor whether she should close her store, give her peaches away to passing refugees, and join the exodus; or, do as her neighbor advocates – stay and sell her wares to the Germans. Her inclination to stay stems mostly from the fact that her son is serving in

---

[35] Golter interview.   [36] Janine and Hélène Flanet interview.
[37] A. Jacques, *Pitié pour les hommes*, 39.
[38] Léon Werth, *33 jours* (Paris: Viviane Hamy, 1992), 15.

the army. She believes that by staying in her village, her son will know where to find her after the war. However, she worries that her failure to depart will be interpreted as an expression of welcome to the invading Germans. Her neighbor encourages Tellier to *stay* in town and sell her peaches at a favorable price: "The Germans will arrive in this heat and be thirsty, they'll give you a good price for your peaches, believe me!"[39] Eventually, Tellier makes the "right" choice. She closes up shop, gives away her peaches to refugees, and joins the mass of compatriots. The story speaks loudly: give away your wares to compatriots even at an economic loss. Profiteering is unpatriotic.

Refugees' search for shelter, perhaps even more than their search for food, underscores the disruption visited upon the daily rituals of comfortable European domesticity. Similar to the vacancies left in Alsace and Lorraine, towns located along the national routes from Reims to Paris to Orléans lay vacant. By day, refugees continued their southerly push, but by night many searched for cover in abandoned homes. After leaving the grandmother in Chartres, Golter and her mother joined the masses crossing the River Loire, but tired of wrestling with the crowd they decided to scout for a place to sleep and found an abandoned house. Golter marveled: "What was extraordinary were all these abandoned houses. A house where there was life one hour, and suddenly, up! There was nothing."[40] A table stood with plates and cups filled to various levels with coffee. The teenager felt as though cadavers lurked in adjacent rooms. The strangeness of the house frightened them so much that they decided that they preferred to sleep under the open sky next to people rather than under a roof with ghosts. Exiting the house, the two happened upon a nurse who was a major in the army. On the road, she had encountered a lost boy of thirteen with whom she was now traveling. Encouraged by the courage of the nurse, and perhaps taking comfort in numbers, the group re-entered the house and decided to set up camp for the night.

The companionship of the nurse and the boy soothed some of Golter's fears, but she remembered this night with lingering pain. All night they heard shouts from the road: "The Germans are coming! They are massacring everyone. Run! Run!" With hindsight, Golter, like many historians, judged that these cries may well have been the work of German agents, planted in the crowd to stir up panic. The cries may have been exaggerated rumors, but Golter and her companions sensed their place in the midst of an attack. Without weapons,

[39] AN 72/AJ/623, Vidalenc papers, Mme Tellier, "Mika," unpublished manuscript.
[40] Golter interview.

the women took unusual measures to prepare to greet the Germans. Fearing they would be raped, the nurse found some Dijon mustard in the kitchen and instructed the women to rub the mustard on their bodies. As Golter explained, the mustard would burn the Germans "as they attempted their rape."[41]

Sexual violence against women by soldiers had transpired in every invasion of World War I according to Alan Kramer.[42] Rape and forced prostitution, argues Tammy Proctor, frequently occurred between 1914 and 1918 in civilian centers near military training camps and sights of invasion and retreat. Yet, in the region of northern France along the Belgian border especially, social stigma surrounded rape, dishonoring a woman and her family. This stigma created, according to Proctor, "complication of where to report such crimes," which, "led to great historical silences on the issue."[43] Despite post-World War I "official" silences surrounding rape, "unofficial" consciousness of civilian women's sexual victimization during World War I wafted through women's communities in the interwar period producing cautionary tales, and home-made anti-rape remedies. Susan Grayzel has found that quiet practices surrounding abortion or placement of unwanted "children of the enemy," were implemented by French women during and after World War I and commemorated in 1920's pulp fiction.[44] The difference between World War I and the invasion of 1940 with regard to sexual violence was that many women of the earlier conflict remained within the structure of home and community. In 1940, displacement exacerbated the vulnerability of women refugees, and further complicated their ability to seek protection within the family structure or report crimes to local police. As we will see, an added complication in 1940 was that French women found themselves embedded within the retreat of one army and the advance of another.

In Golter's memory, the night that she passed in uncertain shelter, melded into the following day's encounter with troops, a fulfillment of her greatest fear. After telling the "mustard segment" of her story, Golter confessed: "We stayed there, but we were really very afraid, you know, very afraid ... the fear was overwhelming." And yet the fear became greater when the women heard soldiers arriving. "Suddenly, we heard their boots. They sounded like ocean liners. We thought we

---

[41] Golter interview.
[42] Horne and Kramer, *German Atrocities, 1914*, 74–76, cited in Proctor, *Civilians in a World at War, 1914–1918*, 125.
[43] Proctor, *Civilians in a World at War, 1914–1918*, 125–126.
[44] Grayzel, *Women's Identities at War*, 60–63, cited in Proctor, *Civilians in a World at War, 1914–1918*, 126.

were lost," she whispered, but "The soldiers were French." "They were retreating," she smiled.[45]

Civilians meet soldiers on the road

On June 17, the prefect of the Eure-et-Loire and future resistance hero, Jean Moulin, waited in his office in Chartres. At 3 am he heard the arrival of tanks and expected Germans, but instead observed fleeing French regiments. At 6 am he saw a regiment of Sénégalais soldiers pass through, seemingly willing to continue the fight rather than be taken prisoner. But by 7 am, a motorcade of German soldiers arrived.[46] The officer assured Moulin that the Germans would respect civilians.

By mid-June, the French military retreat had become a catastrophe as large contingents of soldiers mixed with civilians. The terrible irony for civilians was that they had fled their homes to avoid combat, but in flight their exposure to violence increased as they became engulfed by military units. The illusion of safety on the southern shore of the River Loire faded fast. On Saturday June 15 and Sunday June 16 the Luftwaffe bombed a stream of refugees at La Ferté-Saint-Aubin and claimed ninety-eight dead and a number of wounded.[47] Perhaps the Luftwaffe had not received the order to respect civilians as promised to Moulin.

Personal encounters on the road between fleeing civilians and French or German troops introduced more complex challenges for women than for men. Refugee memories and military reports suggest that the collapse of social and governmental structures were accompanied on the road by the collapse of cultural markers and assumptions that had policed interactions between the two sexes during peacetime. The temporary suspension of these normative rules of male–female conduct proved to be liberating for some refugee women and perilous for others.

Nearly all narrative accounts of civilian–military encounters on the road confirm that the Loire valley served as a geographic convergence point for the two groups. The French hoped that the River Loire would offer a "second front," behind which French troops might regroup to wage a successful resistance. Instead, the Loire set the scene for the collapse of both the military effort and the thinly veiled wall that separated civilians from soldiers. Flanet's experience at the Loire was her first encounter with soldiers. Beyond Orléans, the family, with the rest

---

[45] Golter interview.
[46] Miquel, L'exode 10 mai–20 juin, 308.
[47] Miquel, L'exode 10 mai–20 juin, 288.

of the crowd, pushed toward the river. "There were soldiers all around trying to do something," she recalled. "They were trying to blow up the bridges." Flanet's family and the entire crowd rushed to cross the bridges before the soldiers detonated their explosives. Driving their car next to a truck of soldiers, Flanet recalled, "We had the impression of being safe, but of course we weren't."[48]

Léon Werth captured the humiliation of civilian encounters with the remnants of a defeated French military:

I saw, straggling foot soldiers, without weapons, heads drooping, scraping mud from the bottom of their shoes, sometimes their sandals. They barely avoided collisions with a bicyclist, just skimming a parked car, without appearing to have seen it ... Walking like blind men, like slovenly shadows ... They were strangers to peasants pulling wagons, to city-dwellers in cars, to military formations. They were alone, like beggars who have given up asking for alms.[49]

Werth concluded that most refugees did not yet fully understand that the exhaustion and bewilderment of one stray soldier represented the rule rather than an exception. Refugees formed ungenerous opinions of the courage, character, and stamina of individual soldiers. Yet they still took false reassurance in their company. Describing her experience at the River Loire where she witnessed randomly scattered French troops, Madeline Gohier remarked, "They had lost all reference points, all sense of the 'regular.'" She shook her head, "The rules of life, everything was in the process of *floating*."[50]

Jackie Golter drew somewhat more sympathetic conclusions about the French military. In an episode at the abandoned house, she felt relieved when they discovered that an approaching soldier was French rather than German. But the soldier displayed the fatigue of a weary traveler. He looked Golter in the eye, and then, as if to surrender, he closed his eyes and fell asleep standing up before falling to the ground to sleep.[51] Golter also recalled a separate encounter with a very tired company of retreating troops. At the time, she believed their retreat represented strategic maneuvering rather than signaling defeat. "The civilians mixed with the soldiers," she explained. "We gave them some ham and they kept it." In her mind she had rendered mutual assistance to the tired and demoralized army.[52]

Similarly, soldiers experienced civilians' presence on the road with a mixture of emotions. At one end of the continuum, civilians represented

[48] Janine (née Flanet) De Col interview.
[49] Werth, *33 jours*, 30.   [50] Gohier interview.
[51] Golter interview.   [52] Golter interview.

cumbersome obstacles to military maneuvering. In the middle, civilians appeared as victims in need of soldiers' aid and protection. At the other extreme, civilians heroically helped to rescue soldiers. Soldiers testified to feeling torn between the call to rescue civilians and the requirement of regrouping with their regiments. As the army had feared before the exodus, the sight of retreating civilians caused many soldiers to wonder what had become of their own families. The mingling between soldiers and civilians sometimes reinforced the traditional dependencies between men and women, but as the military situation worsened, civilian women frequently came to the aid of exhausted, malnourished soldiers. When such role reversals occurred, the humiliation of defeat could be exacerbated by the apparent failure of Frenchmen to successfully fulfill their duty as defenders in a resilient patriarchic society.

The mixing of the two groups brought danger to refugees. German and Italian aviators continually strafed fleeing enemy troops, catching civilians in the line of fire. Often, soldiers in trucks offered a lift to tired refugees, not thinking that in so doing they attached refugees to a military target. The Germans later justified the collateral damage to civilians as a product of the fact that French soldiers were retreating among civilians. While firing on civilians violated the customs of war and the Geneva Conventions, the expressed prohibition of using civilians for military cover (difficult to distinguish from giving them a lift) only became codified in postwar international law.[53] This mingling of civilians and soldiers continued to vex international legal experts well into the postwar era as they tried to apply the lessons of the war to improve legal protections for civilians engulfed in combat operations. But identifying a strict distinction between combatant and civilian has proved to be elusive as soldiers and later guerilla fighters honed the tactic of not only using civilians as cover, but concealing their identity dressed as civilians.[54]

Even distant proximity of civilians to soldiers or to military targets could invite danger. On June 10, driving between the Maison de Pommery in Reims and the champagne hideaway in Aviz, Carré witnessed a total of eighteen bombs fall within range of the Aviz train station. The bomb killed fifty refugees waiting on a train headed for Romilly. German aviators, missing their target of a nearby French artillery regiment also hit a refugee walking along the road. During the attack, Carré witnessed one woman suffer a nervous breakdown. On

[53] Mary Ann Glendon, *A World Made New: Eleanor Roosevelt and the Universal Declaration of Human Rights* (New York: Random House, 2002), 9–10.

[54] Kinsella, "The Image before the Weapon," 181.

the road to Flavigny, he encountered two men carrying a bombing victim to the town morgue, followed by the man's slightly wounded wife. While the day's bombings demoralized Carré, his morale was temporarily boosted by a formation of French fighter planes in pursuit of the German aggressors.[55] Finally, the intensification of air attacks forced Carré to redefine his sense of the rational, and after a month of work abandon his efforts to salvage more of Pommery's stock.

Other dangers besides bombing lurked for women who sought security traveling with detached French soldiers. Two cases of civilian–military fraternization gone wrong are documented in French military investigations deposited in Jean Vidalenc's papers.[56] A custom had developed on the road whereby soldiers exchanged protection or a ride for civilians' food. The terms of these exchanges could be misinterpreted and actually jeopardize women's safety. On June 16, corporals Bordet and Mourgues of the retreating 107th Infantry Regiment happened upon a group of refugees fleeing Epinal. Among the crowd was a small group of girls with blonde hair. According to Bordet, the girls resembled the type, "that one sees in the villages near the Maginot Line who say nothing and speak in an incomprehensible local dialect."[57]

Bordet and Morgues stopped to eat rations and noticed the girls watching them. After some hesitation the oldest girl asked if Bordet would sell them some food since they had not had anything to eat in two days. Bordet invited the girls to join them, feeling flattered to be addressed as, "Mister Soldier." The two soldiers testified that they had told the girls how they had lost their regiment. After sharing a small feast, the girls asked if they could follow the soldiers. The group began a collective journey on foot toward the south. By evening, they arrived in a village where the soldiers were able to trade their uniforms for civilian clothes. Less than an hour after departing the village, they heard the sound of a motorcade. Bordet and Morgues ran into a small forest where they dug a hole to bury their guns, scratched off the "D.P." painted on their helmets, and hid their military identification papers in the girls' purses. But both Mourgues and Bordet kept their money, tucking their bills under folds in their ties, and keeping five or six francs in their pockets. Their display of quick thinking and adventurism sufficed, according to Bordet, to "make us masters of the team."[58]

---

[55] René Carré, unpublished journal.
[56] AN 72/AJ/623, Vidalenc papers, extract from testimony of Chief Corporal Bordet of 107th RIF, 1943.
[57] Vidalenc papers, extract from testimony of Chief Corporal Bordet.
[58] Vidalenc papers, extract from testimony of Chief Corporal Bordet.

For two days and two nights the girls accompanied the soldiers "calmly." Nearing Culmont (near Dijon), the girls and their two protectors settled down in a small hamlet. Bordet's description of the ensuing events demonstrates the confused expectations that could lead to violence when soldiers fraternized with civilians:

We passed two days in the shelter with these little ones, enough time to make them pay in kind. Two let themselves go without any difficulty, even though one was a virgin, the third one didn't want to do it, but she ended by succumbing like the others after Mourgues threatened to cut off rations to the entire group, all the same her friends had to hold her down the first time.[59]

Describing an incident that to most represents rape, the corporal delivered a surprisingly candid testimony, void of any recognition of possible wrongdoing. Economically destitute, lost, and without adult supervision, the girls found themselves betrayed by two French soldiers in whom they had placed their trust.

The second case attributed the "spirit of national pride" as motivation for women reluctantly submitting to soldiers' advances. Retreating in a military truck through the forest of Bigny (Cher) on June 17, a group of French soldiers offered a ride to another group of young girls. When the truck and its passengers stopped to rest, the soldiers fed the young girls, gave them something to drink, and finally, "all had their turn." As one soldier frankly described:

Six girls had the air of knowing the music, but the eight others were as virgin-like as possible. None of them were really 'raped,' despite the uncomfortable conditions of the woods and the truck. The eldest must have been 22 years old and she explained to Maupetit that she had decided, like her friends, to give herself to a Frenchman because it was the only thing they could do for the soldiers and as such, the Germans, if they caught them, wouldn't get anything but leftovers.[60]

The soldier tried to persuade the investigators that the girls' primary motivation was fulfilling their patriotic duty. The testimony concludes with the admission that the girls had been drinking heavily without much food, but that in fact the event was a celebratory one. Before crossing the River Loire the girls were still virgins and afterward, "they became women." So complete was this identity transformation, according to the soldier's testimony, that the girls adopted the title, "Women of Poncelet," to commemorate the place where they had entered into womanhood.

---

[59] Vidalenc papers, extract from testimony of Chief Corporal Bordet.
[60] AN 72/AJ/623, Vidalenc papers, "Un aspect de l'exode le 17 juin 1940 dans le Cher," 1941.

These episodes show that exodus rapes were not just mythic nightmares, but the reality confronted by itinerant refugee women and girls. Ironically, the two accounts represent encounters with "friendly fire," not enemy soldiers. Golter's story about the application of mustard and the alleged patriotic act of the girls on the truck were designed to rob German soldiers of the pleasure of stealing French girls' virginity. These testimonies document how French women coped with the threat and reality of rape. For the soldiers, the sexual exchanges, whether coerced or voluntary, seemed acceptable, even as they happened in the context of the military retreat. Obviously, the fact that the military held inquiries into the matters suggests that someone lodged a complaint. Unfortunately, the incomplete record does not include a military judgment or testimony by the women themselves.

An alternate interpretation of the willingness of the "women of Poncelet" to engage in sexual encounters with French soldiers (if, indeed, they did so willingly) is that, with the collapse of society, women felt released from the prescriptions of traditional morality and embraced the opportunity to explore their sexuality at a moment that might have seemed like a "last chance" before death. Popular fiction of the late postwar era presents depictions of both sexual liberation and sexual violation during the exodus. In her novel, *The Blue Bicycle*, Régine Déforges tells the story of one family's exodus and experience under the German Occupation. In a key romantic scene, the exodus is the catalyst for the consummation of the love between Léa and her childhood sweetheart, Mathius. Mathius, a soldier lost from his regiment, finds Léa alone on the road. With bombs exploding around them, Léa and Mathius overcome inhibitions and class differences to explore their sexual desires. Mathius, a "servant" in the employment of Léa's family, avows his forbidden love and asks for her hand in marriage, but Léa refuses. For Léa the exodus offered the pretext to discover her sexuality, and the collapse of society's structures allowed her to cross class boundaries. The story supports the novel's claimed causes of France's collapse: undisciplined soldiers; unsupportive civilians; unpatriotic workers; and sexually liberated women.

After the war, French Army psychiatrists commissioned a study to identify the origins and consequences of stress on combatants and civilians. Their findings support the conclusion that rape occurred more widely than historians have discussed. The report concluded that first fatigue, then hunger served as the primary causes of soldier stress and "hysteria" witnessed during the retreat. Consumption of alcohol ranked third as a cause for unleashing hysteria among civilians and combatants. These deprivations or indulgences figured heavily in the reshaping of behavioral norms on the road. The study unveiled other information about women's experience that perplexed and seemed to agitate army psychiatrists. They summarized their findings from interviews with women at refugee centers with a dismissive conclusion: "All the fantastic stories of rape are undoubtedly caused by the presence, among many of our ill women, of a mystical delirium."[61] Despite the evidence to the contrary, army psychiatrists attributed reports of civilian rape to hunger and fatigue, not to soldiers' combat stress.

These narratives about sexual encounters during the exodus contribute to understanding the emergence of an informal discourse about the acceptability of French women "giving themselves," to French soldiers.[62] While rape of French women by German soldiers loomed as a large fear, rapes of French women by French soldiers did occur. This fact establishes the validity of women's fear and experience of rape, but challenges the nationalist assumptions defining who rapists were. Did French military officers leading investigations conclude that it was more tolerable for French men to "take the virginity" of French women, than for German men to do the same? Did French women feel any less violated because their aggressors were French? More importantly perhaps for historians, why did the evidence of these rapes, as well as the French Army psychiatrists' report, remain in the personal papers of Vidalenc? Rather than using these testimonies to raise these questions in his 1957 study of the exodus, Vidalenc deposited them in the archive. Thus, in a fashion similar to that for World War I, the historical discussion of the rape of French women during the invasion has largely disappeared from public record. It is important that historians mark the frequency of narratives of real and imagined rape during the exodus so as to open the doors for further investigation into the sexual violation of refugees throughout the entire war. Only in this way can historians of women, and of military conflict, begin to better understand the variety

---

[61] AN 72/AJ/623, Vidalenc papers, "Observations of a medical psychiatrist from Paris, retreated to Fleury les Aubains and transmitted by Abbé Guillame Ardan by Olivier."

[62] Françoise Leclerc and Michele Wendling have pioneered research on the history of "Les femmes tondues." See unpublished paper, "Les femmes devant les Cours de Justice à la Libération: éléments d'une recherche," presented at the conference, "Féminismes et Nazisme: colloque en hommage à Rita Thalmann," Paris, December 10–12, 1992. Leclerc and Wendling report that in the official tallies of the Liberation purges, 29,401 persons were detained in French prisons for having collaborated; 6,091 were women. Leclerc and Wendling argue that these figures force historians to consider women's collaboration in a framework larger than just "collaboration de sexe," even if most were prosecuted by the court of justice only for the crime, "intelligence avec l'ennemi."

of threats to civilian women's security consequent of displacement and fraternization or mixing with soldiers.

The exposure of French women's sexual vulnerability in unguarded, public spaces during the invasion and exodus may help us to understand the attempt under Vichy to foster policies intended to restore a more traditional definition of sexual conduct. The National Revolution's policies would equate loyalty to France and resistance to the Occupation with abstention from sexual or romantic contact with the enemy. Additionally, Vichy would attempt to re-establish traditional sexual norms that reserved sexual activity for the dominion of marriage, with child-bearing as the goal. Women's exposure to sexual violation during the invasion may suggest why French women did resort to abortion during the Occupation; the existence of which is evidenced by Vichy's repressive policies to end the practice with the execution of Marie-Louise Giraud, most vividly remembered in Claude Chabrol's 1988 film, *Une Affaire de Femmes*.

Happily not all encounters between civilians and soldiers involved scenarios of rape and "stolen virginity." Soldiers often grieved over how civilians appeared in worse physical condition than combatants. Retreating from the east by way of Dermeulle, one soldier testified:

All the refugees began to retreat and at this moment a young girl came to ask if we had a place for her in our group because she could no longer walk. There was a small boy, with a broken leg, wrapped in bandages, in the care of a nurse ... There was a small girl of 15 years, who had [suffered] such losses due to fatigue that she had begun to hemorrhage and someone had palmed her off to a quack to soothe her, but he could not keep her and had evacuated her on a stretcher with another wounded child and two other injured people.[63]

Refugees' and soldiers' narratives influenced strong judgments in postwar debates concerning the propriety of conduct by either group. Vidalenc interviewed one veteran who judged: "The war ended in a sort of cowardice, as plenty of officers as well as soldiers and these people just accepted the defeat. They saved their skins. The rest is history."[64] The term "cowardliness" is most frequently attributed to soldiers. The accusation of cowardliness among civilians and the French people as a whole occupies a larger place in discussions about resistance to the Germans during the period of Occupation. In the immediate aftermath of the defeat, soldiers felt betrayed by civilians' resignation and believed that they interfered with the army's mobility. Civilians felt betrayed by soldiers, who they thought had given up the fight. Neither

[63] AN 72/AJ/623, Vidalenc papers, Soldier's testimony, transcribed in 1941.
[64] Vidalenc Papers, Soldier's testimony.

representation adequately captured the complexity of combatant and non-combatant experience.

Pointing fingers, allocating blame

With the departure of the government from Paris on June 10 and the virtual collapse of the news distribution services, critiques of government officials, which were virtually absent from most newspapers, spread throughout the countryside. Appalled by the military's policy of destroying telephone and electric lines in evacuated towns, Carré judged the military's competency: "Either these people [the military] were imbeciles having no idea of contemporary tactics for waging war, or they were criminals needing to be punished."[65] René Baudouin's memoir captured in its title, "A Rumor in the Hail of Bullets," the atmosphere of mutual critique and suspicion. On the road to Auxerre, Baudouin had encountered a range of popular complaints founded in reality or generated from fiction. A false, but much circulated critique professed, "Paul Reynaud has fled and taken off with the national lottery."[66] A more accurate critique accused: "Paul Reynaud has better things to worry about. He is busy divorcing his wife and remarrying."[67] In fact, Reynaud's private dealings frustrated his colleagues including Bullitt, who despised Reynaud's mistress, the comtesse of Portes, and who told President Roosevelt:

The people of France who are fighting with an absolute selflessness deserve better at this moment than to be ruled by a Prime Minister's mistress – not even a King's! In the end she will be shot. Meanwhile she will rule the roost.[68]

Meanwhile, contempt for Reynaud, who daily battled with Weygand and Pétain to keep the French military in the game, was somewhat mitigated by the growing fear among refugees that agents of the Fifth Column worked among them to defeat France's morale. Indeed, the belief in the Fifth Column shook refugees' confidence in their neighbors, deepening popular suspicions and setting the stage for the variety of political and personal denunciations that would characterize life under the Occupation.[69]

---

[65] René Carré, unpublished journal, 79–80.
[66] René Baudouin, "Un rumeur dans la mitraille," in *Le Choc de 1940*, republished in *Paris Match*, Paris, 1990, 90–91.
[67] Baudouin, "Un rumeur dans la mitraille."
[68] Bullitt, *For the President*, 453.
[69] The back-biting atmosphere of the Vichy regime was artfully captured in the controversial 1943 Henri-Georges Clouzot film, *Le Corbeau* (The Raven).

The alarmist temperament took hold of most refugees and carried over to their complex and conflicting feelings about German soldiers. The Armistice further muddied French political and popular interpretations of the German victor. Werth's opening sentence of his memoir records the most frequently repeated sentence used to describe the Germans' behavior during the exodus: "It was the period when they were 'correct.'"[70] He then adds, "which precede the period when they would give us lessons in politeness."[71] Yet, in 1940, most refugees seemed willing to divorce the living German foot soldiers from the German fighter pilots and enthusiastic Nazis whose fire slaughtered unprotected civilian masses. Golter's testimony suggests how, and possibly why, common French refugees could believe that the Germans on the ground meant them no harm. "There wasn't any terror," she recalled, referring to her first real, as opposed to imagined, encounter with German soldiers. "In fact, the really horrible things that followed didn't necessarily come from the Germans, but from the French Milice." She recounted: "Me, I saw this German arrive [at Angoulême] and he saw this little girl. He was so moved because the little girl resembled his own little girl and he took out a photo from his pocket to show her. He had some candy. He wanted to give it to the little girl, but her parents didn't want him to." Willing to temporarily forget that German policies resulted in the deportation of members of her family to Auschwitz, Golter offered: "The Germans had orders. They obeyed, but there were many who weren't Nazis."[72]

Indeed, as the German Army pressed further south and French military resistance faded, German soldiers adopted a more relaxed approach in villages and on the road. Casual situations where Germans minded their own affairs and melded into the crowds eased many refugees' anxieties. The French also found ways to rebuild their own shattered sense of cultural superiority. Cuisine provided an arena where the French could still beat the invaders. Flanet, who first encountered Germans at a soup kitchen outside Orléans, later encountered them in a restaurant. She fondly recounted: "We were in a seafood restaurant and there were several German soldiers there. Since there is no sea in Germany, they had no idea how to eat shellfish." She laughed at the memory and used her hands to demonstrate how the German soldiers futilely pounded and pulled at the shells.[73]

In the wake of defeat, a narrative emerged honoring Germans for their correct behavior and superior military skills, but maintaining

---

[70] Werth, *33 jours*, iii.   [71] Werth, *33 jours*, iii.
[72] Golter interview.   [73] Janine (née Flanet) De Col interview.

the thesis of French cultural and political superiority. Postwar memoirs emphasized German faux pas and allowed the nation to cling to a thread of self-respect, cultural pride, and probably most importantly for survival – humor. In Vercor's resistance novel, *Silence of the Sea*, the author depicted Germans as capable of acting with civility. They might even possess great talents, like the piano-playing antihero of *Silence of the Sea*. But Vercor sent a warning to his compatriots: resist the superficial charms of the occupier and work to unmask the Teutonic conqueror. Unveiling the crimes of German Nazism and militarism required a new degree of mass political consciousness and prolonged exposure to the German occupying methods. Although German émigré writers such as Lion Feuchtwanger had tried to warn French readers of the brutal methods of Nazism, the military invasion itself seemed to validate a belief in the technological superiority of their opponent, who had proved to be better equipped and more disciplined. It would take exposure to the tools of occupation – forced labor, deportation, hostage-taking, and civilian execution – to convince the French masses of the link between average German soldiers and the violence of Nazi ideology. Eventually, as the reality of defeat set in, an atmosphere of strife expanded like a fog, obscuring the bonds of national brotherhood (fraternité) that had united many refugees on the road.

Conclusion

The intersection of aerial bombing, civilian displacement, disintegration of family networks, and loss of community, happening under the larger umbrella of government collapse, assaulted the dignity of French and Benelux refugees. The sense of uncertainty, fear, and betrayal generated by the German terror campaign is vividly described in a range of wartime testimonies and postwar literary sources. Not surprisingly, violence occupies center stage in both contemporary and postwar refugee narratives. The outrage and fear sparked by exposure to low-flying planes which strafed innocent civilians, figures as the most enduring image commemorated in refugee narratives. Having endured the traumatic event, many survivors felt compelled to record their individual memoirs, while interviewees exhibited a sense of urgency to express their recollections after years of forgetting. However, few of these accounts of the exodus demonstrated a broader historical awareness of the link between France's military defeat, refugee crisis, and Nazism's application of a system of regularized violence and terror against civilians.

Refugees could identify the human suffering. Soldiers could credit the military innovation and effective application of the Blitzkrieg. But few accounts recognized that violence and terror were the backbone of the Nazi governing system. In short, the German invasion did not immediately illicit a critique of fascism, rather, if anything, it confirmed for many the deep criticisms of the dying republic.

The most interesting feature of both contemporary and postwar accounts about wartime violence is the absence of a concept or language of human rights' violations. This absence underscores that the international legal language of human rights, which forms present-day understandings of distinctions between violence against combatants and non-combatants, developed wide circulation only very late in the postwar period. While that language is derived from the violations of human rights suffered by victims of the Holocaust, it has failed in large measure to capture and incorporate the experience of millions of civilian victims of bombing during World War II. Without a rights language to denounce their victimization, exodus survivors remained alienated from an understanding of their experience within a larger historical framework that gave birth to the concepts of crimes against humanity and victims of aggressive war. Instead, even the memories described here and recorded in the postwar period remain caged within a vocabulary of disbelief, betrayal, and vulnerability. This fact suggests that the Nuremberg trials, which codified the concept of crimes against humanity and prosecuted the Germans for waging aggressive war, failed to raise wartime civilians' consciousness about the violation of their status as innocents. Instead, the narratives catalog "losses" suffered by the French people and the French nation, rather than "atrocities" committed against civilian victims.

"Loss" is the second most dominant theme in exodus survivors' memories. Anxiety produced by the separation of loved ones from family and friends gives way to a sense of grief and enduring regret, infused in refugee survivors' narratives. But the concept of loss reinforces the sense of emotional damage, rather than articulating a principle of legal violation. In this sense, the destruction of the family and the fragmentation of the nation caused by mass displacement fostered a sense of sadness rather than outrage.

For families who lost loved ones, especially small children, their feelings invite a comparison to the passions experienced by family members of soldiers lost, "missing in action" (MIA). The French population experienced this concept of "missing in action" for soldiers captured by the German Army, but perhaps equally for civilians lost from one another on the road. Military historians know that for military families, no worse fate exists than to have a family member listed as "MIA." For mothers who lost small children, a sense of having contributed directly or accidentally to their child's loss exacerbated the sense of vulnerability, exposure, and ultimately guilt, but it also implicated them in their own loss, however slightly, perhaps removing blame from the true culprit, the war.[74]

Another different particularization of the experience of loss forms part of the narratives of female refugees. International legal scholar, Rhonda Copelon, describes rape as, "a loss of their [women's] world, with the loss of self, with the loss of community, and with marginalization in diaspora." These losses to women's sense of personal security find expression in many individual accounts and government reports.[75] While it has not been a major topic for historical analysis in the post-war historiography on the invasion, rape certainly was a consequence of total war. Systematized by the Red Army in Poland and Germany in 1945 and by Serbians in Bosnia in the 1990s, rape has evolved as a weapon of humiliation in the on-going psychological war against civilians. Exodus testimonials about rape reveal a continuity of experience from the period of World War I, but show how the added problem of mass displacement further exacerbated women refugees' sexual vulnerability during World War II.[76]

Displacement and the national emergency it caused readied government officials to sign the Armistice with Germany. In Pétain's capitulation speech to the French people, he cited the tragedy unfolding on the roads of France. Weary from weeks of walking, uprooted from their homes, and constantly in search of shelter and food, the refugees welcomed the Armistice. However, as the battle of France ended in a French defeat and the first wave of violence waned, refugees struggled

---

[74] Joy Damousi, *Living with the Aftermath: Trauma, Nostalgia and Grief in Post-war Australia* (New York: Cambridge University Press, 2001).

[75] See Rhonda Copelon, "Surfacing Gender: Re-engraving Crimes Against Women in Humanitarian Law," in Nicole Dombrowski (ed.), *Women and War in the Twentieth Century: Enlisted With or Without Consent* (New York: Garland, 1999 (reprinted Routledge: 2004)), 334. Copelon addresses Serbian raping of Bosnian Muslim women in the 1990s, but her overall project is to secure a specific place for gender within international law's definition of crimes against humanity.

[76] Annette Becker described a phenomenon of "amnesia," about wartime atrocities, particularly atrocities against women in public discussion and post-World War I commemorations. See Becker, *14–19*, 45.

less to dodge bullets and more to meet the fundamental requirements of daily existence. While many recollections recount experiences of camaraderie and a sense of national cohesion on the road; competition and fragmentation appeared once refugees settled into villages and towns that lacked the resources to meet their survival needs.

Part II

Refugees, rights, and return in a divided land

Figure 2. Refugees applying for permission to repatriate home
(courtesy of the US Library of Congress).

Map 3. Departments of France

5 Provincial towns feed and shelter refugees

On Sunday, June 16, Patricia Guillot traveled on foot, keeping an eye on her daughter and two sons. Her children trudged along, mixing among the mass of refugees. As the family approached a bridge crossing the River Loire, planes appeared and bombed the bridge.[1] As fire fell upon the crowd, and smoke, ash, and dust clouded the air refugees scattered in all directions. Ten-year-old Robert Guillot followed his older siblings who ran in the opposite direction from their mother. After the dust settled, Guillot began the search for her children. She located the older children, but Robert was missing. Frightened, the siblings sadly confessed, they had let go of Robert's hand in the confusion. For a day the family refused to leave the site of the attack, searching everywhere for the lost boy. A medic finally informed Guillot that a medical transport unit had placed a group of children on an evacuation train sent to Brive-la-Gaillarde in Corrèze.

Immediately, the Guillot family set course for Brive, but unrecorded circumstances must have prevented their reaching Corrèze. Perhaps they were trapped north of the Line of Demarcation, which came into force with the Armistice on June 25. Two months later, the mayor of Brive received a letter transmitted by the Service of Refugees in Paris. In the letter, Guillot described every detail of Robert's appearance and inquired whether he had arrived in Brive on the hospital train of June 16 from "St. Satur" (sic).[2] The mother's letter captured the grief she felt for her lost son. Trucks of refugee children did arrive in Brive and other destinations in the south-west during the summer of 1940. Local volunteers and government officials worked tirelessly to care for refugees and reunite lost persons with their families; but, the number of problems

---

[1] AMBG, Series H/IV/98, Mme Guillot to mayor of Brive-la-Gaillarde, August 12, 1940. Her letter records, "pont de St Satur." The author cannot find this bridge, and estimates that the family was probably attempting to cross the Loire between Saumur and Sainte-Maure-de-Tourain. Guillot's letter was among 290 similar letters in one archive.

[2] AMBG, Series H/IV/98, Mme Guillot to mayor of Brive-la-Gaillarde.

caused by the crisis exceeded the material and human resources available. Sadly, Madame Guillot's letter remained unopened and unread for almost fifty years, filed in a box of about sixty similarly unopened inquiries. Robert Guillot's name did not appear among the names of refugees listed on the relief rolls of Corrèze, compiled from June to August 1940.[3]

The Armistice ended combat hostilities for French military men; but for millions of French and foreign families, the battle to reunite with loved ones only intensified as the military conflict wound down. Staff shortages and other priorities prevented the mayor of Brive from replying to Madame Guillot. Despite this seemingly cold example of negligence in responding to a mother's inquiries for a lost child, Brivists and Corrézians made laudable efforts to accommodate the roughly 250,000 refugees who passed through or settled in Corrèze in the summer of 1940.[4]

Corrèze: an example of regional pride and national solidarity

The provision of local relief in Corrèze between May and August of 1940 tested the crisis response readiness of southern prefects, mayors, and volunteer organizations. Successful crisis management depended as much on the availability of material and human resources, as it did on the political and economic conditions of each southern department. In welcoming and later "absorbing" refugees into their towns and villages, host communities drew guidance from experiences with Spanish Civil War refugees.[5] Multiple factors shaped the relationship between host and refugee communities in Corrèze. The attitudes of prefects toward issues of social welfare, as embodied in refugee allocations, formed the most important element in the ability of refugees to find long-term asylum in a given department. Similar to Shannon Fogg's findings for

---

[3] It was difficult to determine whether the name contained two l's or an r. However, no Guillot or Guirot was found on the refugee roles of Corrèze.

[4] The number of refugees who actually resided in Corrèze is hard to calculate. In June 1940, the prefectoral reports count 120,000 refugees, excluding "those who temporarily passed through Corrèze on their way to locations further south." In prefectoral reports submitted to the Service of Refugees after the war, the number of refugees who collected services in Corrèze was estimated at 215,000. Given the fact that Brive-la-Gaillarde served as a railway transfer station for trains from the south traveling to the Line of Demarcation, Corrèze experienced large, short-term influxes of refugees, some of whom disembarked and attempted to stay in Corrèze. See AMBG, Series H/IV.

[5] "Absorption" was the Vichy government's term to describe the long-term integration of refugees into host communities.

nearby Haute-Vienne and Creuse, a tradition of left-leaning politics in Corrèze, valuing social rights and equality, shaped the response of host communities to refugees.[6] The practices and politics of mayoral staffs who delivered front-line refugee services, was the second most significant factor in determining how well refugees integrated into a local community. Less important to refugees' survival, but important for their morale, was the reception given to them by local volunteer organizations. In June and July 1940, the chaos in overpopulated southern towns matched the chaos experienced on the roads, as a newly formed national government, a reorganized Service of Refugees, local mayoral staffs, and community volunteer associations struggled to coordinate delivery of refugee services. While political and cultural traditions conditioned host community responses, refugees' own cultural and political attitudes shaped their expectations and choices regarding their displacement.

As a department situated within the greater Limousin and Auvergne region, which hosted approximately 1 million of the 8 million refugees (Table 2), Corrèze developed responses to the refugee crisis that shared characteristics with the responses in surrounding departments such as Lot, Cantal, Creuse, and Aveyron. As the Occupation dragged on, Corrézian respect for equality formed a foundation for managing long-term extension of asylum to French and foreign refugees. In contrast, Dordogne, Haute-Garonne, and Tarn exhibited stronger elements of xenophobia and hostility to outsiders, due in large part to the influx of Spanish refugees during the Spanish Civil War. In Corrèze, the surrounding departments of the Limousin, and the greater southwest region, the most significant sources of stress for refugee and host community relations included changes in local government leadership; receipt of national directives from Vichy regarding relief distribution and refugee repatriation; German policies of partition and discrimination enforced at the Line of Demarcation; and as Fogg suggests, competition for scarce resources in each department.

After June 22, while the new cabinet digested the particulars of the Armistice Agreement and reorganized political authority, the exodus continued. The Wehrmacht also continued to fortify its hold over France's Atlantic coast. On June 20, the Luftwaffe bombed Bordeaux four times. NBC correspondent in Bordeaux, Helen Hiett, reported that "two of the bombs scored hits on refugee shelters."[7] Bordeaux's

---

[6] Fogg, *Politics of Everyday Life in Vichy France*, 18.
[7] Associated Press, "Refugee-Crowded Bordeaux Bombed Four Times by Nazis," *Baltimore Sun*, Thursday, June 20, 1940, 2.

Table 2. *Departmental and regional refugee counts for the second and third weeks of June 1940*

Region	Departments	Total
Limousin	Haute-Vienne/Vienne (180,000), Creuse (80,000), Corrèze (120,000)	380,000
Auvergne	Puy-de-Dôme (115,000), Allier (160,000), Cantal (40,000), Haute-Loire (70,000)	385,000
Poitou-Charentes	Charente/Charente Maritime (395,000)	395,000
Aquitaine	Gironde (380,000), Landes (80,000), Dordogne (150,000), Lot-et-Garonne (60,000), Pyrénées-Atlantiques (85,000)	755,000
Midi-Pyrénées	Tarn (70,000), Lot (80,000), Aveyron (95,000), Tarn-et-Garonne (80,000), Haute-Garonne (140,000), Hautes-Pyrénées (50,000), Ariège (35,000)	550,000
Languedoc-Roussillon	Hérault (175,000), Gard (140,000), Lozère (70,000), Aude (90,000)	475,000
Bretagne	Finistère (190,000), Côtes-du-Nord (196,000), Ille-et-Vilaine (210,000), Morbihan (210,000)	806,000
Pays de la Loire	Vendée (140,000), Maine-et-Loire (120,000), Mayenne (225,000), Sarthe (160,000)	645,000
Centre	Eure-et-Loir (75,000), Loir-et-Cher (130,000), Indre-et-Loire (95,000), Loiret (120,000), Indre (100,000)	520,000
Nord-Pas-de-Calais	Nord (120,000), Pas-de-Calais (100,000)	220,000
Picardié	Somme (40,000), Oise (30,000)	70,000
Champagne-Ardennes	Marne (10,000), Aube (5,000), Haute-Marne (20,000)	35,000
Bourgogne	Nièvre (120,000), Saône-et-Loire (90,000), Yonne (95,000), Côte d'Or (70,000)	375,000
Total		5,611,000

Source: AN F/1a/3660, Report, Service of Refugees. The Service of Refugees compiled this list by requesting prefects to submit weekly department refugee counts. These numbers, then, represent the numbers counted from June 1 to June 24, 1940. Prefects complained bitterly that they did not have the staff available to undertake such a census of refugees. By the end of July, the prefect of Corrèze had calculated a number closer to 200,000 refugees as opposed to the 120,000 reported in June.

normal population of 250,000 was estimated to have multiplied five times. The raid forced refugees to renew flight further into the southwestern interior.

Refugee concentrations throughout France changed daily, and prefects and mayors faced a daunting task trying to track and count the moving populations. Prefects protested against the Service of Refugees' required weekly refugee population reports, which they called, "an impossible task" at a time when their staff were working day and night to feed and shelter the arriving refugees. The new home of the Service of Refugees, Pau (Pyrénées-Atlantiques), was itself flooded with refugees fleeing departments near the Italian border. The Service of Refugees also required that mayors and prefects submit detailed passenger train rosters to French and German officials. Those rosters recorded weekly refugee numbers, but excluded refugees who traveled by car, or on foot, or were stuck on trains. Still, summer applications for relief and for repatriation provided lists that offer a fairly firm sense of the geographic distribution of refugees. Prefects in Finistère, Côtes-du-Nord, Ille-et-Vilaine and Morbihan reported a refugee influx of 806,000 people. Traveling down the coast toward Spain or ports in Bordeaux, the two coastal regions of Poitou-Charentes and Aquitaine reported 1,956,000 refugees by the third week of June. In France's heartland, the Auvergne and Limousin accommodated 765,000 refugees. Further south, Midi-Pyrénées and Languedoc-Roussillon sheltered approximately 1,025,000 refugees.[8] These populations, especially those located in the departments around the territory that would become host to the Line of Demarcation, continued to disperse swiftly as the hostilities concluded.

On June 22, as a consequence of the partitioning of France, retreating refugees flooded into Limousin, Auvergne, Midi-Pyréneés, and Aquitaine from the coastal departments falling within the emerging "German Occupied Zone." Corrèze had witnessed the initial passage of refugees headed for destinations further south, such as Spain and the Pyrénées, but it never experienced the greatest concentrations of refugees. However, two major waves of refugees brought the peak refugee population to approximately 250,000 in this small and lightly populated area. A jagged terrain of old mountains and valleys, inhabited by only 250,000 people at a concentration of only 43 people per square kilometer, the Corrèze more than doubled its population in June 1940.[9] The economic and social strains caused by refugees in the Corrèze were similar to those experienced in departments west of the Limousin and to the south. Due to its central location, the Corrèze sat at the

---

[8] AN F/1a/1560, Report, Service of Refugees, June and July 1940.
[9] *Annuaire-Almanac du Commerce* (Paris: Didot-Bottin, 1948), 16. According to 1948 statistics, when the population would have been expected to have returned to normal, the Corrèze recorded 254,601 inhabitants. One can assume that this number was slightly elevated from the prewar period due to the return of demobilized soldiers and PoWs.

crossroads of reverberations from the refugee crisis originating in the newly closed-off Occupied Zone.

Both the train from Paris and the national highway passed through Brive-la-Gaillarde, the department's business and transportation hub. In 1940, Brive and Tulle, the Corrèze's administrative capital, stood as little more than agricultural towns where peasants and artisans packaged and sold the region's bounty: foie gras, truffles, walnuts, apples, and nut liqueurs. Industry within the region was limited to the paper mills that thrived on the rich forestlands of northern Corrèze. The Manufactory of Arms in Tulle was one of the only local concerns that directly contributed to the war effort. Corrèze had experienced small intrusions from the outside world as early as April 1940 when the Manufactory of Arms of Levallois evacuated its personnel and equipment from Paris to a location near Brive. This relocation introduced a small population of women war workers and a few conscripted male workers into the local economy. Corrèzians also felt the impact of military mobilization, as the department's young men moved to the front. Brive-la-Gaillarde offered two regiments to the war effort: the 126th Regular Active Infantry (RI) sent soldiers to the front and the 326th Reserve Unit recruited Brivists.[10] However, besides the armament factory and the shortage of agricultural labor, life in the Corrèze had remained fairly untouched by the war until the trickle of refugees grew to a deluge.

Politically, the economic pressures of the late 1920s and 1930s radicalized elements of the departmental electorate, so that in the 1936 legislative elections, 15,000 Corrèzians cast their ballots for the French Communist Party (Parti communiste français, PCF), eroding the support of France's Socialist Party (Parti socialiste français, PSF), and to a lesser degree, the Radical Party.[11] These prewar political divisions, which were exacerbated in the aftermath of defeat, are exemplified by two leaders. Senator Henri Queuille championed political ideals that reflected the middle-of-the-road republican values defended by his Radical Party. His personal interests focused on the rational management of the French nation. He participated in the organization of French agriculture during the interwar period, completing rural electrification while he led the Ministry of Agriculture. Queuille resisted the growing extremism of the right and left in France, but failed, like many men in his party, to recognize the allure the fringe held for his countrymen.

---

[10] René Vigier, *Brive pendant la guerre: héros, victimes, traîtres* (Pouzet: Éditions, 1954), 17.

[11] Vigier, *Brive pendant la guerre*, 70.

Queuille's fiercest political rival hailed from the increasingly popular political extreme. When Queuille won election to the Senate, Maurice Vazeilles, a communist, replaced him in the Chamber of Deputies. Vazeilles defended Corrèze's increasingly left-leaning cooperative-oriented farmers and the small set of industrial workers who embraced a vision of communal rights. Communism's allure for the electorate pushed Queuille to recognize the need for social and economic reorganization during the depression years, and eventually he helped to strengthen the cooperative system of agricultural production.

During the Phoney War, Queuille spent his energies working as Minister of Supply. Not wanting to unleash hardship on the French people unless war threatened, he rejected all suggestions of strict rationing. France might have weathered the invasion better had he adopted a more aggressive program for preparing French food reserves for war. While Queuille participated in government decisions at the highest level, Vazeilles sat in prison. Judged guilty of treason for not breaking with the PCF in September 1939, Vazeilles was among the fifty-one communist deputies who refused to leave the party after the signing of the Stalin–Hitler Pact in August 1939. Vazeilles and the fifty other deputies sent a letter, dated October 1, 1939, to Édouard Herriot denouncing France's declaration of war as, "joining British imperialism against German imperialism."[12] Despite critical, eye-witness accounts published by fellow intellectuals, such as André Gide whose *Retour de l'URSS* criticized Stalinism, the rank and file of Corrézian communists stood loyally behind the Soviet Union.[13] Not until Hitler launched his invasion of the Soviet Union in Operation Barbarossa on June 22, 1941 would a majority of adherents to French communism join the resistance against Nazism.[14] Despite the foreign relations' naivety of Corrèzian communists, they quickly brought their collectivist theories to aid and absorb their department's displaced refugees.

After he was indicted before the War Council of Paris on October 9, 1939, Vazeilles began to correspond with Queuille. Imprisoned, Vazeilles appealed to Queuille: "I reference my loyal conduct, courteous, next to

---

[12] De Tarr, *Henri Queuille en son temps*, 273. De Tarr suggests that Queuille remained fiercely anti-communist, but recognized the relations that joined him to Vazeilles.

[13] For reading on interwar French intellectuals' view of the Soviet Union see Tony Judt, *Un passé imparfait: les intellectuels en France: 1944–1956* (Paris: Fayard, 1992). For a discussion of Stalin's program to "catch up and overtake" the western economies, see Stephen Kotkin, *Magnetic Mountain: Stalinism as a Civilization* (Berkeley, CA: California University Press, 1995). Also Hosking, *The First Socialist Society*.

[14] André Gide's *Le retours de l'URSS (Return from the USSR)* (Paris: Gallimard) appeared in France in 1936 and condemned Stalin's agricultural policies and repression of intellectuals. Faithfuls of the PCF rejected Gide's accounts.

you, since I was elected deputy ... twenty years of fighting together, each with our different temperaments, for the same region."[15] Eventually, Queuille wrote to Prime Minister Daladier, a Radical Party colleague, urging Daladier to consider Vazeilles' health. Due to his health and Queuille's lobbying, Vazeilles had his life sentence commuted to four years. Vazeilles' incarceration placed communists in Corrèze on alert. Experiencing the early manifestations of political repression under the Third Republic, communists in Corrèze stood more prepared to organize against occupation and Vichy repression as it unfolded.

Queuille's and Vazeilles' hold on elected office symbolizes two important political trends in Corrèze on the eve of war: struggling Radical-republicanism/Radical-socialism and nascent communism.[16] The political convictions and divisions of interwar Corrèze resurfaced during the refugee crisis and shaped local responses to Vichy. Ironically, Queuille would later flee France, rally behind Charles de Gaulle, and thus join Vazailles as a designated enemy of the French government.

At the moment of the exodus, Queuille left Bordeaux for Corrèze to witness that, "The turmoil of my little village was at its peak."[17] Queuille's arrival in Corrèze marked a bitter homecoming. Having retreated from Paris with Paul Reynaud's government, Queuille initially thought he would relocate the Ministry of Supply to Pouges-les-Eaux in Nièvre to keep the military fed. However, as the military situation worsened, Queuille joined the retreating Council of Ministers to determine the fate of France. They had first debated capitulation on June 12 at Cangè and then again at Bordeaux on June 16.[18] There, Queuille supported Vice-President of the Council Camille Chautemps, and Minister of Information Ludovic-Oscar Frossard, in their ambiguous proposal to, "pursue discussions" with the Germans on the possible conditions of an armistice. After the vote, Reynaud quit the cabinet, widening the political division within the government. With the collapse of Reynaud's government, Queuille decided to return to Corrèze. The car ride from Bordeaux to Corrèze marked one of the saddest experiences of his life. Queuille passed through Gurat in Charente, where he joined his wife and daughter who had left Paris earlier in the

---

[15] De Tarr, *Henri Queuille en son temps*, 273.
[16] The Radical Party formed in the 1880s and secured its hold on power after the defeat of Napoleon III. For more than two decades it worked to separate church and state in France, while defending its staunchly anti-monarchist position. After the Law on Separation of Church and State was passed in 1905, the Radical Party lost focus according to many historians.
[17] De Tarr, *Henri Queuille en son temps*, 297.
[18] De Tarr, *Henri Queuille en son temps*, 288.

month. From his sedan he witnessed the shambles of his country: "On all the blocked roads, the troops retreated in complete disorder, often abandoned by their commanding officers. Weapons of all kinds were left in their place and in every small hamlet, civilians searched for a roof and something to eat." Queuille further lamented: "We had bread for one day only. The population had already tripled from peacetime. The refugees, whose numbers increased by the minute, were sheltered in all available spaces."[19]

Queuille was among the first to cross the emerging "Line of Demarcation" and observe the proliferation of German checkpoints and roadblocks, which created an extensive system of circulation controls. Corrèze found itself situated south of the Line of Demarcation in the territory that would soon be called the "Free," or "Non-Occupied" Zone. Once drawn and fortified, the Line would serve as the geographical border and administrative tool implemented by the Germans to sift through the mass of refugees. As France's ministers later discovered, the German terms for an armistice turned out to be more severe than even Pétain had imagined. "Article 2" of the Armistice agreement imposed France's partition into two administrative zones, making population movement, communication, self-government, and economic recovery a daunting, if not impossible task. However, as Eric Alary notes, the Armistice said nothing about the subdivisions that the German military later imposed on French territory, creating zones forbidden to French officials and civilians seeking repatriation.[20]

In June, as the countryside became geographically diced by roadblocks, barbed wire, and border patrols, political divisions widened at both national and local levels. At the national level, the most important political divides were between those ministers who would follow Chautemps into a government directed by Pétain, and those who would follow Reynaud's example and leave the government. Some ministers embarked for North Africa. Some returned to their homes. Others answered de Gaulle's June 18 broadcast from Britain calling for a rejection of the Armistice.

On June 17, 1940, Pétain addressed the French people and the world in the context of the growing refugee crisis, and the failure of the military defense. He solemnly announced to the nation an end to one struggle and the beginning of another. "In these harrowing times," he conceded, "I think of the unfortunate refugees who, in a state of

[19] De Tarr, *Henri Queuille en son temps*, 297. De Tarr quotes from Queuille's wartime journal.
[20] Alary, *La ligne de démarcation: 1940–1944*, 24.

complete destitution, cross our highways. I express to them my compassion and my solicitude. It is with a broken heart that I say to you today, it is necessary to attempt to end the combat."[21]

The new national government organized itself after the reconvened parliament voted full powers to Pétain on July 10. Historically, July 10, 1940 represents a much more tragic day for France and the West than even June 16 or June 22; for on this day, in desperation and in isolation, the French defeated their country's hard-earned republic. At the July 10 assembly of the Parliament, Queuille struck his typical middle-of-the-road position and abstained from the vote. Corrèze's National Assembly deputies Spinasse, Roumageon, and Peschadour voted to invest Pétain with full powers. Senator Labrousse and Deputy Jaubert voted against Pétain. Vazeilles had lost his right to vote.[22] Having abstained, Queuille lost any possibility of winning a ministerial post in the new regime. Ironically, his loss of power translated into new strength as the Occupation wore on.

Unlike Queuille, Robert Schuman chose to temporarily accompany Chautemps into Pétain's government. The growth of the refugee crisis contributed to Schuman's decision. The military capitulation, as well as the injunction to "Halt the exodus!" issued by Pétain's Minister of the Interior, Louis Pommery, forced prefects and mayors to find solutions to the many challenges posed by the Armistice. From June 18 to September 30, local officials in the provinces worked to address seemingly unsolvable problems: where would refugees be housed? Who or what branch of government would pay for refugees' long-term housing, food, medical and travel expenses? How long would refugees be allowed to stay in departments and cities different from their primary residences? Would the Germans allow refugees to return to their homes? On June 17, the government ordered all train travel to stop, attempting to end any further refugee movement along the railways. Disobedient SNCF conductors continued to drive trains to the south and many refugees continued by foot. Others decided to settle in the towns where they had stopped.

In a power vacuum, local officials craft relief schemes

Before Vichy and the Germans could impose their more ideologically driven solutions on the refugee crisis, ordinary citizens and civic-minded groups spontaneously pieced together assistance schemes that

---

[21] Pétain's speech reprinted in *Le Corrèzien*, 182-T.78, June 18, 1940.
[22] Vigier, *Brive pendant la guerre*, 24–25.

attempted to offer universal aid to the displaced. Local newspaper editorials suggest that the refugee crisis concerned citizens more than the consequences of defeat. On June 22, the *Chronique de Brive* ran an editorial, not about capitulation, but about potatoes. A spike in the price of potatoes fueled animosity between refugees and locals. On that day, a half kilo sold for 1.50 francs, almost reasonable compared with the 2.50 francs the previous week. Both prices, according to the editorialist, robbed refugees and residents, since normally potatoes sold for 60 centimes per kilo. The paper cautioned residents not to blame the refugees for the rise in prices, but to hold responsible the true culprits: the prefect and the mayors who should order the police to crack down on merchants.[23]

In Brive, crisis management was complicated by an administrative shake-up. When the crisis began, Henri Chapelle served as Brive's mayor. First elected in 1925, Chapelle led Brive's municipal government until the collapse of the Third Republic. According to local historian, René Vigier, the government sought to remove Chapelle by sanctioning him for "a mis-appreciation of the rules of abnegation and a failure of selflessness required as an example of all those who solicit and accept the heavy weight of public service."[24] Vigier believes that these charges were vague at best, and simply provided a pretext to install a more ideologically reliable partner as mayor. Louis Miginiac, a well-known lawyer, succeeded Chapelle on July 12, 1940.[25] In November, however, a complete overhaul of municipal government took place when Vichy published a decree suspending the terms of all elected municipal officials. By a similar ministerial decree of March 17, 1941, an entirely new municipal assembly formed in Brive, without any popular mandate. The Vichy-appointed municipal council stood in marked contrast to any Third Republic local assembly: three women were appointed to the city council. It is a tragic irony, that in the middle of France's democratic demise, women first entered the ranks of municipal administration. Vichy finally bestowed official reappointment of Miginiac in a decree issued on June 7, 1941 naming him mayor of Brive-la-Gaillarde and four other Vichy supporters as deputy mayors.[26]

---

[23] *Chronique de Brive*, June 22, 1940, Musée Edmond Michelet, Brive-la-Gaillarde.

[24] Vigier, *Brive pendant la guerre*, 28: "la méconnaissance de certaines règles d'abnégation, de désintéressement et d'exemple qui doivent guider tous ceux qui sollicitent ou acceptent la lourde charge de s'occuper de la chose publique."

[25] Bernard Murat, *Le passeur de mémoire: histoire des maires de Brive-la-Gaillarde* (Brive-la-Gaillarde: Les 3 épis, 1997), annex. Documents suggest Miginiac did not actually replace Chapelle until the fall of 1940.

[26] Vigier, *Brive pendant la guerre*, 28–29. Named as "adjoints" were: M. Escande and M. Goutines, Dr. Coussieu, M. Amblard, Chief of Police.

In Tulle, known for the production of the fabric most often worn by
ballerinas and for the manufacturing of arms, the municipality's elected
leaders came from the center-left. The mayor of Tulle, Jacques de
Chammard, first elected to office in 1925, managed to survive the early
political shifts and held on to office until 1943 when Colonel Gabriel
Bouty replaced him.[27] Shifts in municipal, departmental, and national
authority took place constantly during partition and Occupation, making the Vichy period, according to Robert Paxton, one of the most
unstable periods of French history since the Terror. In Tulle and Brive,
as elsewhere in the Free Zone, instability at the top reverberated at the
local level and subjected refugees to an environment of rapidly changing policies.

When refugees arrived in Corrèze in numbers that grew to 120,000 in
June and doubled by July, Alfred Papinot, the departmental prefect had
served in the French administration for over twenty years.[28] He began
his posting to Corrèze in 1936. Perhaps his experience in the Public
Health and Welfare administration prepared him to address the growing crisis in his department. Between May and August 1940, Papinot
administered the crisis in Corrèze, insisting on compassion and equality in dealing with refugee affairs.[29] He worked feverishly with mayors,
national officials, and volunteer organizations to assist refugees and to
calm residents' anxieties about the dangers and discomforts brought by
the population deluge. Until his replacement in September 1940 with
Vichy-appointed Ferdinand Musso, Papinot drew on his experiential
knowledge of the refugee problem to inform his decisions regarding the
two central issues of the crisis: the allocation of refugee relief and the
repatriation of refugees to the Occupied Zone.

A key obstacle to overcoming the crisis was the shortage of housing.
Leaders in Corrèze understood that housing refugees in private residences, as opposed to camps – a practice initiated during the Spanish
Civil War – usually meant better health, better food, and increased
security for refugees.[30] The prefect and mayors progressively resorted
to periodic requisitioning of housing and supplies when the crisis

---

[27] C. Mazenc, *Qui est qui en Corrèze* (Tulle, 1983), annex.
[28] ADC 1E/DEP/272–399 and AMBG, Series H/IV.
[29] AN, *Dictionnaire biographique des préfets* (Paris: Archives Nationales, 1994), 424.
  Refugee figures for June and July 1940 come from AN F/1a/3660, Report to the
  Director of the Service of Refugees.
[30] For a history of concentration camps in France, see Grynberg, *Les camps de honte*.
  Grynberg argues, as have others, that concentration camps for refugees, French and
  foreign alike, have mistakenly been believed to be the creation of the Vichy regime.
  The Third Republic, not Vichy, established the first system of internment camps.

exhausted hospitality. National requisitioning of private property such as cattle, farm equipment, and cars began in September 1939 during the evacuations of Alsace and Lorraine. Owners often contested the sum of compensation for their property, but had few avenues for appeal.

Chapelle initially tried to avoid fueling tensions by organizing a partial requisitioning of housing that placed refugees in private homes, hotels, schools, or churches; but permitted the proprietor to set the fee. Local officials cautioned proprietors against fleecing refugees, but refugees' complaints suggest that not all proprietors complied. At the June 1 meeting of the Municipal Council of Brive, Chapelle stressed the need to house the "unexpected" refugees.[31] *Le Petit Gaillard* warned of expanding requisitions, recommending that readers rent empty spaces immediately, before they lost the option of choosing their tenants and naming their price.[32]

Underscoring the increasingly interventionist nature of the state, Papinot ordered the unthinkable in a small French department. On June 19, he issued an emergency decree to keep all food stores open twenty-four hours a day to ensure the feeding of evacuees.[33] Fearful of assaults by mobs of hungry refugees, shop owners in Brive requested, and received, twenty-four-hour police protection.[34] Besides issuing directives to meet refugees' needs, officials acted to "protect" locals, or at least to calm their worries. Local political organizations entered the effort. Socialists invited their constituencies to receive the refugees with pity and sympathy, and converted all constituent sectional meeting spaces into welcome centers. Party leaders encouraged party members to help men and women find work, especially for those refugees originally from the Corrèze. Pronouncing their principles of "equality and fraternity," the Socialists called for equitable treatment of refugees in housing, demanding that residents should lodge refugees "from the most modest bedroom to the largest chateau."[35]

In Corrèze, a notable Catholic influence still existed in 1940. In Brive, refugee services received the indispensable assistance of a local notable, Edmond Michelet.[36] Michelet subscribed to the kind of social

[31] *La Voix Corrèzienne*, 219-T.3, "Bi-Hebdomadaire départemental d'information: Organe du Socialisme et de la Démocratie, " June 1, 1940.

[32] *Le Petit Gaillard*, May 30, 1940.

[33] *Le Petit Gaillard*, June 19, 1940.

[34] AMBG, Series H/IV/98, mayor to police commissioner of Brive, June 19, 1940.

[35] *La Voix Corrèzienne*, 219-T.3, June 8, 1940.

[36] The National Assembly resurrected an old World War I law for organizing public assistance. Secours National (National Assistance) received funding to allow localities to prepare for wartime public emergency assistance.

Catholicism that allowed him to organize across the fracturing party lines. During the course of the war, Michelet first oversaw the rescue effort of refugees in his department, then ignited a determined moral resistance to the Vichy regime that would eventually end in his arrest and deportation to Dachau. During the summer of 1940, Michelet's leadership within the rescue community probably accounts for the vigorous participation of Catholic, Protestant, and later Jewish, volunteers in relief efforts.[37]

In Tulle, the League of Catholic Women's Action announced the formation of a drop-in exchange between local citizens and refugees for sheets, utensils, diapers, and other sundries.[38] At the regional level, the Committee of Assistance to Refugees in Bordeaux attempted to organize women throughout the south-west to sew clothes, sheets, and other necessities. The Bordeaux committee actually offered to pay women up to 5 francs per hour for their work.[39] Such attempts at regional coordination became impossible once the partition dividing departments made the distribution of aid between zones illegal.

To rally the spirit of aid, Brivists organized a public fundraiser at the Cinéma Rex in early June. All profits from a "very attractive program," were to be given to the Refugee Welcome Committee.[40] Across the Atlantic, American Red Cross National Chairman, Norman H. Davis, worked to assure donors that their contributions would not fall into Nazi hands:

> While conditions for rendering relief may change, the policy of the American Red Cross remains the same. Cessation of hostilities in France does not diminish the terrible suffering and needs of refugees. We, therefore intend to continue to extend all possible relief, but only upon condition that we have liberty of action and protection so as to ensure that our aid goes solely to those French men, women and children and refugees for whom it is intended.[41]

As Bullitt had observed to Roosevelt, voluntary aid organizations could simply not meet the needs of the mass of refugees. However, volunteer efforts served to boost refugee morale and deliver crucial, if incomplete, services.

---

[37] Vigier, *Brive pendant la guerre*, 20. See also Edmond Michelet, *Rue de la Liberté: Dachau, 1943–1945* (Genève: Éditions Famot, 1975). Michelet survived his imprisonment and emerged as one of the moral leaders of postwar France. His writings and committed action gained him a ministerial post under de Gaulle.

[38] *Le Corrèzien*, 182-T.78, June 14, 1940.

[39] *Le Petit Gaillard*, "Quotidien Républicain d'informations Brivistes et Régionales," June 5, 1940.

[40] *Le Petit Gaillard*, Saturday, June 1, 1940.

[41] "Fund not to Fall into Nazi Hands," *Baltimore Sun*, June 18, 1940, 26.

Misinformation persists

As in the north, war reports in southern papers did not match reality. Similar doses of censored reporting colored the accounts of front-line action delivered to Corrézians. On June 3, in Brive, *Le Petit Gaillard* printed reports on northern battle action that fostered a false sense of security, assuring its readers with optimistic headlines: "Our Line of Resistance is Solidly Established."[42] Front-page articles hailed the fortitude of the Maginot Line in defending the Somme. Reporters downplayed German gains writing: "The outskirts of Amiens are in the hands of the Germans who could only keep hold of a small bell tower on the other side of the banks."[43]

The first news of the attacks on Paris reached the Corrèze on June 4. By June 5, with the German advance encroaching upon Paris, Corrézian understandings of the war showed a new realism. The paper amended casualty figures upward to 254 dead and 625 wounded.[44] Even though civilians from the Marne evacuated on May 10, not until June 10 did *Le Corrézien* inform readers that enemy ground forces had entered the region of Champagne. On June 12, the arrival of two German armored divisions on the outskirts of Reims confirmed the enemy advance.[45] Finally, rather than trying to minimize the seriousness of German destruction to civilian centers, broadcast journalists derided German reports that insisted air attacks only targeted French aerodromes, asking: "Who would ever believe that groups of planes, dropping thousands of bombs over a region as vast as the Parisian metropolis, could exclusively hit military targets?"[46]

Reports of large-scale bombings of northern civilian centers triggered sentiments of patriotism and empathy for first-wave refugees. The significance of the Parisian bombings for the refugee crisis was threefold: they cleared the capital, thus increasing the number of refugees fleeing from the north; they inspired realistic reporting, until air attacks forced newspapers in the north to close shop; and they awakened the more battle-remote regions of the country to the reality of the impending defeat. Readers made the connection: with Paris moving south along France's rail and roadways, the situation in Corrèze would surely worsen.

La Voix Corrézienne, the bi-weekly PSF newspaper, first reported on the influx of weary war refugees on May 25. In the waiting room of

---

[42] *Le Petit Gaillard*, June 3, 1940.   [43] *Le Petit Gaillard*, June 3, 1940.
[44] *Le Petit Gaillard*, June 5, 1940.
[45] *Le Corrézien*, 182-T.78, June 12, 1940.
[46] *Le Petit Gaillard*, June 5, 1940.

the small train station, city officials and Red Cross volunteers installed the first canteen to feed "refugees of passage," persons intending to travel further south to permanent shelter. A team of Brivist relief workers called upon the "charity of all our compatriots," to make dishes and donations of food, clothing, or cash for arriving refugees.[47] Local officials asked that volunteers willing to house individuals for an evening or two, contact the mayor's office.[48] Such appeals to local tolerance for foreigners contradicted the state-launched vigilance campaign of 1939 that raised civilians' suspicion of all community outsiders. Government requests of private citizens to open their homes not only to French refugees, but especially to foreigners, made perfect sense from a humanitarian perspective, but further eroded the collapsing boundaries between private and public life. In the end, the crisis brought the war to an unsuspecting southern France in a way that opened the south to the entry of regional and foreign differences as never before witnessed in its modern history.

The Red Cross inaugurated and expanded a variety of different refugee services. Reynaud's government had designated the American Red Cross as the coordinator of relief aid in affiliation with French political and religious organizations. Other participating relief organizations included the League of Societies of the Red Cross based in Geneva, Switzerland, the Central Committee of the French Red Cross, and the International Red Cross. Reynaud's announcement of an increased role for the American Red Cross reached the provinces via radio. In his communiqué, Reynaud lauded the efforts of the American Red Cross at the crucial moment when, "children are being killed in the arms of their mothers and old people are passing away among ruins." Reynaud added, "in the moment when one sees only the action of forces of death and destruction, the American Red Cross arrives in superior force, the force of victory: the spirit of mutual aid and humanity."[49] In truth, the American Red Cross experienced difficulty arriving in the south after the German seizure of Bordeaux. On June 21, the Germans refused safe passage to an American Red Cross "mercy ship" loaded with refugee relief and headed to Bordeaux, redirecting the captain to Bilbao, Spain.[50]

While relief structures present in urban areas or towns that hosted main-line railway stations attempted to meet the needs of most

---

[47] *La Voix Corrézienne*, 219-T.3, Saturday, May 25, 1940.
[48] *La Voix Corrézienne*, 219-T.3, Saturday, May 25, 1940.
[49] *Le Petit Gaillard*, Monday, June 3, 1940.
[50] "Mercy ship ordered to head for Bilbao," *Baltimore Sun*, June 21, 1940, 10.

settling and passing refugees, small towns absorbed refugee overflows. Soudaine-Lavindadière, a small hamlet, took the lead, announcing its willingness to accept 163 refugees. The village of Gourdon-Murat offered to send a bus to welcome eighty-three refugees.[51] Commune leaders literally counted beds and estimated exactly how many refugees their small communities could properly host.

On May 26, Chapelle called a meeting of the town council to form an official "Welcoming Committee" and to address the growing needs of the refugees. Local women moved into positions of authority to begin the task of organizing relief efforts. Madame Verdeaux became the committee's president; Madame Labare became vice-president; and Madame Gerbant volunteered as treasurer.[52] Within forty-eight hours the committee had managed to collect 3,500 francs to supplement a 500-franc gift given by a special delegation. The committee directed the money to the purchase of bedding, clothes (especially shoes), and general provisions.[53] Concern about public health and the spread of disease spurred public officials to construct makeshift baths and showers outside the train station.[54]

In Tulle, the local Association of French Ladies coordinated with the Refugee Welcome Committee to establish auxiliary hospitals and rest centers as weary refugees arrived in Tulle, sent from Brive.[55] The American Red Cross and the Welcoming Committee of Brive installed triage units in several key areas to alleviate pressure on the one local hospital. "Expert nurses" in these improvised clinics treated refugees for general fatigue, heat exhaustion, and dehydration. Volunteers transported more seriously wounded refugees to local hospitals. The hospital records of Brive suggest that among the female population, 63 percent of the 480 females admitted between March 1940 and November 1940 were refugees.[56] Only two refugee patients listed wounds from bombings as a cause for seeking care. Nervous troubles counted as the cause for hospitalization among seven women.

Medical staff in the southern departments competed with the north for foreign relief workers, as many health workers remained trapped in the north. We do not have any hard statistics on the total number of civilians who died as a consequence of the exodus, although Pierre

---

[51] "Mercy ship ordered to head for Bilbao," *Baltimore Sun*, 10.
[52] *La Voix Corrézienne*, 219-T.3, June 1, 1940.
[53] *La Voix Corrézienne*, 219-T.3, June 1, 1940.
[54] *La Voix Corrézienne*, 219-T.3, June 1, 1940.
[55] *Le Corrézien*, 182-T.78, June 11, 1940.
[56] AMBG, "L'Hôpital de Brive: L'enregistrement de juin 1940."

Miquel has recently offered an approximation of 100,000 dead or missing.[57] Statistics of the number of refugees who perished due to injuries or illness related to displacement offer an impressionistic picture. A report submitted by the prefect of Corrèze to the Minister of the Interior in 1942 attributed 218 deaths between June and July 1940 to conditions created by the exodus. Among the civilian dead, the report counted 85 women and 115 men. The deaths seem to have fallen most heavily upon the elderly. Among women who perished, thirty-five were between the ages of forty-one and sixty, and twenty-five were aged over sixty. The male death toll fell similarly across the age spectrum. The largest concentration of male dead, fifty, fell in the age range of sixty years and older.[58] The 218 refugee deaths reported in Corrèze represent less than one-tenth of a percent (0.087 percent) of the entire community of refugees. This can be considered a conservative departmental average, especially since no German or Italian planes bombed civilian targets in Corrèze. Extended across 8 million refugees, this would indicate that about 7,026 civilians died as a consequence of the exodus, a massacre, even by today's inflated standards. The real number is probably somewhat higher, since this estimate came from a department that did not experience bombing or overcrowding to the same degree as departments within the Charente and Aquitaine regions. General statistics estimate that 267,000 French civilians died between 1939 and 1945 as a consequence of the war, but do not specify how many of these deaths were women or children.[59] Importantly, these statistics and anecdotal testimonies confirm that hospitals and medical staff were overwhelmed by the displacement crisis.

For women, not all refugee medical emergencies stemmed solely from the war. The psychological stress, physical exhaustion, and lack of food and water aggravated the normal discomfort and problems experienced by pregnant women. One nurse described the particular pain of a pregnant woman arriving in Brive with her three small children after days

[57] Miquel approximates that 100,000 individuals died or disappeared during the exodus. Miquel, *l'exode de 10 mai–20 juin 1940*, postscript.

[58] ADC, Series 69/W/2434, Report filed with the Minister of the Interior, November 11, 1942.

[59] http://en.wikipedia.org/wiki/World_War_II_casualties#endnote_France,   accessed July 10, 2006. Wikipedia offers the following break-down. Out of a population of 41,700,000 the French lost 212,000 soldiers and 267,000 civilians from 1939 to 1945. The breakdown is as follows: battle of France, 92,000; Western Front 1940–1944, 58,000; PoWs, 40,000; Alsatians and Lorrainers conscripted to the German Army, 30,000–40,000. Among civilian casualties: 20,000 civilian combatants (Resistance fighters); 15,000 Roma people; 83,000 Jewish deportees; 120,000 civilian victims of military action. Total loss of life is estimated at 562,000 combatants and non-combatants which produces 13.5 deaths per 1,000 people.

on the road. The nurse remembered the woman being in enormous pain when she arrived at the clinic in a state of advanced labor. After only minutes of arriving at the clinic, the mother gave birth, on a camping cot, to a "ravishing young girl."[60] Indeed, the hospital in Brive kept separate records for the maternity ward. Between May and September 1940, 117 refugees gave birth to their babies in Brive alone.[61] Because the crisis lasted throughout the summer, most pregnant women from the north in their final trimester had no choice but to deliver their babies in unfamiliar towns.

Concentration camps

Beginning in June, and continuing throughout the period of partition and Occupation, a camp system grew to supplement private housing schemes. The concentration camp offered one solution to the problem of providing lodging for arriving refugees. Mark Mazower insists that by the start of the war, concentration camps, a tool of political repression and social control, had become quite the norm across Europe; the Nazi camps housing between 25,000 and 50,000 individuals during the 1930s and the Soviet gulags containing millions.[62] Concentration camps first began to multiply in France's south-west region to accommodate the Spanish republican refugees fleeing Franco's fascists. From the Pyrénées to as far north as Haute-Vienne, many of these camps still, in 1940, quartered lingering Spanish refugees. With the influx of French and Belgian refugees, locals reflexively directed refugees to the lightly occupied barracks of these containment facilities. By November 1940, Renée Poznanski reports that "a commission on camp statistics for the Coordinating Committee of the organizations providing relief to foreign internees and refugees in France reported that there were at least 53,610 people in French camps"; presumably in both zones.[63] By 1943, the "Free Zone" would operate approximately 115 internment centers.[64]

---

[60] *Le Petit Gaillard*, June 5, 1940.

[61] AMBG, "L'Hôpital de Brive: L'enregistrement de juin 1940." All the women listed a department other than Corrèze as their department of primary residence, thus I have assumed that they figured among the refugee population.

[62] Mark Mazower, *The Dark Continent. Europe's Twentieth Century* (New York: Knopf, 1998), 38.

[63] Poznanski, *Jews in France during World War II*, 175.

[64] Soulignac, *Les camps d'internement en Limousin*, 16. Soulignac identifies twenty-two additional camps in the Non-Occupied Zone beyond those studied by Anne Grynberg in *Les camps de la honte*.

Barbed wire fences wrapped around posts in the middle of a field segmented the rural landscapes, separating human space from animal pasture. Inside the fence, wooden barracks capped with corrugated tin roofs sheltered cement or earthen floors, grass mattresses, and hand-pumped showers. Here refugees could eat and sleep, undisturbed by animals, and unobserved by townspeople busily trying to preserve normalcy. The internment camps in Haute-Vienne, just north of Corrèze, reached full capacity in June 1940.[65] Similar centers reopened at Évaux-les-Bains and Boussac in Creuse and Doux and Auchère in Corrèze. These camps first accommodated all types of refugees, but after November 1940, quickly evolved into containment facilities or "surveillance centers" for French men and foreigners declared as "undesirable" or "excluded."[66] In summer 1940, refugees lobbied to be sheltered in their own apartments, in schools, or in the private homes of generous Corréziens; however, many would have no choice but to turn to the camp system as at least a temporary form of shelter.

By the end of June, the refugee crisis had already taken a toll on the public treasury. The Service of Refugees' prewar plans had not calculated the possibility of a multinational, prolonged displacement crisis, and no clear protocol for assigning financial responsibility for the crisis existed.

In June, the amounts and eligibility requirements for refugee allotments could vary from town to town. Establishing a uniform policy for refugee allocations only transpired once a national government fully re-emerged in mid-July. In the meantime, refugees began to articulate expectations for state assistance to finance food, housing, and travel costs, which extended the language and demands for protection from the pre-flight period, to the experience of displacement.

Late June and early July presented prefects and mayors with challenges, but also flexibility before the new Vichy government or German authorities tightened the grip on policy. Locally improvised solutions frequently worked to the advantage of refugees. But locally administered policies could sometimes swing the other way, exposing refugees to the whims of a particular community's charitable feeling. Expanding upon the Schuman program that had been established for Alsatian and Lorrainer evacuees, the mayor of Brive instituted a new system of relief that entitled *all* displaced persons, regardless of department or country of origin, to receipt of cash assistance. Adults could collect the sum of 10 francs per day and children under thirteen could collect 6 francs per

---

[65] Soulignac, *Les camps d'internement en Limousin*, 26, 49.
[66] Soulignac, *Les camps d'internement en Limousin*, 26.

day.[67] With the announcement of a system of refugee relief, universally payable to all refugees, the mayor of Brive adopted a financial burden that could be financed only through national reimbursements.

Prefect Papinot instructed mayors to continue paying cash advances to each refugee during the period from July 1 to July 15. He also gave the first policy regarding in-kind aid, ordering that: "if evacuees are housed in hotels, the municipal treasury will reimburse each hotel upon receipt of the bill for each refugee."[68] The same was to be true with regard to reimbursement of bakers for bread given to refugees. But in a strict fiscal warning, the prefect cautioned that the rules required that in no case, whether for provisions in-kind aid or for housing provided by hotels should the sum paid per day, per refugee, exceed 10 francs for adults and 6 francs for children. In Corrèze alone, with a refugee count of 250,000 at the peak of the crisis, this rate yielded a daily cost of almost 2,500,000 francs. This did not include other expenses, such as construction of temporary lodging, mattresses for shelters, utensils for public canteens, or clothes for the neediest refugees, which mayors could order from the state store that had been opened in Tulle. The prefect's policy anticipated a definable end to the crisis. He stipulated that all allocations were to be terminated as of September 1, 1940, based on that being the tentative refugee repatriation date for the Corrèze.[69] At this point in the crisis, the Service of Refugees and many of the local governments ran budgetary deficits. No one really knew when and how the bill for the crisis would be paid. By late 1940, the government began to collect taxes again, but department prefects complained throughout the Occupation about strapped financial resources. The Service of Refugees would attempt to deliver the bill to the German occupying authority, but the Germans agreed to cover costs pertaining to their operations only.

Universal accessibility to refugee relief seemed to be an obvious and desirable policy, at least from the point of view of Papinot and the mayors of Corrèze. However, universal distribution created administrative headaches, experienced by administrators and refugees alike, that would soon obscure – particularly for government functionaries – the human rights aspect of relief. For the mayor of Brive, his immediate concern stemmed from the need to prevent an assault upon his municipal headquarters by an on-rush of refugees. To avoid public disorder

---

[67] AMBG, Series H/IV/98.
[68] ADC, Series 1E/DEP/272/399, Memo, Tulle, July 3, 1940 from Prefect Papinot to mayors of Corrèze.
[69] ADC, Series 1E/DEP/272/399, Memo, Tulle, July 3, 1940.

the commissioner of police was charged to provide surveillance at City Hall on June 29 and 30 to oversee the transfer of what he described as, "large sums of money."[70]

Expansion of a system of cash assistance to refugees touched off complaints from residents of Corrèze concerned about the possibility of refugee abuse of local hospitality. Residents began to see their charity, combined with cash payments to refugees, not as an entitlement owed to their displaced compatriots, but as a gift or privilege that demanded expressions of gratitude and oaths of honest stewardship. Monsieur Roumajon, the Secretary of the Welcome Committee of Brive, conveyed residents' concerns to the mayor:

Refugees all request cash allotments but continue to benefit from in-kind assistance. It would be worthwhile, from my perspective, to imagine, before cash assistance is distributed, a means of discriminating between refugees who have no resources and, as in the past, have enjoyed free meals, and those who have received cash advances.[71]

Roumajon's letter implied that refugees receiving cash allowances should be made to pay for their own meals. He anticipated emerging problems of how to determine which refugees should receive cash as opposed to in-kind aid, unemployment benefits, or military benefits.

By the end of June, most refugees, homeless and unemployed since mid-May, had depleted their personal cash reserves. Although many refugees had attempted to pack up everything, most had discarded all but the most essential belongings along the road and had no cash to purchase daily supplies. Despite refugees' obvious destitution, from the very beginning of the cash relief program's existence, Frenchmen argued over eligibility and entitlement. Conversations and debates about the breadth of refugee relief also drew upon interwar political debates about government welfare entitlement programs and unemployment compensation. It seemed inherent in the nature of refugee relief that the program would foster categories of entitlement and exclusion.

Two central problems emerged: the universality of relief eligibility and the duration of the paid assistance program. For refugees, the threat of exclusion from relief allocation eligibility translated into forced return to the Occupied Zone. More simply, without state aid, refugees could not afford to finance long-term displacement. The Germans continued to prohibit the transfer of property, including bank transfers, from one zone to the other throughout the highpoint of the crisis. Restricting

---

[70] AMBG, Series H/IV/98, Memo, June 27, 1940.
[71] AMBG, Series H/IV/98, letter signed, M. Roumajon, Sécrétaire du Comité d'accueil.

relief thus forced refugees to return to the Occupied Zone to face an uncertain future under German authority. Many national officials, who assumed roles in Pétain's government, hoped to encourage refugees to return to the Occupied Zone, believing that once refugees returned home, life could resume "normally," and the government could avoid a further draw-down of the public treasury. On June 26, *Le Corrézien* published a notice to relocated workers, stating that they would be eligible for refugee assistance, but only until refugees re-established contact with their employer, at which time officials expected employers to pay unemployment compensation to help sustain uprooted workers.[72]

Some Vichy politicians expounded upon the moral depravity of unemployment compensation. On July 5, *Le Corrézien* quoted Vichy's Secretary of Labor, Charles Pomaret: "The politics of unemployment allocations must disappear from our national economy." Pomaret chastised workers who did not work, but collected unemployment benefits. The minister believed only soldiers and veterans should qualify for receipt of state assistance. He anticipated Vichy's "Work, Family, Country" slogan insisting: "Today's government refuses to accept the idea of unemployment and above all rewarded unemployment; it exalts the idea of the necessity of work."[73] Pomaret's words announced that entitlements of all kind, refugee or unemployment, contradicted the new regime's ethic of self-sufficiency, sacrifice, and hard work. Vichy's work ethic sounded strikingly similar to the Nazis' "Strength Through Joy" volunteerist work programs designed to absorb, but not pay, the masses of unemployed.

Origins of refugee classifications

On July 3, Papinot attempted to rationalize the distribution of relief in his department. His first comprehensive directive to mayors about distribution of cash payments referenced earlier directives issued by the Service of Refugees. The first task mayors faced was a procedural one: to gather, on monthly rosters, personal information about each refugee who submitted a request for assistance. The information requested included: refugees' name, date of birth, place of origin, sex, marital status, occupation, number of children, date of departure, nationality, and race. The resulting tables provided excellent catalogues of information about refugees.

[72] *Le Corrézien*, 182-T.78, June 26, 1940.
[73] *Le Corrézien*, 182-T.78, July 5, 1940.

In July the prefect sent copies of an affidavit issued by Vichy that required each refugee to verify his race as "aryenne ou israélite." This policy predated the September 1940 statutes mandating the registration of Jews with the state in occupied territories.[74] Because displaced Jewish refugees needed the assistance, they most likely registered more uniformly than those required to submit to the census in the Occupied Zone on October 20, 1940.[75] Thus, began the process of establishing refugee rosters that grouped individuals in categories based on national identity, departmental or regional identity, and racial/religious status. Refugee registration also began the process of sorting individuals and creating subgroups of refugees to be ranked for receipt of government services that ranged from receipt of cash payments, to assistance with employment placement, to eligibility for repatriation. Application for refugee relief forced refugees to disclose their racial, ethnic, and class status to state agencies. Identity disclosures, mandated by the rules governing application for refugee relief, would provide the necessary information for the implementation of discriminatory policies regarding not only relief payment, but also eligibility for subsidized housing, repatriation, employment, and property restitution.

It is important to remember a few facts regarding the history and purpose of the adoption of population classification systems. Use of such identity markers in summer 1940 represented continuity with similar policies adopted under the Third Republic during the interwar years. In the 1920s and after 1933, Mary Dewhurst Lewis finds that French immigration officials created a variety of different categories.[76] Lewis argues that even once Léon Blum encouraged his Popular Front Government to take a "liberal stance" on refugee policy, municipal police in cities like Marseilles and Lyons would deny refugee status and reclassify foreigners in ways that limited their economic and political status in France, or worse, resulted in expulsion.[77] As the government developed bureaucratic tools to track the flow of immigrants from Russia, Poland, Romania, and Greece during the 1920s, French officials created forms to register immigrants' nationality, occupation, and other information deemed pertinent to considerations of extending visas or naturalization privileges. According to Anne Grynberg, French officials did not ask immigrants to declare their confessional or racial status on the forms used in the 1920s, making it difficult to know how many

---

[74] ADC, Series W/522, W/66, dated July 1940.
[75] Poznanski, *Jews in France during World War II*, 31.
[76] Lewis, *Boundaries of the Republic*, 184–185.
[77] Lewis, *Boundaries of the Republic*, 180–181.

European Jews immigrated to France during this period.[78] However, with the ascension of Hitler to power in Germany, the French state began to require refugees to declare themselves Jewish, or "Israélite." Chautemps initiated the procedure when he asked the French government on April 20, 1933 to open French borders to German Jews seeking asylum in France. He requested that Foreign Service officers working in Germany treat visa demands from German Jews in the most "liberal spirit."[79] Even if German Jews arrived at the border without passports or visas, Chautemps ordered prefects to admit them. Hence, in the spirit of extending asylum to German Jewish refugees fleeing Nazi Germany, the French state adopted a procedure whereby refugees declared their racial, confessional, or, in a few cases, political identity.

In July 1940, the innovation in the Vichy-issued declaration form was the requirement that *all* refugee aid applicants swear under oath whether they were "aryenne ou israélite." Most functionaries and refugees probably assumed that this declaration represented a continuation or clarification of policies already in practice under the Third Republic. Only in August, when repatriation began, would the declarations begin to have exclusionary meaning for the return options available to different refugees; exclusions that could prove life-saving.

During the summer of 1940, the oath-signing requirement did not seem to generate any protest from refugees. While refugees of all backgrounds wrote complaints to prefects and mayors about a variety of issues, extensive research found no case of a refugee objecting to the oath. The absence of objections to signing the affidavit is consistent with reactions by Jews and non-Jews to identity disclosure requirements implemented wherever the Germans assumed administrative authority. Indeed, as we will see, the Germans required the signing of the affidavit to ensure that Jews did *not* return to the Occupied Zone. However, it is important to note that the fact that the forms required *all* applicants for refugee relief to declare themselves confirms that, by late June, most refugees had become aware of government policies to classify them along racial, regional, economic, and religious lines. By the time the Germans agreed to open the Line of Demarcation for repatriation, many refugees had learned to eschew identity disclosure for a multitude of reasons.

---

[78] Grynberg, *Les camps de honte*, 22.
[79] Archives de la préfecture de police de Paris, Dossier 407. Cited first by Gilbert Badia et al., *Les Barbelés de l'exil* (Grenoble: Presses universitaires de Grenoble, 1979). Quoted here from Grynberg, *Les camps de honte*, 26.

In June and July 1940, departmental and local administrations, host communities, and French national authorities all wished for universal refugee repatriation. Seventy years later, it is hard to imagine why anyone would have chosen to return to German-occupied territory. However, at the time only the Germans, and some refugees, rejected the idea of complete and universal repatriation to the Occupied Zone. Expectations about the timing of repatriation colored policymakers' and refugees' initiatives regarding employment, housing, and allocations through August. While most refugees voiced a desire for a swift return to their homes in the Occupied Territories without consideration of the political or economic consequences, a smaller group of refugees expressed uncertainty about either what to do or where to go. Alsatians and Lorrainers felt most confident remaining in the south, especially after the Reich formally expelled Alsatian Jews and Francophiles from Alsace on July 16 and then annexed the territory on August 4.[80] Yet some Alsatians and Lorrainers did choose to return to the annexed territory. Because so many refugees *did* hope to return to their homes, they began to imagine life in the Occupied Zone as somehow better or simpler than life in the Free Zone. Prohibition of communication between the two zones made it difficult for refugees and officials alike to imagine the destruction of northern towns brought by continued Allied bombing.

Temporarily re-located to Pau (Basses-Pyrénées) in the Non-Occupied Zone, Schuman issued, on June 26, the first statement by a member of the national government regarding refugee repatriation. *Le Petit Gaillard* and other papers carried Schuman's words of assurance that the Armistice included stipulations for returning refugees to their homes. Schuman urged refugees to remain in the towns where they now resided to wait while the government worked with the Germans to re-establish lines of communication and networks of transportation.[81] On July 2, Schuman updated officials and refugees, announcing that the Germans continued to prevent train travel between the Occupied and the Non-Occupied zones, preferring to first repatriate refugees displaced within the Occupied Zone. Southern refugees experienced the announcement as a disappointment. In anticipation that the Germans would soon rescind the interdiction of travel between the two zones, Schuman ordered officials at the SNCF to begin drawing up train schedules to transport refugees from south to north.[82] Despite his

---

[80] Poznanski, *Jews in France during World War II*, 27.
[81] Robert Schuman, quoted in *Le Petit Gaillard*, June 26, 1940.
[82] *Le Corrézien*, 182-T.78, July 2, 1940.

aggressive efforts to repatriate refugees, an action supported by Pétain, the new government replaced Schuman as Director of the Service of Refugees within days. Schuman's replacement, a retired prefect named Louis Florintin Marlier, had emerged as one of the most important negotiators between Vichy and the Germans in the first days of the Occupation.

Repatriation, as discussed in the following chapter, topped the list of priorities for negotiations between the Germans and the Vichy government. Throughout the summer, discussion of repatriation preoccupied Vichy officials, refugees, and mayors. By July, another very important service, the lost family locator service, coordinated by the Service of Refugees and supported by municipal newspapers, began to function and contributed to refugees' decisions concerning where to go.

'I lost my child on the road': family reconciliation as a right to return

The Center for Family Regrouping was established in Paris on May 29, 1940; however, after the evacuation of Paris, the tracking of family members became decentralized. Refugees often filed their names, department of origin, names of traveling companions, and temporary addresses with the host town Chamber of Commerce and newspaper.[83] Throughout the summer local newspapers published names of missing refugees, organized by department of origin. As missing-person lists became longer and newspapers became scarcer, lost persons' bureaux in each municipality tried to publicize and exchange refugee lists. After the signing of the Armistice, the Paris branch of the Service of Refugees reopened its lost person locator service, but the prohibition on communication between the two zones meant that it could respond only to claims filed within the Occupied Zone. In the Free Zone on July 2, the department of the Marne announced in newspaper advertisements that the prefecture had relocated to Albi in Tarn. Paul Marchandeau invited refugees from the Marne to send missing-person inquiries to his office in the Girls' Normal School in Albi.[84]

News about demobilized soldiers or prisoners of war (PoW) was also difficult to obtain. Sarah Fishman puts the number of soldiers killed in the battle of France at 92,000 and the PoW population at 1,800,000.[85] Many families waited weeks or months to learn about the fate of PoW husbands and sons. After June 10, following the near total disintegration

---

[83] *Le Petit Gaillard*, May 29, 1940.   [84] *Le Corrézien*, 182-T.78, July 2, 1940.
[85] Fishman, *We Will Wait*, 27.

of military organization, the French Army was unable to keep track of soldiers' locations. Preoccupied with the war against Britain, the Germans were slow to release information about prisoner's conditions, holding back information in many cases until November 1940. Madame Dufay, a Belgian mother traveling with her four children, wandered the streets of Brive waiting to depart to a more southerly destination. Since the outbreak of war she had been without news of her husband, a soldier in the Belgian Army. Suddenly, looking across the road, she recognized a soldier from her husband's regiment. She approached the soldier to ask whether he knew her husband. "Wait here," said the soldier, "I'll go and look for him." Within minutes the entire family was reunited.[86] While such serendipitous reunions surely occurred, the sealing of the Line of Demarcation made these occasions rare.

The Line of Demarcation imposed the most serious obstacle to interzonal family reunification. On July 10, the Post Telegraph and Telephone (PTT) service, reorganized in Vichy under the Ministry of Communication, established a service in the Non-Occupied Zone for "dispersed families." In the Non-Occupied Zone, the information bureau attempted to centralize refugees' efforts to locate lost family members. Unfortunately, the service had the reverse problem of its Paris-based twin. The Germans allowed the Vichy bureau to function only in the Non-Occupied Zone.[87] To facilitate family reunification, as well as efforts to re-establish economic exchanges between the two zones, Vichy would prioritize negotiations dedicated to easing travel and communication between the two zones.

Political uncertainty, displacement, and sky-rocketing food prices fueled the already present atmosphere of mutual distrust. Northerners brought with them cultural and regional differences foreign to southerners. Soon, Brivists renamed the displaced of France's dairy land, "Mr. and Mrs. Cheese," to describe the refugees' preferences for butter and Camembert. These preferences were in contrast to southern regional tastes for olive oil, goat's cheese, and stronger productions such as Roquefort.[88] Light-hearted in intent, the barbs made of northern refugees' customs also manifested a sharper note of distrust and suspicion. Vichy politicians capitalized on, and institutionalized, the mistrust, requiring prefects to closely monitor refugees' activities and submit monthly reports to the Minister of the Interior. The government encouraged local residents to report suspicious activity among

---

[86] *Le Petit Gaillard*, May 28, 1940.
[87] *Le Corrézien*, 182-T.78, July 10, 1940.
[88] Soulignac, *Les camps d'internement en Limousin*, 26.

refugees, as it had before the exodus. Local police surveillance targeted potential communist agitation and foreign refugees. Soon programs to monitor foreign refugee communities expanded to police French citizens as well.

Refugees' dependence upon state-issued relief facilitated police surveillance of refugee communities. Refugee surveillance activities, however, were not a Vichy-specific innovation. During the Third Republic after waves of refugees arrived in 1938 in the wake of Munich and Kristallnacht, Daladier's government created a special border police and authorized "detention centers for dangerous foreigners," such as the one at Les Milles.[89] As the crisis spilled into July, the new Pétain government pressed local bureaucrats to monitor more vigorously, and more effectively contain the mobile population. From its inception, Vichy rightly feared that the refugee population would act as an incubator for political opposition. By virtue of having to interact with government officials on a daily basis, refugees soon developed a litany of mild complaints against the government. Hence, by late July, the Minister of the Interior directed prefects and mayors to employ several initiatives for keeping an eye on refugees and guiding refugees' activities.

Foreign refugees especially came into direct communication with government officials due to the need to exchange currency. For Belgian refugees, numbering nearly 2 million, along with 70,000 Luxembourgeois and 50,000 Dutch citizens, currency conversion was their lifeline to independent living.[90] Fearing a draw on the money supply, French authorities quickly imposed restrictions on currency exchange. As of May 29, the government limited Belgians to exchanging 2,000 Belgian francs per person every fifteen days, with a maximum of 5,000 Belgian francs per family every fifteen days.[91] Arno Mayer, the noted historian of Europe, was a young refugee from Luxembourg in 1940. He remembered that his family had swiftly left Luxembourg in the night of May 9, armed with only a suitcase full of Luxembourgian francs. The Mayer family luckily exchanged their francs immediately upon entering France, before the imposition of restrictions. The converted currency helped the Mayer family eventually reach the United States.[92]

As early in the crisis as late May and mid-June, before the state began distribution of allocations to refugees, many foreign refugees reverted to a barter economy. The near collapse of the international monetary exchange system further added to foreign refugees' dependence upon

---

[89] Lewis, *Boundaries of the Republic*, 228.
[90] *Le Petit Gaillard*, June 5, 1940.   [91] *Le Petit Gaillard*, May 29, 1940.
[92] Interview with Arno Mayer, Princeton, New Jersey, 1996.

French government officials. To exchange funds, they found themselves continually needing to verify their identity and disclose their residence. Out of these exchanges, an aggressive program of tracking developed to monitor the status of German, Swiss, and Eastern European refugees and naturalized citizens in southern localities. An editorial in the Tulle daily *Le Corrézien* warned: "Foreigners living in France, like Frenchmen themselves, must save the endangered fatherland."[93] Ironically, many foreigners who did apply for military duty in Paris later told stories of being turned away; and those who managed to enlist often received inferior equipment.

Other policies imposed restrictions on foreigners that French nationals also experienced. To stem car travel by foreigners, local authorities impounded all vehicles owned by foreign refugees once the refugees had determined to "settle" in a particular French town; but local authorities also requisitioned French-owned cars. Slightly more discriminating, national directives prohibited the sale of gas to foreign travelers, but soon gas rationing affected most refugees. On June 10, no foreign refugee was allowed to move from one community to another without an official "sauf-conduit," a pass to be issued by the local Service of Refugees. A similar decree ordered all foreigners to deposit all arms and munitions, including hunting rifles, at the police commissioner's headquarters. This policy directive spoke to fears that foreigners might mount an overthrow of French authorities inspired by Italy's entry into the war.

"Work makes us independent": local officials recruit refugee labor

Prior to the Armistice, refugee labor constituted a potential military resource. Although hardly a conscripted labor program, the Refugee Placement Bureau was created on June 1, 1940 by the Minister of Labor as part of the effort to continue war production and monitor foreign refugees.[94] The Placement Bureau required French, Belgian, Dutch, and Luxembourgeois refugees to file a summary of their work credentials and aptitude in different industries, notably those related to national defense. The published notices assured foreigners that they would receive equal pay with French workers. The Confédération Générale du Travail (CGT) of Belgium also set up an agreement with the CGT of France to monitor employment, and help families find lodging and contact lost family members. On June 1, Belgium's Minister of Public

[93] *Le Corrézien*, 182-T.78, June 6, 1940.   [94] *La Voix Corrézienne*, June 1, 1940.

Health urged Belgian "men and women alike" to quickly enroll at French work placement offices to continue with the war effort.[95] French farm laborers were also required to register in work placement programs. In Corrèze, the Bureau of Refugee Farmers was one of the first refugee-specific services to be created on May 21.[96] Primarily an agricultural region, Corrézian employers sought manual agricultural laborers. Local agriculture had suffered the greatest loss of labor since the mobilization of soldiers and defense workers began in 1938. However, matching farmers with refugees, most of whom came from an urban, industrial background caused friction. Many urban workers were not accustomed to low agricultural wages and felt exploited by the situation. In mid-June the mayor of Brive encouraged rural farmers to hire refugee laborers who had the physical ability for farm work but lacked formal training.[97]

Absorption of refugees by agricultural enterprises helped to resolve both a material and a morale problem. Reports submitted to the Minister of the Interior estimated projected expenditures for work programs targeted at demobilized soldiers and refugees. Table 3 shows Papinot's projected expenses for a fiscal year beginning in August 1940 for the Corrèze. He requested 6,790,000 francs for potable water and food, but nothing for housing or cash payments. Papinot's total credit request amounted to 15,000,000 francs.

The monthly prefect reports do not provide concrete costs of refugee relief incurred in each department, but they do indicate the philosophy of how to manage surplus refugee labor. In August, prefects hoped that repatriation would end the need for refugee cash distributions, and thus did not include refugee allocations in their projected costs. Refugee and demobilized soldiers' labor could fuel reconstruction projects and general infrastructure improvement through state-funded work programs that paid them salaries, eliminating the necessity to dispense relief payments.

Employees of the French state, especially railway employees, represented an easily transplanted category of refugee worker. Refugee railway workers easily integrated into local branch operations, transporting refugees by train, delivering information about the German Army's advance, and eventually participating in refugee repatriation to the Occupied Zone. Displaced government workers eagerly reported to the local branch department of their service in hopes

[95] *La Voix Corrézienne*, June 1, 1940.
[96] *La Voix Corrézienne*, June 12, 1940.
[97] AMBG, Series H/IV, Memo, mayor of Brive, June 16, 1940.

Table 3. *Declaration of incurred and planned expenses for "Work Programs for Demobilized Soldiers and Refugees," prefect of Corrèze, Alfred Papinot, August 3, 1940*

Type of expense	Estimated cost
Rural roads	5,177,000 francs
Food and potable water	6,790,000 francs
Rural electrification	12,778,000 francs
Agricultural improvements	2,552,000 francs
Regular workers' pay (general)	134,000 work days/10 months
Agricultural and non-skilled labor	89,000 days/10 months
Departmental roads and bridges	300,000 worker days/per year
Estimated credit request	15,000,000 francs

Source: AN F/1c/III/1147, Office of the Prefect of the Corrèze. Credit request from Prefect Papinot to the Under Secretary of the Minister of the Interior at Vichy, August 3, 1940.

of receiving some restitution for lost wages, but were usually disappointed. While work offered refugees a means to establish financial independence from state-funded refugee assistance, it also exposed them to greater scrutiny. Once repatriation began, local officials used relief and employment registration lists to locate refugees and enforce their return.

"No money left to buy shoes": refugees record woes and demand rights

By late June, material deprivation substituted for the bombs, which had initially threatened civilians' lives. Civilians wrote to lodge their complaints and demand state assistance. In Brive and Tulle, refugees petitioned the mayors' offices in such volume that volunteers and employed staff could not open, much less respond to, all the in-coming mail. This reality preserved treasures for historians and posterity. Gauthier Kleber, a refugee from the Parisian working-class suburb of St. Denis, recorded in his request for shoes or slippers, the toll the exodus had taken on his family. During an aerial bombing of Étampes (Loiret), his family had lost all their belongings, escaping with their lives, but nothing else. Kleber's children walked the remainder of the 500-km journey to Brive in bare feet! One of his children suffered a deviated vertebrae and required enormous medical care. Their daily refugee allocation paid for food, but left nothing to purchase shoes and other necessities.

Kleber requested that the mayor please provide any additional assistance possible to help alleviate his family's misfortune.[98]

On June 14, Charles Bourreoue of Belgium solicited the mayor's help in establishing an avenue of employment for the Belgian expatriate community. The director of a Belgian galosh manufactory, Bourreoue desired the mayor's assistance in identifying a suitable site in Brive to begin manufacturing galoshes. He believed that several experienced Belgian galosh workers had relocated to Brive.[99] While Bourreoue's ambitions might appear slightly misguided given the dry climate of Corrèze in mid-June, his entrepreneurial spirit suggests the optimism embraced by many refugees and their awareness of the need to construct long-term solutions to combat financial ruin.

Gulla Carmelo, a carnival worker from Troyes (Aube), wrote to the commissioner of police requesting permission to launch a luggage-carrying service at the train station. Carmelo had been charging other refugees for porter services when railway representatives required that he apply for a business permit. Carmelo's request documented his experience in the exodus. Due to an illness, the army had discharged him in December 1939. The unmarried twenty-six-year-old left Troyes with his two younger sisters. Robbers had stolen their money and personal items during the exodus, leaving them destitute. A porter service would, "allow me to make a bit of money to buy us some new clothes since you know it is beginning to get a little cold in the evenings."[100] Carmelo's experience illustrates how readily locals referred refugees to police, even those attempting to gain economic independence and diminish reliance upon the state.

When displaced employers settled in the south, they frequently tapped authorities and refugee networks to locate former employees. Monsieur Merlin, director of Demico, an armament factory evacuated from the Yonne, hoped the mayor of Brive could help reunite his dispersed workforce and contribute to the war effort. Merlin explained that he resided at St. Mer-la-Bouille with much of the factory machinery. He, and several members of his staff, had successfully evacuated Demico's workforce, composed mainly of women traveling with their children. During the chaotic retreat Merlin was separated from a few employees. He sought assistance in tracking his staff, and finding a space to begin manufacturing. Merlin's request suggested

[98] AMBG, Series H/IV, letter dated July 18, 1940.
[99] AMBG, Series H/IV, letter dated June 14, 1940, Lisle-sur-Tarne. AMBG, Series H/IV, letter dated July 18, 1940.
[100] AMBG, Series H/IV, Guerre 1939–40, letter, August 17, 1940.

how profoundly committed some Frenchmen felt toward a continued armed resistance.[101]

Workers tried to find their employers as well. One female employee of the armaments manufacturer, Chernard-et-Walcker, tried to track down her husband, a conscripted laborer of the firm. He had disappeared during the bombing of Blois (Loir-et-Cher) when military authorities had closed the road that he had run down seeking shelter. Since Chernard-et-Walcker had retreated to Brive, she wrote to Brive's mayor: "I desperately need my husband to come find me because I have absolutely no money left." Unfortunately for her family, she forgot to sign her name or give a return address, suggesting stress and perhaps a low level of education.[102]

Refugees' flexibility proved to be important both for their own economic survival and in terms of how the host community perceived their willingness to contribute, rather than merely be assisted. Newspaper classifieds were filled with refugee solicitations for employment. Women especially promoted themselves as flexible, multitalented workers. One blurb boasted: "Refugee from Nord, single, serious, middle-school certificate [brevet], can sew, provide child care, be a female companion, or a housemaid: city or countryside acceptable."[103] Employment offerings included jobs whose skill-sets traditionally fell to one of the sexes, but remained open to either. One posting advertised: "French or Allied refugees of either sex with a professional interest in the fabrication of sheets, drapes and linens, or tin makers, boiler makers or cutlery makers, who have not yet found employment to present themselves at the supply office of the garment industry, 22 rue Bansac in Clermont-Ferrand."[104] In one sense, jobs for women such as those advertised for work in Clermont-Ferrand (Puy-de-Dôme) offered refugees the opportunity to supplement their families' refugee allocations. Often, however, women refugees found themselves in charge of destitute families with hungry children, living outside the structure provided by school or neighborhoods. For these women, expanded family responsibilities made seeking employment in a different town very difficult.

As the displacement crisis endured, a desire to ease the financial burden of the crisis on southern municipalities resulted in overly rapid movements to curtail some of the diverse forms of refugee assistance developed in June and July. State assistance did serve refugees' needs,

---

101 AMBG, Series H/IV, letter, July 2, 1940.
102 AMBG, Series H/IV, letter, Chatelleraut, June 27, 1940.
103 *Le Corrézien*, 182-T.78, June 25, 1940.
104 *Le Corrézien*, 182-T.78, June 6, 1940.

while only slightly limiting their autonomy to exercise choice about their own destiny. But by August new, or re-minted, national functionaries entered into the policy mix, bringing a desired uniformity to refugee services, but often at the cost of refugees' individual sovereignty.

Monsieur Louis Rouel wrote to Brive's mayor in response to the announcement that, as of August 2, refugees receiving cash allowances would be asked to pay for their daily meals. Monsieur Rouel objected arguing:

Having submitted a request to receive a refugee allotment on July 8, my wife and myself [and child] have still received nothing. We have absolutely no resources and live with my mother who only receives six francs per day. Four of us live off ten francs per day. We beseech you to continue the free meals at the canteen because we will not be able to pay for them ourselves.[105]

Conclusion

In Corrèze, local residents had extended a warm welcome to all segments of the refugee population. Individuals opened their homes to refugees, and local businesses attempted to absorb the surplus labor. Local women's groups improvised relief efforts and harnessed the community to deliver the maximum aid available within the department, staking out for themselves a leadership role in the chaos of a collapsed state.

Alongside host community sympathy and good will, failure to "resolve" the crisis began to provoke criticism of refugees. A few southerners complained: "Refugees wanted too much cheese and butter." "Alsatians spoke with a German, not a French accent," locals observed. "Refugees swindled the public treasury," writers to Corrézian editorial pages accused.

Evidence suggests that tolerance for refugees, and especially foreign refugees, varied from department to department. In the upper Limousin, scarcity of food and competitive marketing of local products, mingled with ostracizing identity markers eroded refugee–host relations.[106] Papinot's administration extended aid to all refugees regardless of class or national origin, race, or regional identity. Refugees residing in Gironde, Landes, and Pyrénées-Orientales expressed frustration and, in a few cases, fear over the hostility that public officials and private residents voiced toward them. To be fair, these departments had

---

[105] AMBG, Series H/IV, letter dated August 2, 1940 from M. and Mme Louis Rouel, refugees from Reims.
[106] Fogg, *Politics of Everyday Life in Vichy France*, 84.

served as the primary hosts to approximately 400,000 Spanish refugees flooding out of Spain throughout the mid-1930s. The mayors of Corrèze, as well as Prefect Papinot, extended invitations to many refugees who requested relocation to Corrèze from other departments. The Corrèze's left-leaning prewar political traditions did matter in making the Corrèze a more welcoming center for refugees than neighboring departments to the south.

As the crisis wore on, taking an increased toll on the public treasury, French men and women of all classes waited to see how, under the conditions of the Armistice, the French tax structure would re-emerge. Financing the crisis concerned all parties except the Germans, who stated that the costs belonged to the French. Thus, even in Corrèze, enthusiasm for refugee repatriation to the Occupied Zone gained support in the context of the depletion of public finances, and the growing scarcity of local resources such as food and shelter. By the end of July, the Pétain government decided to bring the crisis to an end and return the mass of refugees to their homes. The national administration replaced Schuman with Marlier. The new Director of the Service of Refugees embraced his main obligation: the repatriation of all refugees residing south of the Line of Demarcation to the Occupied Zone. He would even press the Germans to allow repatriation of refugees to the newly delimited "Forbidden Zone," which included Pas-de-Calais and Nord.

The local prefectoral and mayoral administrations initially welcomed foreigners and French men and women equally. Mayors and prefects relied upon and expanded the inadequate, but still model, relief structures drafted to accommodate Alsatian and Lorrainer evacuees from 1939.

Marshal Pétain's new government brought its own political agenda to address the refugee crisis. In Corrèze, the immediate consequence was the substitution of Ferdinand Musso for Papinot in September and the eventual purging of Henri Queuille from his mayoral seat in Neuvic. This purging of municipal and departmental authorities ultimately had an effect on the local policies drafted to manage the refugee crisis. Vichy's refugee policies would emerge alongside a vision for French reconstruction. Papinot's system of universal eligibility for refugee allocations fell victim to the proliferation of ideologically determined categories of relief entitlement.

Women's experience and actions

Women in host towns in France, and in cities across the Atlantic, also found paths toward empowerment, engaging in political and civic relief activities in the midst of war. In Brive-la-Gaillarde, local women moved into positions of authority while organizing the relief effort. They became first-responders in the national emergency. Among refugee women, young, unmarried women refugees possessed a limited advantage over their married and elderly counterparts. They could easily find volunteer jobs in the emerging rescue and relief infrastructure. In Tulle, where armaments production continued during the summer, independent women could also find employment, earning enough money to pay room and board and perhaps defer the need to return to the Occupied Zone. Working-class and peasant married women who had families and whose husbands were in the military, became dependent on state assistance and as such had fewer choices available to them, especially regarding repatriation to the Occupied Zone.

The state's delivery of services was a double-edged sword for displaced civilians. Dependency on the state subjected refugees to a set of state requirements, such as enrollment in obligatory refugee work programs. Dependency on the state also exposed refugees to surveillance programs that could ultimately limit their choices as to where and how they might live out the war and Occupation. Jewish and foreign refugee women who could not return to the Occupied Zone even if they wished to, enjoyed the extension of state relief, but they later became exposed to the dangers that accompanied being registered under an increasingly repressive authoritarian regime. Eventually, the policies that helped them survive would facilitate their persecution.

The experience of refugee women and women in the host communities echo the findings about narrowing options for economic and political activity for women uncovered by Miranda Pollard, Hanna Diamond, and Shannon Fogg. But it must be emphasized that refugee women's unique position of dependency on state relief within the Free Zone also offered them an opportunity to continue to articulate their demands upon the state for assistance. This allowed them to influence and structure, in a limited way, wartime and Occupation-time relief policy. As dependants, women became increasingly politicized during the refugee crisis and the Occupation, arguably about bread and butter issues as Hanna Diamond and Margaret Collins Weitz have both shown; but also in relation to processes linked to relief and restitution issues.[107] They experienced the exodus, defeat, and occupation as directly as had soldiers. This reality gained them a status comparable with veteran soldiers in the public imagination after the defeat. But a countercurrent ran against them as well: French refugees began to develop a sense that their government and compatriots treated them as somehow less

---

[107] Weitz, *Sisters in the Resistance*.

"French" than non-displaced citizens. The term "internally displaced person" (IDP) had not yet become a staple of the vocabulary of human-itarian crisis and international law, or of refugees. However, French refugees experienced a growing sense of themselves as outsiders within their own country, dependent upon the state for refugee allocations and upon strangers for tolerance and kindness, gradually building their consciousness as "internally displaced persons."[108] As the crisis wore on, French refugees, especially women, pressed for the enhancement of the programs and for protections afforded international refugees during war, and contributed to the developing postwar concept of the need to improve and institutionalize protections to civilian non-combatants.

---

[108] For a discussion of political and legal structures that emerged in the postwar era to define displaced persons (DPs) see Cohen, *In War's Wake*.

6   Paving the road for refugees' return

Marie Limousin must have been exhausted! She was twenty-two years old, six months pregnant, and traveling alone with her two-year-old daughter. On June 12, 1940 she had joined one of the last evacuation groups leaving Bar-le-Duc (Meuse) in Lorraine and made the trip south to the department of Lozère where she joined 70,000 other refugees.[1] By mid-August, Marie must have wanted to return to Bar-le-Duc and the Germans had agreed to allow the French to begin refugee repatriation. Marie received a laissez-passer (travel permit) to cross the Line of Demarcation. Initially all seemed well. By September 1, Marie and her daughter had traveled 704 km from Mende (Lozère) to Reims (Marne) in the Occupied Zone. However, German authorities stopped her and informed her that she could not return to Bar-le-Duc. Perhaps Marie did not *qualify* as *eligible* to repatriate to Lorraine, since only Lorrainers who would have qualified for German citizenship prior to 1919 could return to the newly annexed territory. Possibly, she refused to sign an oath of loyalty to the Reich, required of all returning Alsatians and Lorrainers. Perhaps she was Jewish, and hence also prohibited from reintegration. Whatever the reason, the German border patrols forced Marie to return to the refugee staging center in Reims, which was overcrowded with refugees similarly refused re-entry permission to restricted zones in Ardennes, Aisne, Pas-de-Calais, and Nord. But shortly after Marie's return to Reims, on September 11, Marnais officials placed the pregnant mother and her daughter on yet another train destined for Nantes, 516 km to the west. Nantes, located near the Atlantic coast of France, fell within a newly designated restricted zone. Two days later, authorities expelled Marie from Nantes and sent her on a 381-km train trip to Paris. By some miracle, after completing this two-week tour de France, Marie and her daughter found their way to the office of the prefect of the

[1] AN F/60/1507, Report, Service of Refugees, July 1940.

department of the Seine. Hungry and at the limit of her strength, Marie Limousin nearly collapsed.[2]

Moved by frustration and pity, the prefect of the Seine recorded the specifics of Limousin's odyssey in an unusually long and detailed report. It went to General Léon Fornel de la Laurencie, a French Armistice official who held the title, "General of the French Army Corps and Delegate of the French Government in the Occupied Territories." La Laurencie was the top military official empowered to negotiate problems arising from Occupation policy within the Occupied Zone.[3] Interzonal problems did not technically fall under la Laurencie's umbrella. Still, the prefect wanted to press upon the general the gravity of Limousin's case, and gain permission for her to remain in Paris. The prefect also wanted to communicate another urgent point: since August 31, 1940, prefects in the Free Zone had stopped distributing refugee relief payments, forcing floods of refugees into the Occupied Zone. Not knowing whether the withholding of payments was a legitimate policy (it was not), the Seine prefect insisted that the measure had resulted in a large number of refugees attempting to return to occupied areas where the Germans had restricted or prohibited refugee re-entry. Distressed refugees were thus congregating in Paris, turned back by the Germans from checkpoints all along the borders of the newly designated "Forbidden Zones."[4]

Miscommunication between branches of the French government regarding civilian security and refugee relief and return was now exacerbated by the presence of French administration operating in two zones, and the addition of a German administrative authority. Civilian refugees' security, health, and well-being were being compromised by new forms of bureaucratic miscommunication, the proliferation of subpartitioned zones of exclusion, and whimsical starts and stops to refugee repatriation. Rather than being a solution to the displacement crisis, repatriation introduced a new chapter in the enduring humanitarian disaster. As the challenges shifted back from the south to the north, German occupying authorities projected an image of mastery and charged the French with responsibility for the glitches in refugee return. Through the fall of 1940, German officials and Vichy representatives sparred in negotiations, continually redefining the terms of refugee repatriation,

---

[2] AN F/1a/3660. prefect of the Seine to the General of the Corps of the French Army. September 13, 1940.
[3] La Laurencie was an outspoken opponent of communism, and worked behind the scenes to weaken efforts to create a strong Franco-Soviet military alliance. See Crémieux-Brilhac, *Les français de l'an 40 II*, 510–512.
[4] Crémieux-Brilhac, *Les français de l'an 40 II*, 510–512.

passage across the Line of Demarcation and spheres of German and French authority. Led by General Otto von Stülpnagel, the Germans organized to continue the war against Great Britain, which required harnessing French industry, and thus French labor, to German wartime needs. In on-going talks between Vichy representatives and the German Armistice Commission, French leaders attempted to exploit German interests, such as having an industrial labor force return to the Forbidden Zone, and win to their advantage policies connected to areas of ambiguity created by the Armistice agreement.

Between July and September 1940, Franco-German negotiations, an unequal exchange between the occupier and the occupied, progressed with both sides seeking to shape the new conditions of cohabitation and establish rules and structures that would meet their needs. To resolve the worsening refugee and repatriation crisis, the Vichy government turned to the Service of Refugees. Rather than rely on its former Director, Robert Schuman, Vichy appointed a seasoned career man to claim the title, Préfet honoraire, Délégué spécial pour les Réfugiés (Honorary Prefect and Special Representative for Refugees). Louis Marlier thus became the chief diplomat, invested with full powers to negotiate terms with the German Armistice Commission in Paris for the repatriation of the approximately 7 million stranded French and foreign refugees. The operational issues of the service fell under the responsibility of a series of directors, beginning with Director Andrieux, and then to a weakly empowered successor, Director Lassalle-Séré. Meanwhile, Marlier crafted policy and communicated directives to the Minister of the Interior and to the prefects in both zones.[5] His efforts greatly influenced refugee reintegration and the policies and practices enforcing the partition of France. Marlier's career and his ambiguous wartime achievements have thus far escaped historical discussion and analysis despite their enormous impact upon the restructuring of the French population and management of foreign refugees.

Out of retirement: Louis Florentin Marlier answers a call to serve

Marlier became the man charged with returning the shattered and dispersed men and women of France to their homes. His emergence early in the Occupation as a new, but important functionary can be wrongly interpreted as an indication that he was a devotee of Pétain's ideas for

[5] AN F/1a/3660, M. Lassalle-Séré, Note from the Director of the Service of Refugees, Paris, December 10, 1940.

National Revolution. However, further investigation reveals a more complex and engaging man of state whose experience guided France through some of its most difficult times. Most historians today would agree that to have followed de Gaulle into British exile required extraordinary foresight and defiance that the majority of the French people lacked in June 1940. The historical reaction to the Gaullist resistance myth has effectively obscured a more common reality: the battle of France consumed the lives of 92,000 French soldiers and German troops captured and imprisoned 1,800,000 more.[6] These battle-experienced men did not enjoy the luxury of choosing exile. They stood defeated, as did their country. Marlier does not quite fit Robert Paxton's characterization of leaders of "occupation fascism," which called forth in the context of defeat and collaboration, "all the losers of the previous governing system."[7]

Marlier does not possess a headline profile in the annals of contemporary French history. Yet his career under the Third Republic and his service during the Occupation merit attention and reveal complexities about some of the men who served under Pétain.[8] In summer 1940, Marlier, then aged sixty-three, agreed to leave his retirement that had come after years of service to the French state, but with an insufficient accumulation of years as a prefect to guarantee him full draw on his pension. Part of his decision to leave retirement might have been financial. But why did Vichy call on Marlier, a "prefect of the Left," and endow him with full powers to negotiate the particulars of the Armistice agreement regarding the passage of the Line of Demarcation? What credentials made Marlier the man to choose for the enormous task of repatriating 7 million displaced persons and to negotiate, on a day-to-day basis, the fate of expulsees and permanent refugees?

Born on September 21, 1877, Marlier's life ran parallel to that of the Third Republic. His generation grew up during the Belle Époque and lived with an assurance of the republican victory, but many felt torn by the lingering problem of how to reconcile church–state relations and mitigate class strife under the new, more democratic system. A native of the northern border department of Aisne, Marlier descended from a

---

[6] Fishman, *We Will Wait*, 27. Martin Alexander reports slightly different figures: losses, 123,000 French troops killed (370,000 casualties); 1.6 million French PoW, but 84 percent after the Armistice of June 25. Martin S. Alexander, "The Republic at War: The French Army and the Fight for France, 1939–1940," Lecture, University of Birmingham, June 2006.

[7] Robert O. Paxton, *The Anatomy of Fascism* (New York: Vintage Press, 2005), 114.

[8] Burrin, *France under the Germans*. For discussions about wartime moral relativism and the Holocaust see Christopher Browning, *Ordinary Men: Reserve Police Battalion 101 and the Final Solution in Poland* (New York: Harper Perennial, 1992).

Catholic family of modest means. Still, Marlier earned an undergraduate degree in letters and a postgraduate degree in law. It would be hard to imagine that for Marlier, the Third Republic meant anything less than an assurance of equal opportunity.

Marlier's family life determined his public career at many junctures. In 1902, he married Jeanne Amelie Stephanie Mailliet, who also came from a modest background. The union was always marked by financial strain, producing riches only in the form of a child, Madeleine Céline Marlier. Madeleine grew up moving around the French empire. In her adult life, she married two prefects, evidencing the completion of her family's climb from humble obscurity and the social connections attached to interwar bureaucratic service.

Having first served in the military from 1897 to 1901, Marlier re-entered military service during World War I like most men of his generation. He was wounded in combat, and his service and courage gained the attention of military and government superiors. On the recommendation of General Henri-Victor Buat, Marlier received a letter of recognition from the Minister of the Interior, Théodore Steeg, and his star began to rise. On July 14, 1919 he received the citation of the Order of the Nation in recognition of his wartime achievements. The French government daily bulletin, *The Official Journal*, described Marlier as: "A model of courage, of modesty, and of useful actions. During the enemy advance, and throughout the entire campaign, he volunteered himself to scout the most exposed positions, proving his absolute disregard for danger."[9]

In the aftermath of World War I, Marlier developed his credentials as an architect of reconstruction; the expertise that Vichy would later tap. His family's home, as well as his entire department, Aisne, suffered complete devastation during the war. In April 1918 the prefect of Aisne named Marlier General Secretary of his department. A year later, he added the oversight of the reconstruction of the department of Pas-de-Calais to his list of responsibilities. This post-World War I training period prepared Marlier for his role in overseeing the evacuation of Pas-de-Calais.

In Pas-de-Calais, Marlier impressed the prefect, Robert Leullier, who wrote a strong letter of support in 1920 to promote Marlier into the prefectoral core. Leullier commended: "Marlier had always chosen public service against many lucrative private offers despite his difficult financial circumstances and heavy family obligations to his wife,

[9] AN F/1bis/807.

daughter, mother and grandmother."[10] Noting the seventeen-hour days Marlier worked, and underscoring the human qualities Marlier brought to his expanded responsibilities as "Overseer of the Reconstruction of the Formerly Occupied Territories" (of World War I), Leullier further praised: "He brings to his work with distressed communities an energy despite the demanding and difficult circumstances these people face given their losses and their reduced means."[11]

At the age of forty-one, Marlier had risen to the position of General Secretary for the Reconstruction of the Regions Stricken by the Events of the War, which put him in charge of reconstruction in the east; an enormous assignment involving the rebuilding of railways, waterways, bridges, roads, and neighborhoods. He also oversaw the restitution process, investigating and approving claims made by residents whose farms and businesses had suffered damage between 1914 and 1918. Perhaps it was during this period that he perfected his German language skills, skills that would later serve him in his assignment under Vichy.

He later served as prefect in Orne (Algeria) and Corsica. In 1927 he was sent to ease local tensions in Ajaccio. His transfer papers held the signature of Raimond Poincaré, President of the Republic. In Corsica, Marlier met with virulent opposition, especially from local journalists writing for the *Bastia-Journal*. The journalist Jehan, accused Marlier of sinning against a prefect's obligation to "administer" rather than "make" policy.[12] He charged that Marlier mishandled fire relief funds and, more seriously, that Marlier manipulated the local votes for the 1928 elections to the National Assembly in favor of the Party of Democrats and Social Republicans.

The files give no indication as to whether Marlier's move a year later to the prefecture of Oran in Algeria came as a result of his success or failure to stare down local opposition in Corsica. Regardless, he served in the colonial climate in Algeria from 1929 to 1934, where certainly he would have encountered the administrative problems and frameworks for dealing with individuals and groups claiming a variety of rights and exercising civil exclusions, an issue he would confront during his tenure at the Service of Refugees.

Marlier returned to the European continent in 1934, where he became the prefect in the department of Lot-et-Garonne. Correspondence reveals that, between 1934 and 1937, bitterness and a sense of personal desperation began to envelop Marlier. Also, by 1937 his administration

---

[10] AN F/1bis/807, Robert Leullier to Minister of the Interior, Arras, March 17, 1920.
[11] AN F/1bis/807, Robert Leullier to Minister of the Interior.
[12] Jehan, "Des maintenant, il sera a bon de fouiller dans les archives, de mettre le nez dans les comptes des Travaux Publics; de verifier la distribution de secours aux sinistres de derniers incendies," *Bastia Journal*, May 2, 1928.

began to feel the tremors from the Spanish Civil War. Marlier had to respond to problems regarding the provision of asylum to Spanish refugees, a tense and difficult problem in the departments of the southwest that left an imprint on regional attitudes and policies toward the exodus.

In September 1936, the new government of Léon Blum threatened to dismiss prefects earning more than 125,000 francs a year, which Marlier's salary slightly surpassed. The Deputy wrote that:

Marlier should not be included in the list of prefects to be forced into early retirement because he is a prefect of the Left and the former Director of Security who has had strong disputes with Action Française [a French fascist paramilitary group of the 1930s]. I promised him that I would call his case to your attention and ask you to examine the possibility of another solution, because he is without a personal fortune.[13]

Finally, in 1937, Marlier received word that he would be given recognition of a full career as prefect by adding one year of colonial service to draw a sum of 39,000 francs. In fact, the sum fell below a desired full payout, but Marlier settled for the offer and retired.

After his retirement, Marlier's supporters continued to look after him. On November 11, 1937 the government conferred the distinction "Honorary Prefect." While the Party of Democratic and Social Republicans had ceased to be a major force in 1940, it is clear that Marlier had close ties with Radical Party members who chose to follow Pétain. Although the archives provide no clear evidence, one might assume that Chautemps, Vice President of the Council under Reynaud, and an advocate for the Armistice, recruited Marlier from retirement. Chautemps' signature appears throughout Marlier's career file, suggesting that he would have known of Marlier's reconstruction expertise. Rather than thinking he took a turn to the right, it seems more probable that Marlier, the prefect of the Left, was more of an administrative expert than an ideologue. At a moment of devastation for France, Marlier returned to service on July 5, 1940.[14]

Destiny designed by bureaucracy: the Service of Refugees under Occupation

The Service of Refugees began an administrative reorganization as Marlier assumed his duties early in July. Maurice Lagrange, honorary

---

[13] AN F/1bis/807, Chamber of Deputies, National Assembly of France to M. Verlomme, September 22, 1936.

[14] AN F/1bis/807. Marlier died at age 81 on November 14, 1958; Jeanne Amelie, aged 79, died on December 4, 1959.

Conseiller d'État, explained in his postwar testimony that the new government, felt that "It was imperative to create a centralized authority ... with all necessary powers to resolve the traffic jam of refugees persisting in the non-occupied zone. This had been the failure of the Central Service of Refugees during the Phoney War."[15] Hence, the government created twenty-one general secretary posts, one of which was the General Secretary of Refugees that fell under the Minister of the Interior. Initially, Andrieux occupied that position, which facilitated the return of the administrative arm of the Service of Refugees to Paris from Pau (Pyrénées-Atlantiques).[16] On July 12, 1940, Andrieux sent a note to Léon Noël, the Ambassador of the French Government to the Administration of the Occupied Territories. Andrieux requested that Noël assist in securing the return of the Service of Refugee's administration to Paris, noting, a bit prematurely, that Marlier had already obtained assurances from the Germans that the return of state functionaries to the Occupied Zone would meet with their approval. Andrieux tasked Pierre Caron, the President of the National Archives of France, with the mission of repatriating the voluminous papers of the Service of Refugees to Paris.[17]

During July, the Service attempted to reassemble its prewar team under Marlier's new leadership. The Service of Refugees formed another link in the transmission of Vichy policy. Marlier communicated, often directly, but sometimes through the Minister of the Interior, with prefects in the Occupied and Free zones. The reconstituted Service emulated Schuman's effort to centralize policies and directives regarding housing, clothing, food, and cash benefits, but with much more authority. Marlier constructed a centralized decision-making process in which a uniformity of policy issued from Paris, filtered first through Vichy, then through the Armistice Commission and, if approved, down to the prefects in each zone. Of course, application of those policies happened less neatly and frequently differed from department to department and town to town. The location of the Service in Paris allowed Marlier to cultivate a strong, independent status in relation to the Ministry of the Interior, located in Vichy. This geographic and administrative space allowed for policy adaptation and, in many cases, defiance.

Paris-based operations, charged with overseeing a colossal humanitarian emergency, had a single second-class office manager and a small

[15] AN AJ/72/2004, Dossier 5, Maurice Lagrange, Honorary Minister of State, "Le répatriement des Refugiés après l'Exode: Juillet–Septembre 1940," 8.
[16] AN AJ/72/2004, Maurice Lagrange, "Le répatriement des Refugiés."
[17] AN F/1a/3660, Lassalle-Séré, "December 10, 1940 Note."

staff. One person received and delivered mail; a Herculean task since refugees within the Occupied Zone sent daily inquiries to the Service regarding lost family members. Another agent worked with the general media. One staffer liaised with the Minister of the Interior, while another liaised with the other ministries and the Armistice Commission; a job that was too big for one person. One staffer took charge of the relations between Paris and Marlier's Special Delegation. A separate office collected statistics such as the weekly counts of refugee populations in each department. There was one deputy prefect, a writer, three clerks, one typist, two office boys, and one errand boy. Marlier had a personal staff that included two writers and three clerks.

The Service's housing division responded to housing matters from the Paris office, dealing with a wide range of issues, including management of housing centers; questions of expulsions; camp administration; relations with workers; and coordination with the Secours National, the French Red Cross and American relief services, and the Red Cross in Geneva. The division of "Reclassement" (worker re-education) dealt with job training of refugees in the Free Zone; relations with the Ministry of Industrial Production and the Minister of Agriculture; all questions regarding foreigners; and all affairs concerning refugees especially in the Occupied Zone. The Transportation division worked on questions regarding repatriation, especially railway organization. To accomplish this task, the bureau employed one person in Paris and one person in Vichy. Questions of finance fell to the lieutenant prefect in Paris and his staff. He wrote: "Chartered as an ad-hoc service, we have always been under funded."[18] While the head of transportation at the Service of Refugees routed information concerning train departures and issuance of laissez-passer, the SNCF scheduled return trains and the German border control checked or issued identity papers. The Service of Refugees had its hand in a multitude of tasks relating to repatriation as well as to economic renewal. For months after France's defeat, the Service of Refugees lay at the heart of national reconstruction.

On August 2, 1940, after a month of negotiations, the Service of Refugees received its official mandate: "To return all 'approved refugees' to their places of origin." Created as a Vichy government cabinet post, but reorganized under the French Armistice Services' Delegate-General of the French Government in Occupied Territories (Délégation générale du Gouvernement français pour les territoires occupés, DGGFTO), the Service depended upon the DGGFTO's leaders for approval of its actions. The Service coordinated its activities

---

[18] AN F/1a/3660, Lassalle-Séré, "December 10, 1940 Note."

through Noël's and La Laurencie's liaison with the German command in France, but Marlier also entered into one-on-one negotiation with the Germans.

The August decree restored an independent budget to the Service of Refugees and mapped out an internal structure. Vichy appointed a director to exercise operations under Marlier's lead. The Germans agreed to allow Vichy to establish two offices: one in Paris and another at Vichy, with a small regional office in Clermont-Ferrand.[19] The Service essentially acted as a link between the Minister of the Interior located in Vichy, and the Armistice Commission, located in Paris. Marlier's responsibility was to defend French interests regarding the partitioning of France and hence the repatriation of refugees. But, because the repatriation issue stemmed directly from principles governing the enforcement of the Line of Demarcation, Marlier's powers of negotiation extended to matters governing the monitoring of the partition and all passage between the two zones.

All power lies with the Armistice Commission: Marlier negotiates a return

The Armistice Commission held its first meeting on repatriation on July 5, 1940 at the Hôtel Majestic in Paris a month ahead of the Service of Refugees' official reorganization.[20] Although General Otto von Stülpnagel only took over as head of the Militärbefehlshaber in Frankreich (MBF), the chief German military authority over France, in October 1940, he represented Germany at the July 5 meeting.[21] The Armistice Commission held virtually all authority over Occupation policy. However, it had to consult with German occupation offices in Belgium, and with Berlin on military matters, ideological issues, or policies whose jurisdiction extended beyond French borders, such as repatriation of Belgian refugees. Several German officials presided over the meeting, led by President von Pfeffer, who was President of the Occupied Zone; he was accompanied by General von Streccius, the Official Representative of the Head of the German Army, and Minister Schmidt, the Head of German Administration. General Charles Huntziger had negotiated the Armistice for the French and held the title of President of the Armistice Commission for the French, but did

---

[19] AN F/1a/3660, "On the Subject of the Activity of the Service of Refugees," 1941.
[20] AN F/1a/3660, Minutes for the Service of Refugees' Meeting at the Hôtel Majestic, Paris, July 5, 1940.
[21] Gildea, *Marianne in Chains*, 30.

not participate directly in repatriation negotiations. Instead, Marlier was empowered to negotiate a repatriation settlement with Huntziger's full authority. At the first meeting, the atmosphere was cold and formal. The Germans showed themselves determined to frustrate French ambitions to achieve a complete and rapid repatriation of all refugees. As far as the Germans were concerned, the Line of Demarcation sealed traffic between the two zones.

A description of the partitioning of French territory by the Line of Demarcation is essential to understanding repatriation negotiations. French officials' postwar memoirs suggest that not even Pétain believed that the Germans would impose such a harsh punishment on the French. To strictly partition the country and prohibit the government from returning to Paris seemed unimaginable not only to Reynaud, but also to others who supported an Armistice, like Queuille and Schuman. The Line of Demarcation restricted population movement and eventually reshuffled not only spatial configurations, but also individual and collective identities. Immediately after the Armistice's conditions took effect at 12.35 am on June 25, French and German personnel began construction of a physical and administrative border that spanned 2,000 km from Saint-Jean-Pied-de-Port in the Basses-Pyrénées (now Pyrénées-Atlantiques) to Geneva, Switzerland. Its length and impact outstripped even the Maginot Line. Article 2 of the Armistice loosely described a "line of demarcation," but remained mute about its exact configuration.[22] The "green line," as Germans first called the Line of Demarcation, divided German occupied territory from Free France. Eventually policed by 5,460 predominantly French guards, the Line partitioned thirteen departments and reconfigured the geopolitical contour of France.[23] The subdivided departments included Ain, Jura, Saône-et-Loire, Allier, Cher, Loir-et-Cher, Indre-et-Loire, Vienne, Charente, Dordogne, Gironde, Landes, and Basses-Pyrénées. At the beginning of July, authorities did not know whether a fourteenth department would be divided, and they had few instructions regarding which towns would be cut by the Line.[24] Vichy lay in the southernmost region of Allier, one of the divided thirteen departments. In the north of Allier sat the town of Moulins, which would serve as a kind of "Checkpoint Charlie" for passage between the Occupied and the Non-Occupied zones. The Armistice Agreement offered no specifics about

---

[22] Alary, *La ligne de démarcation: 1940–1944*, 27.
[23] Alary, *La ligne de démarcation: 1940–1944*, 49; Souleau, *La ligne de démarcation en Gironde*, 330.
[24] Alary, *La ligne de démarcation: 1940–1944*, 26.

how business and administration would be conducted in the partitioned departments, nor did it offer explanation about interzonal trade.

From the beginning of Armistice discussions, the Germans disagreed among themselves about the wisdom of dividing France and allowing a zone of self-governance. Hitler insisted to Mussolini on conceding to the French a national government, with a considerable part of the French mainland remaining unoccupied by German or Italian forces.[25] Eric Alary's work has cast new light on the historical understanding of the Line of Demarcation, and traces the slow evolution of the idea of the Line within various German political and military camps. Opponents argued that patrolling the Line would burden German military personnel, which is one reason the Armistice Commission wanted to limit points of passage along it. From a security perspective, some Germans, such as Joseph Goebbels, feared the Free Zone would serve as a training ground for resistance fighters who might launch guerrilla attacks in the Occupied Zone. General Charles Huntziger's thinking, although practical in concern, aligned with Hitler's dream of redrawing the European map. Hitler hoped to revive a "Germanité" that laid claim to French territory in three ways: annexation, the creation of protectorates, and the formation of colonies.[26] Hence, the Third Reich annexed Alsace and Lorraine. The departments Pas-de-Calais, Nord, Aisne, and Ardennes served as types of experimental colonies, being designated for military operations or for the resettlement of ethnic Germans from the Reich. The Occupied Zone formed part of a protectorate, although the forms of requisitioning that took place left the relationship open to definitions that leaned toward colonization. The "Free Zone" did not fit into any of these categories, which should have warned Vichy leaders of its threatened longevity.

General Falkenhausen, commander of the German Military Administration in Belgium made practical and ideological arguments for partition and annexation. He recommended several subdivisions of French territory to facilitate military operations along the English Channel coast. Falkenhausen lobbied for the administrative attachment of Pas-de-Calais and Nord, which he believed were essential positions for launching an invasion of the British Isles. On the ideological front, he contended that the northern European territory, including Belgium and the Low Countries, belonged to a Germanic heritage and should be considered part of a larger Germany. Alary points out that

---

[25] The author is grateful to an anonymous reviewer for *Holocaust and Genocide Studies* for sharing information about Hitler's discussions with Mussolini.

[26] Alary, *La ligne de démarcation: 1940–1944*, 32.

Falkenhausen's ideas were drawn from the nineteenth-century German geographer, Friedrich Ratzel.[27] Ratzel reasoned that: "In denying a state [nation] its spatial particularity: she is deprived of the means for maintaining her power."[28] Based on Ratzel's analysis, the Germans believed that, by dicing France into small administrative morsels, they would "deprive France of the means for maintaining her power." We can understand how Goebbels' camp could have initially lost the partition argument. Hence, the Germans who advocated the creation of a "Free Zone," believed that allowing a token puppet state to exist apart from its industrial base, mineral resources, and capital city, would offer an illusion of a viable nation. They further believed that French troops in the colonies, including North Africa, and the French Navy would remain loyal to this puppet state. Rather than dismantling French power after the defeat, the Germans intended to use what was left for their own war efforts.

For the first two years of Occupation, the partition worked as the Germans expected. However, partitioning had other effects, as Goebbels' camp imagined. Hitler had blundered in thinking that he could keep French colonies and the remaining military forces loyal to the French government, thus, preventing them from joining a government in exile, let alone the British camp. The Germans' ultimate miscalculation lay in their belief that men and women, defined by their borders, would accept the German redefinition of their space, and by association, their own identities and allegiances. During the two years that the Line functioned, it gave life to new ideas of resistance and transgression, destroying old sentiments of unity and regional cohesiveness. For a time, the Line offered the Germans a tool for imposing Lebensraum and for occupying France, but it also galvanized French resistance and extended asylum to increasingly endangered individuals and communities. By 1941, it was the only viable, non-fascist asylum remaining on the continent besides Switzerland. (This excludes Vichy from being classified as fully fascist based on Paxton's criteria for occupied, collaborationist regimes.[29])

Falkenhausen also prevailed on subdivision of the Occupied Zone. The designation of Pas-de-Calais and Nord for military operations held life-changing consequences for refugee populations native to those departments. The Germans decided to capitalize on the fact that

[27] Alary, *La ligne de démarcation: 1940–1944*, 27–28, 36.
[28] Friedrich Ratzel, *Géopolitiques et stratégies* (Paris : Fayard, 1923), cited in Alary, *La ligne de démarcation: 1940–1944*, 36.
[29] Paxton, *Anatomy of Fascism*, 116–117.

residents of the north-east had conveniently evacuated the territory. They did not have to implement large-scale forced population removal or carry out ethnic cleansing as they would do in the east. The absence of residents made the process of building fortifications and setting up military operations advance more smoothly than if the entire population had remained in place. Soldiers billeted in refugees' houses without the social discomfort of having to negotiate for space in civilian residents' homes. To enforce their control over the Channel and Atlantic coastal territory, the German military drew another subdivision within their zone of occupation, complete with policed checkpoints designed to monitor and restrict refugee re-entry to the "Forbidden Zone."

The Germans used additional subdivisions to designate areas open for the return of French refugees, as well as areas restricted to the return of refugees. These subdivisions were called "Reserved Zones." Alary maintains that the French deeply resented, and failed to understand, the proliferation of subdivisions within the German Occupied Zone. Military arguments did not suffice since, operationally, Falkenhausen only needed the coast and roads servicing shore points. The lines patrolled by German border guards seemed completely arbitrary to most French officials and rejected refugees. The Germans, for their part, continually debated how to enforce the "Reserved Zones" and "Forbidden Zone," and whether or not to erase or extend the dividing lines. Mounting a futile resistance, the French repeatedly advanced the argument that the Armistice Agreement and international law did not provide for the subdivision of occupied nations.[30] While Marlier and the French authorities resisted the rules governing fortification and control of passage of the Line, tricking French and German border patrols became the dangerous rebellion of refugees moving in both directions.

By July, the Germans had carved a total of four main subdivisions on the French map: the Southern Barrage (Loire linie); the Line of Demarcation of Article 2 of the Armistice; the Median Line (Mittellinie or Seine-Marne linie); and the North-East Line. In redrawing the map of continental Europe, the Germans created a new set of core–periphery relationships. Berlin became the new European core, and France was reduced to a peripheral political and economic entity. The great bonus of the battle of France, besides the victory over the French military, was to have geographically displaced the center of French government and power from Paris to the hinterlands of Vichy.

The divisions of French territory became one of the main topics of negotiation between Marlier's team and the German officials on the

---

[30] Alary, *La ligne de démarcation: 1940–1944*, 30.

Armistice Commission.[31] The French attempted throughout the early period of the Occupation to contest the legality of the subdivisions according to international law, which in 1940 held few specifics about the rules of occupation and territorial subdivision.[32] Given the benefit to the Germans for military operations and providing security, it is remarkable that the Germans even agreed to sit down at the table to negotiate refugee repatriation.

Early efforts at repatriation

The July 5 meeting lasted only an hour, but it established the dynamics and articulated the issues between the Service of Refugees and the Armistice Commission. The French delegation advanced nine requests regarding the repatriation of refugees and passage between the two zones. Marlier first requested permission to return government officials to the Occupied Zone, reflecting Vichy's desire to rebuild local governments in the north; the first step toward full repatriation. Facing communication and infrastructure problems, and desiring assistance in restoring damaged sewage, electrical, and telephone equipment, the Germans welcomed repatriation of departmental prefect staffs, but did not agree that this should set in motion a mass return. Marlier conveniently misinterpreted German intentions.

Marlier's main directive from Vichy was to pressure the Germans to allow fluid passage of people and materials between the two zones. Von Streccius, the German chief negotiator, expressed a grave reluctance to even begin the flow of traffic between the zones. Pointing out the imperative of German security, he argued that unrestricted interzonal travel would cause surveillance problems for the Germans.[33] As a result, von Streccius tabled Marlier's requests to improve postal delivery and telephone service between zones. He also wanted to delay the passage of National Assembly deputies and senators from the Occupied Zone to Vichy. Henri Queuille had successfully traveled from Bordeaux to Corrèze, but only because he did so before the Germans began enforcing the Line of Demarcation.

---

[31] Alary, *La ligne de démarcation: 1940–1944*, 30.

[32] Gildea argues that the Germans did attempt to rule by law, but insists: "The rules of the Occupation thus evolved according to case law rather than legal principle ... In order to protect the security of the military, the Germans established a network of military courts to administer martial law. Any action deemed to threaten German military security was brought before the military court." Gildea, *Marianne in Chains*, 37.

[33] AN F/1a/3660, "Minutes from the meeting at the Hôtel Majestic," Paris, July 5, 1940.

Von Streccius, agreed "in principal" to Marlier's requests to repatriate functionaries, but took the first recorded opportunity to decree that the Germans would not allow the return of communist or Jewish officials to government posts or to the occupied territories.[34] Marlier assured the Germans that communists had already been divested of their electoral mandates at all levels: municipal, arrondissement (county/city district), general council (regional district), and the National Assembly. Marlier objected in purely legal terms to von Streccius' suggestion to effectively revoke Jewish officials from public office and remove them from repatriation rosters. He said: "Regarding the Israélites, French law does not make distinctions based upon the religion of its functionaries and elected officials. A functionary or an elected official cannot be removed from office except according to conditions stated in French laws."[35] Marlier further protested that: "anti-Israélite policies were not part of the language of the conventions of the Armistice."[36] Von Streccius suggested "tabling" the Jewish question indefinitely, knowing that regardless of French protest, the point would not be renegotiated. These discussions marked the first exchange between French and German officials concerning racial exclusions with regard to repatriation policy.[37] This conversation concerned elected officials, but von Streccius likely anticipated that the principle would soon extend to all Jewish refugees. The French had articulated their opposition to the exclusions, but on this issue the Germans held them hostage to Vichy's broader repatriation goals. The first meeting about refugee repatriation came to an abrupt end when von Streccius announced that he had "heard enough discussion," and would consider official approval of the French requests.[38]

Two days after the meeting, having received no official German approval for any of the repatriation terms, Marlier urged the Minister of the Interior to order preparations to repatriate municipal, departmental, and national employees to the Occupied Zone. In departments and towns in the Free Zone, mayors and SNCF rail personnel hurried to organize the repatriation of state functionaries and small business owners. A Ministry of the Interior notice to prefects of Free Zone departments, dated July 7, 1940, ordered all Occupied Zone prefects, general secretaries, subprefects, and administrative personnel back

---

[34] AN F/1a/3660, Minutes from the meeting at the Hôtel Majestic.
[35] AN/F/1a/3660, Minutes from the meeting at the Hôtel Majestic.
[36] AN F/1a/3660, Minutes from the meeting at the Hôtel Majestic.
[37] AN F/1a/3660, Minutes from the meeting at the Hôtel Majestic.
[38] AN F/1a/3660, Minutes from the meeting at the Hôtel Majestic.

to their posts in the Occupied Zone.[39] Posters glued to walls in public places throughout the south warned civil servants that: "refusal to return to the Occupied Zone would be considered the equivalent to the resignation of one's job."[40]

Marlier would continue to oppose exclusions from the Occupied Zone based on ethnic, national, and religious identity. Nevertheless, the Germans began to enforce these exclusions, however unevenly, and the French would unevenly follow the German lead. On July 30, 1940, the office of the French Secretary of State at the Ministry of the Interior instructed prefects in the Free Zone *not* to issue authorization for Jews or those of mixed bloods to cross the Line of Demarcation.[41] Yet the conflicting directives regarding eligibility to cross the Line were sent by, and to, different branches of the French government. French Army archives show that French guards were not told that Jews were among the refugees denied permission to re-enter the Occupied Zone. On September 14, 1940, army authorities at Chateauroux received a note stating that: "Jews could cross the Line, furnished with approved papers, but certain German posts might send them back without any explanation."[42] The ensemble of conflicting documentation confirms that the enforcement of restrictions prohibiting Jews and other excluded persons from crossing the Line of Demarcation did not achieve uniform application during the early months of occupation and repatriation.

Outside the conference room, German troops used French labor to begin fortifying the Line; but it would take months to establish surveillance along the 2,000-km border. Ultimately, the Germans delegated the job of patrolling the border to the French, with the exception of staffing of established crossing stations. The French complained that they did not receive adequate resources from the Germans to patrol the Line. The French hoped to recruit 7,000 guards to work the border, but Vichy never provided funding to employ more than 5,460.[43] French and German authorities exchanged serial correspondence to determine exactly where the Line would bifurcate a city or a single farmer's field. Only in December of 1941 did the Institut Géographique National, located in Paris, issue a map tracing the agreed route of the Line.[44]

[39] AN F/1a/3660, Note, dated Paris, July 7, 1940.
[40] AN F/1a/3660, Note, dated Paris, July 7, 1940.
[41] ADC 528/W/4, Secretary of State for the Interior, Circular, July 30, 1940.
[42] SHAT, 1P9, EMA, 2ème Bureau, "Note pour le franchissement de la ligne de démarcation," Chateauroux, September 14, 1940, quoted in Alary, *La ligne de démarcation: 1940–1944*, 60.
[43] Alary, *La ligne de démarcation: 1940–1944*, 49.
[44] Alary, *La ligne de démarcation: 1940–1944*, 56.

For Vichy, repatriation was the prerequisite to the resumption of full economic recovery in the north as well as the south. The French mistakenly believed that the Armistice Agreement intended the same objective. Hanna Diamond explains that Article 16 of the Armistice: "required the French government to organize the return of refugees to the Occupied territories with the agreement of the competent German services."[45] She suggests that the Germans were eager to facilitate the return of refugees to the Occupied Zone; but if that had been the case at the moment of victory, it had quickly ceased to be the German position. Marlier spent much of July, August, and September trying to persuade the Germans to allow repatriation to proceed at a steady pace. He advanced arguments he thought might appeal to German self-interest, stressing the value of French labor for alleviating the prospect of winter shortages in the Occupied Zone. He urged von Streccius to concede to the rapid repatriation of farmers and all agricultural and alimentary workers in order to feed the German Army. Among this group he included proprietors of small shops, such as bakers and butchers. The Germans, eager themselves to extract whatever possible from French agricultural production, readily conceded to Marlier's requests regarding the return of agricultural workers. However, they hesitated to approve the return of small agricultural property owners wanting to reclaim their farms in Aisne, Ardennes, and Nord. Land redistribution in the north-east was a key component in Germany's attempt at economic colonization of northern France. Operation Ostland aimed to settle ethnic Germans in the area in a pilot program for similar strategies planned for eastern Europe. Having suffered the loss of his home during Germany's World War I invasion, and having managed the reconstruction of the territory, the renewed German assault on Aisne must have pained and angered Marlier; perhaps accounting for his determination to challenge German exclusions from this particular region.

Von Streccius tried to appear obliging by granting approval to less controversial requests for the return of doctors, midwives, and pharmacists, as well as those capable of assessing damage to the infrastructure of northern cities. Indeed, the Germans would argue among themselves about how many French workers they wished to repatriate to the mining areas of Nord. When it later became clear that German labor would be needed to enforce military occupation, and to fight the war with the Soviet Union, they were forced to reconsider policies of excluding miners from returning to the Forbidden Zone.

---

[45] J. Lagrange, "Rapatriement des réfugiés après l'exode," *Revue d'histoire de la Deuxième Guerre mondiale* (1977), 43, cited in Diamond, *Fleeing Hitler*, 148.

With regard to repatriation, correspondence between Marlier and the Ministry of the Interior is striking for what is absent. French officials never discussed the conditions under which repatriated refugees might live. Communication throughout France faltered, and the Germans restricted entry to some areas in the north, but surely the French held reports about the destruction levied on towns in the north. Still, the question of whether repatriation was a sound policy, and for whom it would work, never entered into internal policy discussions. Indeed, in September 1940, as the Allies bombed Le Havre and Dieppe in the Forbidden Zone, forcing an emergency evacuation of the few remaining residents, Marlier's team continued to push for the lifting of restrictions on refugee repatriation to the Forbidden Zone.[46]

Marlier's determination to pressure the Germans to accelerate repatriation, and Vichy's willingness to support his recommendations, raise questions about Vichy's motivations and refugees' desires. Why did Vichy want to repatriate its civil servants and France's population to Occupied Territory? Why did Marlier push so hard to open the Line of Demarcation to refugee passage? Why would refugees want to repatriate to the Occupied Zone? Should they not have considered themselves fortunate to land in the Free Zone? Contemporary knowledge of the German Occupation and the harsh realities of the war's end color these questions. However, one must consider the viewpoint of Marie Limousin and others. Mothers juggled family responsibilities while sheltered in public school lunch rooms in strange places like Brive-la-Gaillarde. Families ate meals twice a day at the train station canteen. Often, they had received no word about their husbands, fathers, and brothers in over two months since the invasion began. Mothers and children had no sweaters for chilly evenings, no shoes without holes, and no money. Even if they had money, it would have done little good because shoe supplies were so short that any available shoes were priced astronomically highly. Thus, it is easy to imagine why a refugee might think of nothing else besides returning to their home in occupied France, Belgium, or Luxembourg. The language of the "right to evacuation" and the "right to shelter" that civilian women had marshaled to pressure the government to improve home front security prior to the invasion, now served them in their demands for refugee aid and petitions for return to their homes. Unfortunately, many did not understand that Britain and Germany continued to wage battle in the skies of northern France.

---

[46] AN F/60/1507, "Summary of the history of evacuations in Nord and Pas-de-Calais," to DGGFTO from Louis Marlier, March 2, 1941, note 1293.

Fortifying and controlling the Line of Demarcation

The Line of Demarcation's success in ensuring German security rested in limiting the number of crossing points. On July 7, French officials told state functionaries to prepare for repatriation, as soon German authorities intended to release acceptable routes for travel to the Occupied Territory by foot, bicycle, automobile, or train.[47] On July 11, Ambassador Léon Noël received German instructions and reported that they included an "invitation" to establish an office to distribute laissez-passers at Moulins (Alliers). Moulins sat 452 km from Bordeaux, where some of the greatest refugee concentrations lingered, and 297 km from Paris. It was hardly a convenient location. The Germans insisted that Moulins would be the only allowed point of entry to the Occupied Zone. At Moulins, Chief of Staff Auleb reported that French and then German border guards would establish a checkpoint for examining the credentials of all refugees applying for re-entry.[48] In addition, the Moulins office would be responsible for submitting a daily list of persons entering the Occupied Zone to the German command. This list was to contain the name, profession, race, organization to which the person "belonged," and purpose of the refugee's voyage.[49]

Along a 2,000-km border, there existed only one point of entry. The establishment of a single point of entry and a monitoring station at Moulins held dual significance: first, it allowed both sides to monitor the flow of people; and, second, the requirement of assigning every traveler an identity card and a laissez-passer, categorized each according to profession and race, marking an important step toward the surveillance of the populations in both zones. Most refugees passing through Moulins would have already registered with the state as a consequence of receiving refugee allocations and railway tickets. Issuing of laissez-passer at Moulins reinforced both the Germans' and Vichy's ability to monitor individuals and restrict the movement of refugees. Monitoring refugees' identities and enforcing German categories of exclusion at Moulins thus became a significant act of cooperation between the new French regime and the German authorities regarding the reordering of national space.

Marlier met again with the Armistice Commission on July 13 in the hope of widening and accelerating repatriation. Replacing von Streccius as head of the hearings, von Pfeffer received Marlier's complaints.

---

[47] AN F/60/1507, "Summary of the history of evacuations in Nord and Pas-de-Calais."
[48] AN F/1a/3660, letter signed by Chief of Staff Auleb, dated July 11, 1940.
[49] AN F/1a/3660, letter signed by Chief of Staff Auleb.

Topping the list were the restrictions on communication between the two zones. Von Pfeffer reported that letters and visitors requesting information about individual refugees' families and government repatriation policies inundated his office.[50] He appointed the Society of the French Red Cross, the Belgian and Luxembourg Red Cross, the French Bureau of Refugees, and the Belgian Ambassador to France to propose a system for improving communication between the zones and for determining the status of foreign refugees. The latter endeavor especially interested the Germans, who had insisted upon Armistice Article 19 requiring the French to hand over "all the Germans whom they, the Nazis, 'wanted.'"[51] Lion Feuchtwanger, among other notable German refugees, sat in a temporary internment camp at San Nicola (Gard), when a fellow refugee handed him a newspaper in late June, which reported the French agreement. For Feuchtwanger, enforcement of Article 19 was a life or death matter. He remembered processing the news:

My knees trembled. I read no further. "All Germans whom the Nazis wanted." For years past the Nazis had been calling me their Enemy Number One in their speeches and newspapers. If they turned in a list of "wanted" persons my name would surely be near the top ... It was the third time in a short period that I had felt death near at hand.[52]

Was the provision of lists of foreigners the price Marlier paid von Pfeffer to allow postal services between the two zones?[53] It was finally agreed that the French Red Cross would act as a neutral agent, moving letters and information between zones, thus assuming a key role in establishing contact between separated families and friends. Von Pfeffer agreed to allow the Red Cross to set up an office in Paris to supervise postal services. Belgian and Luxembourgeois citizens, he directed, should send their mail to the Belgian services in France. Pierre Caron, President of France's National Archives, was charged with overseeing the establishment of the Red Cross postal bureau.[54] By July 29, three offices (in Paris, Bourges, and Vichy) would be established to transfer mail between zones.[55] Von Pfeffer required more scrutiny over

---

[50] AN F/1a/3660, Minutes of meeting at the Hôtel Majestic, July 13, 1940. Numbers are unavailable for July 13, but by August 1, the Armistice Commission received 500 letters per day requesting information about PoWs and missing civilians. Alary, *La ligne de démarcation: 1940–1944*, 69.
[51] Feuchtwanger, *Devil in France*, 173.
[52] Feuchtwanger, *Devil in France*, 174.
[53] AN F/1a/3660, Minutes of meeting at the Hôtel Majestic, July 13, 1940.
[54] *Journal Official*, July 15, 1940.
[55] Alary, *La ligne de démarcation: 1940–1944*, 69.

correspondence between the Service of Refugees at Clermont-Ferrand and Paris, insisting that a percentage of interagency letters transmitted from the Free Zone to the Occupied Zone be translated into German and kept on file.[56] This policy created more work than either side could handle. By September 26, all communication was limited to preprinted postcards that refugees could purchase for 0.90 centimes. The cards allowed refugees to check a list of choices:

> ____ I am not dead.
> ____ in good health.
> ____ in prison.
> ____ without news of _____.
> ____ the family is well.
> ____ we received _____.
> ____ entering school.
> ____ affectionately _____.[57]

On July 17, in evidence of the eagerness of French officials to begin the repatriation process, Marlier, in collaboration with the Chief of French Military Administration, Monsieur Parisius, disseminated a proposed schedule of trains to all Free Zone prefects. The plan was designed to repatriate refugees by departments of origin. First priority was given to residents of Paris and those from the departments of the Seine, Seine-et-Oise, and Seine-et-Marne. Marlier issued these plans without German approval and knowing that the departures would create a terrible bottleneck at Moulins. In a July 19 directive to all prefects titled, "Return in Parts of the Occupied Zone Currently Authorized," Marlier gave the green light for repatriation, mentioning few of the German restrictions articulated by von Streccius.[58] The note is significant in three ways. First, Marlier outlined the geographical subdivisions of the Occupied Zone for the first time to prefects in both zones. Second, he specifically listed the professions permitted to return to the "Non-Restricted Occupied Zone" and those permitted to return to the "Restricted Occupied Zone." The list of approved refugees included farmers, farm workers, agricultural professionals, manure merchants, blacksmiths, wheelwrights, metal merchants, and mechanics able to repair agricultural equipment. Marlier's list does not mention exclusion of native farmers of the Restricted Zone – an exclusion stipulated by the

[56] AN F/1a/3660, Minutes of meeting at the Hôtel Majestic, July 13, 1940.
[57] Alary, *La ligne de démarcation: 1940–1944*, 70.
[58] AN F/1a/3660, Central Service of Refugees, President of the Council to prefects, "Return in Parts of the Occupied Zone Currently Authorized," July 19, 1940.

Germans on July 5. Third, the memo makes no mention of the exclusion of Jews, communists, those of mixed bloods, or foreigners from the Occupied Zone. Furthermore, the July 19 memo makes no mention of the fate of thousands of Alsatian and Lorrainer refugees, such as Marie Limousin. The directive does specify that all demobilized soldiers could return to their homes. It also cautions that no refugees may pass through Paris.

The memo raises questions: did the Service wish to openly defy German restrictions?; did they wish to create confusion, allowing excluded categories to travel to the Line of Demarcation, thus forcing the Germans to enforce the exclusions themselves? In the second two weeks of July, the French directives coming from the Service of Refugees did not direct prefects to enforce German categories of exclusions. By July 30, other branches of the French state and the occupying apparatus moved to "clarify" policy. However, ambiguity regarding refugee exclusions would reign throughout the fall of 1940. Only after weighing more of the historical record can we determine whether Marlier intentionally created this ambiguity so as to avoid enforcing German policy.

Despite the fact that his July 19 memo indicated that trains would be routed around Paris beginning on July 22, Marlier scheduled two trains to depart daily for Paris from seven departure points around the hexagon: Bordeaux, Nantes, Brest, Clermont-Ferrand, Tours, Toulouse, and Marseille. To facilitate the passage of these trains, Huntziger sent a petition to German officials requesting the opening of multiple points of passage in addition to the checkpoint at Moulins. In the same request, Chief of Staff Auleb sought to persuade German officials to reconsider the "one way only" policy of passage. He requested that repatriated business executives be allowed to travel back and forth between zones in order to report to Vichy on the material conditions and extent of property damage in the north.[59] Between July 22 and July 27 trains boarded refugees in the south and moved them toward Moulins for passage through the Line. At Moulins, refugees would board a train for Paris. After less than five days, the Germans ordered the entire program suspended. They informed Marlier that they required more time to implement security procedures. They assured the Service of Refugees that the trains would begin running again on August 2, 1940.[60]

[59] AN F/1a/3660, Memo, July 18, 1940.
[60] Pierre Durand, *La SNCF pendant la guerre, 1939–1945* (Paris: PUF, 1969), 130, cited in Alary, *La ligne de démarcation 1940–1944*, 6. AN F/60/1507, Service of the Armistice to Minister of National Defense, Circular, August 24, 1940.

Conclusion

The negotiations between the Vichy regime and the German Armistice Commission for the return of the approximate 7 million refugees to the Occupied Zone in France and the Benelux countries formed the foundation for the second phase of the refugee crisis. These negotiations marked the national government's efforts to resume control of local crisis management within the larger context of accelerating national reconstruction.

Four parties emerged during these negotiations to shape relief and repatriation policy: Vichy delegates, German Armistice representatives, local officials, and refugees. Between July and September 1940, the Honorary Prefect and Special Delegate for the Refugees, Louis Marlier, promoted a policy of refugee repatriation. Vichy hoped that refugee repatriation would speed up political and economic reconstruction in the north; relieve pressure on Free Zone communities to feed and house refugees; extinguish the potential for resistance movements to grow among displaced communities; and resist the strict partitioning of "Free France" from "German Occupied France."

Temporary refugee "settlement" in various departments on both sides of the Line of Demarcation introduced the second phase of the crisis where people and policies stagnated, reconsidering the wisdom of repatriation. Factions arose within the refugee community as regional, political, religious, national, and ethnic differences influenced how well refugees might thread through the new weave of Occupied and Free France. The Germans quickly capitalized on the opportunities presented to them with regard to refugee repatriation. Creating multiple regional partitions within French territory and the Benelux countries that served as the basis for accelerating population relocation schemes, they began refusing Channel coast residents the right of return. By clearing the Forbidden Zone, they hoped to secure military operations along the Channel and Atlantic coast; transfer French property in the north to German settler populations; and, in a Machiavellian way, curb French ambitions for economic and political reconstruction.

This chapter thus importantly modifies the historiography on the Holocaust in France, producing evidence that racial selection began at the Line of Demarcation as early as July 15, 1940. It identifies the French Service of Refugees' rejection of that policy, but also its failure to make universal repatriation a precondition of any repatriation. This practice bought time for displaced racial minorities who would become targets for repression, arrest, and deportation from the Occupied Zone. The Line of Demarcation emerged as a fundamental tool in the racialization of bureaucratic practices in France that ultimately contributed to the German project of ethnic cleansing in western Europe. Significantly, this chapter describes how the Line of Demarcation, operating as a selection point for refugee repatriation back to the German Occupied Zone, functioned as an integral component to the larger project of racial and ethnic segregation facilitated by partitioning France into smaller geographic zones.

By tracing the relationship between occupation operations and consciousness-building, we see that a complete understanding about what German occupation would mean for different segments of the population revealed itself over a period of time and through civilians' and French officials' interactions with German negotiators and military personnel. In exchanges with French authorities, as well as with German occupying officials, many civilians began to reformulate the notions of individual and collective security that they had relied upon prior to the invasion, adapting these concepts to the new context of occupation and partition. The preinvasion concept of the "right to relocation" away from war's impending violence, slowly transformed into a desire to exercise a "right to asylum" in the Free Zone or a "right to return" to the Occupied Zone.

7 German exclusions inaugurate a policy of ethnic cleansing

Emila Zrim cleaned houses for a living. For four years she had worked for the Rebière family in Enghien-les-Bains (Seine-et-Oise). Monsieur Rebière, a member of the Legion of Honor, had recently retired as the Principal Inspector of the SNCF railway. On June 16, the Rebière family joined the exodus, heading for refuge in Brive-la-Gaillarde. Zrim, had immigrated from Yugoslavia and with no family in France, departed with her employer. A Rebière cousin, Madame Cordelier, welcomed her cousins and Zrim to Brive.[1] By July 23, the Rebière family had made the 502-km trip back to Enghien-les-Bains in the Occupied Zone, presumably by car since train repatriation had not yet started. Once home in the Occupied Zone, they sent a letter across the Line of Demarcation to the mayor of Brive, petitioning for the return of Zrim. It explained that their cousin "graciously hosted" Zrim, but only in the short term.[2] Monsieur Rebière urged Brive's mayor to repatriate Zrim to Seine-et-Oise where her home and her job awaited her.

All the petitions in the world could not assist Mayor Louis Miginiac of Brive in repatriating Zrim to the Occupied Zone as she held foreign citizenship.[3] The best Miginiac could do would be to "forget" to check her papers and hope that German authorities at the Line of Demarcation would do the same. Throughout the summer and early fall of 1940, the Germans refused to issue laissez-passer to any foreigners. They made exceptions for German nationals and Swiss citizens who previously resided in the Occupied Zone. To survive, Zrim would have to count on the continued generosity of Cordelier, hope to continue to receive a refugee allocation, and possibly sell her domestic services to a family in Brive. Her fate was in the hands of Brivists. For residents of France's south-west, forces greater than their individual

---

[1] AMBG, Series H/IV. J. F. M. Rebière to the mayor of Brive, July 23, 1940.
[2] AMBG, Series H/IV. J. F. M. Rebière to the mayor of Brive, July 23, 1940.
[3] Louis Miginiac replaced Mayor Henri Chapelle on June 12, 1940. Miginiac served until August 16, 1944, when a ministerial decree revoked his office. Murat, *Le passeur de Mémoire*, 20.

and collective wills would determine their ability to provide long-term accommodation to the displaced masses.

Between July and October 1940, the partitioning of France, combined with enforcement of regulations restricting population movement substantially limited refugees' choices for long-term relocation and survival. During this period, the Armistice Commission expanded the categories of persons excluded from re-entry to the Occupied Zone, forcing Free Zone communities to adopt policies and develop ways to absorb the permanently displaced populations. Host departments employed a variety of strategies, including ignoring German rules, restricting repatriation, placing refugees in private homes, and converting refugee shelters into permanent facilities. The best shelters allowed refugees the right to come and go as they pleased; the worst sentenced restricted refugees to long-term imprisonment in containment centers focused on surveillance and policing rather than on relief and rescue. As German categories of exclusion expanded, jeopardizing specific groups in the Occupied Zone, the Free Zone began receiving clandestine transfers and German expulsees. Prefects in the Free Zone thus adopted the same language and categories of exclusion in determining policies toward these marginalized refugees. The universalistic refugee relief and rescue policies adopted in the early stages of the summer crisis narrowed their eligibility criteria based upon a refugee's ethnic, racial, political, national, or geographic identity.

Enforcing exclusions at the Line of Demarcation

On July 4, 1940, the Ministry of the Interior, perhaps anticipating the exclusion of foreigners from the Occupied Zone, sent a memo to all prefects encouraging department officials to immediately return all foreigners to the departments from which they had traveled. Vichy may have hoped to reduce the concentration of foreigners in the Free Zone. Maybe they believed the Germans would enter into the process of sending foreigners back to their home countries.[4] Regardless of Vichy's desires, the Germans had already set in place a practice of refusing foreigners re-entry to any departments in the Occupied Zone.

Examination of the application of policies of social, political, economic, and geographic exclusion reveals how the different arms of local, Vichy, and German authority, intentionally or unintentionally, combined practices that marginalized and jeopardized displaced civilians. The exclusion of refugees established the basis for more radicalized

---

[4] Peschanski, *La France des camps*, 163.

policies of political and ethnic cleansing adopted by the Germans and Vichy in 1941 and 1942. The terms of exclusion influenced how local governments and host communities treated foreign and Jewish refugees. In both zones, repatriation facilitated each regime's efforts to separate "undesirable" groups from French society. Women and children belonging to excluded categories suffered particular hardships. Refugees' testimonies show how the permanently displaced attempted to accommodate, and resist, exclusionary relief, resettlement, and repatriation policies. The Germans enforced exclusions at the Line of Demarcation and in the subpartitions of the Occupied Zone. The frequent disregard of German regulations by refugees and French officials provoked German interruptions of the entire repatriation program.

The three top categories of people excluded from the Occupied Zone – communists, Jews, and foreigners (including Belgians) – represented the same categories that Vichy desired to exclude from the Free Zone. The French inclination toward excluding communists and foreigners from public life predated the defeat and Vichy's rise to power. Internment camps had already been established to house suspicious foreigners and "militant communists." Perhaps ironically, by excluding a broad set of "undesirables" from the Occupied Zone, the Germans beat the French at a game they had initiated. The Germans forced the French to adopt policies of *inclusion* to absorb persons excluded from the Occupied Zone. Initially, the French unsuccessfully engaged in defiance, attempting to repatriate persons defined by the Germans as "non-repatriable." The Germans insisted that if the French wished refugee repatriation to move forward, then they must submit to the hard task of self-discipline. The disagreements between the two sides subjected refugees to a roller-coaster ride that endured until the Germans sealed the Line of Demarcation on November 1, 1940.

Belgians

On July 5, Marlier had not pressed von Streccius to suspend the policy to exclude Belgians from convoys traveling to the Occupied Zone, hoping to offer repatriation priority to French citizens and to avoid a deluge of Belgian refugees arriving in Paris.[5] The Germans had no interest in allowing trains to pass between the French and Belgian border, potentially interfering with military operations. However, Belgian Prime Minister Hubert Pierlot and Foreign Minister Paul Henri Spaak

---

[5] AN F/1a/3660, Chief of Staff, Paris, July 17, 1940.

worked tirelessly to secure the return of Belgian refugees.[6] At train stations many foreign refugees worked their way onto trains. Departmental and municipal officials had more reason than national officials to look the other way as foreigners defied German orders and slipped on board trains. The Benelux country refugees had arrived in France in early May, and by August many of them faced a choice between economic ruin or recruitment into French labor brigades. Belgians expressed anxiety about the uncertainty of their political and economic status and pressed for the right to return.

During the summer of 1940, the French interned most Belgian civilians in camps, not as a product of xenophobic feeling, but because using existing camps seemed practical. By centralizing the location of Belgians, prefects could more easily make them comply with government requirements. Refugees needed to register for group work programs, repatriation, and refugee assistance. Arguing that prefects were not applying a politics of xenophobia in housing foreign refugees in camps is not to say that some foreign refugees did not encounter xenophobia. A policy to monitor and arrest foreigners emerged at the same time as the larger crisis unfolded and also resulted in the imprisonment of targeted foreigners in camps.

One subgroup of Belgians that organized early to press for return were Belgian communists. Jean Fonteyne, who had defended the French communists tried for their support of the Soviet Union after the signing of the Stalin–Hitler Non-Aggression Pact, now championed the cause of the Belgian communists. Fonteyne petitioned both the French and German authorities to allow Belgian communists to repatriate to Belgium. Fonteyne now received the backing of the French government, eager to repatriate Belgian communists to their homeland. The Germans refused. Surprisingly, however, before the end of 1940 the Germans slightly reversed their position, permitting the repatriation of female Belgian communists who had been interned at Gurs (Pyrénées-Atlantiques) and at Saint-Cyprien (Pyrénées-Orientales). Fonteyne could not secure the same return for the men interned at Le Vernet (Ariège).[7] In this case, women benefited from the assumption that they posed no political threat – a gender stereotype the French Resistance later exploited.[8]

[6] "Belgian Cabinet Ended," *New York Times*, September 16, 1940, 8.
[7] Peschanski, *La France des camps*, 154–155. Report on the activity of Belgian communists interned in the camp of Le Vernet in June and July 1940, CRCEDHC 545/4/1a; Report of Jean Fonteyne, CRCEDHC (Moscow) 495/74/520.
[8] Schwartz, "*Partisanes* and Gender Politics in Vichy France,", 309.

French officials also tabled repatriation for French citizens who lived in Belgium prior to May 9, 1940. On September 2, 1940, General Huntziger's office wrote to General Weygand, Minister of National Defense at Vichy, advising: "It is preferable to reserve a request to the German Armistice Commission for the return of French compatriots to Belgium ... rather than going in for a certain loss, I think it's better to postpone requests."[9] Huntzinger's letter shows a growing emphasis by French officials on scoring policy "wins" against the Germans and avoiding further humiliating losses. Over the year, the French would achieve partial success in repatriating French citizens to Belgium. Out of approximately 70,000 French citizens who had participated in the May 1940 exodus from Belgium, an estimated 40,000 had been repatriated to Belgium by June 1941.[10]

Belgian Jews fared no better than Belgian communists in their efforts to gain speedy repatriation to Belgium. Initially, some Belgian Jews found themselves lodged at Saint-Cyprien where they lived in deplorable conditions, but enjoyed the freedom to come and go from the camp.[11] The fate of Belgians and Belgian Jews residing in France fueled negotiations between the French Service of Refugees, the German Armistice Commission, the Militärbefehlshaber office in Brussels, and the Belgian ambassador to the Occupied Territories throughout 1940 and 1941. The Germans finally approved repatriation for the majority of Belgians in September 1940. On September 16, 1940 the Belgian Cabinet disbanded, claiming credit for returning 1,200,000 Belgian citizens to their homeland.[12]

Other foreign nationalities

Poles, Romanians, Czechs, Russians, Greeks, and Yugoslavs created a tapestry of eastern and central European ethnicities that blanketed France's south. During the interwar years, some had become naturalized French citizens, but this did not necessarily protect them from discrimination.[13] Furthermore, on July 22, 1940, Vichy formed a commission to review the awards of citizenship made to foreigners since

[9] AN F/60/1507, General Charles Huntziger to Minister of Defense at Vichy, Wiesbaden, September 2, 1940.
[10] AN F/60/1507, DGGFTO to Admiral of the Fleet, Secretary of State for Foreign Policy, Political Directorate – Armistice, June 19, 1941.
[11] Peschanski, *La France des camps*, 154.
[12] "Belgian Cabinet Ended," *New York Times*, September 16, 1940, 8.
[13] Julie Fette, "Avocats et médecins xénophobes (1919–1939)," in André Gueslin and Dominique Kalifa (eds.), *Les exclus en Europe* (Paris: Éditions de l'Atelier, 1999), 345–357.

August 1927 when the National Assembly had adopted a more lenient naturalization law.[14]

Eastern European refugees from Paris came only a year after the French had forced the repatriation of eastern European combatants of the International Brigades, who had fled to Perpignan after the victory of Franco's Nationalists in Spain. French officials in the south feared the growing Trotskyite presence identified with the International Brigades, and, hence, pushed for repatriation of all foreigners.[15] Also, while eastern European refugee populations did not approach the numbers of Benelux refugees, their presence seemed larger due to their linguistic differences and cultural practices. In Brive, for example, December 1940 figures recorded 146 foreigners among a total of 877 refugees remaining in the commune. French refugees always constituted the majority within the residual refugee population, but local rhetoric often suggested the opposite.[16]

The propensity to repatriate foreigners from departments in the southwest predated the exodus and was not limited to eastern Europeans. In 1938, the Plan Cian, which proposed the repatriation of Italian immigrants to Italy, was debated in the National Assembly.[17] The decree of June 10, 1940, recognizing Italy as a belligerent and calling for the arrest of or oaths of loyalty to be sworn by Italians living on French soil, resulted in the arrest of approximately 4,700 out of an estimated 700,000 Italians living in France. Reynaud's collapsing government interned nearly 4,000 Italians in the camp at Saint-Cyprien (Pyrénées-Orientales) and 700 in a facility at Nîmes.[18]

Alsatians and Lorrainers

Alsatians and Lorrainers had benefited from early evacuation programs, and thousands had established residences in the south before the exodus gained full momentum. However, about 20 percent of the residents of the region did not flee until the final hours before the German invasion. This latter group competed with the mass of refugees to find housing and jobs in host communities. On August 2, 1940, the Reich annexed Alsace and Lorraine. Alsace fell under the direction of Gauleiter,

---

[14] Susan Zuccotti, *The Holocaust, the French, and the Jews* (New York: Basic Books, 1993), 52. Zuccotti cites the *Journal Official*, July 23, 1940: 4,587.
[15] Peschanski, *La France des camps*, 50–55.
[16] ADC 1E/DEP/272.398, Prefect Musso to mayors of Brive and Tulle, December 12, 1940, and October 1941.
[17] Peschanski, *La France des camps*, 33–34.
[18] Peschanski, *La France des camps*, 152.

Robert Wagner, and Lorraine under the authority of Gauleiter, Joseph Bürckel.[19] Germans refused to issue laissez-passer to Alsatians or Lorrainers who would not swear an oath of loyalty to the Reich and accept Reich citizenship. They refused admission of Jews from Alsace and Lorraine and created an ambiguous category defined as Alsatians and Lorrainers without proof of German blood. To qualify for admission, the Germans required refugees to provide proof of German heritage prior to 1919. By contrast, the Germans demanded the immediate return of "acceptable" Alsatians and Lorrainers to become new citizens of the Reich. For most Alsatian and Lorrainer men, this new national identity brought with it sure conscription into the German military. They expressed hesitation, and even unwillingness, to return to the annexed territories.

Vichy's policy insisted on the protection of Alsatians and Lorrainers from forced repatriation to the annexed territories, a commitment not extended to any other threatened refugee group. Vichy, and Marlier himself, also worked tirelessly to reunite the permanently displaced Alsatian and Lorrainer refugees with their abandoned property. Property restitution proved an important element in the survival equation of refugees, since acquiring daily necessities was difficult, if not impossible.

Because some "non-qualified" Alsatians and Lorrainers desired to be repatriated to the annexed territories problems arose on various levels. The fact that a portion of Alsace and Lorraine fell within the "Restricted Zone," meant that only selected occupational categories of refugees from Bar-le-Duc (Meuse) were eligible to receive a laissez-passer, angering others wishing to return, but refused readmission due to labor qualifications or "ethnic impurity." The complexity of policy governing Alsatians and Lorrainers earned them the ambiguous status of being considered the "most" disadvantaged *and* deserving refugees in the Free Zone. Vichy's relief policies thus evolved with a clear preference for assisting the distressed and displaced *French* Alsatian and Lorrainer minority community. By mid-September, Alsatians and Lorrainers who refused to take German nationality were expelled. British witnesses, G. and W. Fortune reported: "In some cases they were given only forty-eight hours in which to make up their minds."[20]

---

[19] Peschanski, *La France des camps*, 158. I wish to thank Wendy Lower for sharing her knowledge of Gauleiter Robert Wagner and Gauleiter Joseph Bürckel.

[20] G. and W. Fortune, *Hitler Divided France*, 22.

Free Zone Germans

One group of foreigners that the Germans did wish to repatriate to the Occupied Territory was German nationals. Article 19 of the Armistice Agreement and its corresponding Article 21 signed at Turin, required the French to return all German refugees to the Occupied Zone. The Red Cross reported that 13,500 German civilians had arrived from Belgium in the exodus of May and June. Of approximately 7,500 refugees temporarily interned at Saint-Cyprien in the summer of 1940, the Red Cross recorded 1,000 "Reichsdeutsche."[21] Another 8,000–8,500 German and Austrian civilians arrived at the camp at Gurs (Pyrénées-Atlantiques). Denis Peschanski emphasizes that one of the greatest humiliations of the Armistice was Article 19, which required the French to break with their interwar tradition of extending and ensuring political asylum to Germans who had actively resisted the Nazi regime. The Germans administering the Armistice Commission became very exacting regarding the return to the Occupied Zone of refugees they deemed to be "German nationals," a category that now included eligible Alsatians and Lorrainers. Lion Feuchtwanger, then lingering in a camp at Nîmes recalled: "Every day fresh rumors about the application of the extradition clause circulated through the camp. The Nazis had handed in their list, a list of two thousand names, or rather, no, only forty names; and then, later, none of names of men in the camp was on the list … We believed such rumors."[22]

Residents of the Restricted Zones

The lines of the "Restricted Zone" or "Forbidden Zone" seemed to change continuously. In July and August the Germans admitted administrators, but not refugees to Pas-de-Calais, Nord, Aisne, and Ardennes. Between September and November they denied admission of refugees to the coastal regions of Somme, Seine-Maritime, Haute-Normandie, Calvados, Manche, Ille-et-Vilanne, Côtes-du-Nord, Finistère, and Morbihan. Because thousands of refugees had fled to some of the coastal departments in Brittany, the Germans had to allow repatriation officials to return the displaced refugees from those departments, if they did not come from another restricted zone. In cases where refugees from one restricted zone had taken shelter in another restricted zone, authorities guided those refugees to temporary staging centers

---

[21] Peschanski, *La France des camps*, 153.   [22] Feuchtwanger, *Devil in France*, 236.

in departments like the Oise or the Marne, which fell within the "permitted" Occupied Zone. Rarely did such transfers improve the living conditions for refugees. Indeed, refugee camps in the north became severely overcrowded, sparking complaints from department prefects and relief workers.

Demobilized soldiers

Demobilized soldiers formed another subgroup of refugees. Scattered and now disarmed, these soldiers had the good fortune of not being assembled in PoW camps like the 1,900,000 servicemen who had stayed with their regiments and had fallen captive to the Germans. Provided the French disarmed the soldiers, the Germans allowed them to return to the Occupied Zone. But, as with most policies, impromptu changes would amend the original agreement. When choosing to remain in the south, demobilized soldiers formed a pool of male, French labor, which competed with foreign labor for jobs in the battered economy.

Jews and "mixed bloods"

On July 5, Marlier agreed to von Streiccus' refusal to admit communists to the Occupied Zone, but weakly defended the right of return for French Jews. The Germans tabled the issue of the Jewish right to return, probably so as to avoid scuttling the entire set of negotiations. But in practice, German border guards enforced the exclusion of Jews from the Occupied Zone, sending entire trains back to their point of origin for transporting a single Jewish person. German actions forced the French to attempt to discipline their own repatriation officials. On July 30, in an effort to instill discipline regarding enforcement of racial triage, the Secretary of State for the Minister of the Interior directed Free Zone prefects: "Primo: To avoid passage difficulties at the Line of Demarcation between the Free Zone and the Occupied Zone, I recommend that you avoid placing in route any Jewish, Negro or mixed blood refugees."[23]

In 1953, Maurice Lagrange, a repatriation officer at the Service of Refugees, delivered testimony to the French commission investigating the causes and consequences of France's defeat. Lagrange argued that the Germans intended for the racially discriminatory policies to slow repatriation. "The checkpoints," testified Lagrange, "were responsible for slowing the entire repatriation process; firstly they enforced re-entry

---

[23] ADC 528/W/4, Secretary of State to the Interior, Circular to prefects, July 30, 1940.

restrictions to the 'Forbidden Zones,' and then put in place an entire set of discriminatory categories for permission to re-enter accessible Occupied Territory."[24] Vichy's top leaders knew about the selection process imposed at the Line as evidenced in letters from Henry Lémery to Weygand written on August 11, and one written to Pétain on August 19 by a diverse group of parliamentarians of color.[25] They complained of having been mercilessly rejected from the Occupied Zone at the Line of Demarcation.[26] Lagrange confirmed that: "by mid-August, despite the fact that the Germans did not issue an official decree of Jewish exclusion from the Occupied Zone until November 18, Pétain knew full well of the racial triage taking place at the border in violation of the Armistice agreement."[27] Other than refusing to repatriate any refugees until the Germans lifted the exclusions, French officials had few choices but to comply.

Stop and go traffic

Throughout the Free and Occupied zones, prefects composed "Departmental Committees for Refugee Repatriation" that provided instructions to mayors based on orders from the prefects. In the chain of command between the prefects, repatriation committees, the mayors, and refugees, important decisions regarding refugees' fates could be made in favor or against particular refugees' self-interests. At the prefectoral and mayoral levels, officials decided whether to uphold German occupation policy and French national policy or to ignore them. Feuchtwanger, in his memoir, condemned as "the Devil in France," those French authorities "who simply did not think ahead." The degradation of refugees, especially foreigners, stemmed from "the Devil of indifference."[28]

In Brive, Monsieur Chastre, Director of the "Committee of Refugee Welcome," organized repatriation and coordinated with French military

---

[24] AN AJ/72/2004, Maurice Lagrange, Honorary Councillor of State, "Le repatriement des refugiés après l'exode: juillet–septembre 1940," Extract, Dossier 5.

[25] Lémery was a mulatto senator from Martinique, who worked to cultivate Pétain's return to power. Pertinax, *Gravediggers of France*, 191, 349.

[26] AN AJ/72/2004, Lagrange, Dossier 5.

[27] AN AJ/72/2004, Lagrange, Dossier 5. The exact language was: "Puis commencèrent très vite à apparaître des discriminations raciales, ainsi qu'en font soit par exemple, une lettre de Henry Lémery au Général Weygand du 11 août 1940, ou une lettre au Maréchal du 19 août émanant de divers parlementaires de couleur qui se plaignaient d'être impitoyablement refoulés à la ligne de démarcations, sans parler de Juifs ou présumés tels, bien que l'interdiction officielle à leur égard ne date que du 18 novembre."

[28] Feuchtwanger, *Devil in France*, 40–41.

units of Army C, which functioned along the Line of Demarcation. Army C controlled checkpoint access, verifying refugee convoy lists, and confirming identity papers on the French side en route to Moulins, where they transferred "approved" refugees to the German guards of the Occupied Territories. The Germans repeated many of the same surveillance tasks, mostly to check the work of their French counterparts. This process allowed room for multiple types of intentional and unintentional errors. The most typical structural and organizational problems encountered by repatriation workers included failures to coordinate train schedules between minor and mainline train stations, and failures to verify refugees' identity papers. The looseness of the repatriation structure meant that violations of policy frequently occurred. From August to November 1940, the Germans worked to patch bureaucratic holes in the passage system, and to improve efficiency and effectiveness of identity verification procedures at the checkpoints. They also punished French officials for failure to enforce their control policies. Each month, the repatriation apparatus became more efficient, more rigid, and more dangerous for refugees and officials who attempted to defy German policies.

August

At the beginning of August, the prefect of the Corrèze informed the Secretary of State of the Interior that the return of 16,000 people by car and 7,200 by rail was planned between August 1 and August 10.[29] The mayors of Tulle and Brive sent notices to the refugees informing them of inclusion on the first repatriation list. The notice advised refugees to meet at the train station with their repatriation certificates and two days worth of food and water. Only handbags, bicycles, and baby carriages would be permitted on board. Each passenger – child or adult – would need proof of residence in the Occupied Zone. Round one of repatriation was restricted to residents of the departments of the Seine, Seine-et-Oise, and Seine-et-Marne. Repatriation posters celebrated: "The trip is free!"[30]

However, the Germans again dashed French hopes. After only a week of operations, German officials began to slow trains, rejecting some entirely for bureaucratic slip-ups. On August 13, the Germans suspended all repatriation in the Atlantic Zone, the Central Zone,

---

[29] AN F/1c/III/1147, Telegram from the prefect of the Corrèze to the Secretary of State to the Interior at Vichy, August 3, 1940.
[30] ADC 1E/DEP/272/398, mayoral announcement, Tulle, August 3, 1940.

and the Parisian Zone, sending back one train after another. Two days later, Colonel Paquier, a French Army official overseeing repatriation, accused the Reich of violating the conditions of the Armistice by limiting trains and hindering the repatriation process.[31] Somewhere, someone responded to French complaints, and on that same day, in a complete reversal of German insistence on the one-point of passage rule, they announced planned openings of several new checkpoints. The new checkpoints especially serviced the west coast departments, including openings at Orthez (Basses-Pyrénées), Mont-de-Marsan (Landes), Montpon (Dordogne), Mignaloux (Vienne), Vierzon (Cher), Moulins (Allier), and Paray-le-Monial and Châlon-sur-Saône (Saône-et-Loire).[32] However, the next day the Germans stopped all traffic attempting to cross the Line of Demarcation west of Bléré, located near Tours. Yet by August 20, Paquier had received additional assurances that "in principle" more trains would soon be provided, but no exact date was given.[33]

In his postwar testimony, Lagrange complained about German conduct during this period, observing the tragic irony of the situation. He said that in July, the Germans complained about the French side of operations, accusing the French of being disorganized, of sending trains that were only half-filled, and of failing to coordinate the transfer of refugees between trains. According to Lagrange, the French quickly "mastered their side of the operations" so that the Germans, "could not believe how quickly and orderly the French had improved their repatriation operations." He continued, "In stopping and stalling traffic in mid-August the Germans only wanted to scuttle the remarkable results achieved by the French in only a few days."[34] In contrast to Lagrange's sentiments, the main reason for suspending the mid-August repatriations had less to do with a desire to humiliate the French, and more to do with the preparation for opening the new checkpoints; a demand the French themselves had made in July.[35] The archives challenge Lagrange's testimony and reveal that well into October 1940 the French fell short of full compliance with German demands to present fully packed cars at the Line of Demarcation.

[31] AN F/1c/III/1163, telegram from Colonel Paquier at the Ministry of the Interior to the prefect of the Lot, August 16, 1940.
[32] Alary, *La ligne de démarcation: 1940–1944*, 67.
[33] AN F/1c/III/1163, telegram from Colonel Paquier at the Ministry of the Interior to the prefect of the Lot, August 16, 1940.
[34] Lagrange, "Le rapatriement des refugiés," Dossier 5.
[35] Alary, *La ligne de démarcation: 1940–1944*, 67.

By August 24, national authorities announced that trains would roll once again. Also, the Germans modified their decision about the exclusion of Belgian civilians. The Armistice Commission authorized the allocation of ten trains a day to leave the Free Zone to transport Belgian civilian refugees to Paris. The French welcomed this decision. However, the Chief of Staff of the 7th Region reported only being allowed to send three trains to the checkpoint at Châlon-sur-Saône. When the trains arrived at the Line of Demarcation, the Germans turned them back beginning on August 24 to August 30. The Germans chided the French for mixing Belgian civilians with demobilized Belgian soldiers.[36]

On August 31, the General Commander of the 12th Region, stationed in Limoges, informed the commander in charge of Brive that: "The Germans are returning Belgians between 18 and 45 years of age from checkpoints at the Line of Demarcation ... This measure does not apply to youth traveling with their families, on the condition that they do not leave them in France, and that they have not previously enlisted in reserved or mobilized units."[37] In towns along the Line, mayors built makeshift barracks for rejected Belgian refugees and began to plan for the long-term presence of demobilized Belgian soldiers. The barracks contributed to the geographic marginalization of Belgian foreigners.

Meticulous triage of repatriating refugees slowed the process. On August 28, Colonel Paquin of the Armistice Service wrote to Weygand to inform him that demobilized French soldiers, who fell under a separate categorization from Belgians, would be allocated a total of twenty trains per day. However, the Germans insisted that trains carrying demobilized French soldiers should pass the Line of Demarcation only at the checkpoint established at Moulins, causing more delays.[38] Refugees also frustrated French authorities' efforts. As of August 24, three trains with approximately 3,000 refugees had been scheduled from Brive.[39] However, examining the departures reveals a discrepancy between train bookings and boarding: one train contained 94 persons, a second had 400, and a third held 1,200. Of the 2,900

---

[36] AN F/60/1507. Service of the Armistice to Minister of National Defense, Circular, August 24, 1940.

[37] AMBG, Series H/IV, General Commanding the 12th Region, P.O. Chief of Staff to Lt. Colonel Doublet, Commander of the Canton of Brive, Limoges, August 31, 1940.

[38] AN F/60/1507, Service of the Armistice, Col. Paquin to Minister of National Defense at Vichy, Circular, August 28, 1940.

[39] AMBG, Director of Rapatriation Services to mayors, August 24, 1940.

Table 4. *City of Tulle, applications for repatriation received from refugees originating from regions other than the Paris region, August 10, 1940*

Aube	20	Haute Saône	6	Bas Rhin	46
Côte d'Or	4	Vosges	6	Moselle	13
Saône-et-Loire	1	Sarthe	9	Belfort	29
Indre-et-Loire	12	Maine-et-Loire	10	Meurthe-et-Moselle	13
Loire-et-Cher	1	Vienne	2	Meuse	11
Cher	12	Manche	8	Marne	111
Nièvre	12	Côtes-du-Nord	2	Ardennes	39
Loiret	6	Morbihan	2	Aisne	59
Eure-et-Loire	1	Vendée	2	Somme	13
Eure	12	Charante-Inférieure Ch. Inf.	1	Pas-de-Calais	13
Seine-Inférieure	33	Landes	4	Nord	133
Oise	25	Gironde	1	Calvados	14
Haute Marne	12	Loire Inf.	1	Ille-et-Vilaine	4
Doubs	11	Haut Rhin	5		
Total					747

Source: ADC 1E/DEP/272–399. Table filed in a mayoral report, August 10, 1940.

refugees scheduled to repatriate, 1,200 people failed to show up on their assigned day.[40]

The number of applications for repatriation submitted by non-Parisians in Tulle during the second week of August, illustrates the lack of enthusiasm or confusion refugees felt about repatriation. From the more than 10,000 refugees within the town limits, repeated calls to register for repatriation yielded only 747 applications from refugees of departments outside of the Paris region (Table 4).

Despite the low number of repatriation applications, which suggests a lack of enthusiasm for the idea of returning to live under a German master, there were also refugees who attempted to skip ahead of their turn. In Brive, Inspector of Police Launoy directed a team of municipal employees and volunteers, who verified each returnee's identity papers. Launoy complained that:

Daily we must send away people from Forbidden Zone departments who try to get in on the sly to leave for Paris by any means. I don't even want to talk about the number of refugees who come from surrounding counties, neighboring Brive, who try to leave with our refugees, that is to say, who try to take the place of Brivist refugees on departing trains.[41]

[40] AMBG, Director of Rapatriation Services to mayors, August 24, 1940.
[41] AMBG, Director of Repatriation Services to mayors, August 24, 1940.

Launoy's complaint highlights an important issue for administrators: when refugees from other communes "stole" the limited seats available, "Brivist refugees," had to extend their stay in Brive.

Madame Raynaud's foiled attempt to cross the Line of Demarcation is an example of how a plan that seemed efficient on paper turned out to be chaotic in practice. Following instructions in public announcements about returning to Paris, Raynaud, her three children, her cousin, and her cousin's baby, set out by car to cross the Line. Discouraged by the slow-moving traffic and "the suffering child," the party decided to turn around and drive toward Toulon on the Mediterranean coast, where Raynaud had family. The car ran out of gasoline near Brive and, finding no gas available in Brive, they abandoned the car and made their way by foot. Their story is detailed in a request to the mayor of Brive for permission to extend their stay in the Free Zone indefinitely.[42] A follow-up letter to the mayor indicates that slow-moving traffic may not have been the only reason that Raynaud decided to turn back. She informed the mayor that, since her husband had been taken prisoner of war, she had decided to stay in Toulon; and requested permission to return to Brive to claim her car and obtain a sufficient amount of state-rationed gasoline to drive back to Toulon.[43] The example of Raynaud and others, such as Mlle Yvonne Krauss, who was recorded on one repatriation roster as having refused to leave, suggests that many women continued the practice from the exodus of defying state orders that they considered contrary to the well-being of their family.[44] For cases like Raynaud, financial independence (indicated by automobile ownership) and the ability to stay in a friend's or family's residence enabled refusal to repatriate to the Occupied Zone.

The operation of repatriation services on the local level was a collaboration of local officials and the refugees. Among the refugees were thousands of state functionaries who, while temporarily unpaid, were still employed by the state. These people eagerly volunteered their time and talents to their host community civil service counterparts. Madame Lucette Dourver figured among those volunteering who hoped to have their wages restored. Dourver, a former resident of Paris who arrived in Brive on June 17, 1940, was one of the many women staffing Brive's repatriation effort. As "reward" for helping in the local rescue work,

---

[42] AMBG, Series H/IV, Guerre 1939–40, Madame Raynaud to the mayor of Brive, August 2, 1940.
[43] AMBG, Series H/IV, list by nationalities. Madame Raynaud to Mayor of Brive, Toulon, August 22, 1940.
[44] ADC 1E/DEP/272/398, Tulle, Mayoral repatriation list dated August 2, 1940.

she successfully obtained a letter from the mayor to her employer, then stationed in Lyon, explaining that due to the importance of her services to local repatriation efforts, and because it was "materially impossible" to return to her job, she should stay.[45] The case of Dourver is instructive on multiple levels. First, by staying in Brive (with her husband) she risked the possibility of losing her job in Paris. It is possible that her desire to stay with the repatriation service in Brive served as a pretext for not returning to the Occupied Zone. One might also infer that Dourver found her participation in the repatriating services exciting and demanding, in a way that her job in Paris probably was not. Many women found a sense of fulfillment of their patriotic duty by assisting in the national emergency. Finally, by later arranging the transfer of her salary, Dourver secured the financial means to stay in the Free Zone.

Vichy's aspirations to complete repatriation from the Free Zone by the end of August died when the Germans deferred all repatriation to the region of the Côte-d'Or, the Yonne and the Saône-et-Loire, as well as all regions near Normandy. Furthermore, the Germans refused to discuss the repatriation of refugees from France's north-eastern departments of Aisne and Nord. In August, Interim Prefect Moyen reported to the Minister of the Interior that Corrèze continued to host a refugee population of 85,000, significantly down from the June estimate of 200,000. Of those 85,000, he hoped to repatriate as many as 70,000.[46] Despite all the delays, by the end of August French repatriation authorities claimed that they had repatriated 1,600,000 refugees.[47] Assuming these figures are correct, an additional 4.5 million refugees remained displaced.

September

Marlier's new goal became to complete repatriation by September 30, 1940. Vichy hoped to accelerate the speed of return, so as to establish an unstoppable momentum. The new schedule for September arrived in localities with instructions for authorities to plan daily convoy departures. The instructions gave priority to French refugees, allocated a total of nine trains per day, and included a reminder to ensure that an adequate number of people occupied all seats. These trains would

---

[45] AMBG, Series H/IV, Mayor of Brive-la-Gaillarde, "Certificate of Employment," August 21, 1940.
[46] AN F/1c/III/1147, Office of the Prefect of the Corrèze, prefect of the Corrèze to the Interior Ministry at Vichy, August 31, 1940.
[47] Alary, *La ligne de démarcation: 1940–1944*, 67.

depart from multiple locations including Paray-le-Monial, Limoges, Toulouse, Clermont-Ferrand, and Lyon; and would take advantage of newly established checkpoints at Viezeron and Châlon-sur-Saône in addition to traveling via Moulins. Three other trains were to transport newly eligible Belgian refugees, marking a German concession to French and Belgian lobbying. Luxembourgeois refugees were allotted one train per day. The schedule also hinted that, pending approval, qualifying Alsatians and Lorrainers would have four trains departing daily from Bordeaux and nine trains from other towns in the Free Zone.

September 1940 marked an escalation of the war's violence in the Occupied Zone with a significant intensification of the air war between the British and Germans over the Channel coast. British officials reported that, between September 7 and September 15, 2,000,000 kg of German bombs had dropped on London and 10,000 tons of British shipping had been sunk.[48] British retaliation turned from the defense of London to attacking the French coastline and parts of the occupied interior by mid-September. Around Dunkerque, US reports described: "Fierce flames from the RAF bombs raged, lighting Channel waters and casting a reflection on the calm waters of the Kentish shores."[49] Within the week, Dunkerque was bombed three times, with each raid lasting an hour and destroying fifty ships moored at the docks.

The September 13 instructions to Free Zone prefects made no mention of conditions in the Occupied Zone, and only reminded local authorities that: "no one would be permitted to cross the Line of Demarcation, in either direction unless they had received an ausweis [travel pass]."[50] Furthermore, the Secretary of State to the Minister of the Interior instructed that all requests for ausweis had to be made to the prefect, then submitted to the Service located in Paris, which would present requests to the Germans who retained final approval of every pass issued. This change removed mayors from the approval process for refugee departures, while prefects were to consider as legitimate requests only issued as administrative orders, but *not* motivated by economic and humanitarian concerns. Regarding requests to travel to or from the Forbidden Zones, the Germans cautioned French authorities to submit

[48] Percival Knauth, "Nazis See London Hard Hit by Raids," *New York Times*, September 16, 1940, 1.
[49] James MacDonald, "Channel is Lighted: British Bombers Loose Heightened Offensive on Nazi-held Coast," *New York Times*, September 22, 1940, 1.
[50] AMBG, Series H/IV, Secretary of State, Ministry of the Interior to the prefects of the Free Zone, Vichy, September 13, 1940.

requests of only the most exceptional cases.[51] The Germans hoped that by centralizing the approval to cross the Line of Demarcation, they could exercise more control over reintegration.

Scholars of the Occupation agree that German authorities adopted rules and requirements for requesting ausweis (laissez-passer), designed specifically to dissuade the population from attempting to cross the Line of Demarcation. Between November 1940 and January 1941, the Bordeaux bureau of laissez-passer received 5,100 requests for authorization to pass from the Occupied Zone into the Free Zone.[52] Philippe Souleau reports that only 1,527 passes (29.5 percent) received approval. German officials refused 1,133, and returned 2,440 requests to the French requesting further investigation to verify the legitimacy of the reasons given for crossing the Line.[53]

Slowly in 1941 the Germans began issuing passes for border dwellers wishing to conduct business along the frontier. Laissez-passer to enter the Free Zone granted at the commissariat of La Réole in Gironde, tallied 2,942 in February 1941, 6,151 by July 1941, 9,214 by February 1942, and 12,740 by July 1942. Permissions granted to enter into the Occupied Zone increased from 3,055 in February 1941, to 5,622 in July 1941, to 8,015 in February 1942, and to 13,332 in July 1942.[54]

German authorities also imposed rigorous restrictions on interzonal commercial exchanges. Around Bordeaux, Souleau concludes that the Germans seemed intent on destroying the network of the regional economy. Of sixty-five requests for commercial traffic across the Line of Demarcation in September 1940, officials granted just eight. Between November 1940 and January 1941, border officials granted 174 requests out of 531 submitted. Merchandise prohibited from exchange between zones included wine, alcohol, fish, sanitary products, pharmaceuticals, and construction materials including cement.[55] These restrictions created deep holes in local markets, reducing or eliminating the supply of important food staples in refugee and host community diets. Reporting from the south-west, P. J. Philip described the conditions:

There are villages and little towns in the southwest in which the shops are absolutely bare of all provisions except what comes in from the farms. Sugar,

[51] Secretary of State, Ministry of the Interior to the prefects of the Free Zone, Vichy, September 13, 1940.
[52] Souleau, *La ligne de démarcation en Gironde*, 31.
[53] Souleau, *La ligne de démarcation en Gironde*, 31.
[54] Souleau, *La ligne de démarcation en Gironde*, 33.
[55] Souleau, *La ligne de démarcation en Gironde*, 35.

salt, coffee, chocolate, eggs, matches, flour, cereals, tobacco, even pepper and mustard are scarcely obtainable. In one village shop the writer found the only stock left was some 500 boxes of boot polish.[56]

For French officials, growing shortages in the south trumped increasing bombardments of the north in solidifying determination to continue repatriation.

September operations in Corrèze and the Free Zone

In September 1940, Vichy brought Ferdinand Jêrome Musso from Pyrénées-Orientales to his natal region of Corrèze, which heralded a new attitude toward refugees and prospects for long-term resettlement.[57] In May 1940, Musso had organized relief efforts for the deluge of refugees attempting to flee over the Pyrénées into Spain. He considered himself heroic for issuing exit visas to Jewish refugees like the celebrated French author, Joseph Kessel.[58] In a 1953 memoir titled, *After the Tidal Wave*, Musso recorded his disgust at the time for the fleeing refugees who he thought demonstrated a lack of patriotism and dignity.[59] Perhaps this perspective influenced his occupation-related activities, which resulted in Musso's removal from service, condemnation, and imprisonment by the Court of Angers in 1945. He later received partial amnesty from the Law of August 6, 1953, but his administrative service in Corrèze suggested that he offered Vichy a form of ideological approval and enthusiasm that differed significantly from that of career bureaucrats like Papinot and Marlier.[60]

Musso's approach to repatriation represented a radicalizing shift, reflected by many Vichy officials.[61] At the national level, the new goal for repatriation was to reconstruct the nation along clearly articulated ideological lines. Vichy's September initiatives also realized important policy shifts that added to the bureaucratic structure that would support

[56] P. J. Philip, "France's Shortage of Food Surveyed," *New York Times*, October 17, 1940, 6.
[57] Reynaud, *In the Thick of the Fight*, 608–609, 648–651.
[58] In Joseph Kessel's *Témoins parmi les hommes, vol. 3: L'heure des châtiments* (Paris: Éditions Mondiales, 1956) the protagonist escapes France through the Pyrénées, but only in 1942.
[59] Ferdinand Jêrome Musso. *Après le raz de marée* (Self-published, 1953). Musso claimed that Kessel expressed his thanks by running from the prefect's office to a bookstore in Perpignan, and returning to Musso's office with a signed copy of one of his books.
[60] AN, *Dictionnaire Biographique des Préfets: septembre 1870–mai 1982* (Paris: Presses des Archives nationales de France, 1994), 411.
[61] Paxton, *Vichy France*, 200.

deportations, thus contributing to France's role in the Holocaust.[62] Earlier, in an attempt to improve local operations prior to recommencement of repatriation, Interim Prefect Moyon had ordered Corrèze's mayors to create new lists of all refugees desiring to depart. Like previous lists, these new ones continued to classify refugees according to department of origin (their destination) and the number of family members traveling together. Moyon insisted, "This effort will ensure a good step for repatriating refugees."[63]

Prefects hoped that by meticulously recording the local whereabouts of refugees, they could more easily organize refugees to depart on assigned departure dates and times. This organization was needed since, despite their daily requests to return to the Occupied Zone, refugees continuously missed their scheduled departures so that prefects could not fill trains to capacity. This led to partially filled trains frequently being turned back by German border guards. Musso arrived in Corrèze just in time to exact such obedience from the refugee community. Vichy also equipped Musso and other Free Zone prefects with a new tool for pressuring refugees to honor their assigned repatriation slots: withdrawal of state-funded refugee relief. Already in mid-September numerous prefects in the Free Zone had begun withholding allocations from refugees.

Prefects in the Occupied Zone complained about the effects of withholding refugee allocations from Free Zone refugees. Refugees, ineligible to repatriate to their Forbidden Zone homes and ineligible for relief assistance in the Free Zone, crowded into refugee assistance centers in Paris and other northern cities. On September 17, the Lieutenant Prefect of the department of the Oise wrote one of many letters sent in mid-September to French officials at the Service of Refugees at the Armistice Commission. The letter described the terrible conditions of refugee centers located in the north. In Oise, baroness de Langlade's chateau served as one of the largest camps in the French Army's 2nd Region. The Baroness complained to the Lieutenant Prefect about the conditions in the refugee center, where refugees still lived without running water or light as winter approached. Most windows were broken, having been shattered by earlier bombings. Despite the inability of the center to accommodate the refugees, more arrived daily because

[62] The requirement of Jews to identify themselves on refugee repatriation forms represents a "first step" taken to define who was Jewish. See Zuccotti, *The Holocaust, The French, and the Jews*, 52–53.
[63] AN F/1c/III/1147, Office of the Prefect of the Corrèze, prefect of the Corrèze to the Interior Ministry at Vichy, August 31, 1940.

prefects in the south had terminated their refugee relief allocations. The Lieutenant Prefect hoped that emergency funds could be immediately transferred to Noyon to begin repairs before the deepening of winter.[64]

Perhaps unintentionally, prefects in the Occupied Zone lent support to German policy by demanding that their Free Zone counterparts more thoroughly enforce exclusions. In a September 26 memo, General la Laurencie responded to concerns expressed by the prefect of Seine-et-Oise. The prefect had expressed the need to oppose, "by any means possible," the departure of refugees whose homes were in the Reserved Zones encompassing the departments of the Nord and the east of France.[65] The prefect had also informed la Laurencie that there were a number of refugees trying to get through the Line of Demarcation with the intention of returning to the Forbidden Zones. This caused problems at the Line, including the provision of lodging and feeding refugees in the border departments. La Laurencie assured the prefect that he had communicated his concerns to the Director of the Service of Refugees (Marlier).[66] La Laurencie also recommended that an intervention was necessary from the Occupation Authorities with the prefects of the Free Zones. He felt that it was the Germans' job to impress upon the Free Zone prefects the importance of maintaining refugees in their departments of welcome, or at least to restrict them from leaving except when they could return directly to their homes. He described the fate of disobedient refugees: "They are arrested daily by the Occupying Authorities and placed in camps, even if they have the original approval forms delivered by the local Kommandanturs."[67]

Musso was determined to comply with the new orders. On September 30, he sent instructions to mayors in Corrèze reminding them that that date marked the end of payment of refugee allocations. He set a goal of removing all refugees from Corrèze by the end of the first week of October. Mayors received instructions to clear refugees from all public spaces, including schools.[68] Under no circumstances, Musso warned, should refugees receive in-kind assistance either. The only exceptions to this policy would be for refugees proven to have no personal savings and to be unemployed and ineligible to return to their homes in the

---

[64] AN F/60/1507, Deputy prefect of Oise to the Service of the Armistice, Refugees, Compiègne, Oise, September 17, 1940.
[65] AN F1a/3660, General la Laurencie to the prefecture of Seine-et-Oise, Versailles, September 26, 1940.
[66] General la Laurencie to the prefecture of Seine-et-Oise, September 26, 1940.
[67] General la Laurencie to the prefecture of Seine-et-Oise, September 26, 1940.
[68] ADC 1 E/DEP/272/398, Musso to mayors, Tulle, September 30, 1940.

Forbidden Zone.[69] This heightened pressure to repatriate refugees was fueled by the German declaration that they would definitely seal the Line to passage on November 1, 1940. Free Zone authorities feared that the scarcity of resources in the south foreshadowed a grim winter if refugee concentrations remained high. However, national authorities seemed oblivious to the fact that with agricultural production interrupted for over two months, residents in the north faced a double indemnity: German requisitions of agricultural production and a severely bombed-out infrastructure.

Acceleration to end relief payments and repatriation renews hunt for foreigners

September witnessed an intensification of efforts to locate all foreigners living in the Free Zone. Prefects wished to estimate numbers of refugee dependants who government resources might fund through the winter. Thus, bureaucratic efficiency, rather than xenophobia, anti-Semitism, or ideological zeal motivated southern authorities to more closely monitor refugee communities. Also, renewed repatriation of Belgians on a "stand-by" basis spurred the French to gather excluded Belgians. Musso ordered leaders of refugee committees in each commune of Corrèze to classify refugees according to the following categories: (1) Belgians requesting permission to stay in the Free Zone because they had disseminated anti-German propaganda before the invasion; (2) Belgian Jews or Jews of a different nationality who had resided in Belgium before May 9, 1940; (3) Non-Jewish foreigners of other nationalities residing in Belgium before May 9; (4) Belgian refugees "who presented no inconvenience because they had their own financial resources;" (5) Belgian refugees interned in French concentration camps; and (6) Belgian refugees interned due to previous criminal acts.[70]

Musso did not create these categories. Failure to sort refugees into these categories and remove "undesirables" from repatriation lists, would, if noticed, earn him sanctions from German officials via French government officers. However, compliance with German policies meant that his administration would have to accommodate excluded refugees in Corrèze for the winter. The conundrum caused some prefects to gamble with individual lives and with their own careers. If prefects refused or "erred" in removing excluded refugees from repatriation lists, they might strike a small victory by reducing the number

---

[69] Musso to mayors, Tulle, September 30, 1940.
[70] Musso to mayors, Tulle, September 30, 1940.

of refugees requiring long-term accommodation in their departments. However, they risked a German reprisal: closure of passage at the Line of Demarcation, thus undermining prefects' efforts to clear qualifying refugees from host communities.

On October 11, the prefects of the Free Zone and the divided departments of Allier, Charente, Cher, and Vienne, received a disciplinary memo from the Service of Refugees' Operations Director, Lassalle-Séré. Lassalle-Séré condemned the errors committed at disembarkation points in the south, including failures to properly ticket refugees, check identity papers, and fully board trains. These oversights led to costly traffic jams at the Line of Demarcation. He reiterated: "officials who issued travel papers to Israélites, Poles, Czechs and people of mixed blood ... would receive sanctions."[71] In order to address ambiguous situations, he announced that local officials who could not determine whether a refugee fell into an "included" or an "excluded" category must telephone, before noon each day, the German delegate at Moulins to verify a refugee's status.[72]

This depth of micromanagement caused unnecessary delays in repatriation, which was perhaps the Germans' intention. In Brive, the web of memos, the miscommunication between departments, and the unscheduled arrival of refugee convoys took a toll on the local repatriation staff. A report of the Chief of the Municipal Cabinet charged with the oversight of refugee repatriation offered an example of the problems the exclusions caused. On October 9, a convoy of 109 Mosellian refugees arrived from Hérault at 1 am. The workers in Brive had not received any notice of their arrival and the Hérault staff had not planned for a locomotive to carry the cars to their final destination of Limoges. Furthermore, officials in Hérault had never issued the Mosellians with papers to cross the Line of Demarcation, and the refugees had received no food for their journey. A local volunteer spent the morning traveling to different boulangeries to requisition 100 kg of bread, and organized an effort to gather canned goods and bottled water for the second leg of the refugees' trip. The unexpected arrival of the train from Hérault slowed the planned repatriation schedule from Brive. Refugees scheduled to depart from Brive on October 10 received notice of postponement of travel until October 17. The delay also interrupted transfers of refugees from Cantal and Gers, who had been scheduled to transfer trains headed to the Line of Demarcation that day. Worse, the trains that

---

[71] AMBG, Series H/IV, Lassalle-Séré at the direction of the Service of Refugees at the Ministry of the Interior to the prefects of the Free Zone and the departments of Allier, Charente, Cher, and Vienne, Vichy, October 11, 1940.
[72] AMBG, Series H/IV, Lassalle-Séré, Vichy, October 11, 1940.

arrived as scheduled from Cantal and Gers, arrived without passenger lists. Brivist workers had to re-ticket refugees, issue travel documents, and establish train rosters. Brive's repatriation director said: "Our work would be facilitated if the prefectures of Aude and Pyrénées-Orientales had established passenger rosters and ticketed the Mosellian refugees with tickets for Moselle from the start."[73]

The events of October 9–10, unleashed the frustration of Brive's repatriation team leader. He registered his concerns in a letter to Mayor Miginiac, which made its way to Lasalle-Séré's office at the Ministry of the Interior and back to the departmental prefects in the border departments and the Free Zone. The letter described Brive's repatriation team, which consisted of a group of young female refugees who received 15 francs per day from the mayor's payroll, and "asked for nothing more than an opportunity to serve the mayor and the lieutenant prefect of Brive." It went on to describe how, for over three nights in a row, train after train had rolled through the station – some arriving in the middle of the night. The organizer confessed: "I cannot decently ask these young women to work eight hours during the day, day after day, and then ask them to return to work a 'white night' after resting for only three hours at their home." He elaborated that the women had to come and go during late evening, and early morning hours – times that presented possible dangers to their safety.[74]

Communication between refugees and the branches of state

Throughout September, letters from refugees continued to flow into the municipal offices of Brive and Tulle. Most letters articulated an "either/or" request: "Please, either find me work, or speed up my repatriation." By September 23, Mayor Miginiac of Brive had drafted a standardized letter to send to refugees requesting employment or seeking repatriation. The letter sent to Henri Raout illustrates the limits of local authorities' ability to resolve refugee problems:

Regarding your request for employment, I regret to inform you that presently it is impossible to employ you because I have no openings in my office. On the other hand, in reference to your question concerning repatriation ... I believe that all repatriation will be completed by September 30, 1940.[75]

With the most sincere apologies, Miginiac wished Raout the best of luck in his efforts to survive the wait and enclosed the letter from the

[73] AMBG, Series H/IV, Lassalle-Séré, Vichy, October 11, 1940.
[74] AMBG, Series H/IV, Lassalle-Séré, Vichy, October 11, 1940.
[75] AMBG, Series H/IV, mayor of Brive to M. Henri Raout, September 23, 1940.

Chamber of Commerce of Angère, Raout's city of residence, saying regretfully that even a letter stressing economic concerns would not speed up his return process.[76] Miginiac, like most mayors, feared that Brive would be financially unable to bear the burden of an influx of refugees during the winter months. In compliance with Musso's directive, Miginiac alerted the Director of the Refugee Welcome Committee to strictly enforce the September 30 suspension of aid to refugees *eligible* to be repatriated to Occupied Territory.[77]

Refugee letters sent to the mayor's office also indicate that many refugees resisted repatriation throughout October. On October 28, Mademoiselle Gilberte Schmitt, a nineteen-year-old from Strasbourg living with her aunt in Zurich, Switzerland, wrote to the mayor of Brive to request news of her father, who she believed to be sheltered in Brive. Had he registered in Brive? Had he returned to the Occupied Zone to Strasbourg? If he resided in Brive, could the mayor send her papers to apply for admittance to Brive so she might reunite with him? If he had repatriated to the Occupied Zone, she wished to know the date of his return, but she qualified, "I do not wish to follow him to the Occupied Zone."[78]

Reverse migration from Occupied Zone to Free Zone

The racial and ethnic repression in the north caused many early returnees to the Occupied Zone to reverse their course and seek renewed asylum in the Free Zone. Sometime in early 1942, Simonne Zuckerman, a Parisian Catholic saleswoman, hid herself in the trunk of a car to cross the Line of Demarcation into the Free Zone (an act punishable by death in 1942). Successfully passing one obstacle to imagined "liberty" and security, Zuckerman, who was pregnant at the time, now faced the challenge of survival as a "new" refugee in France's Free Zone. Madame Zuckerman took this risk to her life to join her Jewish husband, Sigmund Zuckerman, a native of Romania and naturalized French citizen, who had escaped Paris for the Free Zone on December 5, 1941.[79]

Sigmund Zuckerman's flight from Paris happened as a result of German policies of racial cleansing in the Occupied Zone that were

---

[76] Mayor of Brive to M. Henri Raout, September 23, 1940.
[77] AMBG, Series H/IV, mayor of Brive to M. Chastre, September 20, 1940.
[78] AMBG, Series H/IV, French Consul General in Zurich to the mayor of Brive on behalf of Mlle Gilberte Schmitt, Zurich, October 28, 1940.
[79] Interview with Simonne's daughter, Hélène Zuckerman Rossi, resident of the Drôme in France via e-mail, August 2004.

accomplished by forced registration, round-up, removal, and intern-ment of Jews, Gypsies, and foreign "undesirables." The first large-scale round-up of foreign-born Jews swept through the Paris neighborhood of Place de la Bastille from August 20 to August 25, 1941, resulting in the internment of 4,230 men at a camp outside the city limits.[80] Zuckerman's flight from Paris occurred one week before German police arrested another group of 743 French Jews in their Parisian homes on December 12, 1941.[81]

While the Germans imposed ethnic cleansing in the Occupied Zone, Vichy officials also explored ways to rescind rights awarded to foreign-ers and Jews during the interwar years. Zuckerman was among the 23,648 French Jews whose citizenship Vichy threatened to revoke as a consequence of the July 22, 1940 law, which authorized the Minister of Justice to establish a commission to revisit and revoke naturalized citi-zenship awards granted from 1927 to 1939.[82] On October 3, 1940, Vichy created Jewish statutes (Statut des juifs). These exclusionary measures removed Jews from several professions, including public service, the armed services, and professions that exercised influence upon public opinion, such as journalism. The Jewish statutes also expanded the def-inition of a Jew such that any person with two or more Jewish grand-parents or a person married to a Jew fell into the excluded categories. Hence, Simonne Zuckerman, despite her Catholic faith, became des-ignated Jewish under the new laws. A French administrative change also held consequences for refugees. On October 18, 1940, the French government granted department prefects the right to "intern, assign to supervised residence or enroll in forced labor any foreign Jews in their department."[83] The change decentralized power and subjected refu-gees to the whims, either charitable or punitive, of local department prefects.

The enforcement of racial and ethnic exclusions in the Occupied Zone had a noticeable impact upon attitudes and policies toward "old" and "new" refugees in the Free Zone. In many cases, the influx of a new wave of refugees increased competition for scarce resources in the Free Zone. The competition for relief aid, housing, food and jobs var-ied from place to place, but structured the struggles of daily life, com-plicating wartime survival for refugees and host community residents alike. A body of policy changes occurring after November 20, 1940

[80] Zuccotti, *The Holocaust, The French and the Jews*, 85–86.
[81] Zuccotti, *The Holocaust, The French and the Jews*, 59.
[82] Zuccotti, *The Holocaust, The French and the Jews*, 53. See n. 13.
[83] Zuccotti, *The Holocaust, The French and the Jews*, 57. Zuccotti cites the *Journal Official*, October 18, 1940: 5,324.

with regard to relief aid distribution, provision of housing, management of unemployment, and the authorization to repatriate, further limited the survival strategies available to refugees in the Free Zone. These changes from Vichy, coupled with the new pressures brought by the radicalization of German-sponsored ethnic cleansing in the Occupied Zone, further eroded the more universalistic and inclusive policies of relief and rescue practiced in the immediate aftermath of the exodus.

Between November 1940 and May 1942, Corrèze's experience typi-fied those of most host departments in the region. After the Germans sealed the Line the refugee populations remained significant for this rural department.[84] Musso reported that, as of December 1, 1940, a total of 25,602 refugees remained out of a July count of 85,000 perman-ent refugees.[85] Corrèze thus held 2.5 percent of France's permanently displaced refugees, a seemingly small number, but significant when compared with a local peacetime population of approximately 200,000. The breakdown by categories of the displaced population is shown in Table 5 and reflects the diversity of refugees. A substantial portion of refugees, 42.5 percent, originated in parts of the Occupied Zone open to the repatriation of all French nationals. Of this group, departmental rolls indicate that only 750 received refugee relief, meaning that 10,130 financed their own asylum and had little reason to be in contact with state authorities. In contrast, a similar number of refugees originated from the Forbidden Zone, but nearly two-thirds of these received aid.[86] Despite the fact that foreigners represented less than 4 percent of the refugees, Vichy policy and local civilian rhetoric disproportionately emphasized the presence of foreign refugees.[87]

As German policies of occupation and partition changed, many ori-ginal refugee categories were subdivided along the shifting geographic subdivision of France. This fragmentation of identity and compart-mentalization of people into manageable categories bears witness to the dehumanization brought about by the war. To be sure, the French state employed categories before the Germans arrived, but the redrawing of the European map and the reordering of humanity that occurred throughout World War II impacted the entire spectrum of Europeans,

---

[84] This is based on the rough estimate of 200,000 native Corrézians and approximately 40,000,000 French men and women.
[85] Musso reported the number 85,000, which significantly differed from earlier esti-mates of approximately 215,000–250,000 refugees.
[86] ADC, Series 1E/DEP/272/398, Report of prefect, December 12, 1940.
[87] The exaggeration of the presence of the "outside, other" is less surprising in the con-text of the French nation trying to reconstitute its national community in the after-math of the defeat and under territorial division.

Table 5. *Reported refugee population in Corrèze, December 1, 1940*

Refugee category	Refugees receiving aid	Self-supported refugees	Totals	Percentage of total
Open Occupied Zone	750	10,130	10,880	42.5
Forbidden Zone	6,630	4,200	10,830	42.3
Alsace and Lorraine	1,199	1,692	2,891	11
Foreign			1,001	3.9
All			25,602	

making survival marginally easier or severely more difficult for individuals and communities depending upon their categorization. As Vichy officials continued to negotiate with the German occupying authority for the reopening of the Line of Demarcation, these categories gained and lost value as negotiating chips in the on-going competition for territorial control. The German categories of exclusion from the Occupied Zone, such as "foreigner," "Israélite," and "mixed bloods," evolved over the duration of the crisis into categories that also negatively marked refugees as politically or economically "undesirable" in the Free Zone.

Between November 1940 and May 1941, regional, class, national, racial, and ethnic categories continued to be the chief means used by Free Zone authorities to track and manage the refugee population. Table 6, showing the refugee figures for Brive-la-Gaillarde for February 1941, exemplifies the monthly reports that prefects were required to submit to the Service of Refugees.[88] Not surprisingly, former residents of Forbidden Zone departments figured most prominently in the refugee population. Among refugees categorized by race and ethnicity, 308 foreign Israélites received aid, outnumbering the 215 French Israélites registered for aid. Table 6 illustrates the repetitions and vague categories that frequently confused local bureaucrats and made precise tracking of the number of refugees receiving aid difficult.[89] Throughout

---

[88] ADC, Series 1E/DEP/272/398, mayor of Brive-la-Gaillarde to prefect of Corrèze, February 12, 1941.

[89] Vigier could not find figures for the number of Jews living in Brive, but cites a prefectural report from September 1942 that showed 1,055 French Jews and 1,475 foreign Jews residing in the whole of Corrèze. The author believes these numbers can only be judged as approximations given the continual movement of refugees within the Free Zone, the inability of officials to commit relief workers to the task of counting refugees, and the growing awareness among Jewish and foreign refugees of the need to stay under the radar of the local government. See Vigier, *Brive pendant la guerre*, 30.

Table 6. *Number of refugees receiving allocations from the municipality of Brive-la-Gaillarde, by department of origin, nationality and/or race, February 1, 1941*

Department of origin	Total number
Aisne	174
Ardennes	69
Bas-Rhin	5
Doubs	20
Haute-Marne	13
Haute-Rhin	2
Haute-Saône	13
Meurthe-et-Moselle	173
Meuse	63
Moselle	20
Nord	265
Pas-de-Calais	45
Seine-Inférieure	13
Somme	14
Vosges	18
Terre de Belfort	8
Aube	12
Eure	6
Indre-et-Loire	1
Manche	2
Marne	19
Morbihan	1
Oise	3
Orne	2
Seine	17
Seine-et-Marne	2
Foreigners of Jewish race from ZI	6
Foreigners from ZO	39
French expatriates	14
Foreigners in ZI	20
French Israélites	215
Foreign Israélites	8
Foreigners from ZO	27
Blacks and Mixed Bloods	12
Foreigners from ZI	9
Foreigners	9
Foreign Israélites (ZI)	38
Czechs and English	9
Foreign Israélites (ZI)	59
Foreign Israélites[a]	197
Non-allocators refugees	3,162[b]

[a] Numbers indicate refugees from Paris and Strasbourg.
[b] Refugees not receiving aid.
ZO = Zone occupée (Occupied Zone).
ZI = Zone interdite (Forbidden Zone).
Source: ADC, Series 522/W/63, mayor of Brive-la-Gaillarde to prefect of Corrèze, February 12, 1941.

1941, Vichy's policies toward these refugees transformed as the public's perception of refugees changed in an environment of mounting political repression in both zones.

As German policy became more rigid around the categories of persons permitted to reside in the Occupied Zone, Vichy officials became more aggressive in their efforts to negotiate a reopening of the Line of Demarcation and a return to a more universalistic policy of readmission to the Occupied Zone. This initiative was, in part, spurred by host communities' and national policymakers' waning tolerance of refugees. During the exodus southern officials described refugees with empathy as helpless women, children, and elderly. Seen as victims of German aggression, the June refugees received a generous expression of compassion and hospitality from local communities. However, by the end of the summer of 1940, reports written by the Service of Refugees and local residents' letters to the mayors of Brive and Tulle described refugees as potential pariahs of the state and a threat to public order. A soft-spoken, but growing intolerance spawned a desire among French officials to clear refugees from host communities. Fearful that refugees' lingering presence in the Free Zone might stir political and social unrest Vichy pressed the Germans to reopen the Line of Demarcation.[90]

Conclusion: German intentions

Initially, the partitioning of France along the Line of Demarcation allowed the Germans to bolster security and limit French economic and political reconstruction. However, in the fall of 1940 the Germans began to use the Line of Demarcation as a tool for performing racial, ethnic, and political triage, a first step toward ethnic cleansing in France. The Germans forced the French to enforce discriminations in the repatriation process, helping to achieve their desired results of aryanization and military domination of the Occupied Zone. Indeed, the Germans adopted a strict disciplinary policy against French bureaucrats who failed to enforce racial and political triage at the Line of Demarcation, turning back fully loaded trains and stopping repatriation for weeks in order to demonstrate the seriousness of their exclusion policies.

By limiting the passage points along the Line of Demarcation, the Germans controlled the pace and the policing of repatriation, and were able to enforce population exclusions from the Occupied Zone. The Germans refined repatriation policy as a tool for engaging the French in

---

[90] For a discussion about the ways in which the ideology and rhetoric of efficiency permeated not only bureaucratic interwar culture in Europe and the United States, but also labor management, see Mary Nolan, *Visions of Modernity: American Business and the Modernization of Germany* (New York: Oxford University Press, 1994).

policies of racial and political discrimination. Foreign, Jewish, and communist refugees, deemed "undesirable" by the Germans, became the permanent charges of the French refugee relief system. This dependency, combined with growing material shortages, contributed to the erosion of the tolerance and good will of host communities toward these marginalized refugees.

While the Germans applied racial and political ideology in structuring their repatriation policies, practical concerns often forced the Germans to retreat from some of their initial propositions. As they secured the Occupied Zone, they allowed repatriation of Belgians and Dutch to their native countries. In need of assistance to repair damage to infrastructure in the still embattled north, they reversed their position on the repatriation of some residents of the Forbidden Zones, a topic explored in the following chapter.

French intentions

Led by Louis Marlier, Vichy advocated for a policy of universal refugee repatriation. However, the French carefully chose their battles, prioritizing the repatriation of the vast majority of French German-authorized refugees, at the expense of the denial of the "right of return" to a significant few. Marlier continued throughout the summer to persuade the German Armistice Commission to repatriate residents of the Forbidden Zones, the Restricted Zones, foreigners, and demobilized soldiers. He worked to ensure the return of Alsatian and Lorrainers who desired repatriation, but also crafted an aggressive policy to facilitate long-term relocation of French citizens who did not wish to return to the annexed territory. Marlier initially opposed the exclusion of Jews from the Occupied Zone, but later became silent on the matter, leaving enforcement of exclusions to the Germans, the Ministry of the Interior, and the DGGFTO office of General la Laurencie.

Below the national level, department prefects and mayors were motivated by practicality rather than ideology. These officials simply could not adequately enforce the exclusionary policies dictated by the Germans and to a lesser degree, Vichy. They lacked the human resources to check identity papers and to reschedule trains that arrived with "undesirables." Like their superiors in Vichy, prefects and mayors had a financial interest in reducing the number of refugees residing in their communities. By enforcing the German exclusions, prefects invited refugees into a state of permanent displacement within their own departments. Facing the financial burdens of maintaining large communities of permanent refugees, prefects and mayors chose to assist willing refugees to repatriate to their homes, even residents of the Forbidden Zones. Some prefects and many mayors turned a blind eye toward excluded refugees who boarded trains in an attempt to repatriate to the Occupied Zone. While this practice might appear as beneficial to both local officials and refugees, it often resulted in the arrest or internment of refugees at the Line of Demarcation, or rejection of entire train-loads of refugees by the Germans. Hence, German exclusions forced French officials to devise policies for absorbing the permanently displaced within the Free Zone.

Refugees: intentions and ironies

Understandably, most refugees wanted to return home; wives hoped to reunite with their demobilized husbands; children needed to return to school. Most refugees could not find jobs in host communities that paid enough money for permanent resettlement; a problem exacerbated by the government's withdrawal of refugee allocations on September 30, 1940 (except for excluded refugees' payments). For married women with children living without their husbands, and frequently without the support of extended family, prolonged displacement in the Free Zone was not a realistic survival option. Even excluded refugees just wanted to return to their homes and restart their lives. Zuccotti estimates that 30,000 Jews repatriated from the exodus, "anxious to resume a semblance of normal life."[91] Those who repatriated clandestinely faced a grim future in the Occupied Zone.

While most refugees wanted to return home, significant numbers elected not to do so. Wives of men held in German PoW camps calculated that they might fare better in the Free Zone. At the very least they would be nearer to the government, the advocate for their husbands' release. Several factors discouraged refugee return: uncertainty about their home and safety; demoralization; injury and illness; fatigue; fear of the Germans. For those refugees excluded from the Occupied Zone, the repatriation process raised consciousness about the consequences of their racial, ethnic, regional, or national identity. As such, they were forced to reconsider how they might reconstruct their lives in the Free Zone. Those who were lucky might enjoy independent financial support, but more often excluded refugees had to find housing and rebuild home life from scratch. In the worst case scenarios they had to accept residence in internment camp facilities. In the next chapter we will

---

[91] Zuccotti, *The Holocaust, The French and The Jews*, 44.

survey the consequences of long-term dependency on state assistance for the permanently displaced.

Ultimately, the reduction in state benefits for permanently displaced refugees worsened their economic condition and dampened their morale. As Vichy accelerated the withdrawal of services, permanently displaced refugees, especially women, sharpened their critique of the new regime and stiffened their resolve to defend refugee subsidies in a language that framed these benefits as "dues owed by the state." The language of entitlement coined during the Phoney War, resurfaced during the refugee crisis, becoming more militant in its claims for compensation to redress the hardships of total war.

8   Disappointment and despair in the Occupied Zone

In October, 1940, Irene Potaufeu returned to Chenay (Marne), having spent five months as a refugee in the Yonne with her mother and three children, aged seven, six and four. Upon returning home, she found not the promised state of normalcy, but an unnatural disaster. Despite laws against pillaging, refugees had squatted in her home; her vegetables had been uprooted and her chickens were gone. Adding to her woes, Potaufeu learned that her husband had been taken to Germany as a PoW. Despite the fall of France's democratic institutions and the occupation of her country by German troops, Potaufeu felt empowered to demand assistance from the highest French official within her reach, the prefect of the Marne. Potaufeu's letter requested a cash payment to mitigate her destitution, "the time has now come for the government to aid all who, at the time they were sent out on the roads, did not receive any aid. Above all, children waiting for their papas should receive aid."[1]

In form and content, Potaufeu's letter followed the practice of French women who staked claims to state aid and protections that began during the run-up to war, and continued through invasion, exodus, displacement, and repatriation. Unsuccessful in claiming refugee relief during the displacement crisis, Potaufeu insisted that the state pay her due monies in arrears. She defined her "right to collect assistance" in terms of a debt the state owed her for the service she had provided to France: "the reproduction of three children." Vichy posters touted the recalibrated language of female honor and duty, defining women's roles in the new, penitent nation as uniquely defined by the vocation of motherhood: "French mothers! Here is support to the nation: Motherhood reunites joy and duty. Motherhood lifts you up. Motherhood will always earn you respect, and sometimes glory. Motherhood makes you more beautiful, healthier, more balanced

---

[1] ADM, Reims Annex, 6 W/R/400/404, Letter, February 10, 1941.

and useful."[2] Invoking the rights and responsibilities of women, as scripted by the regime, Potaufeu asked that the state back up its elevation of the cult of motherhood. She demanded for French mothers the wages of modern warfare, previously reserved for soldiers, widows, and veterans.[3]

Typical of the wartime period, the state espoused lofty ideals, but failed to deliver. Marne's prefect refused Potaufeu's request citing: "her failure to repatriate to the Marne before July 31, 1940." The date was an arbitrary creation of local bureaucracy and actually conflicted with the September 30 deadline designated by the Service of Refugees.[4] The wife of a PoW, Potaufeu actually received two payments from the state of 20 and 50 francs. Frustrated, Potaufeu reiterated: "I am only asking for what is my right and I hope that you have the good heart to help me obtain my due."[5]

Potaufeu unmistakably advanced a concept of refugee rights emanating from women's rights, or more specifically mothers' rights, to just compensation for women's wartime suffering and service. Returnees brought back to the Occupied Zone not only the memory of their struggle to survive German bombardment and displacement in French camps or makeshift shelters, but also carried home their cahier des doléances (list of complaints) against the wartime government. Refugees, and women in particular, learned from each other the terms to employ to advance demands upon their government for wartime compensation and restitution. Through displacement and repatriation, they mastered the language of refugee rights learned as a consequence of Germany and the Allies waging total warfare.

Civilian letters not only demanded state compensation for their suffering, but helped to define the greater historical legal transformation produced by actions now classified as war crimes and crimes against humanity. The emerging postwar law and war conventions attempt to criminalize violations committed against civilian innocents. Civilian complaints defined the horrors of "forced deportation," and "wonton destruction of towns and villages." However, the greater injustices

---

[2] ADM, Chalôns-sur-Marne, Hp7980, Poster, Office of Public Information, Paris, 1941. See Pollard, *Reign of Virtue*, 9–42.

[3] This language stretched beyond the familialism expressed by women in fascist regimes in Italy and Spain. See Victoria de Grazia, *How Fascism Ruled Women: Italy, 1922–1945* (Berkeley, CA: University of California Press, 1992); Paul Preston, *The Spanish Civil War: Reaction, Revolution, and Revenge* (New York: Norton, 1986), 225; Paxton, *Anatomy of Fascism*, 139.

[4] National policy gave the date of return as September 30, 1940 for the cut-off for refugee relief.

[5] ADM, Reims Annex, 6/W/R/400/404, Letter, February 10, 1941.

suffered by civilians, internal displacement and "collateral damage" from aerial bombardment, remained largely permissible in the postwar Geneva Conventions.[6] Yet, in writing letters protesting these crimes, French civilians set the ball moving to better define and conceptualize total warfare's crimes against civilian innocents and the state's obligations to ensure the protection of civilian persons and property. This new consciousness evolved unevenly across Europe. Ironically, Torrie discovered that German civilians organized protests against the very evacuations designed by German authorities to improve civilian protection.[7]

As re-entry to the Occupied Zone wound down by the winter of 1940/41, two important factors shaped civilians reintegration. First, returnees continued to refine their language for expressing demands for state compensation for property destitution. Second, returnees had to re-articulate their demands for civil defense protection in the context of renewed bombardments against civilian centers from British forces along French coastal territory in the Forbidden Zone. Now French government officials had to coordinate with German occupying authorities to meet the continuing challenges of safeguarding the repatriated civilian population from hunger and bombing.

A comparison of refugee reintegration in the Marne with that of the battle-torn, coastal departments of Nord, Pas-de-Calais, and Haute-Normandie, highlights the special challenges of civilian re-entry to the Forbidden Zones. Returnees who slipped past the Germans or gained official approval to repatriate to the Forbidden Zone soon found themselves reiterating demands for protection from bombardment previously made during Germany's invasion. Simultaneously, the exclusion of many returnees from the Forbidden Zone departments, which bordered the Marne, created new mini refugee crises in the Marne and other Occupied Zone departments open to refugee return. German subpartitioning of Occupied Territory and British retaliatory bombing, thus prolonged French coastal refugees' agony.

In the Marne mid-September witnessed the repatriation of a majority of the Marne's residents. But despite Vichy's economic and political aspirations for reconstruction, Marne residents had to pressure local officials to force the German authorities to improve the basic material conditions of occupation. Despite the authoritarian regime's anti-democratic structure and the repression of Occupation, Marne

---

[6] For example, the bombing of the train station in Rennes on June 17, 1940, collateral damage would claim 5,000 refugee lives in one day. See: G. and W. Fortune, *Hitler Divided France*, 16.
[7] Torrie, *"For Their Own Good,"* 35, 49.

returnees reinvigorated the practices of republican petition and political engagement to improve their economic and physical security.[8]

Reintegration of the city of Reims

With the national government in Vichy, the job of resolving returnees' problems and directing political and economic reconstruction fell primarily upon local authorities working with the DGGFTO. Slowly, national agencies, such as the Service of Refugees and the Ministry of Education, began to deliver services in the north, but the bulk of early reconstruction efforts fell to recently returned administrators who lacked the staff and resources for the job.[9]

René Bousquet, the General Secretary of the Marne, was one of the first high-ranking French officials to meet with the Germans.[10] Bousquet later became the infamous Secretary General of the French Police and was charged in 1991 with Crimes against Humanity for his role in the deportation of 76,000 French Jews to German extermination camps.[11] However, in the early days of the Occupation Bousquet served the Ministry of the Interior and, in September 1940, became the Marne's prefect before Vichy appointed Peretti Della Rocca. On July 1, 1940, Bousquet met with German authorities in Châlons-sur-Marne to negotiate return passes for all government personnel of the Marne. André Jozon, still the Marne's prefect, received the passes in Albi (Tarn), and issued return permits to the civil servants with whom he had contact.

Once in Châlons-sur-Marne, in the third week of July, Jozon entered negotiations with the Germans to continue the return of employees of the Roads and Bridges Services, Agricultural Services, and Veterinary Inspection Services.[12] The invasion had devastated roads and bridges, and bombing had almost completely destroyed the towns of Vitry-le-François and Fîsmes. Châlons-sur-Marne, Ste. Menehould, Frère Champenoise, Mourmelon, and Suippes had sustained serious damage, but could be lightly re-inhabited by returnees. During the fall and winter of 1940/41,

[8] Hanna Diamond has also shown that women acted strongly to advance their social rights during the war: Diamond, *Women and the Second World War*.
[9] For a history of French national reconstruction see Danièle Voldman, *La reconstruction des villes française de 1940 à 1954: Histoire d'une politique* (Paris: L'Harmattan, 1997).
[10] AN F/1c/III/1166, Marne, Jozon, Report to Minister of the Interior, July 31, 1940.
[11] Jean-Pierre Husson, "René Bousquet, une personalité ambigue, efface de la mémoire marnaise," *Histoire et mémoire des deux guerres mondiales – CRDP de Champagne-Ardennes*, 2000, available at: www.histoire-memoire.fr.
[12] AN F/1c/III/ 1166, Marne, Jozon, Report to Minister of the Interior, July 31, 1940.

Jozon's principal battle was fought with the Germans and Vichy to obtain financial resources for reconstruction programs.[13]

Emergency responders, who had been among the last to leave Reims, were among the first to return to survey the damage to the water supply, electrical infrastructure, and public buildings. Assisted by a smattering of repatriated municipal councilors, firemen, electricians, and functionaries, they confronted an enormous task. One of the most challenging jobs lay in trying to prepare to feed and shelter a reintegrating population estimated at 125,000 refugees for Reims alone.[14] Paul Marchandeau, mayor of Reims was still located at the other end of the country, but prepared his staff's return from Gaillac (Tarn). On July 15, Marchandeau thanked his hosts, the director of Camp Brena in Gaillac, and the mayor of Albi, saluting the citizens of Gaillac who, "in an overcrowded village, gave the best possible hospitality to the people of Reims."[15] To communicate with employees who had remained headquartered at Nevers (Nièvre), Marchandeau placed reintegration notices in Free Zone newspapers. The shot-in-the-dark locator system actually produced some results. After having read in a Toulousean newspaper that the prefecture of the Marne had set up temporary offices in Albi, François René, a Marne employee, wrote, "I have hurried to send you [Prefect Jozon] my address as quickly as possible."[16]

On September 21, 1940, the City Council of Reims held its first session since May 1. Acting Mayor M. G. Hodin, opened the meeting in the absence of Marchandeau, who did not return from Gaillac until November. Hodin delivered an emotional assessment of France's defeat to twenty-seven repatriated city delegates:

It is not without a strong emotion that I stand before you ... where current events have temporarily called me to serve here in this chamber where we last held session on May 1, 1940 ... My emotion ... grows from the memory of anxiety and sadness, and from the misery of our courageous and brave population, who suffered during this long and painful journey of exodus on these long roads, where from the corners of the north and the east of France, women, children, and elderly harrowingly fled toward exile.[17]

Mayor Hodin invoked the exodus as the symbol of the tragedy suffered by the population of Reims and the nation, drawing upon the evolving narrative which insisted that the peril weighed most heavily upon

[13] AN F/1c/III/1166, Marne, Jozon, Report to Minister of the Interior, July 31, 1940.
[14] AMVR 2183, Circular, July 15, 1940.
[15] AMVR 2183, Marchandeau to Camboulives, mayor of Albi (Tarn), July 15, 1940.
[16] AMVR 2183, Marchandeau to Camboulives, mayor of Albi (Tarn), July 15, 1940.
[17] AMVR, *Bulletin Municipal*, "Séance du 21, September 1940," 242.

women and children. Despite this narrative of women's disproportionate suffering, many women still could not obtain state assistance.
Hodin concisely outlined France's four major challenges to restoring
life to "normal": reduction of unemployment; improved distribution of
rations; establishment of a positive morale, and repatriation of 90,000
refugees to Reims by mid-September.

Efforts to improve daily life

Daily life deprivations seemed impossible to alleviate. Jozon reported
to the Ministry of the Interior that: "he was having the most difficulty
assuring the supply of food to the population."[18] The Marne had only
the basics – canned goods, vegetables, oil, soap, coffee and sugar – to
feed 500,000 Marnais and returnees prohibited from entering the
Forbidden Zone.[19] Bakers could not resume bread production due to a
lack of salt and yeast. Occupied Zone prefects worked to ease shortages
by maximizing the new interdepartmental administrative ties created
during the exodus. Jozon tried to obtain produce from Marne refugee
host cities, Nevers (Nièvre) and Dijon (Côte d'Or).[20] But in September,
the Marne still had no meat. Reims was prohibited from purchasing
beef from its prewar suppliers in the Ardennes, and could no longer
provide meat to 100,000 residents.[21]

Housing shortages multiplied in part because German soldiers had
appropriated many civilian homes and bombs had destroyed others.
Hence, returnees resided in schools and churches, giving them no official residences to list for filing for ration cards. In Reims, the mayor's
office finally abandoned residentially-based rationing, because so many
returnees could not move back into their own homes.[22] The residency
requirements for ration card eligibility produced only a minor bureaucratic wrinkle, but had painful short-term consequences for hungry
families.

In October, national authorities admitted the desperate need to accelerate agricultural production. The Marne was among the departments
where fighting had completely destroyed a significant number of food

---

[18] AN F1/cIII/1166/Marne, Jozon, Report to Minister of the Interior, July 31, 1940.
[19] AN F1/cIII/1166/Marne, René Bousquet to Ministry of the Interior, Report, October 1, 1940.
[20] AN F1/cIII/1166/Marne, René Bousquet to Ministry of the Interior, Report, October 1, 1940.
[21] AN F1/cIII/1166/Marne, Bousquet to Ministry of the Interior, Report, December 1, 1940.
[22] AMVR 3481, Military Authority to mayors, July, 1940.

production companies. Prior to the war, Marne factories were among the most modernized, high-capacity facilities in the country, furnishing ten to twelve departments with food basics.[23] To quantify the destruction, Bousquet explained that a workforce requiring 10,000 employees prior to the invasion had only managed to re-hire 1,000 workers through October. He urged the DGGFTO to commit to re-starting agricultural production, and demanded the resumption of trade with the Forbidden Zone.

Departments subpartitioned by the Line of Demarcation faced the greatest difficulties. Charente, near the Atlantic coast, hosted approximately 300,000 exodus refugees and 100,000 evacuees from Alsace and Lorraine.[24] Partitioned in July 1940, Charente also quartered a large concentration of German troops who exacted heavy requisitions from Charente's food reserves. For example, in August 1940, they demanded 850 kg of butter per day and 650 kg of cheese per day.[25] With the German administrative lines disrupting normal trade patterns, traditional agricultural commerce could not resume to feed returnees or the perpetually displaced. Matters worsened as foot-and-mouth disease spread through thirty-one departments from August through September, with 20,000 farms infected. Charente-Inférieure was one of the hardest hit departments along with Manche, Seine-Inférieure, and Eure. The disease, combated in a coordinated effort by French and German veterinarians, took a deep toll on milk and meat supplies.[26] Faced with food shortages, Charente adopted strict rationing policies as illustrated by Table 7, which shows daily ration allocations in November 1940, when only 6,647 of the original 400,000 refugees remained.[27]

Counter to government promises, refugee repatriation from the department hit hardest by the exodus did not dramatically improve the availability of food for the indigenous population.

In the Marne, the Germans agreed to permit the return of heads of industry, especially leaders of food and agricultural production. Pierre Tetevuide, director of G. Leroy based in Vitry-le-François (Marne), justified his repatriation request, "because our industry is linked to cheese production, which is necessary for feeding the civilian population, we

---

[23] AN F/1c/III/1166, Marne, Bousquet to DGGFTO, Reports, October 1, 1940.
[24] AN F/1c/III/1145, Charente, Prefect Malick, August 1940.
[25] AN F/1c/III/1145, Charente, Prefect Malick, August 1940.
[26] "Livestock Diseases Combated in France," *New York Times*, via Berlin, September 17, 1940, 8.
[27] AN F/1c/III/1145, Charente, Report, November 19, 1940. Of the 6,647 remaining refugees, 4,503 were from the Forbidden Zone and 2,144 were Mosellans refusing repatriation to the Annexed Territories.

Table 7. *Daily rationing in Charente, November 1940*

Food source	Grams per day
Bread	350
Meat	60
Sugar	36
Tea	2
Coffee	15
Salt	15
Vegetables	60
Cheese	125
Marmalade	100

should enjoy first priority among those allowed to return."[28] Noting that repatriation information in the press was frequently in error, Tetevuide requested that the prefect of the Marne secure the necessary papers for his and his employees' return. Most likely, he did not realize that German bombs had destroyed almost the entirety of Vitry-le-François.

As the Marne gradually improved food distribution, Acting Mayor Hodin asked that the population concede priority for milk to nursing mothers and children. The consumption of milk by adults, particularly in café au lait and milk chocolate, contributed to the shortage of milk for children. Thus, Hodin proposed that all adults stop consuming milk for two months, until full production could be assured.[29] By November though, the city had failed to make clear gains in the production of milk. Upon his return, Marchandeau did raise the consumption limits: children below aged three could now receive 1 liter a day; children aged between three and six could consume 750 ml a day; and children aged between six and ten were allowed 250 ml. Only adult pregnant women and mothers breast-feeding infants could consume 500 ml per day.[30] Marchandeau tried to console citizens: "these rules are not intended to favor particular members of the community over others, quite the contrary. Rather, we hope that by bringing a certain discipline to the prevailing conditions ... these rules will ensure as much equality in the present circumstances with regard to all consumers."[31]

[28] ADM 204/M/3110, Pierre Tetevuide to prefect of the Marne (at Albi, Tarn), Tulle (Corrèze), July 18, 1940.
[29] AMVR, *Bulletin Municipal,* "Séance du 21, September 1940," 243.
[30] AMVR, *Bulletin Municipal,* "Séance du 21, September 1940," 380.
[31] AMVR, *Bulletin Municipal,* "Séance du 21, September 1940," 381.

As was the case with food supplies such as meat, north-eastern mayors entered negotiations with the Germans for the right to trade with other occupied departments to obtain supplies of coal and gas. The energy shortage of the winter of 1940/41 had a direct relationship to the refugee crisis and repatriation policy. In September 1940, the Reims municipal government predicted an energy shortage in three months if German authorities continued to halt shipments of coal from the Forbidden Zone. Hodin reported that the Marne's expected coal shipments had not arrived in September 1940. "The war is the main obstacle preventing the arrival of [fuel supplies]. We must live off our reserves, which after three months of hostilities we have nearly exhausted," lamented Hodin.[32] Of the 4,000 tons of coal requested by the municipal government, only 360 tons was delivered, leaving a shortfall of 3,640 tons.

One cause of fuel shortages was the displacement of Forbidden Zone miners, which significantly curtailed the extraction of coal. Vichy initially sought to re-employ the miners in the Free Zone; but the miners, while not necessarily desiring to return to the north, typically refused to work for lower paying farm wages. Vichy economists also understood that skilled miners could be more useful in the north, if only the Germans allowed them to return to the Forbidden Zone. In mid-November 1940, Marlier informed Free Zone prefects that he was working toward German approval for the return of 850 to 1,750 miners to Pas-de-Calais.[33] By January, Marlier had persuaded the German authorities that coal shortages in the north resulted not from inefficient use of transportation but from a lack of labor.[34] The Germans promised to forward Marlier's request to authorities in Berlin, where decisions regarding repatriation to the Forbidden Zone were made. In point of fact, Marlier had seized the opportunity presented by coal shortages in German-occupied territory to negotiate the release of some 15,000 to 17,000 PoW miners to work programs mining coal for the Germans.[35]

In Reims, Hodin predicted that the shortage of coal would force a prioritization between domestic and industrial consumption over the winter. Asserting that the problem resulted from German interference with transportation and not coal production itself, Hodin adopted a different line than the Vichy government and pointed out: "We would like the Kommandantur, to understand the difficulty of our situation, so that he can best assist us and redouble his efforts to obtain for us

---

[32] AMVR, *Bulletin Municipal*, "Séance du 21, September 1940," 245.
[33] AN F/60/1507, Marlier to prefects in the Free Zone, November 21, 1940.
[34] AN F/60/1507, Marlier, Note 989, January 18, 1941.
[35] AN F/60/1507, Marlier, Note 989, January 18, 1941, 2.

this coal which exists elsewhere 'sur le carreau' in the mines of the Nord, but which simply can not easily reach us due to transportation difficulties."[36] The expectation that the German Kommandantur of the Marne would or could actually intervene demonstrated the degree to which local authorities did not yet understand the multiple layers of German Occupation Authority. Of course, the Germans intended to subordinate French civilian needs to the requirements of the German military, but their own ideological fanaticism often undercut their strategic and material needs. The expulsion of 4,000 miners from Lorraine in 1941 simply because they refused to swear an oath of loyalty to the Reich removed skilled laborers from an already depleted workforce. Thus, the coal shortage in the north did not only result from insufficient extraction and disruption of interdepartmental trade by German trafficking policies and Allied bombardment. It also depended on the *will* of the Germans and the displaced miners whose concerns went beyond meeting their duties as fuel suppliers. Civilians learned to care as much about their personal and familial security as the Germans cared about their military security. Ironically, but not surprisingly, the 4,000 Lorrainer miners cared more about their French citizenship than did Vichy, an indication that by the winter of 1940/41, Vichy's commitment to civilians could be eroded by the economic and political pressures of occupation and partition.

Returnees articulate the "right" to compensation for wartime loss

Throughout the fall and winter of 1940/41, returnees wrote to local authorities to criticize the inadequacy of returnee relief benefits and the aid application process. One mother who returned from "exile," Madame Fleury, had appeared at the Bureau d'Assistance (welfare office) in Reims to collect her refugee allocation in arrears:

> I only ask for what is owed to me. I have never asked for it before now. I'm not asking for a handout, but only a little bit of justice from those who have work, for those who have no work. From May 16 to August 28 I have had no work since no one wants to work for the Germans.[37]

An employee at the bureau refused to approve Fleury's request on the grounds of insufficient identification since she possessed only an insurance card and no photo identification card. Fleury's letter actually

---

[36] AMVR, *Bulletin Municipal*, "Séance du 21, September 1940," 245–246.
[37] AMVR 3514, Mme Y. Fleury to mayor of Reims, October 22, 1940.

elevates unemployment to a patriotic act of resistance, and taps another common theme in refugee letters: "But if I were a foreigner, I would surely have more success since they [foreigners] receive help from everywhere, food, lodging, but we, the poor French, it doesn't go well for us."[38]

The economic situation of female returnees worsened on November 30, 1940, when Marchandeau mailed a letter to all married female employees of Reims' civil services:

the Law of October 11, 1940, temporarily prohibits the recruitment of female personnel into Departmental Administration or that of the Commune and other public enterprises. The law stipulates specifically that married female employees, whose husbands earn a living, must be laid off without severance pay. In an effort to enforce this directive I must remove you from the payroll by January 1, 1941.[39]

Traditionalist ideologues hoped to strengthen French male employment by placing men in women's jobs, similar to a strategy adopted in the aftermath of World War I.[40] However, removal from the workforce only made female returnees' survival more difficult.[41] Vichy removed women from state employment simultaneously with termination of their refugee and returnee relief allocations.[42]

Elderly refugees encountered the added obstacles attached to age. Charles Lacan of Vitry-le-François (Marne) continued his efforts through July 1941 to claim monies from the prefect of the Bouche-du-Rhône. Lacan pleaded:

At the time of my departure from Marseille, I believed that my repatriation benefit would be paid to me upon my return to Vitry-le-François, however, after numerous attempts made at the Mayor's office, I have not received any results. As I told you at the beginning of my letter, I am 72 years old and can no longer work.[43]

The prefect of the Bouche-du-Rhône instructed Lacan to appeal again to the prefect of the Marne.

---

[38] AMVR 3514, Mme Y. Fleury to mayor of Reims, October 22, 1940.
[39] AMVR 2185, Marchandeau to all women in municipal service of the city of Reims, November 30, 1940.
[40] Grayzel, *Women's Identities at War*, 224–225.
[41] See Miranda Pollard, "La politique du travail féminin," in Jean-Pierre Azéma and François Bédarida (eds.), *Vichy et les Français* (Paris: Fayard, 1992), 242.
[42] Women's experience of material destitution was often downplayed in postwar discussions by the emphasis on women's "sexual treason" in pursuit of German favoritism, which gained them the punishment of shaved heads. See Virgili, *Shorn Women*.
[43] ADM, Reims depot, 6W/Series/R/628–230, Charles Lacan to the prefect of Bouche-du-Rhône, Vitry-le-François, July 14, 1941.

Clearly, the exodus hastened the physical degeneration of northern France's elderly population. In November 1941, Philippe Aubry of Reims requested that a refugee allocation be sent to him and his wife at their place of retreat:

We cannot return to Reims at this time because we are ill as a consequence of our evacuation, during which we spent three weeks on the roads, ill. We are refugees in a small hamlet of ten houses in Côte d'Or, where nobody will come to our aid because they do not know us. Mr. Prefect, given that we are ill and without any resources, and that we are refugees from the department of the Marne, I thought I might appeal to your good heart to please send us a little help.[44]

Aubry received a negative reply from the Marne's Refugee Allocation Commission on the grounds that awards could not be distributed to refugees living outside the resident department. Linking aid eligibility to a particular residence in the host department or the home department, failed to recognize that the neediest refugees continued to live in a state of dislocation.

Written communications between returning Forbidden Zone refugees and local officials in the Marne testify to the fact that French officials did not apply a uniform policy of distribution of benefits to returnees. Three major factors contributed to returnees' failure to receive assistance: residing outside a department of origin or refuge; difficulty in communicating requests across the Line of Demarcation; and general bad luck. These factors emerged from the larger national policy that forced refugees to curb their dependence on the state and to return to their homes and jobs – regardless of whether their homes or jobs still existed. For women whose husbands were prisoners of war, who could not find work, or whose homes had been destroyed, the random distribution of state aid and cuts in returnee relief payments cast them deeper into economic hardship.

Arbitrary rules for aid distribution compelled widow Pierchon to direct her complaints to Pétain himself. An early returnee to Châlons-sur-Marne on July 6, 1940, Pierchon described her experience:

Following our return to Châlons-sur-Marne, the mayor's office distributed 200 francs of aid per person. They called it, "return money". I was never able to claim these funds either, because the distribution of aid ran out at the letter "O," and my family name begins with "P". Hence I received no aid because my family name begins with the letter "P". This is pretty aggravating, to not receive aid because of that, especially since I have suffered as much since the

---

[44] ADM, Reims depot, 6W/Series/R/628–230, Letter, Champeau-Beau, November 14, 1941.

beginning of the evacuation as people whose family names begin with letters "A" to "O".[45]

Pierchon continued that, as a mother of three, as a widow of a World War I veteran, and as someone without a pension whose house refugees pillaged during the exodus, she should receive a cash benefit from the state. The archive file held no reply to Pierchon's complaint.

Civilians' demands for state entitlements suggest a belief that parents' suffering merited state compensation. Monsieur Morel of Reims, invoked his status as the "father of a large family":

I am the father of a family of 7 children who all live with me. I suffered the pillaging of my house during the evacuation. I cannot possibly afford to buy everything that my family requires which is why I have come to request your distinguished assistance for aid to help me out.[46]

Civilians' petitions attempted to hold the state accountable for the destruction of private property. The widow, Modestine Adélina Galichet, aged seventy-eight, returned to her home fifteen months after her "involuntary stay in the Puy-de-Dôme." Galichet recorded:

I found my house standing, but with tiles broken, the locks picked, latches removed, requiring replacement. Inside, someone had plundered all the essential items in the house. I had two beds which disappeared completely, mattresses, down beds ... covers, pillows, sheets, pocket handkerchiefs, which I now have only one, bought during the exodus. They took clothes and a host of other things that I become aware of on a daily basis when I go to look for something.[47]

Galichet continued to describe the challenges to her survival and inquired why she was not entitled to state aid in these terms:

That is not all ... I had to find some firewood, I had a hard time buying it at 60 francs per stere, plus 25 francs per stere to cut it ... I am 78 years old, do you think I can saw big pieces of wood? And I can't just eat wood. I must go out and find vegetables and feed myself, it's what one does as a housewife. What do you think Mr. Prefect that I have a lot left over given the cost of living? I must ask: why am I not entitled to the same aid given to refugees? Why don't I have a right to this money?[48]

[45] ADM, Reims depot, 6W/Series/R/628–230, Letter, Châlons-sur-Marne, January 26, 1942.

[46] ADM, Reims depot, 6W/Series/R/628–230, Letter, Reims, December 17, 1941.

[47] ADM, Reims depot, 6W/Series/R/628–230, Mme Modestine Galichet to prefect of the Marne, November 19, 1941.

[48] ADM, Reims depot, 6W/Series/R/628–230, Mme Modestine Galichet to prefect of the Marne, November 19, 1941.

The prefect of the Puy-de-Dôme refused Galichet's appeal, saying that she should have repatriated to the Marne in August 1940. Galichet, like so many other civilians, refused to accept the domestic destitution wrought by the war as inevitable, acceptable, or patriotic. More importantly, she refused to allow an authoritarian state, and foreign occupation to silence her voice.

Racial exclusion and property redistribution: Jewish property transfer

For refugees prohibited from returning to the Occupied Zone by German racial laws, their long-term absences produced more severe losses of personal property. French policies that required the redistribution of "abandoned" apartments and houses to repatriated refugees and German soldiers compounded expulsees' losses. The case of Jacques Saadia, a Jewish refugee who fled Reims during the exodus and was excluded from returning to the Occupied Zone, exemplifies the double hardships endured by expulsees. Saadia and his family had taken refuge at St. Étienne (Loire), where he paid 450 francs per month to live in a poorly furnished apartment. Saadia learned that refugees from the Forbidden Zone lived in his apartment in Reims, but he received bills from the gas, electric, and water companies for services rendered to these refugees. Saadia had written to the refugees to request that they send him some of his furniture. They refused, inspiring Saadia to express his anger to the prefect:

I am asking you to tell me what my rights are and what are their's [squatters] in this matter? Do I have to pay gas and electricity for the refugees in my home? They are staying there at the initiative of a neighbor and I get nothing out of it. I am a refugee myself, in the Free Zone. If I have the right to an indemnity, then on what order and who is responsible for paying it?

Do I have the right in these circumstances to have my furniture moved? The Germans must approve it, but can the refugees living in my home prevent it? I wrote to them and asked them to send me a cover and the eiderdown, while leaving them plenty of others. These refugees refused to give them to my friend who I sent to pick them up ... I would be very grateful if you could send me information and counsel me on what to do.[49]

As a Jew of foreign birth, Saadia corresponded with the Vichy state at considerable risk to his own anonymity and personal security. In this case, the investigation uncovered that Saadia was a Syrian-born Jew

---

[49] AMVR 3514, St. Étienne, M. Jacques Saadia to the prefect of the Marne, March 14, 1941.

who had been naturalized in February 1940, which meant that his citizenship stood in jeopardy based on the September 1940 Vichy law. The refugee living in his apartment, Édouard Gillis of the Ardennes, testified that Saadia had given consent to his neighbors to fill the apartment. Gillis claimed to have regularly paid all bills and claimed that the rental company had waived his rent. To complicate matters, Monsieur Millet, the neighbor, claimed to have accepted the burden of paying Saadia's rent on his behalf. In response to the accusation that Gillis failed to honor Saadia's request to send his bedding, Gillis told the police that he urgently needed the sheets and blankets for his own children during the severely cold winter of 1940, since the apartment's windows had been shattered during bombings. Based on the testimony of Gillis and Millet, the police report found against Monsieur Saadia:

Briefly, the complaints made by M. Saadia have been found in large part to be false. He can move his furniture, if he wishes, with approval, with a moving agency. The current occupant is not at all opposed to the removal of his furniture.[50]

Saadia's case reveals one of the many difficulties faced by Jewish refugees in the Free Zone when trying to regulate property claims. The solution of problems through police or state intervention became increasingly worrisome in the latter half of 1940. The "discrete" life that Saadia wished to live in St. Étienne was compromised by the fact that he had to engage authorities to negotiate a resolution to his problem. To complicate matters, the Germans formally prohibited the transfer of Jewish property between zones.[51] In the end, Saadia had no recourse to appeal his loss of property.

Some Jewish refugees did manage to skirt German restrictions and return to Reims after the exodus, but were subjected to increased state surveillance. Evidence of the number of Jewish returnees whose presence was known is revealed in the application of an August 1941 military ordinance prohibiting French Jews from owning radios. The Reims commissioner of police reported to the prefect of the Marne on September 19, 1941 that he had succeeded in obtaining the "voluntary" surrender of nineteen radios from a list of 247 Jewish Rémois.[52]

---

[50] AMVR 3514, Commissioner of police of the 1st Arrondissement to prefect of the Marne, Reims, May 18, 1941.
[51] AN F/60/1507, Minutes of the Conference between Superior Council Heydenreich, representative of Gauleiter Burkel and Louis Marlier, January 14, 1941.
[52] AMVR 3382, Commissioner of the police, Reims to prefect of the Marne, Reims, September 19, 1941.

As refugees returned to their departments of origin, they experienced the growing power of both the state and the German occupiers to intervene in their lives. Alsatians and Lorrainers, who had previously held a privileged and protected status, felt themselves at particular risk in the Occupied Zone. On November 6, 1941, Martin Hubrecht, a refugee from Alsace, wrote to the lieutenant prefect of Reims, expressing his concerns about the growing fear among his displaced compatriots. Hubrecht reported that Alsatian and Lorrainer refugees had received a letter summoning their families to the prefecture in Châlons-sur-Marne in order to receive instructions regarding their repatriation to Alsace. Hubrecht decided not to respond to the "invitation," titled "Consolidation of the German Community," but many of his compatriots had become "crazed" by the letter, worrying that it was an order. Hubrecht urged the lieutenant prefect to declare the letter unofficial, because "it might push them to do something profoundly against their will."[53] The Germans had carefully worded the letter, "offering the opportunity" for refugees to return to Alsace, Lorraine, Luxembourg, or other lands in the German Reich, including compensation during the journey. However, the letter also implied that attendance was obligatory, "you are thanked for arriving on November 18, 1941 at 8:00 a.m., accompanied by all the members of your family who are part of your household."[54]

Distinguishing between mandatory registration and an "invitation" to register for repatriation created confusion. Alsatian and Lorrainer refugees who had returned to the Occupied Zone increasingly understood that returning home meant loss of French citizenship, military conscription for men, and loss of freedom to contract their own labor. For those refugees who desired to return to their homes in Alsace and Lorraine or the Forbidden Zone, they soon learned that the price of return could be greater than freedom and nationality.

Forbidden Zone returnees face prolonged displacement and renewed bombing

Ineligibility to receive "returnee relief" emerged as the first major problem for unauthorized returnees who had managed to cross the Line of Demarcation. The initial "good fortune" of finding an official

---

[53] ADM, Reims depot, 13/W/3-z-386, Martin Hubrecht to lieutenant prefect of Reims, November 6, 1941.

[54] ADM, Reims depot, 13/W/3-z-386, Martin Hubrecht to lieutenant prefect of Reims, November 6, 1941, 2.

willing to ignore a refugee's "forbidden status," soon turned into "bad luck," once in the Forbidden Zone. These returnees entered a state of limbo, disqualified from employment, unable to receive state relief aid, and refused readmission to their homes.[55] Simone Feuilliette, a refugee from Aisne, experienced this condition of virtual statelessness. When she failed to find work in Paris and having exhausted her savings, Feuilliette returned to her parents' residence. On December 24, 1940, she arrived in Reims. She applied for a laissez-passer to cross into the Forbidden Zone. When her request was denied, Feuilliette sought assistance from the mayor's office.[56] The mayor's reply enforced the same principle cited in his rejection of other similar requests:

The only people authorized to come to live in our department are refugees who can prove that they are coming here to join immediate family [spouse or child under 18 years of age]. In any contrary case, we can only issue to refugees a coupon for transportation back to where they came from.[57]

Marie Choin, a sixty-seven-year-old widowed returnee had hoped to return to Carignan (Ardennes) and thus welcomed repatriation from Charente. Choin remained stranded in Reims as a consequence of German authorities' refusal to allow re-entry to the Forbidden Zone. She pleaded for assistance from the city of Reims:

I am a 67-year-old widow without any assistance. Having had to tour all of France, it [France] cannot even give an old woman 10 francs a day so she can live or at least return me to my home.[58]

The commission refused Choin's request on the grounds that she could only move from Charente to Reims to join underage children. Reims could not award her a refugee allocation, and the mayor actually suggested that the sixty-seven-year-old widow try to return to Charente.[59] André Lamarle of Ay (Marne) addressed an inquiry to the prefect of the Marne asking why she should pay taxes since she never received her refugee allocation:

I never settled in a refugee center, we remained on the road the entire time and how we suffered. I have two children one fourteen years old and one eleven and a half and my husband is a prisoner of war in Germany. Now you know why, Monsieur. I make a request of you because now someone sent me my

---

[55] Jews, Alsatians and Lorrainers, and foreigners remained eligible for aid in the Free Zone, conditioned upon enrollment in work programs.
[56] AMVR 3514, Mlle Simone Feuilliette to mayor of Reims, January 7, 1941.
[57] AMVR 3514, Mlle Simone Feuilliette to mayor of Reims, January 7, 1941.
[58] AMVR 3514, mayor of Reims to Mme Choin, March 24, 1941.
[59] AMVR 3514, mayor of Reims to Mme Choin, March 24, 1941.

contribution papers for 1940 [taxes] and I'd like to ask you how am I suppose to pay, given that my husband is a prisoner?[60]

The prefect denied Lamarle's request, simply stating that she did not meet the commission's criteria of "neediness."

Documenting the first wave of repatriation, the *L'Éclaireur de l'Est*, Marchandeau's re-established daily newspaper in Reims, reported in strangely optimistic terms of the "last challenge" faced by refugees returning to the north. The story was about La Maison Rouge, a camp in Vouziers (Ardennes), which housed approximately 2,000 refugees who had been refused re-entry to the Forbidden Zone. The *L'Éclaireur* reported, "thanks to the care of German authorities" the last step in the terrible exodus of French refugees was being made easier. The *L'Éclaireur*'s reporters spun a tale of the "congenial conditions" of camp life, declaring, "Concentration camps, no. Refugee camps, yes: in order to provide those waiting [to return], the best possible conditions – given the state of war."[61] Certainly, if the reporters accurately described the Vouzier camp's conditions, the German camp in the Forbidden Zone sounded like an improvement upon many of the refugee camps operated in France's Free Zone.[62]

The article credited German authorities with the initiative of ensuring healthy, comfortable conditions for returning refugees. What journalists failed to stress was that refugees remained in these camps not by choice, but because of German restrictions on repatriation to the Forbidden Zone – a policy generated by the continuation of the war with Britain. After describing the pleasant conditions in the German refugee camps, the Marne reporter confessed the conditions of the Forbidden Zone: "The cities and villages are completely destroyed; no water flows. The bridges are blown, supplies are limited. The dangers of epidemics threaten."[63]

By contrast, the German authorities hoped to dissuade refugees from demanding repatriation to their homes along the Channel coast, reporting that bread lines stretched a distance of 1 km. German accounts further contrasted the orderliness of the camps to the chaos on Forbidden Zone roads: "Upon their arrival, one is struck by the long lines of wagons carrying everything one might imagine: an interminable line of

---

[60] ADM, Reims depot, 6W/Series/R/628–230, Mme Lemarle to the prefect of the Marne, September 5, 1941.

[61] *L'Éclaireur de l'Est*, No. 9919 Nouvelle Série. Friday, July 19, 1940. Shannon L. Fogg, "The Youngest Refugees: Children, Daily Life, and Material Shortages during the Second World War," paper presented at the French Historical Studies Conference, Stanford University, March 18, 2005.

[62] Fogg, "The Youngest Refugees."   [63] Fogg, "The Youngest Refugees."

horses drink water at the edge of the woods: tents are set up across the prairie."[64] Yet, regardless of these confusing accounts about Forbidden Zone life, refugees chanted in unanimity: "We would like to return to our homes!" According to Captain Meisser, refugees needed to content themselves with the current situation: "Orders are orders and very often the silence that weighs on a rejection does not allow the voicing of the sad, lamentable scene that awaits them at their homes."[65]

The account of the refugee camp at Vouziers attempted to balance praise and critique of German relief efforts. Written at the beginning of the Occupation, before rigid censorship was reapplied to all newspaper reports, this article managed to document refugees' reluctance to settle for the "splendid" conditions of camp life. At the same time, it indirectly gave legitimacy to the German policy of restricting re-entry to certain zones, accurately describing the conditions of northern villages as destroyed. Most official French information circulating in the Free Zone failed to offer details of the destruction in the north. The French journalists' image of German camps captured aspects of a particular truth, but avoided a larger, grimmer reality – that the Germans actually refused to admit the majority of Forbidden Zone returnees even to their camps. Without state aid or the hope of finding employment, these "expulsees," as they became called in popular discourse, wandered between makeshift Red Cross and German-run relocation camps, destitute and without hope.

The dangers created by the red tape returnees encountered trying to gain access to relief benefits or their homes, paled when compared with the dangers Forbidden Zone residents confronted once returned to their homes. British bombing pounded France's Channel coast departments with incredible intensity during the fall and winter of 1940/41. Some government officials assigned to cope with the consequences of bombings knew of the danger, but public discussion about Allied bombing was muted, largely because of poor communication with the Forbidden Zone.[66]

Historical accounts of France's World War II experience highlight the violence of Germany's invasion and the conflict that accompanied Allied liberation in 1944, but Allied bombing between autumn 1940

---

[64] *L'Éclaireur de l'Est*, No. 9919 Nouvelle Série, Friday, July 19, 1940.
[65] *L'Éclaireur de l'Est*, No. 9919 Nouvelle Série, Friday, July 19, 1940.
[66] British bombing did spill beyond the Forbidden Zone, encroaching into French territory around Reims and even Paris. On December 21, British bombers launched attacks in the Marne, destroying sections of the commune of Bazancourt, and demolishing one bridge and a rail line between Reims and Challerange to the east. AN F1/cIII/1166/Marne, Report from prefect of the Marne to DGGFTO, January 1941.

Table 8. *Population figures for Pas-de-Calais and Nord, March 1941*

City	Population pre-May 1940	Population March 1941	Not returned	% Not returned
Dunkerque	31,000	12,000	19,000	61
Rosendael	17,000	16,000	1,000	6
Malo-les-Bains	11,000	7,200	3,800	35
Couderkerque Branche	13,600	10,000	3,600	26
Petite Synthe	7,100	Unknown	Unknown	Unknown
Saint-Pol-sur-Mer	12,700	Unknown	Unknown	Unknown
Cappelle-la-Grande	22,300	15,000	7,300	33
Calais	67,500	49,050	18,450	27
Boulogne-sur-Mer	52,000	30,000	22,000	42

and June 1944 has received far less historical scrutiny. Consider that approximately 19,000 repatriated French coastal civilians died as a consequence of Operation Overlord, the Allies' D-Day invasion.[67] One hypothesis for why refugees in the south did not understand that the Channel coast was a live battleground is that the government wished for refugees to return to their homes, regardless of combat conditions. Civilians and Vichy officials wanted to believe that the Armistice meant that the war was over. This yearning for home and a desire to begin reconstruction altered officials' political judgment and clouded civilians' decision-making processes. Thus, despite the danger, many Forbidden Zone cities had returned to well over 50 percent of their pre-exodus population by March 1941 as shown in Table 8.[68]

The story of British bombing of occupied France documents the inability of civilians to achieve their goal of finding an end to war's violence. Among civilians, a model of response to bombardment evolved in two confusing directions. On the one hand, a similar desire to avoid the effects of war that had propelled civilians onto the road in May 1940, now strangely motivated many refugees to return to a territory that remained embattled. At the same time, civilians who repatriated to

---

[67] Documentary film, *Jour-J du Débarquement à la Libération*, produced by the Mémorial de la Seconde Guerre Mondiale à Caen, offers an excellent video footage of Operation Overlord's destruction of French civilian centers.

[68] Nicole Dombrowski Risser, "The Search for Civilian Safe Spaces: Re-Evacuation of Le Havre, Calais and Dunkerque in Response to British Bombing, September to March, 1940–41," in Patricia Lorcin and Daniel Brewer (eds.), *France and Its Spaces of War* (New York: Palgrave Macmillan, 2009), 63.

their homes in the Forbidden Zone re-entered a cycle of bombardment and evacuation.

A brief survey of bombing in three Forbidden Zone departments, Haute-Normandie, Nord and Pas-de-Calais, illustrates the intense levels of violence that awaited civilian returnees to the Forbidden Zone in the fall and winter of 1940/41, well before Operation Overlord in 1944. In the port cities of Dieppe, Le Havre, Berck, Boulogne-sur-Mer, and Calais, returnees encountered violence that continued unabated despite the proclamation of war's end. Calais endured British bombing sixty-two times between August 1940 and February 1941, averaging eight bombings per month.[69] In Le Havre, Dieppe, and Calais a new "normalcy" established itself that was based upon bombing, evacuation, destruction, and death.

From September 16–28, 1940, the British attacked Le Havre nightly. Ninety-four civilians died and 179 others were injured. In an urgent message to Paris, Le Havre's police commissioner described the destruction: "The two hospitals are completely overflowing with the never stopping inundation of the wounded. The hospitals have no security. One has been hit by a bomb and the staff have moved surgical operations to a more secure spot."[70] Bombs demolished 165 buildings including the stock exchange, City Hall, the post office and the Casernes of Eblé and Kléber.[71] Consequently, the commissioner requested assistance from Marlier at the Service of Refugees in planning the re-evacuation of urban children. "The population Havraise, which had previously evacuated the city in June 1940 is shaken with panic," described the commissioner. "A new exodus has begun, lamentably; we have no means for transportation."[72] Families, described as "stricken by the liveliest terror," took refuge in nearby communes. At dusk each evening, a flood of refugees evacuated the city by foot, in wagons, or on bicycles, finding shelter in fields or woods. "The fear of bombings from ships in the sea accentuates even more the hysteria that has overtaken the entire population," emphasized the commissioner to Marlier.[73] In the paper margins of the Le Havre report, Marlier noted, "Emotion but not panic."[74] The reader wonders what would have qualified as "panic" to this war-seasoned veteran official.

---

[69] AN F/60/1507, Service of Refugees, Marlier to DGGFTO, Report on Evacuations of the Forbidden Zone, March 2, 1941, 8.
[70] AN F/60/1507, Report, "Secours aux populations civiles, victimes de bombardements," from the commissioner of police of Le Havre to Marlier, September 1940.
[71] AN F/60/1507, Report, "Secours aux populations civiles," September 1940.
[72] AN F/60/1507, Report, "Secours aux populations civiles," September 1940.
[73] AN F/60/1507, Report, "Secours aux populations civiles," September 1940.
[74] AN F/60/1507, Report, "Secours aux populations civiles," September 1940.

As September progressed, fires consumed Le Havre. Volunteer reserves that might have helped to fight the fires were depleted by bombing casualties. Civilians able to assist the smattering of emergency workers lacked any formal training. The Germans authorized a regiment of firefighters with family ties in Le Havre to travel from Paris to assist in the struggle to contain the blazes; but they faced an uphill battle since the bombings had completely paralyzed the city's water systems. Le Havre's fire chief ordered a wagon pump from Paris, but the company requested 175,000 francs advance payment which the city could not afford. Le Havre's Mayor Risson emphatically requested that Marlier seek the funds from the DGGFTO.[75]

For the next three and a half years, bombing and evacuation marked the rhythm of daily life in many coastal cities. The most ironic and tragic fact is that, with the majority of exodus refugees returned to their homes, the Service of Refugees now turned toward organizing the re-evacuation of the recently repatriated coastal populations to inland areas of the Occupied Zone. In this second round of attacks and evacuations, civilians and state officials acted in similar ways to May 1940. The differentiated experience between the classes persisted, and the disruption to the economy from daily air raids was equal to, if not worse than, during the German invasion. The state and family emphasis on the rescue of children continued; but now, a much sharper division of opinion emerged between civilians who demanded to "stay home" and those who sought to evacuate. Despite feeling the sustained impact of bombardment, many of civilians felt less convinced of the merits of seeking shelter away from their homes. Also, repatriated civilians were less capable of affording a second round of displacement and unemployment.

The impulse to flee among a significantly growing segment of the youth population did require that the government identify ways to transport young civilians out of bombing zones. Of the nearly 150,000 residents of Le Havre who had returned to their city, approximately 15,000–20,000 attempted to flee the city for shelter in the surrounding countryside each night. Moreover, the increasing damage in places like Dieppe and Le Havre was staggering. On September 28, Marlier recorded that RAF bombers had sacked 950 to 1,000 buildings in Le Havre alone, leaving nearly 12,000 people homeless. Mayor Risson reported that destruction to factories added 1,500 people to his unemployment list, which now totaled 17,000 for the city. Thus, in September 1940, the only fortunate residents of Le Havre were

---

[75] AN F/60/1507, Report, "Secours aux populations civiles," September 1940.

the 15,000 refugees who had never repatriated from the May–June exodus. While those 15,000 residents probably faced hunger and unemployment in Free Zone refugee centers or reintegration centers in the interior of the Occupied Zone, they were not exposed to nightly bombings.

The new round of evacuations was complicated by the fact that the German military had destroyed or closed many northern train routes. Hence, agents sent from Paris to estimate the dimensions of a future evacuation reported meeting 500–600 people, mostly children, walking or riding bikes toward Rouen. Eight hundred elderly people resided in the town's two hospitals. Doctors reported that 500 could survive transport to other locations, but that 300 could not be evacuated.

On the night of September 30, 1940, Mayor Risson ordered evacuation notices posted throughout Le Havre. The posters could have easily been leftovers from the May evacuations. They ordered the departure of the hospitalized, women, children and the elderly. Within hours, the German authorities ordered the notices removed until they received approval of the evacuation plan from the Field Kommandur of Rouen. The added layer of German military approval substituted for the removed layer of French military authority, which had functioned in a similarly obstructionist manner in the May–June crisis. The main difference was that the Germans supported, and, indeed, insisted upon, removing civilians from coastal towns. Rather than opposing evacuation of Le Havre, the Germans focused on where to relocate Forbidden Zone civilians. Marlier's service requested that refugees be sent to Rouen. However, the Germans feared that this move might not be deep enough into the interior to offer long-term shelter. On the other hand, the Germans forbade refugees from crossing the Line of Demarcation into the Free Zone. On this point Vichy and the Germans could agree. Via Marlier's office in Paris, Vichy confirmed that they could accept coastal evacuees in the Free Zone, but *only* if the Germans had absolutely no other means of accommodating them in the Occupied Zone.[76]

In Calais, civilians had few good options for protection. Having been bombed sixty-two times between September 1940 and February 1941, residents oscillated between wanting peace, wanting evacuation, and wanting to remain in their homes. Despite Calais' natural fortifications, the mayor began to seriously reconsider the wisdom of allowing residents to remain in the targeted city after one particularly horrendous attack on February 26, 1941. "Usually," the mayor

---

[76] AN F/60/1507, Letter, Marlier to Mayor Risson, September 28, 1940.

reported, "the British bomb in the evenings."[77] However at 1.15 pm on February 26, several German and British planes engaged in a dog-fight just above a primary school. In the course of the fight, planes released two bombs that fell on the school where pupils were return-ing to class.[78] The events of February 26, 1941 horrified the bomb-stricken neighborhood, but the mayor confirmed that the population remained "courageous and attached to their soil and did not want to leave." One interpretation of Calais residents' resolve to stay in their homes is as a defensive posture. Working people had lost jobs, money, and loved ones during the exodus of May–June 1940. Few could afford to leave the jobs to which they had returned. In a language imbued with class-based understandings, many workers rearticulated the narrative from May that ascribed treason with retreat and identi-fied retreat as a bourgeois dereliction.

In Dunkerque, socioeconomic background determined "courage." The Service of Refugees received a request from the mayor to evacuate 11,000–12,000 children under the age of fourteen. The mayor said that the children of parents with economic means had already been moved from the city. In a census of remaining residents, the remaining 3,882 families were families of dock workers with multiple children who did not have the means to send their children away. Because the primary schools had been destroyed by bombing, the children attended make-shift schools in buildings that remained standing. The mayor stressed that these "schools" did not have any form of bomb shelter other than an ordinary basement.[79]

The destruction of Dunkerque and surrounding areas (Table 9) increased during the spring of 1941 due to bombings that occurred two to three times per day.[80] Unlike the population of Le Havre, which attempted to flee the city each evening, residents of Dunkerque wanted to remain at home. However, in February 1941, the Service of Refugees and the prefect of Nord decided that women and children of the coastal cities should be moved away from the ports. They petitioned the Germans to allow the transfer of 21,000 children and women from the coast to Lille, located marginally closer to the interior.

[77] AN F/60/1507, Service of Refugees, Marlier to DGGFTO, report submitted March 2, 1941, 2–11.

[78] AN F/60/1507, Service of Refugees, Marlier to DGGFTO, report submitted March 2, 1941, 2–11.

[79] AN F/60/1507, Service of Refugees, Marlier to DGGFTO, report submitted March 2, 1941, 2–11.

[80] AN F/60/1507, Service of Refugees, Marlier to DGGFTO, report submitted March 2, 1941, 2–11, in Dombrowski Risser, "Search for Civilian Safe Spaces," 67.

Table 9. *Destruction to Pas-de-Calais and Nord, May 1940–March 1941*

City	Buildings destroyed	Buildings damaged	Evacuated	Wounded	Dead
Dunkerque	3,250	Unknown	19,000	Unknown	1,000/200[a] (6/40) 191 (9/40–3/41)
Rosendael	800	1,500[b] 1,700[c]	1,000	270	520
Boulogne-sur-Mer	720	2,200[b] 2,200[d]	Unknown	350	220

[a] Missing, presumed dead.
[b] Seriously damaged.
[c] Pillaged and temporarily uninhabitable.
[d] Occupied by German troops.
Source: AMVR 3514, Marne prefect to Marne mayors, Circular No. 35, Châlons-sur-Marne, April 29, 1942.

In Boulogne-sur-Mer, 30,000 residents had returned from the pre-invasion population of 52,000. The mayor reported that all middle-class families had evacuated and only families of workers remained behind. The remaining residents included 10,000 children aged under fourteen. The housing situation in Boulogne added additional complications. Of the 9,600 houses in the town, bombing had destroyed 720; 2,200 were damaged and had no water or electricity, and German authorities had requisitioned about 2,200 to lodge their troops. The week of February 22 proved difficult for the residents of Boulogne-sur-Mer as renewed attacks claimed fifteen lives. As a result, 600 residents attempted to leave the town on foot.[81]

Marlier ordered Jean Borotra, celebrated tennis champion and Secretary of General Physical Education and Sports, to plan for an evacuation of 61,000 children, women, and elderly residents.[82] Marlier conceded: "The recommendation to move these children as far away as possible from the hostilities constitutes a minimal solution."[83] The goal for the future would be to enlarge the evacuations to include all women,

[81] Dombrowski Risser, "Search for Civilian Safe Spaces," 67.
[82] AN F/60/1507, Service of Refugees, Marlier to DGGFTO, report submitted March 2, 1941, 2–11. The Germans later imprisoned Borotra at Saxenhausen where he had a cell near Paul Reynaud. See Reynaud, *Thick of the Fight*, 652.
[83] AN F/60/1507, Service of Refugees, Marlier to DGGFTO, report submitted March 2, 1941, 2–11.

children, and the elderly from all towns endangered by bombings, water restrictions, and interruptions to electrical service.

Unfortunately, the May crisis had not persuaded men like Marlier to join visionary military planners such as Lt. Colonel Arsène Vauthier, who wrote in his 1930 pamphlet, *The Aviation Danger and the Future of the Country*, that: "the entire civil population will be placed abruptly on the warfront, despite the efforts of ground army troops, despite all obstacles and all fortifications."[84] While Reims, Paris, and Lille did not experience the same sustained bombings as the port cities, they fell within range of British bombers. Moving populations deep into France's interior to areas like the Corrèze had succeeded in keeping civilians away from the bombs during the initial invasion. By contrast, in April 1940, moving populations a distance of 80 km from Verdun to Reims had gained security for no one. In the aftermath of such a lesson, it is incomprehensible that French security planners replayed the failed policies of the Phoney War (see Table 10).

France's evacuation story came full circle in April 1942. At a conference at the Service of Refugees offices in Paris, Marlier met with German occupation officer, Dr. Kübler. The Service and the Occupation Authorities began to plan for a new evacuation of Parisian children. Bombings in Parisian neighborhoods near factories had increased significantly, and, while officials recognized the growing need to transfer segments of the population to locations in the south, the population remained wary of the government's schemes. Marlier noted that: "Only those [children] of well-off families can and have assured their departure at their own expense, leaving at their own convenience once they have received permission from the proper authorities."[85] The arrival of the summer vacation in a few months offered an opportunity to gain working-class parents' acceptance of the idea to move children out of Paris to designated havens.

The Service of Refugees faced two problems. Marlier feared another mass departure, making the Service reluctant to broadly advertise the departure of Parisian children. "Information distributed to the parents of children," Marlier wrote, "concerning the possibility of their children's departure, has not been accompanied by publicity officially issued from the Service through the channels of the press, such as the radio or newspapers. We wish to avoid a general movement to depart."[86]

---

[84] Lieutenant-Colonel Arsène Vauthier, *Le Danger aérien et l'avenir du pays* (Paris: Berger-Levrault, 1930), 72, quoted in Panchasi, *Future Tense*, 138.
[85] AN F/60/1507, Notes, Conference between Dr. Kübler and Prefect Marlier, April 17–18, 1942, April 22, 1942.
[86] AN F/60/1507, Notes, Conference between Dr. Kübler and Prefect Marlier, 2.

Table 10. *Evacuation plans for Nord and Pas-de-Calais, March 1941*

City	Children (7–14)	Relocation destination
Dunkerque	12,000	Lille
Bray Dunes	5,800	Lille
Loon Plage	11,900	Lille
Grande Synthe	3,500	Lille
Calais	7,300	Unknown
Boulogne-sur-Mer	10,000	Unknown
St. Léonard and St. Martin	2,500	Unknown
Total	53,000	

Source: AMVR 3514, Marne prefect to Marne mayors, Circular No. 35, Châlons-sur-Marne, April 29, 1942, 2.

On the other hand, Marlier feared that parents would again resist sending their children to the interior. Class played a role in parents' fear. "We have confirmed that the last bombings have above all fallen around the families who live closest to the factories already attacked by bombs but which risk being targeted again. It is considered a given that it is working-class families by and large who live in these densely populated neighbourhoods."[87] The complication, according to Marlier was that: "It so happens that these families do not desire to entrust their children with the official administrative services or its workers. Instead they prefer that their children be accompanied by a relative such as a mother, a grandmother, an older sister or a step-parent."[88]

Hence, Marlier conceded that the only way to convince working-class parents to allow the state to evacuate their children would be to offer each family an allocation to permit a parent to live outside his/her normal residence. Marlier suggested that the public welfare agency, Assistance Sociale, issue support to re-evacuated refugees, thereby affirming the necessity of the state to subsidize the evacuation of low-income and working-class civilians. Marlier's acceptance of the idea that state-paid refugee assistance was necessary for low-income civilians to participate in state-sponsored evacuations committed the French state to an important principle with regard to ensuring civilian protection. Although working-class women had long argued that, without state aid, they could not access adequate civilian protection schemes, the

[87] AN F/60/1507, Notes, Conference between Dr. Kübler and Prefect Marlier, 2.
[88] AN F/60/1507, Notes, Conference between Dr. Kübler and Prefect Marlier, 3.

government had resisted this argument. Not until it became an indisputable fact that French working-class populations were suffering a greater proportion of deaths from bombing did the government finally articulate a policy linking state payment of refugee allocations to universal access to civilian protection programs such as evacuations.

As during the initial exodus, most middle-class women enjoyed the freedom from work and poverty that allowed them to accompany their children to distant shelter without the support of state refugee assistance. But as the crisis wore on, even middle-class families wishing to remain in the Free Zone could hardly afford to live out the war on their savings. Jewish families, in particular, found this a daunting task.

Once the Service finally did entice parents to accept assistance and leave Paris, Marlier directed children and parents to the various departments in the south that had again agreed to receive refugees. Cantal agreed to accept 900 Parisians, Haute-Savoie would host 400 children and the towns of Grenoble and Annemasse wished to split 300 evacuees between them. Other willing hosts included the Var, able to accommodate 200–250, and Doubs and Vosges who set no limits. The department designated to accommodate the largest numbers of children was Algeria. Discussion of using overseas' territories as centers of evacuation had died prior to invasion, but with the Germans as the new landlord, some French might have been more willing to travel overseas.

Conclusion

Repatriation to the Occupied Zone did not, as Vichy officials had promised or refugees had hoped, restore life in France to "normal." For repatriated refugees, return to their homes shattered expectations of recreating life as it had been before the defeat. Faced with shortages and hardships upon their return, refugees' letters to municipal and departmental officials in the Marne testify to dashed expectations, frustration with policies governing relief assistance, and dissatisfaction with management of the repatriation process. In the Forbidden Zone, returnees faced the greater threat of daily bombardment, this time by British aircraft.

Returnees to the north spent their time escaping British bombs or fighting to overcome economic destitution. While conditions in the non-restricted part of the Occupied Zone were certainly better than in the Forbidden Zone, few civilians could find the time or energy to enter into resistance against the Germans. Instead, they resisted the reduction of benefits imposed by the French state. Civilian demands upon the state illustrate the degree to which the disappointments of repatriation continued to cultivate a sense of entitlement to compensation. Women, in particular, registered their experience with the state and in the pages of history, articulating their understanding of the state's obligation to stand by them and their children in the storm of war. Their letters, while only occasionally openly hostile, reveal that a large segment of the French population did not willingly accept the conditions of the Armistice or the economic and security terms of the German Occupation. As France's democratic institutions lay dormant, embattled civilians used democracy's tools to petition the state, demand accountability from leaders, and even to press the Germans to consider their security needs. In doing so, French civilians spoke a language of human rights, advancing civilian claims for protection against war's increasingly indiscriminate violence against innocents.

As its work with repatriation slowed, the Service of Refugees and repatriated municipal governments addressed civilian demands. Under the new German "management," and as conditions deteriorated, Occupied Zone officials became less and less tolerant of refugees from other departments remaining in their communities. However, individual policymakers' opinions mattered little, as the Service of Refugees began to dictate solutions to population relocation and relief disbursement. The Service also produced and enforced gender distinctions among civilians.

Gender, age, racial identity, and socioeconomic status significantly influenced the experience of, and ability to, survive prolonged displacement and war's violence. Children remained the most vulnerable members of the returned population. In the Marne they depended upon an uncertain and dramatically reduced milk supply. Their schools were destroyed by bombs and their makeshift substitutes lacked formal bomb shelters. Children stood exposed and vulnerable when they partook in evacuations held under cover of night, but they also suffered when they remained in bombarded towns.

Eventually, officials recognized that working-class men, women, and children could choose to evacuate only if provided with financial assistance, a policy that Marlier finally embraced in 1942. Besides determining who could evacuate for a second time, socioeconomic status appears to have affected which civilians wished to evacuate. In the case of the dock workers of Dunkerque, battle fatigue and an inflated sense of class pride may have clouded their judgment about remaining in a port city, especially one so symbolically important to British forces. The resolve of the Dunkerque dock workers suggests that the equation of departure with treason, rhetoric that appeared early in the invasion, had taken on some political meaning within working-class communities.

Gender, too, divided civilians' aspirations to stay or retreat from British bombardment. As British bombing intensified, French mayors and the Service of Refugees had no choice but to plan for re-evacuation of vulnerable towns. Children and women figured prominently as the designated recipients of re-evacuation schemes. A question that remains unanswered is why the Service limited its discussions of round two evacuations to women and children, especially when returned men in the Forbidden Zones tended to work for the Germans in a direct or indirect capacity. Certainly, the Germans wished to hold on to skilled workers such as miners and metal-workers. French policy continued to support the return of miners to the Forbidden Zone into early 1941, even as the Service planned for evacuations of the northern towns from which the miners had initially escaped.

As the displacement crisis endured through 1941 and 1942, the services and assistance available to refugees diminished, while state policing functions increased. In January 1941, the Office for the Requests of Temporary Assistance to Refugees was closed and its functions consolidated under the Bureau d'Assistance.[89] On March 13, 1942, a directive from the Minister of the Interior again altered repatriation and allocation policy. As of June 1, 1942, all refugees were to be given laissez-passer to return to their department of origin and all refugee allocations would cease. Local officials were instructed to permit no exceptions for refusing repatriation, including previously acceptable ones such as the inability to find work, health problems, or the occupation of one's home by the military or refugees.[90] Three groups remained excused from repatriation: natives of the departments of Haut-Rhin, Bas-Rhin, Moselle, or the littoral zone (coastal towns of the north); Jews who left their homes in the Forbidden Zone before the signing of the Armistice; and refugees whose homes had been offi-cially designated as destroyed.[91] To be included in the latter category, refugees had to present official documentation from the prefect of their department of origin verifying the destruction of their home. The dir-ective dictated that agricultural workers whose land had been seized by German authorities would be engaged collectively by the German Economic Services.[92] Thus, by the summer of 1942, refugees who had stayed away from their homes in either the Occupied or Free Zone,

---

[89] AMVR 2198, Director of the Service of Refugees to mayor of Reims, January 30, 1941.
[90] AMVR 3514, Marne prefect to Marne mayors, Circular No. 35, Châlons-sur-Marne, April 29, 1942.
[91] AMVR 3514, Marne prefect to Marne mayors, Circular No. 35.
[92] AMVR 3514, Marne prefect to Marne mayors, Circular No. 35, 2.

were required to return regardless of the consequences for their liberty, their economic well-being, or their safety.

The termination of refugee assistance on June 1, 1942 marked an end to the work of the Service of Refugees. The hardships that persisted for displaced persons became officially classified as problems of unemployment. By redefining wartime destitution as an unemployment problem, responsibility for refugees' hardship was transferred from the state to refugees, and the state effectively undermined refugees' previous claims to entitlement to compensation for the state's part in contributing to their homelessness. Unemployed persons who failed to accept state-sponsored solutions, such as work programs in Germany (forced labor) or employment in state work teams (e.g., agricultural work collectives in the farm regions of Ardennes, Pas-de-Calais, and Aisne), faced destitution. Still dependent upon state solutions, many refugees were the first to fall victim to the increasingly repressive state measures to "clean up" the unemployment problem or to remove refugees from host communities. Until the war came to an end, French civilians would find limited assurances of either safety or economic security in a war that knew no boundaries.

Conclusion

> there is only one principle in this sphere [the 1949 Geneva Conventions] which has remained unchallenged by civilized states and which must remain undisputed as a dictate both of law and humanity ... non-combatants must not be made the object of attack unrelated to military operations and directed exclusively against them.
>
> Hersch Lauterpacht, 1952[1]

What new historical perspective might be gained from listening to the voices of civilians caught up in the maelstrom of total war, of placing the experience of non-combatants at the center of a study of modern warfare and France's defeat in 1940? What options for survival do families have in wartime in the context of aerial bombardment, displacement, and foreign military occupation? How has the nation-state, in this case France, imagined its obligation to protect civilian innocents from wartime violence? What protections have international law and occupying military powers provided to women and children – civilian non-combatants – living in war zones? How has wartime violence shaped women's citizenship? This study has attempted to analyze civilians' wartime experiences to contribute answers to these pressing historical questions.

The French civilian exodus of 1940 occurred in response to Germany's Blitzkrieg tactics, which combined aerial bombing and swift-paced land invasion, delivered, as Julian Jackson has emphasized, with an unprecedented element of surprise, terrorizing civilians and soldiers, and triggering mass panic.[2] Aerial bombardment was thus the "original sin" causing the exodus; but in the aftermath of the war was possibly credited

---

[1] Hersch Lauterpacht, "The Problem of the Revision of the Law of War," *British Year Book of International Law* No. 29, 1952, reprinted in J. Gardam (ed.), *Humanitarian Law* (Aldershot: Dartmouth Publishing, 1999), 115–116, 107–129. Quoted by Helen M. Kinsella, "The Image Before the Weapon: A Genealogy of the 'Civilian' in International Law and Politics," Ph.D. dissertation, University of Minnesota, July 2004, 304, n. 869.

[2] Jackson, *Fall of France*, 219.

less than failed government planning and was certainly the least punished of the war crimes. Indeed, contemporary military scholars continue to argue that Germany's strategic planning "obviated the need for strategic bombing of civilian targets," and that Hitler's war directives "indicated his inclination to limit the impact of the air war on civilians," so as not to provoke Allied retaliation on German cities.[3] The indictments against German military officers at the postwar Nuremberg trials underscored the degree to which civilians' experience of death and victimization, suffered particularly under aerial bombardment, passed without official condemnation and went virtually unpunished. Telford Taylor has emphasized that Count One of the Indictment against Reich Marshal Hermann Goering, which specified as criminal "the indiscriminate destruction of cities, towns, and villages, and devastation not justified by military necessity," contained no charge of "unlawful aerial bombardment."[4] Goering had built up the Luftwaffe, taken pride in its powerful assault on London, and celebrated its support of German panzer divisions' flattening of France. Yet he argued at his trial that the air force had been used strictly as a defensive weapon. Field Marshal Albert Kesselring, commander of the German air fleet in 1940 further retorted that German bombers were too lightweight and short-ranged to be used as anything but a defensive force.[5] He also pointed out to the prosecution that "The Hague Conventions on land warfare did not provide for the requirements of air warfare."[6] The goal of the German defense at Nuremberg was to challenge the charge of waging aggressive war and insist that the Luftwaffe was designed purely as a defensive tool, not as an offensive tool. The Allies only pushed the question of the Luftwaffe's intent and capabilities to advance their own argument of Germany's intent to wage aggressive war, not to advance their case of crimes against humanity. Telford Taylor dismissed Goering's and Kesselring's testimony, concluding: "To argue that the Luftwaffe was not designed, intended and used offensively was ludicrous."[7] Nevertheless, no defendant at Nuremberg was convicted of "unlawful aerial bombardment." Taylor surmised that the Allied powers wanted to avoid indicting the Germans for aerial bombardment so as to divert attention from their own catastrophic bombing campaigns against cities such as Dresden, Tokyo, Hiroshima, and Nagasaki. But in so doing,

[3] Alexander B. Downes, *Targeting Civilians in War* (Ithaca, NY: Cornell University Press, 2008), 145.
[4] Taylor, *Anatomy of the Nuremberg Trials*, 325.
[5] Taylor, *Anatomy of the Nuremberg Trials*, 238.
[6] Taylor, *Anatomy of the Nuremberg Trials*, 238.
[7] Taylor, *Anatomy of the Nuremberg Trials*, 238.

and surprisingly with French consent, the Allies themselves dealt a brutal blow against postwar prohibitions that might have protected civilian innocents in the future from such wanton disregard for human life, and placed moral constraints on the arms race that erupted with the Cold War. Rather, bombing emerged from World War II as a legal and legitimate tool of war, with its civilian victims being denied justice.

Inadequacies and failures within French civil defense programs included an insufficient supply of bomb shelters, inadequate provisions for evacuated families, limited eligibility for relocation subsidies, and a narrowly defined zone of evacuation. All of these contributed to civilian flight and their endangerment on the exposed roads and railways of France. Conceived prior to the war's outbreak and without similar intensity and scale of bombardment during World War I, the programs established during the Phoney War mitigated what surely would have been an even greater humanitarian crisis had no rescue infrastructure been designed. Planned evacuations certainly reduced, but did not eliminate, civilian exposure to aerial bombardment and the deprivations of displacement. However, the eventual shift in the focus and scope of evacuations came too late to prevent the exodus. Responsibility for the delay rested mostly with military and national political authorities, but some civilians, as well as local officials in host communities, resisted a broadening of evacuation policy during the Phoney War. At the same time, a well-spring of pro-evacuation sentiment bubbled up from civilian residents and mayors residing in northeastern departments.

The military and the government had focused on the evacuation of Alsace and Lorraine in anticipation of a slow-moving land campaign that might engulf the contested region. It was the region's own representative, Robert Schuman, who, in April 1940, finally conceded the need to expand civilian evacuations to include residents of major urban centers. Schuman also began to recognize the socioeconomic roots of civilian reluctance to embrace evacuations. He thus widened the distribution of state aid to evacuees beyond residents of Alsace and Lorraine. Mayors and prefects in the north complained bitterly up until the invasion crisis that the military and civilian authorities at Défense passive were too slow in responding to civilian security concerns. Perhaps ironically, the German authorities who witnessed France's chaotic civilian flight, later attempted to plan more expansive and organized evacuation schemes for their own citizens, which Julia Torrie has shown were resented and resisted by German civilians. Germans were angered by an authoritarian state trespassing further into the already compromised privacy of German family life.[8] In France, when civilians witnessed or read about the advancing attacks, they supported, and even demanded, evacuation.

French civil defense response was a case of "too little too late," and tragically fell behind the shifting paradigm of waging war. It is hard to imagine the logistics and financial investment necessary to move the entire northern urban civilian population out of the reach of aerial bombardment. The task was too large for a state whose resources were already fully committed, as Talbot Imlay has shown, in an effort to defend the nation's borders.[9] Indeed, despite Kesselring's claim that German bombers flew at short ranges, they could reach France's interior and coastal cities such as Bordeaux, limiting the success of any evacuations, which, as Torrie has emphasized, "depended upon a stable roughly delimited combat zone."[10] The speed of the German assault destabilized any clear distinction between battle zone and home front, erasing any imagined "safe space" to which the French could reliably move civilians. Under the Occupation, evacuation planning improved slightly, as Louis Marlier and the Service of Refugees responded to civilian pleas. After 1942, Marlier successfully pressed the Germans into greater support of the evacuation of "returnee residents" of the Forbidden Zone.

As the new methods of warfare placed unprecedented pressures on the state to expand and improve civilian security measures, French civilians also responded to changing historical circumstances, placing demands upon the state to deliver improvements in civilian protection programs. French civilians, mostly women, politicized their demands by infusing letters and petitions with a language of rights and entitlements to protection from war's violence. Civilian women in particular appropriated interwar language used to advance policies of family allocations, mixing in the evolving language of wartime entitlements and human rights, to voice their rights' claims for state protection from wartime violence.[11] During the Phoney War, women's petitions and letters failed to shift civil defense policy quickly enough to make a difference at the moment of invasion. As the displacement crisis endured, and as Vichy and the German occupying authorities coordinated future evacuations, the French government adopted some key principles demanded in early

---

[8] Torrie, *"For Their Own Good,"* 178.
[9] Imlay, *Facing the Second World War*, 363.
[10] Torrie, *"For Their Own Good,"* 9.
[11] De Grazia, *How Fascism Ruled Women*; Pedersen, *Family, Dependence, and the Origins of the Welfare State*; Diamond, *Women and the Second World War in France*.

evacuee complaints. Robert Schuman, host prefects, and, after July, Vichy officials expanded eligibility for refugee allocations. The military shifted its position on evacuations in response to northern prefects and civilian flight. Host department prefects requisitioned public and private rooms to house refugees. However, in the fall of 1940, Pétain's government backed the withdrawal of such supports to encourage eligible refugees to return to the Occupied Zone. When return became possible, Vichy did allot small sums to refugees to cover travel and a fraction of reintegration costs.

Prior to defeat, the state responded to civilians' petitions for improved security to preserve national unity, especially with regard to Alsace and Lorraine. After the signing of the Armistice, Vichy responded to the plight of refugees to avoid the outbreak of social and political unrest. At best, France's civilian security support systems prevented mass starvation and limited, but did not prevent, refugee homelessness. Civilian protection policies did not prevent widespread impoverishment, chaos, the destruction of private property, or the outbreak of illness and epidemic – typhoid was rampant in the areas most heavily bombed, especially in Pas-de-Calais and Nord.

What kind of "rights" did French civilians claim from 1939 to 1945? Were they advancing a set of human rights forged in the crucible of war? If the right to shelter, food, and protection from military violence qualifies as "human rights," then assuredly French civilians made claims to human rights as redefined in the context of war. Were civilians simply formulating their rights in a language of familialism, as Vicky de Grazia has shown was the case for Italian women who tried to garner the best deal for their families from the fascist state? Yes and no. French civilian demands for refugee allocations and returnee compensation were anchored firmly in the experience of the war's disruption of family life. However, the right to evacuate, the right to a refugee allocation, the right to shelter, the right to compensation for damage to one's home, and the right of return were more complex than the articulation of familialism as expressed in Italy. Claims to these rights sprang from the modern methods of waging war, which engulfed civilians' families and property.

In the mass departure, there was an expression of popular dissent. If the state chose to wage war – we might recall that France declared war on Germany – then civilians demanded a new form of compensation for war. It would be overreaching to inscribe pacifist convictions on evacuees' claims and refugees' actions as there is no evidence of a strong anti-militarist or anti-war sentiment in civilians' claims upon the state. Rather, their claims and actions suggest a fervent desire that the state should limit the encroachment of war into the home front. Having failed to rally against war, civilians wished for a return to a form of warfare that distinguished between combat zone and home front. Absent a return of a romanticized notion of traditional warfare, civilians negotiated for greater protections from total warfare's violence.

Samuel Moyen's recent history of human rights suggests that "the right of civilian security from combat" would not fit neatly into the human rights language as it evolved out of the war. Certainly, there is no articulation of a "right to protection against aerial bombardment" – the essential demand of French civilians. However, as Moyen points out, a process has evolved in which "vernacularization of human rights was one in which ordinary people in different places winnowed their demands ... to use them from below in creative and transformative ways."[12] Contemporary international media had discussed German bombing of French civilians employing the term "commission of wartime atrocities." In Europe and the United States, images of the wounded and reports of the mass displacement provoked moral outrage. As Pétain called for the cessation of hostilities on June 16, the Germans were flattening Tours. The *New York Times* focused almost uniquely on the attacks upon civilians: "It was the first bombardment of the city's residential areas."[13] In Bordeaux, Pétain and the remaining cabinet surely received reports that: "Bombs opened huge craters in the center of the residential district ... residents ran across streets into cellars and even into shell holes. Men, women and children – in family groups and alone – darted from luncheon tables for safety."[14] With casualties amounting to 100,000 and 8 million refugees trudging across France under German fire, it seems evident that the government, refugees, and observers understood the German assault as an atrocity.

Between 1939 and 1945 the bombing of civilians provoked international moral outrage as observers decried the Luftwaffe's lack of moral restraint.[15] French, British, Canadian, and American volunteers turned anger and despair into good works, forming voluntary associations to collect clothing, food, and cash for France's refugees. At the level of international organizations, men like Norman H. Davis attempted to raise millions of dollars for the Red Cross relief effort in France. From

---

[12] Samuel Moyen, *The Last Utopia: Human Rights in History* (Cambridge, MA: Belknap Press of Harvard University, 2010), 219.
[13] United Press, "Tours Bombed in 3 Big Raids; Hundreds Hit in Packed Streets," *New York Times*, June 17, 1940, 1.
[14] "Tours Bombed in 3 Big Raids; Hundreds Hit in Packed Streets," *New York Times*, June 17, 1940, 4.
[15] Downes, *Targeting Civilians in War*, 154.

New York to San Francisco, women's groups sponsored relief galas and fashion shows to raise funds to assist French refugees. In France, host department volunteers also responded to the tragedy, affirming a sense of fraternal community in the early weeks of the crisis. Relief workers understood that humanitarian aid was essential to ensure refugees' survival. Narrowly defined, shelter, food, and clothing were basic rights guaranteed under the Third Republic's policies of family allocations. Using Jean Quataert's concept of human rights as historically contingent, we can conclude that bombing and displacement violated these basic rights.[16] Over the course of the crisis refugees' experiences and relief workers' observations sharpened the language of wartime rights. No formal arena existed during the displacement crisis in which civilians could make their voices heard in rights debates.[17] However, civilian women did make their voices heard, crafting in their independent letters and petitions to government agencies their wartime definitions of human rights. Their articulation of wartime human rights enforcement anticipated the need to revise not only state civilian protection programs, but the laws of war. By describing the violation of their persons, property, security, and well-being, they linked the violation of their human rights to the methods of waging war and thereby helped to define a new standard for wartime criminal behavior.

In France, civilians articulated their human rights demands, forming communities that were sometimes "real" in the sense of organized refugee committees or neighborhood petitions, but more often joining a common community of complainants, united only in the physical space of a mayoral or prefectural mailroom. The language they used was certainly gendered to the extent that civilian refugees and the home front were gendered as female, regardless of sex. Despite their isolation, civilians' demands joined what feminist theorist Hilary Footitt calls a gendered linguistic community. Footitt draws upon Richard Rorty's concept of a "contingent community, multifaceted, shifting and viscerally aware of the contingency of its languages of politics."[18] More simply said, although French refugees lacked political organizations and rarely coordinated among themselves, their demands were commonly linked in time and theme, gendered, deeply political, and contingent upon the context of the war. Across the Rhine, German civilian evacuees

---

[16] Jean H. Quataert, "The Gendering of Human Rights in the International Systems of Law in the Twentieth Century," *Essays on Global and Comparative History* (Washington, DC: American Historical Association, 2006), 2.

[17] Quataert, "The Gendering of Human Rights," 2.

[18] Richard Rorty, *Contingency, Irony and Solidarity* (Cambridge University Press, 1989), ch. 3, quoted in Footitt, *Women, Europe and the Languages of Politics*, 31.

did organize in "real" and recognizable political organizations, protesting the terms of wartime evacuations, and mobilizing around the concept of "family sovereignty in evacuation."[19] Simply because the French refugees and evacuees failed to form organized protests, does not mean that historians should consider their individual demands any less political or politically conscious than their organized German counterparts. German civilians in Witten objected to evacuation for many of the same reasons that French civilians demanded it: namely, family preservation. Ironically, in the German case, their military masters, who had waged Blitzkrieg in France and witnessed the havoc bombing had created in French society, knew better than the citizens the necessity of evacuation as a family survival tool under aerial bombardment.[20] French and German civilians' demands shared a desire to preserve the family unit in the time of war and to insist on family security.

While the rights claims of civilian evacuees and refugees met with varying degrees of satisfaction during the war, the immediate postwar response only partially validated their experiences and demands, inscribing the sanctity of the family in the governing objectives for the postwar international order as outlined in the Universal Declaration of Human Rights, adopted on December 10, 1948 by the United Nations. The Declaration predicated its origination on the events of the war, referencing how, "disregard and contempt for human rights have resulted in barbarous acts which have outraged the conscience of mankind."[21] Article 16(3) of the Declaration specified: "The family is the natural and fundamental group unit of society and is entitled to protection by society and the State."[22] However, the Declaration only vaguely referenced wartime threats to family protection, mentioning nothing about "civilians." Article 2 identified and prohibited potential sources of wartime atrocities, insisting on the observance of rights in a potential state of military occupation, declaring: "no distinction shall be made on the basis of the political, jurisdictional or international status of the country or territory." Article 13(1) stated: "Everyone has the right to freedom of movement and residence within the borders of each state," and Article 13(2) added: "Everyone has the right to leave any country, including his own, and to return to his country."[23] These principles recognized many of the violations of the war that had separated families, jeopardized

---

[19] Torrie, "*For Their Own Good*," 127.
[20] Torrie, "*For Their Own Good*," 127.
[21] Universal Declaration of Human Rights, Preamble, in Glendon, *A World Made New*, "Preamble," 310.
[22] Glendon, *A World Made New*, "Article 16(3)," 312.
[23] Glendon, *A World Made New*, "Article 16(3)," 312.

civilian security, and served as the underpinnings for deportation, imprisonment in concentration camps, and extermination.

Just as genocide was not specifically named in the Declaration (although the Genocide Convention was adopted on December 9, 1948), the recognition and naming of bombing as an atrocity went unmentioned. No articles ensured civilians' rights to evacuation, shelter, and relief entitlements during wartime, which are arguably "human rights." Civilians' "rights to protection," also remained vague in the immediate postwar revision of the Geneva Convention. Human rights discussions remained quite independent from the revisions to the laws of war. Moyen's assertion that the Nuremberg trials failed to establish "a morally familiar tradition of responding to mass atrocity," could be extended to the Declaration and the Geneva Convention.[24] Nuremberg did prosecute deportation, enslavement, and hostage-taking as criminal, but the trials were silent on aerial bombing and evasive around genocide; two major causes of wartime civilian deaths.

The wartime social rights and entitlements that emerged as a program for refugee relief and, hence, to use Moyen's phrase, "prevent catastrophe through minimalist norms," disappeared from the postwar rights discussions. The atrocity of bombing, considered a violation of human rights by its wartime victims, was placed under greater international legal constraint only in 1977. International lawmakers realized the most important achievement in this area with the adoption of the 1977 Protocol Additional to the Geneva Conventions of 12 August 1949.[25] The most significant provisions for civilians of the 1977 Protocol lie in Article 48, "Basic rule"; Article 50, "Definition of civilians and civilian population"; and Article 51, "Protection of the civilian population." The "Basic rule" requires signatories to distinguish between the civilian population and combatants.[26] Article 50 rejects one German wartime rationale given for bombing civilians – the presence of retreating soldiers within civilian ranks – specifying that: "The presence within the civilian population of individuals who do not come within the definition of civilians does not deprive the population of its civilian character."[27] Article 51 includes provisions to protect civilians

---

[24] Moyen, *The Last Utopia*, 82.
[25] United Nations, Protocol Additional to the Geneva Conventions of 12 August 1949, and relating to the Protection of Victims of International Armed Conflicts (Protocol 1), adopted June 8, 1977 by the Diplomatic Conference on the Reaffirmation and Development of International Humanitarian Law applicable in Armed Conflicts. Entered into force December 7, 1979, in accordance with Article 95.
[26] Protocol Additional to the Geneva Conventions of 12 August 1949, Article 48, "Basic Rule."
[27] Protocol Additional to the Geneva Conventions of 12 August 1949, Article 50, "Definition of civilians and civilian population," No. 3.

from incidental injury, forbids reprisals against civilians, and prohibits the use of civilians as human shields.[28] Thus, we see that the protections demanded by civilians during World War II were not codified by international lawmakers and signatories to the Geneva Conventions until thirty-two years after the war. We should not consider the delay in criminalizing the bombing of civilians as evidence of a failure of wartime civilians to turn their security demands into legal principles in the immediate aftermath of the war. Rather, we should consider the significance of civilian women's expanding citizenship in the postwar era as having contributed to advancing a principle that Allied leaders resisted articulating in 1949. Along with the expanding human rights agenda of the 1970s, the revision to the laws of war revealed a growing consciousness of the potential for mass annihilation inherent in the arms race of the Cold War, but anchored in the testimonies of atrocities committed during World War II.

At the end of the nineteenth century and through World War I, feminists had agitated jointly for human rights and improvements in the laws of war. Fin de siècle media developed a consciousness of the relationship between war crimes and human rights violations.[29] Quataert explains that:

Graphic visual images of the plight of fellow human beings helped to sustain humanitarian sentiments. The deliberations at The Hague were followed avidly by a growing reading public, which included many individuals and groups beyond the feminists who also were committed to arms limitations and reduction of military burdens.[30]

Quataert argues that new-century feminists believed women's suffrage was a "precondition for a fundamentally more peaceful international world."[31] Politically empowered women would demand that the "very norms of humane warfare were seen to mark the 'civilized' nations off against 'savage' peoples."[32] These feminists linked the effort "to diminish 'the evils of war' [to] part of a broader quest for peace" that would "serve the interests of humanity."[33]

Obviously, the efforts and ambitions of the new-century feminists and peace activists failed to prevent war or limit war's savagery. Interwar feminists, peace activists, and diplomats, such as Aristide Briand and

---

[28] Protocol Additional to the Geneva Conventions of 12 August 1949, Article 51, "Protection of the civilian population."
[29] Francis H. Early, *A World Without War: How US Feminists and Pacifists Resisted World War I* (Syracuse University Press, 1997), 200.
[30] Quataert, "Gendering of Human Rights," 6.
[31] Quataert, "Gendering of Human Rights," 7.
[32] Quataert, "Gendering of Human Rights," 9.
[33] Quataert, "Gendering of Human Rights," 9.

Frank G. Kellogg, embraced peace and revised laws of war in the inter-war years, but their efforts failed to paralyze Germany's march toward rearmament and war. During the war, Germany did selectively respect certain provisions of the Geneva Conventions of 1920, especially in col-laboration with Marlier and the Service of Refugees to evacuate civilians from coastal battle zones. They also selectively honored certain con-ventions pertaining to PoWs. But in general, Germany's World War II record was one of massive disregard for, and violation of, all the inter-national laws and conventions of war established from the first Hague Convention to the Geneva Conventions in 1920. Women's suffrage in the United Kingdom, the Weimar Republic, and the United States following World War I did little to shore up international peace or ensure respect for the revised laws of war. In the aftermath of World War II, many European women, having lived for nearly a decade under the threat and then administration of fascist regimes, were ill-prepared professionally or physically to enter into the debates about human rights and the laws of war. Vera Brittain's anti-bombing campaign was widely criticized in Britain, her position was considered naive and obsolete by the end of the war. Yet civilians' wartime suffering and the particularities of the viola-tion of their basic human rights did receive a measure of recognition in the formulation of the Universal Declaration of Human Rights.

Postwar revisions of the laws of war genuflected to the suffering of bombing victims, but failed to ensure the protection of civilians from future bombing. Protecting civilians became difficult because the war itself had so destroyed the distinction between combatant and non-combatant. Civilians' efforts to flee combat zones, organize self-defense, or actively engage in armed resistance to foreign military occupation jeopardized the sanctity of civilians. Histories that have lionized resistance combatants, including women's histories written about engaged, armed female partisans, must be rethought in order to understand not only civilians' and women's contributions to national defense, but also to the process of militarizing civilians, which calls into question the protections offered civilians by international law. Kinsella points out that engagement by opposition forces in non-traditional forms of guerilla warfare during World War II "eroded the belief in the desirability [among combatants] and necessity of enforcing and maintaining distinctions between combatant and non-combatant."[34] The historical and contemporary confusion of who constitutes a civilian non-combatant and what situations or spaces

---

[34] Kinsella, "Image before the Weapon," 181.

are legitimately defined as combat or non-combat zones has a tremendous impact on present-day law and experience. This unwillingness to specify who is a "civilian" or a "protected person" and enforce the protection of this category of "innocent," has had special repercussions for women and children. Traditionally, women and children fell into the category of the "innocent." In fact, until the 1947 adoption of the IV Geneva Convention, "innocents of war," typically a construct implying the weak, especially "women, children and the elderly," were only protected by the laws of chivalry as articulated in the 1899 "Martens Principle of the Hague Accords." This stated that: "populations and belligerents remain under the protection and empire of the principles of international law as they resulted between civilized nations, from the laws of humanity, and the requirements of public conscience."[35] Current studies in International Law point out the continued weakness of the concept of "civilian" and argue: "it is not until 1949 under the IV Geneva Convention Relative to the Protection of Civilian Persons in Times of War, that the 'civilian' is formally made a subject of treaty law."[36] In both the 1949 and the 1977 agreements, member states, Kinsella shows, are not held to respect civilian protection while waging a military campaign. Thus, while we study the exodus and express outrage and horror at the attack on French and Benelux civilians, we must remember too that strict laws defining and protecting civilians did not yet exist in 1940.

In international law, the concept of "innocence" has been premised upon a concept of "passivity."[37] Historically, the laws of war for civilians have been defined so that: "To be innocent is also to be without the freedom or the agency to act in one's own defense or for one's own life."[38] The principle of discrimination in international law, which distinguishes between civilian non-combatant and combatant for the purposes of applying the protections afforded by international law, reflects a history of ambiguity. Looking back in time as well as surveying present conditions, historians and postwar legal scholars must face the historical outcome: that in fleeing, refugees did not necessarily improve their personal survivability or the inviolability of the category of "non-combatant." Mixing with soldiers on the roads of France, civilian refugees also contributed to the implosion of the battle front into

---

[35] Preamble to the 1899 Hague Convention, cited in Kinsella, "Image before the Weapon," 167.
[36] Kinsella, "Image before the Weapon," 10.
[37] Kinsella, "Image before the Weapon," 300.
[38] Kinsella, "Image before the Weapon," 300.

the home front. They acted both as agents of their survival and agents of their own demise.

In interwar France, civilian innocence, predicated upon an insistence of passivity, found discursive reinforcement in the name of the political institution dedicated to protect civilians: the Défense passive. Despite early efforts by French government officials, such as Robert Schuman, to keep the policies of the Défense passive outside public debate and as de-politicized as possible, French civilians politicized civilian protection programs. Intuitively, if not consciously, they began to understand that maintaining an "apolitical and dependent status," as in previous conflicts, was "both impossible and dangerous to maintain in times of war."[39]

When civilians defied government direction to remain passive and dependent upon the state and the military for their well-being, they also exposed themselves to physical danger and endangered their status as non-combatants. Paradoxically, by taking action and rejecting their assigned passive and dependent status, civilian refugees eroded their condition as "civilian innocent" as they mixed with retreating French soldiers and exposed themselves to the assertions made by the Germans that French refugees had involved themselves in efforts to conceal France's retreating military troops. One complexity in this story of civilians' pursuit of protection is that those civilians who early in the conflict fled in disregard to military and government orders, rendered not only themselves vulnerable, but also the very weak legal category of "civilian" meant to protect them.

The French civilian exodus is a transformational moment in the development of an international consciousness with regard to human rights as linked to refugee rights and civilian wartime protection laws. It is one of the key episodes within both world wars that contributed to the vocabulary for a "politics of protection" that expanded the human rights' principles of the modern period, requiring their extension through wartime.[40] The "language of protection" that continued to evolve through the exodus and its aftermath, informed a postwar "politics of protection" that now articulates a platform of rights of

---

[39] Kinsella, "Image before the Weapon," 300.
[40] Gareth Stedman Jones, *Languages of Class: Studies in English Working Class History, 1832–1982* (Cambridge University Press, 1983). The language of class was not simply a verbalization of perception or the rising to consciousness of an existential fact, as Marxist and sociological traditions have assumed. But neither was it simply an articulation of a cumulative experience of a particular form of class relations. It was constructed and inscribed within a complex rhetoric of metaphorical association, causal inference and imaginative construction," pp 101–102.

the displaced, although it is certainly far from being as coherent and as evolved as the language of class.[41] The language and law of civilian protection continues to evolve and is impacted not only by refugee experiences, but also by ideological transformations in the world of international law. Refugee rights are not an equivalent to civilian non-combatant rights or human rights, nor are women's rights necessarily embedded within civilian and refugees' rights. However, during World War II in France, civilians' experiences as targets of German aggression and as displaced non-combatants, combined with French women's evolving understanding of their social and political rights as family heads and as French citizens to produce a refined concept of civilians' "rights to state protection" during wartime.

Louis Marlier finally acknowledged the relationship between class position and access to security, approving in 1942 the policy to provide working-class civilians residing in bombing zones with refugee allocations in order to allow them to fully participate in civilian evacuations. Marlier's affirmation of this principle represented a transformation in French thinking, which under Schuman had prioritized the distribution of refugee allocations to residents of threatened regions without attention to class.

Personal narratives also capture the particulars of women's hardships as internally displaced persons in 1940. The descriptions of women refugees' struggles in German-occupied France and documentation of their small triumphs contribute to our historical and contemporary understanding of how the experience of displacement is deeply gendered. Violations of family security, war crimes against the domestic sphere, escape articulation within the still too selectively enforced law of international human rights.

French civilian security programs evidenced deeply gendered understandings of the "threat" to national security. Military authorities discounted the psychological and, less forgivably, the material consequences of exposure to air sirens and air warfare. They built limited and underfunded defense programs around a traditional, largely immobile, World War I, soldier-centered view of combat. National authorities, more so than local officials, hesitated in 1940 to make concrete

---

[41] Stedman Jones identified the 1830s as the starting point for the appearance of "languages of class," which gradually coined a vocabulary and hence a political platform for social change and the acquisition of economic rights for the working classes in Britain and Europe. Similarly, the language of human rights discourses on class and economic relations combined with interwar languages of welfare entitlement to produce a wartime concept of state responsibility and civilian rights during wartime.

links between definitions of national defense and civilian defense.[42] Indeed, interwar French military and civilian defense strategists stood before a new threshold of understanding; it was not self-evident how to *coordinate* a defense of national territory and government infrastructure with a mission to protect civilians. As we have seen, civilians too displayed confusion about how best to protect themselves; but they generally realized more clearly and instinctively that their security required new, more aggressive defense initiatives precisely for the purpose of ensuring their "passive" status as civilian non-combatants. Civilians recognized the elimination of traditional gendered concepts of home front and combat zone and took action to preserve or re-establish the old, gendered distinctions.

French military strategists held on to what we might describe as a traditionalist or classic vision of warfare, which was also deeply gendered in terms of perpetuating a vision of separate spheres of mobilization: men on the lines; women behind the lines. The *male* German military leaders adopted a new form of military strategy that sought to erase more completely than had World War I the distinctions between combatant and non-combatant, home front and battle-front, women's space and men's space. Paradoxically, the Germans embraced a strategy of erasing the gendered spaces of war at the same time that German fascist rhetoric emphasized the unique benefits of nurturing and enforcing the distinction between male and female spheres of activity in German daily life. French civil defense planners and military strategists of 1940 remained wedded to a gendered, traditionalist vision of the division of the home front from the battle front, and therefore they planned poorly for the gender-neutral German assault on civilians. It is lamentable for humanity that the French traditionalists' highly gendered and territorially limited vision of warfare died so brutal a death in June 1940, replaced instead by a much more gender-blind, territorially limitless form of inhumane warfare perpetuated to this day by the targeting of civilian population centers for terror campaigns of violence. Let us be clear, however, that even within the process of collapsing the previously gendered differentiated spaces of war, gender continued to construct civilian and policymakers' assumptions about security and survival before, and in the aftermath, of war.

---

[42] National defense protects national borders, government institutions and buildings, military research, production and strategic centers, and privately held munitions plants. Civil defense protects "soft targets," which include civilian neighborhoods, civilian centers, and private property.

The German military and its institutions of occupation thus shattered, at least temporarily, the sanctity of the domestic hearth, and in doing so destabilized French society in the public as well as the private realm. The Third Republic had fought to establish a republican, Rousseauian-style family that enjoyed access to public benefits and supported democratic institutions, such as public schools, working family holidays, and tax benefits for large families. Interwar policies championed motherhood, rewarded high birth rates, extended family allocations, and improved prenatal care for pregnant mothers and postnatal care for infants, demonstrating that the French family formed a cornerstone of the Third Republic. While the Third Republic celebrated women's contribution to the family, it marginalized women from full participation in the public realm to its peril. The German assault on civilian space precipitated the perhaps unintentional, but nevertheless dramatic, attack on the family institution and family life, dealing a significant blow to the Republic as a whole.

One consequence of France's mass flight was that German forces confronted significantly fewer political and administrative obstacles to installing their own bases of operations in northern France, which facilitated the imposition of German administrative control, territorial reorganization, and population re-engineering in occupied territory. Mass civilian displacement provided the Germans with an excellent opportunity to implement population surveillance systems based on the partitioning of conquered territory. They established checkpoints to monitor, police, and ultimately to reclassify itinerant civilians' citizenship status according to German political and racial hierarchies. The analysis here shows the direct and necessary connection between the political and military restructuring of territorial borders and violence against civilians. Through the destruction of neighborhoods, the separation of families, the disruption to food production and distribution that caused civilian hunger, Germany worked to destroy French democratic political institutions at the national and local levels. The dispersal of millions of French families throughout the country disrupted not only domestic tranquility, but accelerated the decline of the French Republic and one of the fundamental institutions that had been forged to bolster it: the republican family. Military conflict provided a cloak for the European Holocaust, facilitating the destruction of Jewish family life, culture, and community institutions. Progressively, as the German occupier coordinated its administrative units with those of the French, the surveillance system designed to segregate Jews, foreigners, and political enemies drew upon French Third Republic administrative procedures and practices developed in the colonies after World War I, and applied overseas and at home to track foreigners and other travelers defined as "undesirable."[43]

A substantial portion of the diverse refugee population initially settled in the departments that fell within the Free Zone; but motivated by growing impoverishment, a hope to return to employment, the desire to reunite with lost family and loved ones, and the necessity of returning children to school, refugees pursued repatriation to the Occupied Zone. However, a smaller, vocal minority did resist forced repatriation. Generally, this group consisted of united families who enjoyed sufficient savings to withstand a few months of unemployment when combined with refugee relief allocations. Ill and fatigued elderly refugees also tried to prolong their stay in the Free Zone. Choosing to remain in the Free Zone, when not officially excluded from the Occupied Zone, frequently contributed to refugees' forfeiture of state-issued return money. Wives of PoWs determined whether to return home based upon how they thought their choice would impact their chances of communicating with their husbands. Excluded Jews and foreigners had no choice but to try to rebuild their lives in the Free Zone. For these permanently displaced refugees, French state refugee relief aid proved crucial. However, as dependents upon refugee allocations from the state, they often unknowingly fell into the bureaucratic apparatus that reconfigured their status in France according to their economic, political, racial, and ethnic composite. As long-term dependents on state aid, a situation that allowed them to survive permanent displacement, these refugees also became easy targets for state-sponsored group employment schemes, local police surveillance initiatives, expulsion to other departments, internment, and eventually for some, forced deportation. Expulsees' dependency upon state aid and their receipt of refugee subsidies produced paradoxes of protection. An important link existed between the failure of a civilian protection scheme, mass dislocation, and racial segregation leading to internment and deportation, thus emphasizing the historical and contemporary importance of understanding the consequences of the uneven application of civil defense and human rights' protection schemes.

The paradoxes of protection experienced by the permanently displaced refugees in the Free Zone and the refugee returnees who repatriated to the Forbidden Zone highlight a number of flaws within the

---

[43] Kathleen A. Keller, "Enemies, Charlatans, and Undesirables: Foreigners under Police Surveillance in French West Africa, 1914–1945," unpublished conference paper presented on the panel, "Power and Practice: Maintaining Control in the French Empire, 1880–1945," at the American Historical Association, Philadelphia, January 6, 2006.

civilian protection programs and humanitarian aid regime that emerged in France during World War II. Throughout the crisis, civilians, other than Alsatians and Lorrainers, lacked a formal institutional structure for articulating their concerns and their needs as civilians and as refugees. In order to voice their complaints or influence policy, civilians and refugees most frequently relied upon the government structures of municipal and departmental administration. Host communities in the Free Zone as well as in the north established refugee councils to review refugee allocation policy and to respond to refugee complaints, but these councils lacked the full power to advocate for refugees.

Only Alsatian and Lorrainer refugees, who enjoyed the advantage of early evacuation, formed representative organizations that lobbied municipal and departmental officials on behalf of their displaced constituency. Alsatian and Lorrainer evacuees did succeed in securing important advantages that assisted them in enduring the hardships of long-term displacement, and they offer a model for how to effectively plan and manage the evacuation of large-scale civilian centers. Another important aspect of the relative success of the Alsatian and Lorrainer refugees is that these communities evacuated intact from their homes and relied upon male community leadership to assist them in their negotiations with local officials in host communities.

When refugees from the north managed to locate their municipal representatives who had, like Paul Marchandeau, established operations in the south, they asked for advice about return to their homes, inquired about the whereabouts of missing family members, and sometimes requested assistance finding employment. Refugees in general lose the advantage of political representation through displacement; but French women refugees lacked political representation before the crisis, and thus were unable to form a united constituency in the south to demand a coordinated government response to their needs. Nevertheless, all refugees, but especially displaced mothers, voiced their demands for state accountability for civilians' protection, which included financial assistance as well as the provision of shelter.

In 1940, the memories of the German occupation of France during World War I fueled a new generation's resolve to avoid a re-enactment of the atrocities of that war. It is perhaps an accident of history that Robert Schuman, the Vice-President of the Cabinet and Director of the Service of Refugees in 1940, presided over the largest refugee crisis in Europe's history despite his efforts to manage civilian security and dislocation. That Schuman emerged as one of the principal advocates of European union in the postwar period, dedicated to joint economic reconstruction between France and Germany as well as the establishment of a

European practice of respect for human rights, speaks to the degree to which the lessons from the refugee crisis extended beyond the civilian masses and impacted government officials.

What lessons did unarmed French civilians take then from World War II? Local planning succeeded best when supported by national policies. Although these policies proved inadequate as the German invasion unfolded, they were foundational and even innovative for their time.

Ultimately, the important lesson the French population of the day learned was that they had to pay for civilian protection. As fundamental to civilian protection as refugee subsidies and evacuations proved to be in France, public debate and sustained media coverage of civilian protection policy proved as crucial to civilian survival as state entitlements. Individual elected officials, like Paul Marchandeau, responded to women's applied pressure, but too slowly and without worry of retribution at the polls. The failure to take women's fears for their families' security seriously confirms that the marginalization of a vocal and active female citizenry from the civil defense planning process mattered terrifically for the outcome of the war. Throughout so much of the crisis individuals made a difference. Mayors like Paul Marchandeau, who had a political record of leaning toward appeasement of German remilitarization, did eventually respond to petitions and changed their position on evacuations, aggressively petitioning the military to allow for the declaration of civilian retreat from Reims. But the military continued to order a censoring of reports about the progress of the military campaign, and issued orders prohibiting the evacuation of civilians from the north. Finally, by mid-May, as the skies became increasingly crowded with French and German aircraft, and as refugees began flowing into France from Belgium, Holland, and Luxembourg, French civilians broke ranks. They disobeyed the military's orders to stand their ground, and northern mayors, faced with chaos, followed suit and began to issue evacuation orders in defiance of military authority. The official order allowed municipal employees, first-responders, and department functionaries to legally retreat to "safer territory." Once the mayors and prefects of the north did mobilize and order evacuations, some structure emerged within the retreat of municipal and department employees. Many traveled to pre-assigned retreat locations in sister cities that were established by mayors working around military authorities. It is impossible to conclude that all civilians would have fared better had they not fled their homes.

By necessity family members' energies, especially that of heads of households, turned increasingly inward toward the reconstruction of private life and away from engagement in civic issues and political resistance. Mothers and individual women refugees continued to employ the language of welfare entitlement and family allocations adopted in the interwar years. They wrestled vigorously with administrators of the Third Republic as well as the authorities of the Vichy state to gain protection for their families. In doing so women and men kept oiled some of the constituent-centered institutions of the Third Republic, challenging dictatorship and German occupation in small ways that had huge meaning for their families and personal sense of integrity and accountability. They soldiered on as citizens in a deeply divided and sorely defeated country. Perhaps understandably, their concerns turned away, for a time, from the desire to wage armed resistance against an enemy who had proven his willingness to destroy civilians as eagerly as soldiers. But as refugees, returnees and ever-threatened civilians, they continued to wage a vocal protest for civilian protection from the violence of war. In so doing, French and Benelux civilian refugees of World War II, made an important historical contribution to the complex task of resisting the wholesale intrusion of war into the domestic sphere.

Coda

By 1945, the Service of Refugees had been merged into the Service of Deportees, Prisoners of War and Refugees, a strong indication of the fate that awaited refugees who had remained dependent upon public monies after June 1942. In 1945, refugees who had not benefited from the Vichy government's normalizing policies surfaced to demand their due. After five years of living life as a refugee, Icek Apelgot wrote to the mayor of Nancy to request one last bit of assistance – a "transportation coupon" – to facilitate his return from exile in Corrèze:

In order to be able to return to my home, I must ask you to send me free transportation coupons for four people to return to Nancy.

I have been a refugee since 1940, and I did not register for refugee relief until the present, because I am Jewish and the Vichy government would have deported me. I would be very obliged to you if I could return to my home, which is why I am now asking for a refugee allocation.

I also need coupons from Nancy to Seine and back to Nancy, so that I may go find my family.[44]

The short, unceremonious letter of Madame L. Levy, written in April 1945 to the mayor of Brive-la-Gaillarde, captures the relief of

[44] ADC 522/W/72, M. I. Apelgot to the mayor of Nancy, Brive, March 3, 1945.

Figure 3. Monument in Père Lachaise Cemetery: "In memory of
878 Jewish men deported from Drancy to Kaunas, Lithuania, and
Reval, Estonia, May 15, 1944" (Dombrowski Risser 2008).

permanently displaced refugees, who yearned for the end of their exodus, their exile and their exchanges with government bureaucracy:

Sir,

Having been a refugee from Paris since the exodus, I am honored to inform you that I have decided to return home with my granddaughter around the fifteenth of May 1945. I would be very grateful if you could please send me the form so that I may return home.[45]

---

[45] AD Corrèze 522/W/72. Mme L. Levy to the mayor of Brive-la-Gaillarde, April 1945.

Bibliography

PRIMARY SOURCES

ARCHIVAL SOURCES

Archives nationales de France, Paris:
  Series F/23, Dossiers 220–236.
  Series F/60, Cabinet militaire, Réfugiés, 1940–1942.
  Series F/60/1507, DGGFTO.
  Series F/1a/1560 and 3660 Direction des réfugiés du Ministère de l'Intérieur, Dossiers 1940–1941.
  Series F/1bis/807, Robert Leullier to Minister of the Interior.
  Series F/1c/III/1145, Rapports de préfets de la Charente.
  Series F/1c/III/1147, Rapports de préfets de la Corrèze.
  Series F/1c/III/1153, Rapports de préfets de la Gard.
  Series F/1c/III/1163, Rapports de préfets de la Loiret et Lot.
  Series F/1c/III/1166, Rapports de préfets de la Marne.
  Series F/1bI/959 and 1102, Dossier Fernand Musso.
  Series F/1bI/822 and 1104, Dossier Alfred Papinot.
  Sous-Séries 72/AJ/623.
  Sous-Séries 72/AJ/2004, Dossier 5, "Le rapatriement des réfugiés après l'exode, juillet–septembre 1940," Étude dactylographiée de Maurice Lagrange, Conseiller d'État honoraire, October 1976.
Archives départementales de la Corrèze, Tulle (Corrèze): Cabinet du Préfet.
Archives départementales de la Marne, Reims Annex, and Châlons-sur-Marne (Marne).
Archives municipales ville de Brive-la-Gaillarde (Corrèze): Series H/IV/98.
Archives municipales ville de Reims (Marne): Series R.
Archives municipales ville de Tulle (Corrèze): Series W.
Bibliothèque Documentation Internationale Contemporaine, Nanterre: Manuscript Collection, World War II.
Bibliothèque historique de la ville de Paris: Manuscript Collection, World War II.
Institut national de l'audiovisuel (INA), Paris.
Musée Edmond Michelet, Brive-la-Gaillarde (Corrèze).

PERSONAL INTERVIEWS (1991–2004)

Brive-la-Gaillarde: Mme Longrin, Malemort (Corrèze) (1992), Mme Dalm (1992), M. Louis Dalm (1992), Mme Sarlin (1992).

New York: Fanny Racine (1992), Nadine Racine Gill (1992), Helen Racine (1992), Professor Aristide Zolberg (1992).

Nyons: Odette Brès (2004), Yvette Brès (2004), Claudine Breton (1992), Mme Hollond (1996), Yvonne Kaneko (2002); Hélène Zuckerman Rossi, Tulette (Bouchet) (July–October, 2004).

Paris: Janine (née Flanet) De Col (1992, 2004), Hélène (née) Flanet (1992), Mme Monique (1992), Jackie Golter (1992), Madéline Gohier (1992).

Princeton, New Jersey: Professor Arno Mayer (1996).

Reims: Claudine Chemla (1992), Mme D'Argent (1992), Françoise Ouzan (1992), Renaud Poirier (1992), Mme Thienot (1992), Sandrine Mary (1992), Mme Gosset (1992).

NEWSPAPERS

Alsace-Lorraine, Musée Historique de la ville de Paris: *Le Lorrain*.
Corrèze:
 Baltimore: *Baltimore Sun*.
 Brive-la-Gaillarde (AMBG): *Chronique de Brive, Le Petit Gaillard, Socialisme et Liberté, Le Travailleur de la Corrèze* (*The Worker of Corrèze*).
 Tulle (ADC à Tulle):
  182-T.78, *Le Corrézien*, 1939–1940.
  182-T.79, *Le Corrézien*, 1941.
  206-T.2, *La Défense Paysanne de la Corrèze*, 1934–1940.
  206-T.3, *La Défense Paysanne de la Corrèze*, 1934–1940.
  206-T.4, *La Défense Paysanne de la Corrèze*, 1934–1940.
  219-T.3, *La Voix Corrézienne*, 1937–1940.
  219-T.4, *La Voix Corrézienne*, 1941.
  224 T.1, *Servir*, 1940.
  244-T.27, *La Croix de la Corrèze*, 1940.
  256-T.5, *La Corrèze Républicaine et Socialiste*, 1936–1940.
  256-T.6, *La Corrèze Républicaine et Socialiste*, 1941.
  285-T.2 and T.5, *Centre-Sports* (Division réservée), 1940–1941.
  284-T.1 and T.5, *Le Bas-Limousin* (Division réservée), 1941.
  307-T.3, *Le Courier du Centre* (Imprimé à Limoges), 1939–1940.
  307-T.4, *Le Courier du Centre* (Imprimé à Limoges), 1939–1940.
  307-T.5 and T.30, *Le Courier du Centre* (Division réservé), 1941.
London: *The Times*.
Marne, Reims: *L'Éclaireur de l'Est, L'Union*.
New York: *Daily News, New York Times*.
Paris: *Le Figaro, Le Journal, Le Monde, Paris Centre, Paris Match, Paris-Soir, La Tribune des Femmes Socialistes, L'Union Nationale des Femmes, La Victoire*.

PUBLISHED GOVERNMENT DOCUMENTS

Assemblé Nationale de la France. *Rapport de La Commission Chargée d'Enquêter sur les événements survenus en France de 1933 à 1945*, vol. 6, No. 2344.

United Nations, Protocol Additional to the Geneva Conventions of 12 August 1949, and relating to the Protection of Victims of International Armed Conflicts (Protocol 1), adopted June 8, 1977 by the Diplomatic Conference on the Reaffirmation and Development of International Humanitarian Law applicable in Armed Conflicts. Entered into force December 7, 1979, in accordance with Article 95.

RADIO

Pétain, Henri Philippe. Président du Conseil, "Conteste les propos de Churchill sur l'armée," June 23, 1940.

"Je fais à la France le don de ma personne," Discours, June 6, 1940.

"La demande d'Armistice," Discours, June 20, 1940.

Reynaud, Paul. "Rationing, A War Weapon," speech broadcast on the BBC, February 29, 1940. Bibliothèque Nationale.

Simone, Mme. "Reportage sur l'arrivée de l'exode à Bordeaux, Juin 1940," June 23, 1940.

MAPS

Annuaire-Almanac du Commerce. Paris: Didot-Bottin, 1948.

Carte de France. Paris: Frédo-Gardoni, 1940.

Index Atlas de France. Rennes: Fabrical-Oberthur, 1991.

"Map of Occupied France." New York: *Daily News*, March 11, 1941.

PUBLISHED AND MANUSCRIPT PRIMARY SOURCES

Albert-Lake, Virginia d'. *An American Heroine in the French Resistance: The Diary and Memoir of Virginia d' Albert-Lake*, ed. Judy Barrett Litoff. New York: Fordham University Press, 2006.

Alexander, Martin S. "The Republic at War: The French Army and the Fight for France, 1939–1940," unpublished manuscript, lecture given at University of Birmingham, June 2006.

Armstrong, Hamilton Fish. *Chronology of Failure: The Last Days of the French Republic*. New York: Macmillan, 1941.

Arnoux, Alexandre. *Hélène et les guerres*. Paris: B. Grasset, 1945.

Assailly, Giselle d'. *S.S.A. Journal d'une conductrice de la section sanitaire automobile*. Paris: Juillard, 1943.

Aubrac, Lucie. *Outwitting the Gestapo*, trans. Konrad Bieber and Betsy Wing. Lincoln, NA: University of Nebraska Press, 1993.

Benoît, Abbé. *Les Journées de juin 1940*. Troyes: Unpublished manuscript, 1941.

Bloch, Marc. *The Strange Defeat: A Statement of Evidence Written in 1940*, trans. Gerard Hopkins. New York: Norton, 1968.

Blond, Georges. *The Marne*. Paris: Les Presses de la Cité, 1962.

Brittain, Vera. *One Voice: Pacifist Writings from the Second World War. Foreword*, ed. Shirley Williams. London: Continuum, 2005.

Bullitt, Orville H. (ed.). *For the President: Personal and Secret: Correspondence between Franklin D. Roosevelt and William C. Bullitt*. Boston, MA: Houghton Mifflin, 1972.

Callil, Carmen. *Bad Faith*. London: Jonathan Cape, 2006.

Camus, Albert. *Actuelles chroniques 1944–1948*. Paris: Gallimard, 1966.

Carré, René. "Unpublished journal," Reims, 1940.

Chambrun, René de. *I Saw France Fall. Will She Rise Again?* New York: Marrow, 1940.

Chastenet, Jacques. *Le drame final 1938–40*. Paris: Hachette, 1963.

Decrest, Jacques. *Les jeunes filles perdues*. Paris: Plon, 1943.

Deighton, Len. "Adieu, Mickey Mouse." Unpublished manuscript.

Delatour, Yves. *Le travail des femmes pendant la première guerre mondiale et ses conséquences sur l'évolution de leur rôle dans la société*. Paris: Français, 1944.

Dumaître, Paule. *Rue Brûle-Maison*. Paris: S. L. Arodan, 1980.

Dutourd, Jean. *Au bon beurre*. Paris: Gallimard, 1952.

Feuchtwanger, Lion. *Simone*, trans. G. A. Hermann. New York: Viking Press, 1944.

The Devil in France: My Encounter with Him in the Summer of 1940, trans. Elisabeth Abbott. New York: Viking Press, 1941.

Filoque, G. Souvenirs d'exode de 1940, de l'occupation allemande et de l'exode de 1944, Archives de Institut de l'Histoire du Temps Présent (IHTP), Paris.

Fogg, Shannon L. "The Youngest Refugees: Children, Daily Life, and Material Shortages during the Second World War," paper presented at the French Historical Studies Conference, Stanford University, March 18, 2005.

Fortune, G. and W. Fortune. *Hitler Divided Europe: A Factual Account of Conditions in Occupied France from the Armistice of June 1940 up to the Total Occupation in November 1942*. London: Macmillan, 1943.

Gandon, Yves. *Destination inconnue: La dispersion*. Paris: R. Laffont, 1975.

Garreau, Albert. *La fuite sur les routes, 1940*. Niort: Imbert Nicholas, 1940.

Geraud, André (Pertinax). *The Gravediggers of France: Gamelin, Daladier, Reynaud, Pétain, and Laval*. Garden City, NY: Doubleday, Doran, 1944.

Germain, José. *Mes catastrophes. Souvenirs*. Paris: La Cousonne littéraire, n.d.

Gide, André. *Le retours de L'URSS (Return from the USSR)*. Paris: Gallimard, 1936.

Giraud, Madeline H. *Jerry dans l'ombre*. Paris: Bibliothèque de Suzette, 1954.

Gisclon, Jean. Ils ouvrirent le bal: la chasse française du 10 mai–24 juin 1940. 1967, Bibliothèque Documentaire Information Contemporaine (BDIC), Toulouse.

Gobert, Lieutenant Alexander. Journal de compagne: 1939–40, Archives of the Institut de l'Histoire du Temps Présent (IHTP), Paris.

Goutard, Colonel A. *The Battle of France, 1940*, trans. Captain A. R. P. Burgess. New York: Ives Washburn, 1959.

Hivert, Madeline. *L'Ouragan*. Paris: Éditions Albatros, 1983.

Huddleston, Sisley. *France, The Tragic Years, 1939–1947: An Eyewitness Account of War, Occupation, and Liberation.* New York: Devin-Adair, 1955.

Hugueville-Diseur, Marcelle. *1940: Toute l'Ardenne sur les routes.* Charlevilles: Unpublished manuscript, 1961.

Humbert, Agnes. *Notre guerre,* trans. Barbara Mellor. New York: Bloomsbury, 2008.

Hunt, Antonia. *Little Resistance: A Teenage English Girl's Adventures in Occupied France.* New York: St. Martin's Press, 1982.

Jacques, Anne. *Pitié pour les hommes.* Paris: Éditions Seuil, 1943.

Jucker, Ninetta. *Curfew in Paris: A Record of the German Occupation.* London: Hogarth Press, 1960.

Keller, Kathleen A. "Enemies, Charlatans, and Undesirables: Foreigners under Police Surveillance in French West Africa, 1914–1945," unpublished conference paper, presented on the panel, "Power and Practice: Maintaining Control in the French Empire, 1880–1945," at the American Historical Association, Philadelphia, January 6, 2006.

Kessel, Joseph. *Army of Shadows,* trans. Haakon Chevalier. New York: Alfred A. Knopf, 1944.

———. *Témoins parmi les hommes, III: L'heure des châtiments.* Paris: Les Éditions Mondiales, 1956.

La Hire, Jean de. *Les horreurs que nous avons vues. La crime des évacuations.* Paris: Tallandeur, 1940.

Laval, Josée, countess R. de Chambrun. *The Unpublished Diary of Pierre Laval.* London: Falcon Press, 1948.

Léca, Dominque. *La rupture de 1940.* Paris: Fayard, 1978.

Leclerc, Françoise and Michele Wendling. "Les femmes devant les cours de Justice à la Libération: éléments d'une recherche," presented at the conference, Féminismes et Nazisme: colloque en hommage à Rita Thalmann," unpublished manuscript, Paris, December 10–12, 1992.

Lesort, Paul André. *Quelques jours de mai–juin 1940: Mémoire, témoignage, histoire.* Paris: Seuil, 1992.

Lowenthal-Felstner, Mary. *To Paint Her Life: Charlotte Salomon in the Nazi Era.* New York: Harper Perennial, 1997.

Massenet, Marthe. *Journal d'une longue nuit.* Paris: Fayard, 1971.

Michelet, Edmond. *Rue de la Liberté: Dachau, 1943–1945.* Geneva: Éditions Famot, 1975.

Musso, Ferdinand Jèrôme. *Après le raz de marée.* Self-published, 1953.

Noël, Léon. *A propos des bombardements aériens du 15 juin 1940.* Auxerre: Imprimerie Coopérative, 1958.

Poggioli, Natale. *Progrès (Le) de la Homme: Journal des réfugiés originaires de Picardie.* Lorient: Éditions Spéciales, 1940.

———. *Sous la tourmente humaine.* Paris: Pensée universelle, 1986.

Queuille, Henri. *Journal de Guerre 7 septembre 1939–8 juin 1940,* ed. Isabel Boussard. Limoges: Presses de l'université de Limoges, 1993.

———. *Journal de Guerre 1943–1944,* eds. Hervé Bastien and Olivier Dard. Paris: Plon and Fondation Charles de Gaulle, 1995.

Renault, Abel. *L'exode mai–juin 1940.* Paris: Flammarion, 1944.

Reynaud, Paul. *Au coeur de la mêlée*. Paris: Flammarion, 1951.
Courage de la France. Bibliothèque Nationale: Flammarion, 1939.
In the Thick of the Fight 1930–45, trans. James D. Lambert. New York: Simon & Schuster, 1955.
Saint-Exupéry, Antoine de. *Flight to Arras*, trans. Lewis Galantière. New York: Reynal & Hitchcock, 1942.
Sevareid, Eric. *Not So Wild a Dream*. New York: Atheneum, [1946] 1976.
Simon, Claude. *La Route des Flandres*. Paris: Les Éditions de Minuit, 1960.
Trouillé, Pierre. *Journal d'un Préfet pendant l'occupation*. Paris: Gallimard, 1964.
Vaucher, Paul. "Evacuation in France," in Richard Padley and Margaret Cole (eds.), *Evacuation Survey: A Report to the Fabian Society*. London: Routledge, 1940.
Villelume, P. *Journal d'une défaite, 23 août 1936–16 juin 1940*. Paris: Fayard, 1976.
von Manstein, Erich. *Lost Victories: The War Memoirs of Hitler's Most Brilliant General*, ed. Martin Blumenson. Munich: Bernard & Graefe Verlag, [1955] 1982.
Werth, Léon. *33 jours*. Paris: Viviane-Hamy, 1992.

PUBLISHED SECONDARY SOURCES

Adler, Karen H. *Jews and Gender in Liberation France*. New York: Cambridge University Press, 2003.
Agnew, John and Stuart Corbridge. *Mastering Space: Hegemony, Territory and International Political Economy*. London: Routledge, 1995.
Alary, Eric. *La ligne de démarcation: 1940–1944*. Paris: Perrin, 2003.
L'exode: Un drame oublié. Paris: Perrin, 2010.
Albistur, Maité, and Daniel Armogathe. *Histoire du féminisme français du moyen âge à nos jour*. Paris: Éditions des femmes, 1977.
Alexander, Martin. "The Fall of France, 1940," in Martel (ed.), *The World War II Reader*, 7–40.
Allwood, Gill and Wadia Khursheed. *Women and Politics in France, 1958–2000*. New York: Routledge, 2000.
Amouroux, Henri. *La vie des français sous l'occupation*. Paris: Librairie Arthème Fayard, 1961.
Le 18 juin 1940. Paris: Fayard, 1964.
Quarante millions de pétainistes: Juin 1940–juin 1941. Paris: Hachette Pluriel, 1988.
Archives nationales de France, Direction. *Dictionnaire Biographique des Préfets*. Paris: Archives nationales, 1994.
Atkin, Nicholas (ed.). *Daily Lives of Civilians in Wartime Twentieth-Century Europe*. Westport, CN: Greenwood Press, 2008.
Audoin-Rouzeau, Stéphane and Annette Becker. *14–18: Understanding the Great War*, trans. Catherine Temerson. New York: Hill & Wang, 2002. *(14–18)*, *Retrouver la guerre*, Bibliothèque des Histoires. Paris: Gallimard, 2000.
Azéma, Jean-Pierre. *1940, l'année terrible*. Paris: Seuil, 1990.

La Collaboration (1940–1944). Paris: Presse universitaires de France, 1975.

"Il y a 50 ans, La guerre 1939–40, L'année terrible," *Le Monde*. August 1, 1989.

Azéma, Jean-Pierre and François Bedarida. *La France des années noires: De la défaite à Vichy*. vol. 1. Paris: Seuil, 1992.

(eds.). *Vichy et les français*. Paris: Fayard, 1992.

Baley, P. "Sauvegarde 28–29," *Influences psychiques de la dernière guerre mondiale* February–March 1949, 5884.

Bartov, Omer. *Mirrors of Destruction: War, Genocide, and Modern Identity*. New York: Oxford University Press, 2002.

Bartov, Omer, Atina Grossmann and Mary Nolan. *Crimes of War: Guilt and Denial in the Twentieth Century*. New York: The New Press, 2002.

Becker, Annette. *Les monuments aux morts: patrimoine et mémoire de la grande guerre*. Paris: Éditions Errance, 1991.

War and Faith: The Religious Imagination in France, 1914–1930, trans. Helen McPhail. New York: Berg, 1998.

Becker, Jean-Jacques. "L'Europe dans la 'drôle de guerre,'" *L'Histoire* 129, January 1990, 10.

The Great War and the French People, trans. Arnold Pomerans. Dover, NH: Berg, 1983.

Bedarida, François. *La stratégie secrète de la drôle de guerre*. Paris: Fondation nationale des sciences politiques, 1979.

Bernard, Philippe and Henri Dubrief. *The Decline of the Third Republic 1914–1938*, trans. Anthony Forster. New York: Cambridge University Press, 1985.

Bertrand Dorléac, Laurence. *L'art de la défaite (1940–1944)*. Paris: Le Seuil, 1993.

Bey, Douglas R. and Jean Lange. "Waiting Wives: Women under Stress," *American Journal of Psychiatry* 131, March 1974, 283–286.

Bolle, Pierre, and Jean Godel (eds.) *Spiritualité, théologie et résistance*. Grenoble: Presse universitaires de Grenoble, 1987.

Boswell, Laird. "Franco-Alsatian Conflict and the Crisis of National Sentiment during the Phoney War," *Journal of Modern History* 71, September 1999, 552.

"From Liberation to Purge Trials in the 'Mythic Provinces': Recasting French Identities in Alsace and Lorraine, 1918–1920," *French Historical Studies* 23(1), Winter 2000, 152, 161–162.

Rural Communism in France 1920–1939. Ithaca, NY: Cornell University Press, 1998.

Bourderon, Roger. "Le ravitaillement et les prix dans le département du Gard (été/automne 1940)," *Revue d'Histoire de la Seconde Guerre mondiale* 79, July 1970, 3760.

"Le régime de Vichy était-il fasciste?" *Revue d'histoire de la deuxième guerre mondiale* 23(91), 1973, 23–45.

Boutet, Gérard. *Ils ont vécu l'occupation*. Paris: Jean-Cyrille Godefoy, 1990.

Brauner, Alfred. *Ces enfants ont vécu la guerre*. Paris: Les Éditions sociales françaises, 1964.

Bridenthal, Renate, *et al*. *When Biology Became Destiny: Women in Weimar and Nazi Germany*. New York: New Feminist Library, 1989.

Broszat, Martin. *The Hitler State: The Foundation and Development of the Internal Structure of the Third Reich*, trans. John W. Hilden. New York: Longman, 1981.

Browning, Christopher. *Ordinary Men: Reserve Police Battalion 101 and the Final Solution in Poland*. New York: Harper, 1992.

Burleigh, Michael and Wippermann. *The Racial State: Germany 1933–1945*. Cambridge: CUP, 1991.

Burrin, Philippe. *France under the Germans: Collaboration and Compromise*, trans. Janet Lloyd. New York: The New Press, 1993.

Cairns, John C. "Along the Road Back to France, 1940," *American Historical Review* 64, April 1959, 583–603.

Campbell, D'Ann. *Women at War with America: Private Lives in a Patriotic Era*. Cambridge, MA: Harvard University Press, 1984.

Caron, Vicki. *Between France and Germany: The Jews of Alsace-Lorraine, 1871–1918*. Stanford University Press, 1988.

Uneasy Asylum: France and the Jewish Refugee Crisis, 1933–1942. Stanford University Press, 1999.

Chalas, Yves. *Vichy et l'imaginaire totalitaire*. Arles: Actes sud, 1985.

Chapman, Herrick. *State Capitalism and Working-Class Radicalism in the French Aircraft Industry*. Berkeley, CA: University of California Press, 1991.

Charbonnel, Jean. *Edmond Michelet*. Mayenne: Beauchesne, 1987.

Chatel, Nicole. *Des femmes dans la Résistance*. Paris: Juilliard, 1972.

Christofferson, Thomas R., with Michael S. Christofferson. *France during World War II: from Defeat to Liberation*. New York: Fordham University Press, 2006.

Cobb, Richard. *French and Germans, Germans and French: A Personal Interpretation of France under Two Occupations, 1914–1918/1940–1944*. Hanover, NH: University Press of New England, 1983.

Cohen, Gerard Daniel. *In War's Wake: Europe's Displaced Persons in the Postwar Order*. New York: Oxford University Press, 2011.

Cointet-Labrousse, Michele. *Vichy et la fascisme*. Brussels: Éditions complexes, 1987.

Copelon, Rhonda. "Surfacing Gender: Re-engraving Crimes Against Women in Humanitarian Law," in Nicole Dombrowski (ed.), *Women and War in the Twentieth Century: Enlisted With or Without Consent*. New York: Routledge, 2004, 334.

Crane, R. F. "Maginot Line," in Bertram M. Gordon (ed.), *Historical Dictionary of World War II France: The Occupation, Vichy and the Resistance, 1938–1946*. Westport, CT: Greenwood Press, 1998, 230.

Crawley, Heaven. *Refugees and Gender: Law and Process*. Bristol: Jordan Publishing, 2001.

Crémieux-Brilhac, Jean Louis. *Les français de l'an 40: ouvriers et soldats*, vols. I and II. Paris: Gallimard, 1990.

Damousi, Joy. *Living with the Aftermath: Trauma, Nostalgia and Grief in Post-war Australia*. New York: Cambridge University Press, 2001.

Dank, Milton. *The French against the French: Collaboration and Resistance*. New York: J. B. Lippincott, 1974.

Daridan, Jean. *Le chemin de la défaite: 1938–1940*. Paris: Plon, 1980.

Darrow, Margaret H. *French Women and the First World War: War Stories of the Home Front*. New York: Berg, 2000.

Davies, Peter. *France and the Second World War: Occupation, Collaboration and Resistance*. London: Routledge, 2001.

Davis, Belinda. "Review Article: Experience, Identity, and Memory: The Legacy of World War I," *The Journal of Modern History* 75, March 2003, 111–131.

De Grazia, Victoria. *How Fascism Ruled Women: Italy, 1922–1945*. Berkeley, CA: University of California Press, 1992.

De Tarr, Francis. *Henri Queuille en son temps 1884–1970*. Paris: La Table Ronde, 1995.

Deak, Istvan, Jan T. Gross, and Tony Judt (eds.). *The Politics of Retribution in Europe: World War II and Its Aftermath*. Princeton University Press, 2000.

Delaunay, Bernard. *Maquis de Corrèze par 120 témoins et combattants*. Paris: Éditions Sociales, 1971.

Mémorial de la Résistance et de la déportation en Corrèze 1940–1945. Edité par le Comité de la Corrèze de l'Association nationale des anciens combattants de la Résistance et ses amis. Brive: ANACR, 1995.

Diamond, Hanna. *Fleeing Hitler*. Oxford University Press, 2007.

Women and the Second World War in France, 1939–1948: Choices and Constraints. London: Longman, 1999.

Dombrowski, Nicole (ed.). *Women and War in the Twentieth Century: Enlisted With or Without Consent*. New York: Garland, 1999 (Routledge, 2004).

Dombrowski Risser, Nicole. "The Search for Civilian Safe Spaces: Re-evacuation of Le Havre, Calais and Dunkerque in Response to British Bombing, September to March, 1940–41," in Patricia Lorcin and Daniel Brewer (eds.), *France and Its Spaces of War*. New York: Palgrave Macmillan, 2009, 63.

Doughty, Robert A. *The Seeds of Disaster: The Development of French Army Doctrine 1919–1939*. Hamden, CT: Archon Books, 1985.

Dower, John. "The Bombed," in Michael J. Hogan (ed.), *Hiroshima in History and Memory*. Cambridge University Press, 1996.

Downes, Alexander B. *Targeting Civilians in War*. Ithaca, NY: Cornell University Press, 2008.

Downs, Laura Lee. "'A Very British Revolution'? L'évacuation des enfants citadins vers les campagnes anglaises 1939–1945," *Vingtième Siècle. Revue d'Histoire* 89, January–March 2006, 47–60.

Childhood in the Promised Land: Working-Class Movements and the Colonies de Vacances in France, 1880–1960. Durham, NC: Duke University Press, 2002.

Manufacturing Inequality: Gender Division in the French and British Metal-working Industries, 1914–1939. Ithaca, NY: Cornell University Press, 1995.

Dumaine, Roger. *"Accueillir les réfugiés était déjà un acte de Résistance." Premier et essor de la Résistance: Edmond Michelet*. Paris: SOS édition, 1952.

Durand, Pierre. *La SNCF pendant la guerre, 1939–1945*. Paris: PUF, 1969.

Duroselle, Jean-Baptiste. *L'Abîme 1939–1945*. Paris: Imprimerie nationale, 1982.

Politique étrangère de la France: La décadence 1932–1939. Paris: Imprimerie nationale, 1979.

Dutailly, Henry. *Les Problèmes de l'armée de terre française (1935–1939)*. Paris: Imprime nationale, 1980.

Early, Francis H. *A World Without War: How US Feminists and Pacifists Resisted World War I*. Syracuse University Press, 1997.

Eck, Hélène (ed.). *La guerre des ondes. Histoire des radios de langue française pendant la deuxième guerre mondiale*. Paris: Armand Colin, 1985.

Fabry, Joseph. *The Next to Final Solution: A Belgian Detention Camp for Hitler Refugees*. New York: Peter Lang, 1991.

Farmer, Sarah. *Martyred Village: Commemorating the 1944 Massacre at Oradour-sur-Glane*. Berkeley, CA: California University Press, 1997.

Fauré, Christian. *Le projet culturel de Vichy. Folklore et révolution nationale (1940–1944)*. Lyon: Presses universitaires de Lyon, 1989.

Ferro, Marc. *Pétain*. Paris: Fayard, 1987.

Fette, Julie. "Avocats et médecins xénophobes (1919–1939)," in André Gueslin and Dominique Kalifa (eds.), *Les exclus en Europe*. Paris: Éditions de l'Atelier, 1999, 345–357.

Fishman, Sarah. "Grand Delusions: The Unintended Consequences of Vichy France's Prisoner of War Propaganda," *Journal of Contemporary History* 26, April 1991, 22954.

The Battle for Children: World War II, Youth Crime, and Juvenile Justice in Twentieth Century France. Cambridge, MA: Harvard University Press, 2002.

We Will Wait: Wives of French Prisoners of War, 1940–1945. New Haven, CT: Yale University Press, 1991.

Fogg, Shannon L. "Refugees and Indifference: The Effects of Shortages on Attitudes towards Jews in France's Limousin Region during World War II," *Holocaust and Genocide Studies* 21(1), Spring 2007, 31–54.

The Politics of Everyday Life in Vichy France. Cambridge University Press, 2009.

"'They are Undesirables': Local and National Responses to Gypsies during World War II," *French Historical Studies* 31(2), Spring 2008, 327–351.

Fondation nationale des sciences politique. *Le gouvernement de Vichy 1940–1942*. Paris: Fondation nationale des sciences politique, 1972.

Fondation nationale des sciences politiques et la Fondation Charles de Gaulle, *Le rétablissement de la légalité républicaine (1944)*. Bruxelles: Éditions Complexe, 1996.

Footitt, Hilary. *War and Liberation in France: Living with the Liberators*. New York: Palgrave Macmillan, 2004.

Women, Europe and the Languages of Politics. London: Continuum, 2002.

Forsythe, David P. *Humanitarian Politics: The International Committee of the Red Cross*. Baltimore, MD: Johns Hopkins University Press, 1977.

Fouché, Pascal. *L'édition française sous l'Occupation (1940–1944)*, vol. 2. Paris: Bibliothèque de littérature française contemporaine de Paris VII, 1987.

Fourcaut, Annie. *Femme à l'usine: Ouvrières et Surintendants dans les entreprises françaises de l'entre-deux-guerres*. Paris: François Maspero, 1982.

Francis, Ania. *Il était des femmes dans la résistance*. Paris: Stock, 1978.

Fussell, Paul. *The Great War and Modern Memory.* New York: Oxford University Press, 1975.

Gardam, J. (ed.). *Humanitarian Law.* Aldershot: Dartmouth Publishing, 1999.

Gellately, Robert. *The Gestapo and German Society: Enforcing Racial Policy 1933–1945.* Oxford: Clarendon Press, 1990.

Gildea, Robert. *Marianne in Chains: Daily Life in the Heart of France during the German Occupation.* New York: Metropolitan Books, 2002.

Gill, James V. "Panhard (A Memoir)," *The Kenyon Review* 15(4), Fall 1993.

Giuliano, Gerard, Jacques Lambert, and Valerie Rostowsky, *Les Ardennais dans La Tourmente: De la mobilisation á l'evacuation.* Charleville-Mezieres: Éditions Terres Ardennaises, 1990.

Glendon, Mary Ann. *A World Made New: Eleanor Roosevelt and the Universal Declaration of Human Rights.* New York: Random House, 2002.

Goldstein, Joshua S. *War and Gender: How Gender Shapes the War System and Vice Versa.* Cambridge University Press, 2003.

Gordon, Bertram M. *Collaborationism in France during the Second World War.* Ithaca, NY: Cornell University Press, 1980.

Gorrara, Clare (ed.). *Modern and Contemporary France*, Special Issue, "Gendering the Occupation," February 1997.
   Women's Representations of the Occupation in Post-'68 France. Basingstoke: Macmillan, 1998.

Grayzel, Susan R. *Women's Identities at War: Gender, Motherhood, and Politics in Britain and France during the First World War.* Chapel Hill, NC: University of North Carolina Press, 1999.

Grynberg, Anne. *Les camps de honte: les internés juifs des camps français (1939–1944).* Paris: Éditions la Découverte, 1991.

Halimi, André. *La Délation sous l'occupation.* Paris: Éditions Alain Moreau, 1983.

Harris, Ruth. "The Child of the Barbarian," *Past and Present* 141, October 1993, 170–206.

Harrisson, Tom. *Living Through the Blitz.* New York: Schocken, 1975.

Hartmann, Susan M. "Prescriptions for Penelope: Literature on Women's Obligations to Returning World War II Veterans," *Women's Studies* 5, 1978.

Hathaway, J. C. *The Status of Refugee Law.* Toronto: Butterworths, 1991.

Hewitt, Leah Dianna. *Remembering the Occupation in French Film: National Identity in Postwar Europe.* New York: Palgrave Macmillan, 2008.

Higonnet, Margaret, Jane Jenson, Sonya Michel, and Margaret Wietz (eds.). *Behind the Lines: Gender and the Two World Wars.* New Haven, CT: Yale University Press, 1987.

Hilden, Patricia. *Working Women and Socialist Politics in France 1888–1914.* Oxford: Clarendon Press, 1986.

Hoffmann, Stanley. "Aspects du Régime de Vichy," *Revue français de science politique* 6(1), 1956, 4449.
   "Collaborationism in France during World War II," *Journal of Modern History* 40(3), 1968, 375–95.
   Duties Beyond Borders: On the Limits and Possibilities of Ethical International Politics. Syracuse University Press, 1981.

"*Paradoxes of the French Political Community.*" In *Search of France*, ed. Stanley Hoffmann *et al.* Cambridge, MA: Harvard University Press, 1963, 1117.

The Ethics and Politics of Humanitarian Intervention. South Bend, IN: University of Notre Dame Press, 1996.

Holborn, Louise W. *The International Refugee Organization: A Specialized Agency of the United Nations: Its History and Work, 1946–52.* London: Oxford University Press, 1956.

Homze, Edward L. *Foreign Labor in Nazi Germany*. Princeton University Press, 1967.

Horne, Alistair. *To Lose a Battle: France 1940.* London: Macmillan, 1969.

Horne, John N. and Alain Kramer. *German Atrocities, 1914: A History of Denial.* New Haven, CT: Yale University Press, 2001.

Hosking, Geoffrey. *The First Socialist Society: A History of the Soviet Union from Within.* Cambridge, MA: Harvard University Press, 1985.

Husson, Jean-Pierre. *La Marne et les Marnais à l'épreuve de la Seconde Guerre mondiale*, vols. 1 and 2. Reims: Presses universitaires de Reims, 1995.

Hyndman, Jennifer. *Managing Displacement: Refugees and the Politics of Humanitarianism.* Minneapolis, MN: University of Minnesota Press, 2000.

Imlay, Talbot. *Facing the Second World War: Strategy, Politics and Economics in Britain and France 1938–1940.* Oxford University Press, 2003.

Jackson, Julian. *France, The Dark Years, 1940–44.* Oxford University Press, 2002.

The Fall of France: The Nazi Invasion of 1940. Oxford University Press, 2003.

Jackson, Robert. *The Fall of France.* London: Arthur Barker, 1975.

Jacoby, Gerhard. *Racial State.* New York: Institute of Jewish Affairs, 1944.

Jones, Gareth Stedman. *Languages of Class: Studies in English Working Class History, 1832–1982.* Cambridge University Press, 1983.

Joutard, Phillippe, Jacques Poujol, and Patrick Cabanel. *Cévennes: Terre de Réfuge, 1940–44.* Levenol: Presse du Languedoc, 1987.

Judt, Tony. *Postwar: A History of Europe since 1945.* New York: Penguin, 2005.

The Burden of Responsibility: Blum, Camus, Aron and the French Twentieth Century. University of Chicago Press, 1998, 47.

"The War between the French," *The Times Literary Supplement*, No. 4,565, September 28–October 4, 1990.

Un passé imparfait: les intellectuels en France: 1944–1956. Paris: Fayard, 1992.

Juillet, P. and P. Moutin. *Psychiatre militaire.* Paris: Masson, 1969.

Karlsgodt, Elizabeth Campbell. "Recycling French Heroes: The Destruction of Bronze Statues under the Vichy Regime," *French Historical Studies* 29(1), Winter 2006, 143–181.

Kedward, H. R. *Occupied France: Collaboration and Resistance 1940–1944.* Oxford University Press, 1985.

Resistance in Vichy France. Oxford: Oxford University Press, 1978.

Kedward, Roderick and Roger Austin (eds.). *Vichy France and the Resistance.* London: Croom Helm, 1985.

Kitson, Simon. "From Enthusiasm to Disenchantment: the French Police and the Vichy regime, 1940–1944," *Contemporary European History* 2(3), 2002, 371–390.

Kladstrup, Donald and Petie Kladstrup. *Wine and War: The French, the Nazis, and the Battle for France's Greatest Treasure.* New York: Broadway, 2002.

Klarsfeld, Serge. *Vichy–Auschwitz. Le rôle de Vichy dans la solution finale de la question juive en France, 1942.* Paris: Fayard, 1983.

Kleiman, Laurence and Florence Rochefort. *L'égalité en marche: Le féminisme sous la Troisième République.* Paris: Presses de la Fondation Nationale des Sciences Politique, 1989.

Koonz, Claudia. *Mothers in the Fatherland: Women, the Family and Nazi Politics.* New York: St. Martin's Press, 1987.

Koreman, Megan. *The Expectation of Justice France 1944–46.* Durham, NC: Duke University Press, 1999.

Kotkin, Stephen. *Magnetic Mountain: Stalinism as a Civilization.* Berkeley, CA: California University Press, 1995.

Kuisel, Richard. *Capitalism and the State in Modern France.* Cambridge University Press, 1981.

Kulischer, Eugene M. *Europe on the Move: War and Population Changes, 1917–47.* New York: Columbia University Press, 1948.

Laborie, Pierre. *L'opinion française sous Vichy.* Pairs: Seuil, 1990.

Lacan, Jacques. "La psychiatrie anglaise et la guerre," *L'évolution psychiatrique* 1, 1947, 293–318.

Lagrange, J. "Rapatriement des réfugiés après l'exode," *Revue d'histoire de la Deuxième Guerre mondiale* (1977), 43.

Lahaw, Gallya. *Immigration and Politics in the New Europe: Reinventing Borders.* Cambridge University Press, 2004.

Larson, Eric V. and Bogdan Savych. *Misfortunes of War: Press and Public Reactions to Civilian Deaths in Wartime.* Santa Monica, CA: RAND Corporation, Project Air Force, 2007.

Léca, Dominique. *La Rupture de 1940.* Paris: Fayard, 1978.

Leff, Mark. "The Politics of Sacrifice on the American Home Front in World War II," in Martel (ed.), *The World War II Reader*, 336–358.

Levine, Philippa and Susan R. Grayzel (eds.). *Gender, Labor, War and Empire: Essays on Modern Britain.* Basingstoke: Palgrave Macmillan, 2009.

Levy, Claude. *Les Nouveaux Temps et l'idéologie de la collaboration.* Paris: Presse de la Fondation nationale des sciences politiques, 1974.

Lewis, Mary Dewhurst. *The Boundaries of the Republic: Migrant Rights and the Limits of Universalism in France, 1918–1940.* Stanford University Press, 2007.

Lindenberg, Daniel. *Les Années souterraines (1937–1947).* Paris: Presses universitaires de Reims, 1989.

Lindqvist, Sven. *A History of Bombing.* New York: The New Press, 2003.

Loescher, Gil. *Refugee Movements and International Security. Adelphi Paper 268.* London: The International Institute for Strategic Studies, 1992.
    The UNHCR and World Politics: A Perilous Path. Oxford University Press, 2001.

Loiseaux, Gerard. *La Littérature de la défaite et de la collaboration.* Paris: Publications de la Sorbonne, 1984.

Lorcin, Patricia M. E. and Daniel Brewer (eds.). *France and Its Spaces of War: Experience, Memory, Image.* New York: Palgrave Macmillan, 2009.

Lottman, Herbert R. *Petain: Hero or Traitor, the Untold Story.* New York: William Morrow, 1985.

Lower, Wendy. "A New Ordering of Space and Race: Nazi Colonial Dreams in Zhytomyr, Ukraine, 1941–1944," *German Studies Review* 25(2), May 2002, 227–254.

    Nazi Empire-Building and the Holocaust in Ukraine. Chapel Hill, NC: North Carolina University Press, 2005.

Marrus, Michael R. (ed.). *The Nuremberg War Crimes Trial 1945–46: A Documentary History.* Boston, MA: Bedford/St. Martin's Press, 1997.

    The Unwanted: European Refugees in the Twentieth Century. New York: Oxford University Press, 1985.

Marrus, Michael and Robert O. Paxton. "The Nazis and Jews in Occupied Western Europe, 1940–44," *The Journal of Modern History* 54(4), December 1982, 687–714.

    Vichy France and the Jews. New York: Oxford University Press, 1981.

Martel, Gordon (ed.). *The World War II Reader.* New York: Routledge, 2004.

Martens, Stefan and L'Institut historique allemand de Paris. *La France et La Belgique sous L'Occupation Allemande 1940–1944: Les fonds allemands conservés au Centre historique des Archives nationales.* Paris: Presses des Archives nationales de France, 2002.

Marwick, Arthur. *War and Social Change in the Twentieth Century.* New York: St. Martin's Press, 1974.

Mazenc, C. *Qui est qui en Corrèze.* Tulle, 1983.

Mazower, Mark. *The Dark Continent. Europe's Twentieth Century.* New York: Knopf, 1998.

McEnaney, Laura. *Civil Defense Begins at Home: Militarization Meets Everyday Life in the Fifties.* Princeton University Press, 2000.

McMillan, James. *France and Women 1789–1914.* New York: Routledge, 2000.

McPhail, Helen. *The Long Silence: Civilian Life under the German Occupation of Northern France, 1914–1918.* London: I. B. Tauris, 1999.

Melman, Billie. *Borderlines: Genders and Identities in War and Peace, 1870–1930.* London: Routledge, 1998.

Meyssignac, Marcel. *Comment Tulle ne fut pas Oradour: Le drame de Tulle au fil de trois journées tragiques: 7–9 juin 1944.* Brive: Chastrusse, 1994.

Michel, Henri. *La Défaite de la France.* Paris: Presses universitaires de France, 1980.

    La drôle de guerre. Paris: Fondation nationale des sciences politiques, 1979.

    Pétain, Laval, Darlan, Trois politiques? Paris: Flammarion, 1972.

Michelet, Claude. *Mon Père Edmond Michelet.* Paris: Presses de la Cité, 1971.

Michman, Dan. *Belgium and the Holocaust: Jews, Belgians, Germans.* Jerusalem: Yad Vashem, 1998.

Milza, Pierre. *Fascisme Français.* Saint Amand: Flammarion, 1990.

    Fascismes et idéologies réactionnaires en Europe. 1919–1945. Paris: Armand Colin, 1969.

Miquel, Pierre. *L'exode 10 mai–20 juin 1940.* Paris: Plon, 2003.

Moyen, Samuel. *The Last Utopia: Human Rights in History.* Cambridge, MA: Belknap Press of Harvard University, 2010.

Murat, Bernard. *Le passeur de mémoire: Histoire des maires de Brive-la-Gaillarde.* Brive-la-Gaillarde: Les 3 épis, 1997.

Nabulsi, Karma. *Traditions of War: Occupation, Resistance, and the Law.* Oxford University Press, 1999.

Neumann, Iver B. *Uses of the Other: "The East" in European Identity Formation.* Minneapolis, MN: University of Minnesota Press, 1999.

Newman, Edward, Jodnne Van Selm, *et al. Refugees and Forced Displacement: International Security, Human Vulnerability, and the State.* New York: United Nations University Press, 2003.

Nolan, Mary. *Visions of Modernity: American Business and the Modernization of Germany.* New York: Oxford University Press, 1994.

Nora, Pierre. *Les Lieux de mémoire, tome I, La République, tome II, La nation.* 3 vols. Paris: Gallimard, 1984, 1986.

Ollier, Nicole. *L'exode sur les routes de l'an 40.* Paris: R. Laffont, 1970.

Ory, Pascal. *Les Collaborateurs 1940–1945.* Paris: Seuil, 1976.

Ousby, Ian. *Occupation: The Ordeal of France 1940–1944.* New York: St. Martin's Press, 1998.

Panchasi, Roxanne. *Future Tense: The Culture of Anticipation in France between the Wars.* Ithaca, NY: Cornell University Press, 2009.

Passerini, Luisa. *Fascism in Popular Memory: The Cultural Experience of the Turin Working Class.* Cambridge University Press, 1987.

Paxton, Robert O. *The Anatomy of Fascism.* New York: Vintage, 2005.

 Vichy France: Old Guard and New Order, 1940–1944. New York: Columbia University Press, 1982.

Pedersen, Susan. *Family, Dependence, and the Origins of the Welfare State: Britain and France, 1914–1945.* Cambridge University Press, 1993.

Pellus, Daniel. *La Marne dans la guerre 1939/1945.* Lecoteau: Éditions Horvath, 1987.

 1944: la Libération de Reims. Reims: Matôt-Braine S.A., 1984.

Pernet, Jacques and Michel Hubert. *Reims: A l'heure Américaine 1944–1946.* Reims: Atelier Graphique de Reims, 1990.

Perrot, Michelle (ed.). *A History of Private Life: From the Fires of Revolution to the Great War,* trans. Arthur Goldhammer. Cambridge, MA: Belknap Press, 1990.

Peschanski, Denis. *De l'exil à la résistance: réfugiés et immigrés d'Europe Centrale en France, 1933–1945.* Saint-Denis: Presses universitaires de Vincennes, 1989.

 La France des camps: l'internement, 1938–1946. Paris: Gallimard, 2002.

 Le Sang de L'Étranger, Les immigrés de la MOI dans la Résistance. Paris: Fayard, 1989.

 Vichy 1940–44: contrôle et exclusion. Bruxelles: Éditions Complexe, 1997.

Petersen, Roger D. *Understanding Ethnic Violence: Fear, Hatred and Resentment in Twentieth-Century Eastern Europe.* Cambridge University Press, 2004.

PitoisDehu, Marie Agnes. *L'Aisne dans la guerre: 1939–45.* Le Coteau: Éditions Horvath, 1986.

Poidevin, Raymond. *Robert Schuman, homme d'État, 1886–1963.* Paris: Imprimerie nationale, 1985.

Pollard, Miranda, "La politique du travail féminin," in Azéma and Bédarida (eds.), *Vichy et les Français.* Paris: Fayard, 1992, 242.

Reign of Virtue: Mobilizing Gender in Vichy France. University of Chicago Press, 1998.

Poznanski, Renée. *Jews in France during World War II,* trans. Nathan Bracher. Hanover, NH: University Press of New England, 2001.

Preston, Paul. *The Spanish Civil War: Reaction, Revolution, and Revenge.* New York: Norton, 1986.

Proctor, Tammy M. *Civilians in a World at War 1914–1918.* New York University Press, 2010.

Proudfoot, Malcolm J. *European Refugees, 1939–52: A Study in Forced Population Movement.* London, Faber & Faber, 1957.

Quataert, Jean H. "The Gendering of Human Rights in the International Systems of Law in the Twentieth Century," *Essays on Global and Comparative History.* Washington, DC: American Historical Association, 2006.

Quincy, Guy (ed.). *La Corrèze de 1919 à 1939.* Tulle: Archives départementales de la Corrèze, 1986.

Ratzel, Friedrich. *Géopolitiques et stratégies.* Paris: Fayard, 1923.

Rayski, Adam. *Le choix des juifs sous Vichy entre soumission et résistance.* Paris: la Découverte, 1992.

Rémond, René. *La droite en France de 1815 à nos jours.* Paris: Aubier, 1954.

Rémy, Colonel. *La ligne de démarcation,* vols. I–VII. Paris: Presse Pocket, 1973.

Rioux, Jean-François (ed.). *La vie culturelle sous Vichy.* Brussels: Complexe, 1990.

Roberts, Mary Louise. *Civilization without Sexes: Reconstructing Gender in Post-War France, 1918–1928.* Chicago University Press, 1994.

Rosanvallon, Pierre. *L'état en France: de 1789 à nos jours.* Paris: Seuil, 1990.

Rossignol, Dominique. *Histoire de la propagande en France de 1940 à 1944: L'utopie Pétain.* Paris: Les Belles Lettres, 1992.

Rossilandi, Guy. *La drôle de Guerre.* Paris: Armand Colin, 1988.

Rousso, Henry. "L'activité industrielle en France de 1940 à 1944: Economie 'nouvelle' et occupation allemande," *Bulletin de l'Institut d'histoire du temps Présent* 38, December 1989, 2568.

La Collaboration. Paris: Éditions MA, 1987.

Le Syndrome de Vichy: 1944–198 ... Paris: Seuil, 1987.

Schleunes, Karl A. *The Twisted Road to Auschwitz: Nazi Policy toward German Jews 1933–1938.* Urbana Champagne, IL: University of Illinois Press, 1970.

Schwartz, Paula, "*Partisanes* and Gender Politics in Vichy France," in Martel (ed.), *The World War II Reader,* 296–316.

Scott, Joan W. *Gender and the Politics of History.* New York: Columbia University Press, 1988.

Only Paradoxes to Offer: French Feminists and the Rights of Man. Cambridge, MA: Harvard University Press, 1997.

Shephard, Ben. *A War of Nerves: Soldiers and Psychiatrists in the Twentieth Century.* Cambridge, MA: Harvard University Press, 2002.

Siegel, Mona. *The Moral Disarmament of France: Education, Pacifism and Patriotism, 1914–1940.* Cambridge University Press, 2004.

Singer, Claude. *Vichy, l'université et les juifs. Les silences et la mémoire.* Paris: Les Belles Lettres, 1992.

Sirinelli, Jean-François. *Intellectuels et passions françaises: Manifestes et pétitions au XXe siècle*. Paris: Fayard, 1990.

Société des Lettres, Science et Arts de la Corrèze. *Les parlementaires Limousins sous la IIIe République: Actes du Colloque tenu à Tulle le 6 mai 1990*. Tulle: Archives de la France, 1992.

Soucy, Robert J. *French Fascism: The First Wave 1924–1933*. New Haven, CT: Yale University Press, 1986.

"French Fascist Intellectuals in the 1930's: An Old New Left?" *French Historical Studies* 8(3), Spring 1974, 445–458.

"The Nature of Fascism in France," *Journal of Contemporary History* 1(1), 1966, 2754.

Souleau, Philippe. *La ligne de démarcation en Gironde: Occupation, Résistance et société 1940–1944*. Périgueux: Fanlac, 1998.

Soulignac, Yves. *Les camps d'internement en Limousin, 1939–1945*. Saint-Paul: Soulignac, 1995.

Steiner, Niklaus (ed.). *Problems of Protection: The UNHCR, Refugees and Human Rights*. London: Routledge, 2003.

Sternhell, Zeev. *La droite révolutionnaire, 1885–1914: Les origines françaises du fascisme*. Paris: Seuil, 1978.

Sweets, John. *Choices in Vichy France*. New York: Oxford University Press, 1986.

Taylor, Lynne. *Between Resistance and Collaboration: Popular Protest in Northern France, 1940–1944*. Basingstoke: Macmillan, 1999.

Taylor, Telford. *The Anatomy of the Nuremberg Trials*. Boston, MA: Little, Brown, 1992.

Terrenoire, Louis. *Edmond Michelet Mon Ami*. Paris: Nouvelle Cité, 1992.

Thalmann, Rita (ed.). *Femmes et Fascisme*. Paris: Éditions Tierce, 1986.

La mise au pas. Idéologie et stratégie sécuritaire dans la France occupée. Paris: Fayard, 1991.

Théabaud, Françoise. *Quand nos grandes mères donnaient la vie: La maternité en France dans l'entre-deux-guerres*. Lyon: Presses universitaires de Lyon, 1986.

Torrie, Julia S. *"For Their Own Good": Civilian Evacuations in Germany and France, 1939–1945*. New York: Berghahn Books, 2010.

VanderWolk, William. "Whose Memory is This?: Patrick Modiano's Historical Method," in Martine Guyot-Bender and William VanderWolk (eds.), *Paradigms of Memory: The Occupation and Other Histories in the Novels of Patrick Modiano*. New York: Peter Lang, 1998, 60.

Veillon, Dominique. *La collaboration. Textes et débats*. Paris: Hachette, 1984.

La mode sous l'Occupation. Paris: Payot, 1990.

Venner, Dominique. *Histoire de la collaboration*. Paris: Pygmalion, 2000.

Vidalenc, Jean. *L'exode du mai–juin 1940*. Paris: Presses universitaires de France, 1957.

Vigier, René. *Brive pendant la guerre: héros, victimes, traîtres*. Pouzet: Éditions, 1954.

Vinen, Richard. *The Unfree French: Life under the Occupation*. London: Penguin/ Allen Lane, 2005.

Virgili, Fabrice. *Shorn Women: Gender and Punishment in Liberation France*, trans. John Flower. Oxford: Berg, 2002.

Voldman, Danièle. *La reconstruction des villes française de 1940 à 1954: Histoire d'une politique*. Paris: L'Harmattan, 1997.

Walker. R. B. J. *Inside/Outside: International Relations as Political Theory*. Cambridge University Press, 1993.

Weber, Eugen. *Action française*. Stanford University Press, 1962.

Webster, Paul. *Pétain's Crime: The Full Story of French Collaboration in the Holocaust*. London: Macmillan, 1990.

Weitz, Margaret Collins. *Sisters in the Resistance: How Women Fought to Free France 1940–1945*. New York: John Wiley, 1995.

Wieviorka, Annette. *Déportation et génocide: Entre la mémoire et l'oublie*. Paris: Plon, 1992.

Williams, John. *The Ides of May: The Defeat of France, May–June 1940*. New York: Knopf, 1968.

Winock, Michel. "Français, voulez-vous résister à Hitler?" *L'Histoire* 129, January 1990, 18.

Winter, J. M. *Remembering War: The Great War between Memory and History in the Twentieth Century*. New Haven, CT: Yale University Press, 2006.

Sites of Memory, Sites of Mourning: The Great War in European Cultural History. Cambridge University Press, 1995.

The Upheaval of War: Family, Work and Welfare in Europe, 1914–1918. eds. Richard Wall and Jay Winter. Cambridge University Press, 1988.

Wylie, Laurence. *Village in the Vaucluse*, 3rd edn. Cambridge, MA: Harvard University Press, 1974.

Zaretsky, Robert. *Nîmes at War: Religion, Politics and Public Opinion in the Gard, 1938–1944*. University Park, PN: Pennsylvania State University Press, 1995.

Zuccotti, Susan. *The Holocaust, The French, and The Jews*. New York: Basic Books, 1993.

THESES

Dombrowski, Nicole Ann. "Beyond the Battlefield: The French Civilian Exodus of May–June 1940," Ph.D. dissertation, New York University, 1995.

Kinsella, Helen M. "The Image before the Weapon: A Genealogy of the 'Civilian' in International Law and Politics," Ph.D. dissertation, University of Minnesota, July 2004.

Index